FAMINE

'A major achievement, a masterpiece'

Liam O'Flaherty

Liam O'Flaherty titles published by Wolfhound Press:

The Pedlar's Revenge and Other Stories (1976)
All Things Come of Age: A Rabbit Story (1977) – for children
The Test of Courage (1977) – for children
The Ecstasy of Angus (1978) – a novella
Famine (1979) – a novel
The Black Soul (1981) – a novel
Shame the Devil (1981) – autobiography
Short Stories by Liam O'Flaherty (1982)
The Wilderness (1978, 1986) – a novel
Skerrett (1977, 1988) – a novel
The Assassin (1983, 1988) – a novel
Insurrection (1988) – a novel
Thy Neighbour's Wife (1992) – a novel

Limited first editions, handbound, signed and numbered:

The Pedlar's Revenge and Other Stories (1976)
The Wilderness (1978)

FAMINE

Liam O'Flaherty

WOLFHOUND PRESS

Published by Wolfhound Press
an Imprint of Merlin Publishing
16 Upper Pembroke Street, Dublin 2, Ireland
Tel: + 353 1 676 4373
Fax: + 353 1 676 4368
publishing@merlin.ie
www.merlin-publishing.com

ISBN 1-903582-20-2

A catalogue record for this book is available from the British Library.

20 19 18 17 16 15 14

Cover Design by sin é design
Typeset by Gough Typesetting Services, Dublin
Printed in Denmark by Nørhaven Paperback A/S

To John Ford

Liam O'Flaherty was born on the Aran Islands, in 1896. His rebellious ideals were nurtured by his Fenian father while his *seanchaí* mother infused him with a deep love of nature.

In 1917, World War I left O'Flaherty severely shell-shocked. He travelled the world before joining the Republicans in 1920 to fight the Irish Free State government. O'Flaherty fled Ireland after the Civil War.

In London, he started writing for Jonathan Cape and produced an astonishing number of books. Aside from their intrinsic literary value his books are a crucial sociological study; charting the ways and beliefs of a peasant world before they were lost forever.

Liam O'Flaherty died in Dublin in 1984.

CHAPTER I

THE COCKS HAD just heralded the break of day when the first clap of thunder burst above Black Valley. Its echoes rolled along the steep, cavernous, mountain slopes for fully half a minute.

Brian Kilmartin sat up with a jerk. He had been lying awake in bed, waiting for the rheumatism to ease in his bones.

"Blood an ouns!" he said.

He turned to his wife, who lay still asleep beside him. He shook her so violently that she awoke with a cry of fright.

"Jesus, Mary and Joseph!" she said, peering at him through the rheum of sleep that webbed her eyelids. "What is it?"

"Thunder," said Brian, as he sprang from the bed to the floor.

She opened wide her lips and listened to the dying chimes that tinkled in a far-off cave. Before it had faded into silence another clap came rolling through the firmament.

"Glory be to God," she said, crossing herself.

Brian groaned and clutched his right knee as he touched the floor. Then he limped to the window in his shirt and looked out, scratching his thigh. He could hear the patter of rain.

"Pooh!" he said. "It's coming down in bucketfuls. Nice day for it, too, and we going to thresh the oats. Get up and light the fire, Maggie."

He began to pull on his trousers, groaning with pain. His wife reached for her skirt that hung over the end of the bed. She thrust her head through it. Brian hurried into the kitchen and drew the bolt of the front door. A dog began to whine. As soon as the door was thrown open, the dog, whose shaggy hide was speckled with peat ashes from lying all night on the hearth, dashed through Brian's legs and scampered into the yard, barking joyously.

"Merciful God!" said Brian. "What a morning!"

He was seventy-one years old. As he looked at the sky, he grinned, exposing gums that had only two yellow teeth in them and drawing the skin tightly, as if stitched, about his piercing blue eyes. His eyes and his long, hooked nose gave his bony, bronzed face a hawk-like appearance. He appeared to be all bone, a tall, thin wisp of a man, full of energy.

"This rain," he said in a loud voice, so that his wife could hear him, "will be the ruin of the Valley."

The rain now fell from the sky in a wild torrent. Grey, mountainous clouds lurched along with hanging tails, from which the flood of water poured upon the sombre earth amid the crashing pearls of thunder. There was an ominous silence beneath the dull, fierce patter of the rain and the rumbling of the thunder. The air was sultry. The yard was creased with rills that flowed down the incline to the dunghill in the far corner. The pigs' trough, perched on the flat top of a boulder beside the door, had already filled with rain water and was overflowing.

The dog cocked his hind leg against the boulder but dropped it again and went whining back to the hearth. The old man drew in a deep breath, shrugged his shoulders angrily and also went to the hearth. He took his rosary beads from a peg in the chimney wall. He kicked aside the dog, which was shaking its hide on the hearth stone. Then he knelt with his arms resting on a stool and began to recite his morning prayers, yawning and groaning as he prayed. The weather had made his rheumatism worse this morning.

Maggie came out of the bedroom shivering. Even though it was sultry outside, the air in the house was chilly. She limped on her naked feet across the earthen floor, glancing timidly out the open door at the rain. Then she crouched on her heels at the hearth to prepare the fire. Three pigs that lay on a bed of straw in the corner by the fire-place, within a square pen made by two stretched logs, awoke and began to whine when they heard the rattle of her tongs on the hearth stone, as she raked the live embers of turf from the ashes that had covered them during the night. Fowl in a coop by the open door began to cackle.

The old man did not stay long at his prayers. After a final yawn he got to his feet smartly. Then he turned on the pigs, crying:

"Huh! You ruffians! You're going to get the wash of your lives now."

He kicked them with his bare feet, while he shook his rosary beads and yelled. They sat up in their straw, with their heads close together, watching him with stupid curiosity and grunting quietly, but refusing to move. Then the dog leaped at them suddenly. He bit one of them on the rump. Immediately they all squealed and fled from their straw. They ran across the floor stiffly, their little feet creaking under their heavy bodies, leaving a stench and wisps of straw in their trail. They collided in the doorway and bit at one another. Then they dashed out into the yard, where they ran about in the rain, tossing their flatulent gullets and grunting in ecstasy, as the parasites were washed from their itching hides.

"Phew!" said the old man. " I don't know which stinks the most, them or the hens."

"They pay the rent, poor beasts," Maggie said timidly.

"Who asked you to speak?" Brian retorted.

He raised the trap door of the hen coop.

"Is it out in the rain you're going to send them?" said Maggie.

"They can go into the little house," he said. "Kush, you devils. It was the smell in this house that turned Michael's stomach last night. Kush. Put out this coop, woman, and get it washed. Throw out the pigs' bed and put new straw in its place and scatter lime on the floor."

"Have I ten hands?" she said.

"Wake your daughter-in-law, then," he shouted. "Does she get her bread from Heaven?"

"Ho! Ho! You devil," came a strong, deep voice from the bedroom on the left. "Isn't it yourself has the fine, free pipe this morning?"

The old man snorted in reply to this voice and shooed at the hens. One by one, slowly, they came out of their coop. They spread their wings, stretched their legs and shook themselves. They wiped their beaks on the floor, first one side and then the other, as if to sharpen them for the day's picking. The old man waited impatiently until the last one had left the coop and then he tried to shoo them into the yard. That, however, was a difficult matter. It was only after the dog and his wife joined him that the screaming hens and their cock could be made to face the rainy yard. Then he went out to open the door of the barn for them to take shelter there.

Maggie lowered a large pot of potatoes that had been hanging on the pot-hooks over the fire all night. Then she knelt against a stool to say her prayers. She was nine years younger than her husband but she looked older. She was very fat, with pale, unhealthy cheeks, over which her untidy grey hair lay in strands. Her grey eyes were deeply sunk. The skin had darkened about them and the lids, closed in prayer, were lined with little pink veins. There was a coquettish down on her upper lip. As she knelt, with her elbows on the stool, her body was huddled in a round, clumsy heap, with her bare feet protruding from the edge of her red petticoat. Her heels were quite black.

Brian re-entered the house, coughing and shaking the rain off his clothes. She opened her eyes, looked at him mournfully and said:

"You shouldn't go out into the wet yard in your bare feet."

"Don't spend the morning there," he answered. "Throw out the ashes. Why don't you wake Mary? Call Thomsy, too. There's work to be done, woman."

She struck her breast three times, made the sign of the Cross with her face to the roof, kissed her beads and rose slowly.

The old man sat down in the corner of the hearth, took his socks from a peg and began to rub their soles together, while he dried his wet feet at the quickly kindling fire.

Great lumps of soot, loosened by the rain that entered above, fell down the chimney into the fire, or else on to the lid of the pot. When a lump of soot fell into the fire, jets of flame sprang up from the peat to lick it. Then a little cloud of acrid smoke eddied out from the fire into the kitchen.

It was now quite light, but the kitchen remained in gloom, as there was no window and the door was so small that it admitted very little of the sombre morning. The roof was barely visible. Up there, the long slabs of turf that covered the rafters sagged downwards. This part of the house had been built for nearly a hundred years and the walls could no longer hold their innumerable coats of limewash. Here and there, the covering had split, showing a mass of brownish dust within each wound. Above the fire-place the wall had turned dark with peat smoke. A heavy fur of soot lay on the chimney wall and along the handle of the pot-hooks. The earthen floor had got uneven with long use. It was pocked with holes. A door led into the principal bedroom, where the old couple had slept, opposite the fire-place. Another door, beside the fire-place, led into the smaller bedroom. Still another door opened on to the south side of the house, to be used when the wind blew from the north, as there was no porch. There were two lofts. The one above the hearth was stacked with sods of turf. The other, over the large bedroom, looked empty. The end of a ladder protruded from its edge.

When Brian had pulled on his socks he went back into his bedroom. Now the light in the room was much stronger. On one side was the big four-poster bed in which the old couple had slept. In a corner there was a smaller bed, very low and narrow. Brian's youngest son, Michael, lay on this bed, with the clothes up about his ears.

"Well?" whispered the old man tenderly. "How are you to-day?"

A dry cough sounded in the bed. Then the clothes were pushed back from the young man's face. He sat up against the pillow.

"How would I be?" he grumbled. "Waked up at the crack of dawn by your shouting."

"Maybe it was the thunder that woke you," said Brian contritely.

It was odd the way his fierce manner had changed suddenly to one of humility and gentleness. Michael did not respond to this tenderness. He stared gloomily at the little window, down whose solitary pane of glass beady streams of rain, like pale worms, were winding.

"It's raining," he said.

"It is," said the old man, coming closer to the bed on tip-toe. "Maybe you should stay in bed to-day and give your cold a chance to get better."

"Stay in bed?" said Michael indignantly. "Why so? Aren't we going to thresh the oats?"

"Huh!" said Brian. "True for you. I was forgetting that."

He laughed in pretended ridicule of the idea that his son should stay in bed while there was work to be done. His laugh was cut short as Michael was taken with a fit of coughing. The old man clenched his fists and trembled, as he watched Michael writhe under the patched quilt. The young man's face, as he coughed, assumed the blatant mask of the disease from which he suffered. On his hollow, yellowish cheeks, two bright spots, like red paint, appeared as if by magic. His blue eyes became unhealthily bright, like the eyes of a madman in an accession of frenzy. A light perspiration appeared on his forehead. His fair hair, hanging down over his forehead, looked damp. He wore a half grown beard, auburn in colour, which gave his face a Christlike appearance, the Christ in agony on the Cross. Yet his hands, clutching the quilt as he coughed, looked healthy and powerful. So did his broad chest, heaving up and down rapidly, like the chest of a man trying to escape from a wrestler's grip. Poor boy! He was in the grip of a wrestler from whom escape was impossible.

As he watched, the father's sorrow clutched his bosom, just like the living germs that tore at his beloved boy's lungs. Brian at that moment could not believe in his usual pretence that Michael merely suffered from a cold that would soon pass. Listening to that hacking cough, the outcome was all too manifest. That same cough had snatched five of his children in their childhood. And now, of the four that remained, Michael had it.

"You better try to sleep anyhow until breakfast-time," he said when the fit of coughing had ceased.

Michael mumbled something and lay back. The old man sighed and went on tip-toe out of the room. His other son, Martin, was now in the kitchen.

"Ho! You old devil," Martin said merrily, "what got under your hide this morning?"

"Have you no feeling for your sick brother?" the father said.

"It's little feeling you have for anybody," said Martin, "roaring about the house like a hyena."

He laughed and strode out into the yard. Indifferent to the rain, he raised his arms above his head and cried:

"Hey! Did you ever see such a flood of rain?"

Then he ran across the yard in his bare feet, uttering cries of pretended pain. The old man went to the hearth and began to pull on his boots.

"How is he?" Maggie said timidly, as she prepared the can to milk the cow.

"Why don't you go in and ask him?" said the old man. "It wasn't from me he got it."

"God forgive you," said the poor woman, bursting into tears and putting her apron to her face.

Martin came back into the house, singing a snatch of song, which died on his lips as he saw his mother in tears.

"What ails you, mother?" he said fiercely.

"Nothing, treasure," she said, taking a heather broom from the back door.

Martin looked angrily at his father and said:

"What did you say to her?"

With his boots still unlaced, the old man jumped to his feet, strode to the dressers, took the milk-can and left the house. Martin shouted after him:

"You are asking for the stick, you…"

"Hush, darling," said Maggie. "There's no use arguing with him."

Martin looked at her, tightening his belt. He was very like his father, but much taller, well over six feet in height. He had the same long head and nose, fierce blue eyes and bony, bronzed cheeks. A fine looking man, with the chest and shoulders of an athlete. He went up to his mother and hugged her.

"Never mind," he said. "One of these days I'll tame him."

With a sack over his shoulders, the old man ran around the gable of the house to a little paddock, where there was a sort of byre, built against a rock in the corner. The rain now came down worse than before. Steam rose from the earth. The thunder had ceased. A black cow, tied to the wall of the byre by a rope halter, lowed when she saw him approach. He crouched under her and began to milk. When a little of the milk had fallen into the can, he dipped his thumb in the froth and made the sign of the Cross on the cow's thigh. Then he continued to milk steadily with both hands, while the cow chewed her cud.

The murmur of the falling milk and the sweet smell that rose from its billowing white froth soon softened his temper. His face looked gentle.

The rain no longer sounded menacing. Its myriad drops fell, tumultuously, on the earth, as a droning lullaby that banished care and sorrow.

CHAPTER II

WHEN HE RETURNED to the kitchen with the milk, the old man found Martin talking to his young wife at the dressers. She was pouring buttermilk into mugs for the breakfast, while she listened to her husband's whispered nonsense. They had only been married a month and they were still in the first flush of their desire. They looked really beautiful together, but the sight of them angered the old man. Martin had married this Mary Gleeson against his father's wish, she being the daughter of the local weaver and therefore, in the old man's opinion, a social inferior. Added to that, her beauty appeared to him improper in the wife of a peasant.

She was truly a beautiful woman. Her shining, black hair, which she wore in a long plait that reached to her waist, like a girl, would alone have made her outstanding, by its extraordinary richness and profusion. Tall and slim, she had perfectly moulded limbs and bosom. Her mouth was voluptuous and then her eyes counteracted that voluptuousness by their startling brilliance. They gave subtlety to her beauty.

Becoming aware of the old man's harsh stare, she took the mugs of buttermilk to the form near the hearth where breakfast was laid. She moved gracefully, with a swinging of her hips within her red frieze skirt. Her breasts stood out stiff against her tight bodice. Her husband's eyes followed her, drunk with unsatisfied love.

"Is Thomsy not up yet?" grumbled the old man.

"I called him twice," Maggie said, as she prepared food for the pigs in the trough by the back door. "Thomsy, come on down to your breakfast."

A groan came from the empty loft.

"Huh!" said Brian. "The drunken ruffian!"

He and Martin sat down to the form on stools and crossed themselves. On the form there was a wide dish made of willow rods. It had a flat bottom and upright sides, circular in shape. It was stacked with steaming potatoes. Mugs of buttermilk stood on the form on either side of the dish. In the centre of the potatoes there was a small wooden bowl of salt and water. There were knives with pointed ends for skinning the potatoes.

"God have mercy on us," suddenly cried a hoarse voice from the loft.

Martin laughed.

"Do you hear the groans of him?" he cried. "Oh! Boys, it must have been powerful stuff surely that you drank, Thomsy. Come down and tell the people about it."

"Don't torment him now," said Maggie, "or he'll get up and clear off again for days."

While she mixed their food for the pigs with a large cudgel, the greedy animals pushed against her, grunting. She had to pause now and again in order to drive them back. The hens had also collected about her, hovering on the outskirts of the pigs and making sudden forays. When one of them got a piece of potato, she scurried off, with widespread wings. The dog sat eagerly watching the table, uttering a short bark now and again. A black cat, his tail perpendicular, whined and rubbed his sides against Mary's shins, as she stood at the dressers straining the new milk.

Martin and his father began to eat rapidly. Even while he ate, the young man could not take his eyes off his wife and he smiled dreamily, as if rapt in the contemplation of some delicious pleasure. The old man's face, on the contrary, had got to look quite savage at the sight of food. His gnarled hand, the fingers stiff with rheumatism, the great knuckles scarred like the bark of an old tree, the back ridged with a mass of bluish veins, shook as it reached out to take a potato from the dish. He sliced the potato into four parts, took one part on the tip of his knife, dipped it in the salty water and swallowed it hurriedly, hardly chewing at all. Then he took a mouthful of the buttermilk. While he ate he looked about him furtively, as if afraid that somebody might snatch his food before it touched his lips.

Thomsy, Maggie's brother, now appeared at the edge of the loft. He crouched on his hands and knees, looking down in a forlorn manner. His face seemed to be all beard, with a thick nose and very red lips stuck in the middle. His cheeks also were very red. He wore a tattered, blue, woollen cap, with a round tassel at the top. Curly, grey hair hung down his forehead from beneath the rim of this cap and then continued round his face, increasing in bulk until it became a tangled bush of great depth beneath his chin. The chin itself was bare and there was hardly any hair on his upper lip. The unbearded parts of his face were as red as a berry except his forehead, which was white and deeply furrowed. His eyes were so small that it was almost impossible to see them under their bushy grey brows. Perched on the edge of the dark loft, huddled together, he looked like a dwarf, although he was of ordinary size. The great quantity of rags that he wore made him look as broad as he was long.

"Ga! Maggie asthore," he cried, "will you cut down a snipther of dog-fish and put it on the tongs for me? I'm so bad with the craw sickness that I don't know am I dead or alive."

"Devil mend you," said Brian. "If you didn't make a pig of yourself with poitheen yesterday you wouldn't have the poith to-day."

"Ah! God help me," said Thomsy, "sure I couldn't resist the temptation, bad cess to it, seeing lashings of it around. A whole keg he had, a ten-gallon keg, all to put a gravestone over his mother. 'Faith, Pat Healy knows how to treat his dead mother properly and no doubt about it."

He threw down the end of the ladder to the floor and timidly put his foot on the rung, shaking as the result of the alcohol he had consumed. His feet were covered with sacking, fashioned into the shape of shoes. His clothes were tied together with a rope at the waist.

"Where would Pat Healy get the money for a keg to put a gravestone over his mother?" said Martin. "He had no more than three gallons for her funeral last year."

"Wasn't he in England the spring of this year," said Thomsy, "working on them railways they are making?"

"True for you," said Maggie. "They get as much as two shillings a day in England, making the iron roads, or so they say. Poor man! Isn't he foolish to throw away all that great riches and it hard earned?"

"Ten roaring gallons he had," said Thomsy, as he reached the end of the ladder.

"God forgive you," said Maggie, throwing a strip of dog-fish on the tongs. "It's a sin to boast about that waste."

"Blood an ouns," said Martin, "I was a fool to miss it. It was how I thought there wouldn't be anything to drink."

"Thank God you did," said Mary.

Martin laughed. The old man stopped eating and looked fiercely at Mary and thought:

"She's only a month in the house, but she's beginning to interfere already."

"A custom is a custom," he said aloud. "Good or bad, it's well to live up to it."

Mary looked at him and her eyes hardened. She took a seat at the form and crossed herself. Thomsy waddled down to the hearth.

"What's that in the saucepan?" he said.

"It's a hen egg for Michael," Maggie said, as she crouched over the saucepan, in which the water was beginning to bubble.

"God keep sickness from us," said Thomsy, "though it's funny that the poor have to be sick before they get coddled. I was never sick in my life, so it's a one-sided kind of thanks I have to give the Lord."

"Pooh!" said Brian. "You're lucky to get your keep, not to mind coddling."

"Musha," said Thomsy plaintively, "it would be a strange world where a man couldn't take shelter and nourishment in his father's house."

This had been his father's house, although Kilmartin had added the large bedroom and the barn. When Maggie was eighteen, her parents, two brothers and four sisters were all carried off by typhus, leaving her and Thomsy with this cabin and ten acres of land. She married Brian Kilmartin, who was a stranger without relatives in the district, but with a little money which he had earned as a spalpeen or migratory labourer. Thomsy was then a child of eight. He surrendered his share of the land to Brian in return for his keep. As almost invariably happens in these cases, he had become completely degenerate and was treated with contempt by everybody. When he earned a few pence for doing odd jobs in the district, he got drunk and stayed away until the money was all spent. In fact, he was a byword all over Black Valley and mothers used to threaten naughty children with his fate, saying:

"If you carry on like that, you'll be another Thomsy Hynes when you grow."

As soon as the strip of dog-fish had been broiled a little, Thomsy took it off the tongs and began to eat it, making grimaces as the intense saltiness of the fish bit his palate. After eating a few mouthfuls he threw the remainder to the dog. Then he came to the form and swallowed a mug of buttermilk.

"Ah!" he said with delight. "There's no cure like it."

At this moment, Michael appeared from the bedroom. Immediately, the atmosphere became strained and there was silence except for the grunting of the pigs, which were on their way to the door after finishing their meal. He looked much better now that he was dressed and on his feet. He was twenty-four, one year younger than Martin. They were both about the same height, but Michael was less robust, more slender and with a countenance which sickness had made look refined. His eyes, also, were blue and wild. The hectic flush on his hollow cheeks made them look quite mad. He had a nose like his mother, short and turned up at the end.

"You should have stayed in bed," said his mother timidly, "on this terrible day."

"What for?" he retorted.

He pushed aside the pigs, which stood grunting in the doorway, nosing the air outside, their bellies round with food. Then he swelled out his chest, drew in a deep breath, suppressed a cough and said:

"The rain is stopping."

Nobody answered him. Like most people who suffer from his complaint, he was over sensitive and the rest of the household were afraid to make any remark, lest he might construe it into a reference to his illness. He came down to the form, crossed himself and began to eat the egg which his mother put before him. He devoured the egg rapidly and then, with the suddenness of people who suffer like him, his countenance changed to an expression of radiant happiness and enthusiasm. Now his face had a girlish beauty.

"Did you bring back any of the poitheen?" he said to Thomsy. "A round of it would be great to drive out this cold I have."

"Not a drop a mhac," said Thomsy, as he lit the stump of an old clay pipe. "Indeed, if I had itself, I'd have it drunk this morning as soon as I awoke."

Suddenly, the dog, which was licking the sides of the pigs' trough, paused, listened, cocked his ears, raised the fur along his back, yelped and darted out into the yard, scattering particles of food from his jaws as he barked. He plunged out the door through a flock of hens that had gathered there, sending them flying in all directions with a great, shrill cackling.

"Oscar," shouted Martin, "come back here. Lie down, Oscar."

"Huh!" said Brian. "A dog is a good judge of people. He hates that thieving witch."

"God forgive you," said Maggie. "You shouldn't bite at the poor like a dog."

"Huh!" said Brian. "The poor! If you had your way we'd be in the workhouse, throwing food and drink to the beggars of the county."

The dog came back with his fur still on end and his tail between his legs. Looking behind him and smothering a final bark, he returned to the trough.

"God save all here," said a voice at the door.

"And you, too, Sally," said Maggie.

Sally O'Hanlon, silently, on bare feet, like a ghost, edged round the door-post into the kitchen. She was a tiny woman, about forty-four, with hardly any breasts, and a round, protruding stomach. Her sallow face was withered like an old potato and her features were so small that they gave her face the vacant expression of a pick-pocket. She wore a man's knitted cap, from under which her brown hair hung down dishevelled. It was turning grey at the temples. She had turned up her tattered red skirt about her head, as a protection against the rain. Her under-skirt, of white flannel, also very ragged, had become spotted with mud during her progress to the house. Her hands were hidden under the folds of her upturned skirt, concealing something. Her feet were tiny, very straight and narrow and exceedingly dirty. As soon as she had saluted the household, she crouched on her heels by the wall to the left of the door.

"You're out early this morning," said Martin.

"I have to be, God help me," she said. "The poor are like the birds. They have to be out with the dawn foraging for their little ones."

"What news have you got?" said Michael gaily.

"Well! Then," she said, "God forgive me, I have bad news."

They all looked at her with interest. She rapped out her words with great speed and energy.

"It's this strange disease," she said, "that the people are talking about and how it's spreading over the country, destroying the potatoes of the people."

"The blight?" said Brian. "What news of it is there, woman?"

"It struck Glenaree yesterday," she said.

"May God deny your words," said Maggie, crossing herself.

The old man jumped to his feet and looked at Sally fiercely, as if the poor woman had deliberately, by her own contrivance, brought the blight to Glenaree. It was the next valley to the east, separated from Black Valley by a narrow ridge of mountain. If the disease had reached Glenaree, then Black Valley could hardly escape.

"Where did you hear this?" he said.

"Patsy was over there yesterday," she said, "seeing could he hear of any work. It was late last night when he came back, for he stayed mending baskets in a house. He said the blight was all over the glen. There is a smell from some gardens that would make a person sick."

The old man listened to this speech with his mouth wide open. He remained perfectly still for a few moments after she had finished speaking. Then he closed his mouth, chewed a little, grabbed his hat, clapped it on his pate and dashed out of the house in silence.

"Where are you going?" said Maggie.

"He'd go anywhere after a bad smell," said Michael gaily.

"Don't make fun of disaster," said Thomsy.

"Arrah! Devil take the blight," said Michael. "Sure, if the potatoes rot in the ground itself, we won't be any worse off than we are. What is our life in any case, but hunger and hardship, like any dog? Give us a tune out of your mouth, Sally, and let us dance a jig to show the devil we're not afraid of his blight."

"Musha, God bless you, asthore," said Sally, "it's yourself

has the heart that's stronger than misfortune. I would and welcome, a mhac, only the children are crying with the hunger. They had nothing since noon yesterday. Patsy brought back a grain of oatmeal that I have on the fire and it's how I came over, God spare ye, to see could ye…"

"Give me the can," said Mary, getting to her feet.

"May God increase all the best you have in the house," said Sally, "and may you never feel the lash of hunger laid to your Christian backs."

She handed Mary a quart can which she brought from beneath the folds of her upturned skirt. Mary took the can to the dressers and put fresh milk in it, while Maggie, in a plaintive voice, said that the poor should take no credit for helping the poor, for it was so that God ordained it.

"God bless you, in any case, for being God fearing," said Sally, fervently. "Since we came into this valley eight years ago, evicted out of house and home in the county Tipperary, you have saved us from hunger time and again, Maggie Kilmartin, not to speak of your good man giving us a garden on half. And sure, if the bowl of fate turned, we'd do the same for you. When I had a house and land, many people came to my door and none were turned from it with empty hands."

She went on talking rapidly while Mary brought her the milk and what was left of the potatoes in the dish. Then she delivered a final blessing on the house and went her way, walking in a very graceful manner and cocking up her little rump behind.

"Come on, Thomsy," said Martin, "we have to make a start."

"It's little humour I'm in, 'faith," said Thomsy, "to lift a hand over the skutching stone to-day."

They went out, followed by Michael, who turned on his mother an indignant look when she tried to prevent him going to work.

"There he is," said Maggie, when they had left the house,

"so headstrong that he'll listen to nobody. Now we have to start cleaning this house, darling."

Mary looked at her mother-in-law tenderly.

"May you get the reward in heaven that's been denied you for your goodness on this earth," she said.

Maggie turned aside and blew her nose violently into her apron to hide her emotion.

CHAPTER III

THE RAIN HAD now lessened and the sky had begun to clear in patches as the three men came into the yard.

"Ugh!" Martin said, as he looked up the Valley. "I wish the first man that settled here had broken his neck before he reached it."

"Ga! There are worse places in the world," said Thomsy.

They both crouched and ran through the rain around the gable of the house. Michael stood for a few moments looking up the Valley.

It stretched northwards for a mile, a narrow crater between sheer mountain slopes. Up above were the naked granite peaks, encircled by their shifting wreaths of mist. Then, like the hide of a half shorn animal, came the fur of gorse and heather that covered the lower slopes, down to the little fields that were scattered about the Valley's bed; tiny fields bound with stone fences and a thatched white-walled cabin here and there. From the Black Lake, perched loftily among the peaks at the northern end, the Ghost river flowed south in triumphant flood through rocky gulches. Its roar was like martial music with the flood.

Beside the cattle shed stood the barn where the oats were stacked. It opened on to a flat, rocky plateau facing the east and overlooking the river, which flowed about three hundred yards below it. As Michael reached the barn door, Martin pointed downwards and said: "Look at himself down there. He's running around like a dog on the scent of a rabbit."

The old man was hurrying around the fence of a potato garden that lay beneath the barn, beyond a little field where the black cow was now grazing. The old man did indeed look like an animal tracking its prey, as he stooped over the fence, smelt, ran on to another spot, stooped and smelt, crouching, his face sideways from the rain. His old frieze overshirt had turned dark with moisture.

"Ga! Brother," said Thomsy in the doorway of the barn, as he pulled off his outer shirt, "how could he see anything in this rain, with everything turned black? Isn't it little brown spots that come on the leaves? Them that has seen it on the stricken lands say that little brown spots come on the leaves and then…"

"It's a smell," Martin said. "It begins with a smell."

"That old devil down there will catch his death from cold," Michael said.

"Come on up out of the rain," he shouted at his father.

The old man paid no attention. The three men went into the barn and prepared for work. The oats sheaves were stacked on one side. They cleared the earthen floor on the other side and set out a ring of stones. In the centre of this ring they put a large round block of granite, against which they began to skutch the sheaves. They swung down the sheaves on the block of granite, striking in rotation. When the grain had all been struck out of the ears, they hurled the empty sheaves into the far corner. The air soon became full of dust as the chaff flew about. Michael began to cough. It was obvious that the work was too much for him.

"Take it easy, man alive," Thomsy said to him. "If you go on like that, making a mule of yourself, your cold'll never get better."

Michael said nothing, but brought down his sheaf angrily on the block.

"Ga! Brother," continued Thomsy, "when you first got that cold in spring and we putting down the potatoes, I told you to lie up or it would be the worse for you. You paid no heed to my words, bad cess to you for a headstrong man. You think your strength is greater than the powers of nature, but the ague in your bones turned into a cough in spite of your strength. Then again you stayed out in the rain drinking at Patch Daly's funeral last month and…"

"Shut up or I'll hit you," Michael shouted suddenly.

" 'Faith, then, I will," said Thomsy calmly, "for there's no sense in giving advice to a fool."

"He's right, Michael," said Martin. "You should take it easy while you have your cold."

"Let him that's as good as me skutch as many," said Michael furiously.

"Devil take you, then," said Martin. "Sure, we're only talking for your good. We all know what you can do, your share of work with any man on two legs in the parish. Have sense, man."

Michael was going to make a further angry retort when he was taken with a violent fit of coughing. He had to stagger against the wall, gripping his chest and bent double. The other two watched him anxiously while the paroxysm lasted. When it was over, he wiped his mouth on his sleeve, stared at them in a peculiar manner and then returned to his work with still greater speed. He looked quite deranged, as he tried by sheer force of will to conquer the germs that were devouring him.

The old man came into the barn looking as happy as a child. As he stripped off his bawneen he cried:

"There's no sign of it yet in any case."

"That's good," Martin said. "It's foolish to pay any heed to Sally. She's the greatest liar in the parish."

"They don't know what it is, or where it came from," said Thomsy.

"The sergeant said it came from foreign parts," said Brian. "It's a class of plague that destroys all before it."

They made room for him at the block and he began to skutch. Now they all worked in silence for a long time, until Michael was taken with another bout of coughing. This bout was much more severe than the last. They watched him anxiously, particularly the old man. The old man's face was in agony. He had seen his other children go like that. He knew the full implication of those convulsions.

"It's this dust that's doing it," he said timidly. "Go on into the house and tell your mother to give you a hot drink."

Michael straightened himself, stopped coughing for a moment and looked at his father, as if about to make a reply. Before he had time to speak, however, he suddenly put his hands to his mouth and rushed out of the barn.

"It's no use saying anything to him," said Thomsy. "He's as headstrong as a pig."

The old man sighed and brought down his sheaf limply on the block.

"God have mercy on him," he whispered.

Michael returned, wiping his mouth on his sleeve and looking about him furtively. Nobody spoke. He looked dreadful. Except for a bright, red spot on either cheek, his face was deadly pale. The rings around his eyes were quite black. He trembled as he strode up to the block. Yet he seized his sheaf and resumed his work with his previous energy. After the first few blows, he gasped and a thin wisp of blood trickled on to his lower lip. He hurriedly wiped it away, looked around him aggressively and continued to work. Except for his loud breathing it would be hard to notice anything unusual in his condition. Now he was not straining himself to outdo the others, after the manner of a weakling, or one eager to prove his strength. He swung his sheaves with an easy rhythm, like a strong man in the prime of his health.

At noon, however, when Mary came to announce dinner, a sudden weariness possessed him. With downcast head, he walked back to the house, went immediately to his room and threw himself on the bed. The others took their seats by the form and began their meal, which was now oat porridge and new milk. The mother, noticing that he did not come, went into the bedroom. To her horror she found him sobbing aloud, as he lay face downwards.

"Oh! My treasure," she said, running to him, "what's the matter?"

He did not answer but continued to sob. The sound rent her heart. Even though he had always been delicate, his nature had hitherto been too proud to show any outward mark of suffering. She had never even seen him wince as a child, when he fell and cut himself, or met with any of the other little misfortunes that cause children to shed tears. And now in his manhood he was sobbing like a girl. She called her husband, who hurried into the room with his fists clenched.

"We had better take his clothes off and put him to bed," he said.

"You shouldn't have let him work," she said.

"How could I stop him?" said Brian angrily.

"Don't shout at me," she cried hysterically.

"Go and make him a hot drink," he retorted. "This is no time for throwing blame."

Tears streamed down Maggie's cheeks as she returned to the kitchen. She had over-worked all morning and now this shock, together with her husband's ill-temper, was too much for her. She took a saucepan off the dressers and began to pour milk into it.

"What's the matter?" said Martin.

Maggie began to sob aloud. Mary jumped up and took the saucepan from her.

"Go and sit down," she said. "I'll do it."

The old woman sat down in the hearth corner, threw her apron over her head and rocked herself, weeping.

"Crying will do no good," said Martin, who continued to eat moodily.

He and Thomsy hurried through their meal and left the house in silence. They had been working some time when the old man joined them.

"How is he now?" Martin said.

"He's fallen asleep," said the old man.

In about an hour they had finished threshing. Then Brian and Thomsy began to carry the heap of grain out to a flat rock in front of the barn, while Martin went to the house for a dish to sift the chaff. The rain had now given way to radiant sunshine and there was a faint breeze, making it ideal weather for gleaning.

Mary was spinning in the yard and Martin stood to watch her, smiling rapturously. Her spinning was like a dance. First she took a roll of the carded wool from the board between the wheel and the spindle frame. She fixed the roll carefully to the end of the spun thread. Then she drew back gently, the roll in one hand, the other hand reaching for the wheel. A slow, gentle turn of the wheel stretched out the roll. Then she went over it with her fingers, straightening out the lumps, strengthening it where it was weak, making it even. Then again she spun the wheel, this time more quickly, so that it hummed. Now a humming sound also came from the thread and as she turned the wheel, she bent and raised her body, just like a slinger swinging to hurl a stone from his sling. Finally, she drew the spun thread smartly to her shoulder and let it run up the spindle. Then she stooped to take another roll of the carded wool.

Martin crept up behind without her hearing him. Suddenly he pounced on her and clutched her in his arms. She uttered a little cry of fright and turned round in his embrace.

"You shouldn't frighten me like that," she whispered.

She panted and her eyes wandered over his face, soft with desire.

"Don't tire yourself too much," he whispered, "because it will be a long time yet before my love can give you any rest."

"Arrah! Be off with you," she said. "You have too easy a tongue."

"Thank God for it," said Martin, "for what else seduced you? Tell me that now, you that had all the rich men of the parish after you."

"Let me work, will you?" she said. "I have to finish this spinning for after supper. The loom is waiting for it at my father's house."

He released her and said seriously:

"How is Michael?"

"He's asleep."

"Poor man," said Martin, "isn't it a pity? Why do we ever grumble at anything as long as we have our health and our eyes to see the sunbeams dancing on the river water?"

"It's a pity surely," said Mary. "Poor Michael! It's not a land slave he should have been born, but a rhyming poet at the court of some high king. God gave him poor harness to drag the load of poverty, and what good to him in his dreaming mind, that would make your mouth water at the lovely stories he tells?"

Martin sighed and took the dish over to the flat rock, while Mary continued her spinning. A heap of grain had already been spilled on the rock. He filled the dish, held it out in front of his face and then tipped it into the wind. The heavy grain pattered like hail-stones on to the rock, while the chaff flew away on the breeze.

"How is he now?" said Brian, coming out with another load.

"Sleeping," Martin said.

"Ha!" said the old man. "This is the finest crop I have seen in years."

Late in the afternoon, they had all the oats packed into bags, while the empty sheaves were divided into two stacks, the light straw for thatching the house and barn, the heavier straw for cattle feed and for bedding. They were about to return to the house when Martin sniffed the air and said:

"That's queer."

"What is it?" the old man said.

"That smell," said Martin. "Can't you smell something queer?"

"Ga! Brother," said Thomsy, sniffing, "I smell something, but maybe it's my own breath after yesterday."

"Blood an ouns!" said the old man. "Would it be the blight? Where is it coming from?"

"From up there," said Martin, pointing towards the north, from which a faint breeze was blowing. "Phew! It's stinking. It's from Patch Hernon's share up there. Look. There are people looking over a wall into his garden."

They all looked at the garden towards which he pointed. The sun's rays now came slantwise through a gap between two high peaks on the west, gilding the sombre Valley with a gorgeous light. The vast shadows on the mountains made a ghostly pattern of extraordinary beauty. Now the dim colours of the gorse, the heather and the decaying green of the potato stalks were brought forth. The white walls and faded thatch of the cabins that stretched in a crooked row from where they stood to the Valley's end, above the western bank of the stream, all shone in the brilliant evening light. Even the parched grass and the stubble of the shorn oat fields stood out distinctly against the solemn darkness of the unlighted mountain caverns. Down below, the roaring torrent cascaded from the Black Lake through narrow, rocky gorges, until it widened below the house to a deep pool that was now yellow and turbulent with a press of water, its banks fringed with a swirling rime of froth and jetsam gathered by the flood.

"It's Patch Hernon's share sure enough," said Martin. "I'll go up and see what's wrong."

"Whist!" said the old man. "Don't you hear?"

The sound of a woman's wailing reached their ears. Martin set off at a run towards the north. The old man returned to the house with the dish.

"Where is Martin going?" Mary said to him anxiously.

She also had heard the wailing. The old man did not answer. Michael appeared in the doorway. The old man stared at him and said:

"I thought you were in bed."

"I'm all right now," Michael said. "Where is Martin going?"

"I'm afraid it's the blight that has struck Patch Hernon's share," said the old man. "Why didn't you stay in your bed?"

Michael stared dreamily towards the north and said nothing. Then he shrugged his shoulders and strode across the yard, like a man sleep-walking, while his father and Mary stared after him. He passed into the lane and then paused, as if uncertain whither to turn. The lane ran from end to end of the Valley.

"Where are you going, Michael?" the old man called out at last.

"Visiting," Michael said.

Then he suddenly turned towards the south. Maggie had now come to the door and Thomsy appeared round the corner of the gable. Just before he passed out of sight beyond the house, Michael looked towards Thomsy and said, smiling in a strange way:

"Come on visiting with me, Thomsy."

"For God's sake, stop him," said Maggie.

"Why didn't you stop him?" said Brian.

"He got up unknown to me," said Maggie. "I was in the little room."

"Go on with him," the old man said to Thomsy. "It's plain where he's going. I know he has two shillings on him since the lambs were sold. Try to keep him from fighting when he has the poitheen drunk."

"Ga! Brother," said Thomsy, "I'll do my best."

"God have mercy on us," said Maggie, making the sign of the Cross.

After supper, which was eaten in a gloomy silence, Martin and Mary took the thread to the weaver's house. It was quite late when they returned. Michael and Thomsy were still absent. The old man was terribly worried. He sat in the corner of the hearth, dangling his rosary beads. Maggie sat knitting in the opposite corner. The pigs were snoring loudly on their fresh straw.

"Did you see any sign of them?" Brian said.

"Say your rosary and go to bed," Martin said. "You'll see no sign of them to-night."

"Have you no heart in you?" said the old man. "I don't believe you'd care if your brother died on the road."

Before Martin could answer, Maggie took her stool and said:

"In the name of God, let us kneel down and say the rosary. There's no use waiting."

While the old man led the recitation of the rosary, he kept pausing to listen to sounds outside, the barking of a dog, or the call of a night bird. When the prayers were finished, Maggie put a dish of warm water before the hearth for them to wash their feet. The old man washed his feet first. While he was drying them at the fire, the sound of singing reached their ears.

"That's him," said the old man excitedly.

They all listened. The air was painfully sad and the words were equally so.

"You'll see me walk at night upon the mountain,
And you'll hear my voice at noon down by the stream…"

They all knew the song, called "The Ghost's Lament". The old man pretended to be pleased by the singing.

"Hech!" he said. "Hasn't he got a fine voice?"

"Holy Virgin! He has drink taken," Mary whispered to Maggie.

"Go on into bed, asthore," Maggie said. "Don't be afraid of him."

Martin hurriedly dried his feet and pulled on his shoes once more. Michael was a difficult man to deal with when he had been drinking. Mary, clutching her bosom, went into her bedroom and closed the door. The old man followed Martin into the yard. Michael had now stopped singing. He was helping Thomsy over the stile into the yard.

"Ga! Brother," said Thomsy, "I'm that heavy I can't lift myself."

"Let me get hold of him," Martin said, seizing Thomsy by the shoulder.

"Let him alone," said Michael, pushing Martin aside violently.

"All right, then," said Martin gently. "Have it your own way."

Thomsy belched and then hurtled over the stile into the yard, where he lay in a heap, grunting. Martin returned to the house.

"He's out of his mind," he said to his mother. "I'm leaving him alone."

"Go on in with Mary," the mother said. "We'll take care of him."

Martin went into his bedroom. It was pitch dark there, the little window being covered with a curtain.

"Where are you, Mary?" he said.

She answered him from the bed. He groped his way over to her and took her in his arms. She was sobbing.

"Fasten the door," she said. "I'm afraid of him."

He got up and drew the bolt of the door.

"Take your clothes off and get into bed," he whispered. "You needn't be afraid. Michael is the kindest person in the world, but he's out of his mind on account of his sickness, poor creature."

They stripped and got into bed. Locked in his arms, Mary no longer felt afraid. Thomsy and Michael were now in the kitchen and the old couple were trying to get them into a reasonable frame of mind. Michael kept singing snatches of song.

"Let me sing," he cried. "I have only a little while to sing. Maybe in the grave I'll sing too, only my songs will be shining flowers that will grow over me. Let me sing, father, and let you hold my hand."

For a long time, they made a fearful din in the kitchen, singing and hurtling about the place. The pigs and fowl were disturbed and added to the tumult. Finally the old couple managed to quieten them. They all went to bed.

"Why are you shaking, Mary?" Martin whispered. "You're shaking like a leaf."

"I wish we had a house for ourselves," Mary said.

"Never you fear," Martin said. "You'll get used to this house and then you'll be happy."

"I'm happy, darling, but I wish we were alone, with nobody else in our house."

Martin fell asleep, but Mary lay awake a long time, listening to the squeaking of a marsh bird, a sound like the snapping of scissors. Now and again she felt Martin shaking in his sleep, as if he were laughing at something.

CHAPTER IV

BY THE FOLLOWING morning the blight had spread over nearly all the potato fields in Black Valley. However, except on Patch Hernon's crop, which was the first to be affected, it did not look very serious. Hernon's crop seemed completely destroyed and there was a stench from his fields. All the people decided to begin digging at once.

Patsy O'Hanlon and his wife came to help the Kilmartins. The O'Hanlons were merely squatters in the Valley. As Kilmartin allowed them to plant one field with potatoes, in return for half the yield, they generally helped him with his work. There were a considerable number like them about the place, people evicted from their holdings elsewhere.

Kilmartin decided to begin digging in the field that bordered on the river. Sally O'Hanlon set to work clearing the decayed stalks and the weeds from the ridges, in order to make digging easier for the men. Martin was the first to throw out a spade full of earth. He held up the roots, with their little cluster of potatoes.

"These are not touched yet in any case," he said with joy. "And a fine crop they look too."

"Praised be God!" said the old man.

" 'Faith, then," said Thomsy, "these are as small as marbles."

He tipped the potatoes he had dug into a little heap with the edge of his spade.

"Oh! Well!" said O'Hanlon. "Big or little it's best to dig them before the blight gets at them."

He was about the same age as his wife and strangely like her, with a wrinkled face the colour of parchment. However, he lacked her energy and he was miserably thin. It seemed an effort for him to plunge his spade into the ground and he spoke in the sad, ineffectual way of a person who has given up all hope.

"Did ye drink a lot last night?" said the old man to Thomsy.

He was very cheerful this morning, as Michael had slept well during the night and was still asleep. He had great hopes that the crude whisky might shake up the man's constitution and set him on the road to health. It often happened with a man going into a decline that a night of drinking put new life into him.

"Ga! Brother," said Thomsy, "don't talk to me about it. That man can drink a barrel of it."

"Huh!" said the old man. "He can do his share at most things."

"Phew!" said Sally. "The stalk that's touched by it is as rotten as dung. Look. The stem breaks off when you lay a finger on it."

"Bend your backs," said the old man curtly. "Whatever it is, we'll get the better of it by digging them. Poor Patch Hernon is likely to lose the lot."

In spite of the smell of the blight it was very pleasant working down there by the river, whose music was loud in their ears. The wind had the crisp freshness of autumn. After the rain of the previous day the sky was spotless. People were digging potatoes all over the Valley. Now and again a shout came along on the air, or the rasping sound of a stone rubbing the clinging moist earth from a spade. Then again a curlew would call, or a cow would low. It was very beautiful down there.

They worked steadily until noon when Mary came with dinner.

"Is Michael still asleep?" the old man said.

She had a dish of potatoes on her head and a can of milk in her hand. The potatoes were covered with a cloth, through which steam arose.

"No," she said. "He's up now."

They sat down to eat by the river bank, where there was a grassy lane between the potato ridges and the sandy edge of the pool.

"Any sign of them rotting?" she asked when they had begun to eat.

"Only an odd one," Martin said. "Nearly all of them are as God made them."

"It's twenty-four years now," Brian said, "since this garden was sown last. Bad luck it had, too. It was a year of flood."

They hurried through the meal and then returned to their digging. Before going back to work, Sally O'Hanlon whispered to Mary. Mary nodded and then Sally waved towards three little heads that were peering over a fence in the distance. The three heads were those of her children. They came running down to the river bank behind the fence, making a wide detour, like wild animals afraid of coming too near human beings. They paused several times and their mother had to re-assure them by beckoning each time they halted. Finally, they came rushing along through the tall grass and fell upon the remains of the meal.

They devoured even the skins of the potatoes and what was left of the salt and water. They scraped the bottom of the dish with their grimy fingers, to pick out any tiny morsel that had got wedged between the woven willow rods. When there was absolutely nothing left, they sat huddled together by the empty dish, snuffling and wiping their noses on their sleeves.

One was a boy of fourteen. The other two were girls, of eight and ten respectively. The boy, who had suffered from rickets, was no bigger than his sisters. Indeed, they were all under-sized and emaciated. Their faces were unlike those of children. The queer, unholy wisdom begotten of hunger had already made them look old and unhappy. They all wore red petticoats. In addition, the boy wore the remnants of a man's waistcoat.

When Mary, who had been scouring the milk can with

sand by the river's edge, returned to pick up the dish and the cloth, the children scurried away in fright. They halted at a distance and squatted once more, hoping that something more might be given to them.

"Poor little creatures," Mary thought, as she watched them run away. "It's terrible that little children should be hungry like that."

Suddenly she heard a loud cry from the house. She looked and saw Maggie in the yard above, waving excitedly.

"What is it?" Martin shouted.

Maggie could not make herself understood at that distance. She kept waving her arms. Martin dropped his spade and ran out of the garden. They all followed him. Mary came last. She was afraid to find out what had happened. A terrible fear oppressed her suddenly, a fear that her young love was going to be destroyed by an imminent disaster.

The wind was beginning to have the tang of winter in it, as it swept through the Valley with its persistent whisper. The cold hand of winter was about to touch the earth. And she felt that this destroying hand, icy, with immovable grasp, would destroy her and her lover.

As she was walking slowly across the little field where the black cow was grazing, Martin came running towards her from the house.

"I'm going for the doctor," he cried.

"What happened?"

"At the back of the house," he panted as he hurried past. "I found him lying in a pool of blood. He coughed up blood."

She halted and stared at the cow, which was lowing nervously, excited by the running of the people. The hip bones of the poor animal stuck out in a horrid fashion. Nothing for her to eat. The grass of the little field had been already shorn so closely that the black earth was naked in patches.

Mary suddenly wanted to scream and to cry out to God in revolt against the tortures of this poverty. Immediately she was taken by a great fear of having sinned. Meekly, she crossed herself and begged God to forgive her. Then peace descended on her.

The sound of the wind passing through the Valley became caressing and it whispered a gentle lullaby that drowned sorrow. Its never-ending sound was soothing like the unintelligible words muttered by the priest on the altar, coming from somewhere in the vast spaces of eternity.

CHAPTER V

DR. HYNES CAME early in the afternoon on the black mare that Martin had brought to fetch him. The mare was very wild and quite unused to a saddle, since the old man and his sons rode her barebacked, except for a piece of cloth to protect the crutch from her spine. Thus, when she found the doctor on her back, together with a saddle, and a bit between her jaws, she bolted from the village of Crom at a headlong gallop. The doctor was a poor horseman and was unable to get the wild animal under control, until she came in sight of Kilmartin's house, when she broke into a trot, snorting and dripping with lather.

A crowd waited for him in the lane outside the house. Doctors were still a novelty in that year of Our Lord 1845. The people still regarded them merely as "gentlemen", from whom the poor creatures felt entitled to beg a copper or a favour. Even though Dr. Hynes was the son of John Hynes, the shopkeeper, who had been born in Black Valley, they still regarded him as a "gentleman", because of his position. They crowded around his panting horse, seizing his stirrups, his reins and even the tails of his coat.

Their rags, their filth, their coarse expressions and excited gestures repelled and embarrassed him, as he felt conscious that his own father had begun like one of them, before he escaped from the serfdom of a tenant farmer's life to become a huckster. Nobody is more repelled by the sordidness of extreme poverty than the child of parents who were born in it.

Brian had put on a clean bawneen to receive the doctor. He had also put on his Sunday boots and these being too small for him, he cut rather a ludicrous figure, as he ran out into the lane, bent almost double, limping, his wrinkled face contracted into a grin of pain, which he meant to be a smile of welcome. The mare whinnied when she saw him. Then she stood still with her neck stretched forward, a heavy lather dripping from her jaw, where the unaccustomed bit had chafed her. With his hat in his hand, the old man took the mare's head. The mare, to show her gratitude for delivery from the strange rider that had terrified her by his clumsy seat, caressed Brian's shoulder with her slavering snout. He led her up to the door, dropping curtseys and muttering a profuse welcome.

It was funny to see him behave with such abject humility, considering how dour he was ordinarily, when dealing with his own kind.

"Are you the sick man's father?" said the doctor, striving to be distant and dignified, although he found it hard to speak on account of the way his teeth chattered.

"Yes, your honour," said Brian. "God bless your honour for coming in such a hurry. 'Faith, you're a fine rider, God spare your health."

He helped the doctor to dismount by offering his bent knee and his shoulder. In his excitement, however, added to the fact that the doctor was very stiff after his ride and could only move his limbs with difficulty, Brian impeded the descent instead of helping it. The result was that the doctor finally lurched from the horse's back into a pool of water that had remained by the door after the previous day's rain. He splashed the muddy water up on to his breeches.

"Lord save us from harm," cried Maggie in a horrified tone from the doorway. "Your elegant clothes are ruined, sir."

She ran forward, holding out her apron. She began to rub the mud from his breeches, but only succeeded in fouling some more of the cloth. The doctor flushed and felt very angry, but quite helpless.

"That will do, my good woman," he said. "Where is the sick man?"

"This way, sir," cried Brian, rushing past him into the

house. "Bend your head, your honour, for the door is low."

This warning was entirely unnecessary, as Dr. Hynes was very short in stature, unlike the tall, lanky Kilmartins. In spite of his youth, for he was only twenty-five, he was beginning to be a podgy little man. His frock coat bulged slightly at the waist and his thighs seemed like to burst the seams of his breeches. He had rather a furtive expression, probably owing to the smallness of his mouth and eyes. As a result, he looked by no means handsome, although he had beautiful golden hair, curly and luxuriant. Even that, however, looked out of keeping with the rest of him.

Carrying his little bag, he walked scowling, very stiff and wide-legged, into the house. Immediately he began to sniff. The pigs and their bed had been removed. So had the fowl coop. The lime which had been scattered on the floor during the previous morning had made the air quite sanitary, compared to what it was ordinarily. Even so, there was an undoubted stench. Standing in the doorway of her bedroom, Mary noticed the doctor sniff and felt terribly ashamed. The doctor caught sight of her, as his eyes roamed about. She saw him start slightly. His little, yellowish eyes widened a little, startled by her unexpected beauty. She dropped her eyes and turned hurriedly into her room. He moved to follow her, thinking the patient was there, but Brian stopped him.

"This way, your honour," said Brian, tugging at the doctor's coat.

He led the doctor into the other bedroom. Here the smell was quite as pronounced as in the kitchen, but it was of a different kind. It was the heavy odour of unwashed bodies and of human breath that had been unable to find an exit and had grown stale, swaying around in a confined space. The tiny window, of course, did not open and the door, also very small, was generally closed. To the inhabitants of the house, this condition of the air was normal, but it was offensive to the doctor.

"Open that window," he said curtly.

Brian and Maggie looked at one another with open mouths. The doctor had to repeat the order, still more curtly, before Brian, with a nervous lurch forward and a further curtsey, said that the window did not open.

"Well! Then, in God's name," said the doctor angrily, "throw that door wide open. Get some air into the room. How do you expect a sick man to get better in a room like this?"

" 'Faith, sir," said Maggie humbly, "sure it's the same air that we do always breathe."

"Silly people," thought the doctor, going over to the bed.

"Where's the pain?" he said curtly, drawing back the clothes from Michael's chest.

But Michael clutched at the clothes and replaced them, gripping them with rigid fingers and staring at the doctor with the ferocious stare of a cornered animal.

"I have no pain," he whispered fiercely.

The doctor drew back a pace, discomfited by this extraordinary and unexpected reception. He was by no means a bully, or a rude person. His rude behaviour had been caused by his inability to master the situation in which he had found himself; first of all making a fool of himself on the horse and then being sensitive about his father's origin when confronted with people who called him "your honour". The sick man's defiance brought him back to his normal timid and gentle self. He flushed and lowered his eyes.

"How long has he been ill?" he said to Maggie.

"Since noon, your honour," Maggie said. "He went out to the back of the house and he was gone out no more than a little while when I went around there to the well for a can of water and I found him outside the wall of the little house, lying down, saving your presence, in a pool of his own blood. It was pouring out of his mouth and nose and he lying there unconscious. 'What is it?' I said to him. 'What ails you, darling?'

Never a word did he speak. I called the men and they took him between hands into the house, but he never spoke a word since then, until you spoke to him now, so we don't know what happened to him, except it's from the cold he's had these several months and he that headstrong, sir, that it's beyond our power to make him take his ease."

"I see," said the doctor to Michael. "So you've had a haemorrhage?"

Now that the doctor's attitude had changed, Michael allowed himself to be uncovered. The doctor began his examination.

"Did you give him anything?" he said to Maggie.

"We gave him melted butter," said Brian, "but it only made him sick."

"He threw it up, saving your presence," said Maggie, now beginning to sob.

She was biting her lower lip to keep back her tears. She did not want to commit the impoliteness of weeping in the presence of the doctor.

"Well!" said the doctor, when he had finished his examination. "You're not too bad, young man. We'll see what we can do for you."

After he had given Michael a remedy against haemorrhage, he tried to explain to the old woman how the patient was to be treated. He found that she did not understand a word of what he was saying. The poor woman's instincts as a mother knew that remedies were of no use. She bit her lower lip more fiercely, trying to keep back that loud wail of the despairing peasant.

"Tell Mary what to do, your honour," said Brian. "She has more learning than we have."

He led the doctor out of the sick room, through the kitchen, into the small bedroom, where Mary was still hiding.

"There she is, your honour," he said, pointing to Mary. "Take it down in writing, Mary. She can write a good hand, your honour."

"It's not at all necessary to write anything down," said the doctor.

"It's no bother, sir," said the old man, who seemed determined that his daughter-in-law should show her ability to write. "She's my son's wife. Get your pen and paper, Mary."

In order to humour the old fellow and that he might have more time to observe Mary's beauty, the doctor asked her to write down his instructions. She shyly opened her big marriage box that stood by the wall and took from the top shelf a small sheet of paper, a bottle of ink and a quill pen.

"I'm ready, sir," she said.

The doctor had in the meantime noticed how neat this room was compared to the other. There were even little attempts at decoration and the bed had a curtain about it. The air was fresh, smelling of limewash. He felt unaccountably thrilled and he started when he heard her voice. It was throaty and yet clear, like the music of a mountain torrent. He felt carried away suddenly and looked at her boldly. She would not meet his eyes.

Then he thought with anger of the young man who had cantered up to his father's hotel, where he lived, and cried that his brother had "spat up a gallon of blood." Her husband!

"You don't get much opportunity to use your skill at writing," he said.

"I do, sir, now and again," she said. "At home I used to write letters for people that had relations in America."

"Oh! You're not long married," he said.

"Only a month, your honour," said the old man. "Her father is Barney Gleeson, the weaver. She has another sister, Ellie, over at the Big House. Nineteen she is. They have genius in them, that family of Gleesons. Her father is a great talker about politics. He could give you by rote the history of Ireland and of all the injustice that's been done to the people by the tyrants that are over them."

The old man, usually silent and severe, had become

garrulous and fawning under the influence of his trouble. While he listened to the old man's babbling, the doctor flushed and he felt the blood course wildly through his veins, as he looked at Mary's beauty. He felt ashamed and at the same time utterly abandoned.

"How lovely she is!" he kept thinking. "What a voice!"

After he had left the house, the people again crowded round him, begging, showing their sores, asking for news of the blight and when the Queen's men were going to be driven out of the country, to leave the landlords at their mercy.

"You're one of ourselves," they cried, "a Catholic and a son of the people."

Now he no longer felt angry with them, because of their rags, their filth and their fawning. Under the influence of Mary's beauty and the intoxication of her glorious voice, he felt proud to be of their stock. He was so excited that renewed contact with the mare's spine did not hurt him as he rode away.

CHAPTER VI

AS SOON AS the doctor had left, the pigs and the fowl were brought back to the kitchen. Some of the neighbours stayed to commiserate. In the evening, Mary's father came to enquire after the sick man's health.

"Ah! Musha," said Maggie. "He's only poorly."

"Ah! God help us," Gleeson said.

The weaver was a stout man, with the short, powerful legs peculiar to those of his craft. Although he was sixty-one, there was no grey streak in his rich, curly, brown hair. His face was full and aggressive, with a prominent chin, which made his thick beard protrude like a lever. His thick lips curled outwards. His nose was heavy at the tip, with wide-open nostrils. His blue eyes had an expression of good-humoured ferocity.

"As if the blight wasn't enough for ye, poor people," he continued, lighting his pipe with a coal at the fire, "without this misfortune to come down on ye."

"It's not so bad on our share," Martin said, "but there was terrible talk of it in Crom and I in the village to-day. Your share is bad with it, Patch?"

"Not a sound pratie did I dig to-day," cried Patch Hernon. "They are all rotten. First the cow died on me in the spring, and now this. There's a curse on the land."

This Patch Hernon was married to Brian's eldest surviving daughter, Kitty. He had all the appearance of a demented fellow. Tall and lean, with a closely-cropped skull, his body was continually in exaggerated movement. His hands and his nostrils twitched. He kept tapping the ground, first with one foot and then with another. He shifted about on his seat and jerked his head from side to side, as if avoiding flies that were trying to sting him. His face was clean-shaven, deadly pale, with high cheek-bones and glaring, dark eyes. His rather thick lips were drawn back from his large teeth, in a perpetual, maniacal grin. He had taken a seat by the open door, through which he kept looking, as if he expected the approach of an enemy, or some important message that would compel his instant departure. He addressed his remarks to no one in particular and it seemed that he considered the whole company hostile to him.

"There's a curse on the people," Gleeson said, "not on the land. The land of Ireland is holy and lovely and rich, but the tyrants have taken the rich land from the people and thrown them to live on the western rocks. It's on the bog and moor now that the people of Ireland are living and the bogs breed disease."

"Disease it is, sure enough," said a wandering fiddler called Timoney. "But sure I wouldn't mind it on the praties, but now it has struck your fine son, Brian, whose dancing thighs often brought a tear to my eye at the fair of Crom. I heard he was ailing in the village to-day and I came to see him."

"God bless you, good man," Martin said. "And what news do you bring from your travels?"

The fiddler was a thin old man, with a red nose and watery eyes, wearing a tattered, blue, frock-coat that had belonged to a gentleman.

" 'Faith, I have heard plenty in my travels," he said. "A man was reading out of a newspaper last night in a tavern at Clogher and I fiddling for a shower of men off a Norwegian barque. He read out how the blight is spreading back and forth over all the land and the gardens destroyed with all their crops. A man that was there said the crows would have fine feeding all this winter off the corpses that would be lying dead on the roads."

"God have mercy on us," Maggie whispered.

"But that's nothing, my good woman," Timoney, the

fiddler said, "compared to what I've seen in my young days."

" 'Faith, you've seen queer things and no lie to it," said Patch Hernon, "tramping the country roads with your fiddle, more power to you, although it's yourself that should never bid the time of day to sorrow or misfortune and the great share of joy you leave in your travels, along the highways of the land."

"I remember Ninety-Eight," said the fiddler, raising his voice. "I was at the Races of Castlebar when the French sent the English flying. I've heard the screech at the triangle, too, and I've seen the pitch cap like a mocking crown on the patriot's head and the poor priests flying through the bog with a price on them for any informer to take. Them times are gone, thank God and our great Liberator Daniel O'Connell for it. What does it matter if a few people die of hunger? There's no real persecution no more."

"Hunger'll be nothing new to the natures of the people," said Gleeson. "It's eighteen years since I was on the roads myself, tramping from the hunger in Sligo to this place in Galway here. It was a woeful journey."

"God spare your health," said Thomsy, "you've been a godsend to the parish since you came. It's well I remember the day you came with your good woman and the children on the donkey-cart. Mary there was only a year old at the time."

Mary flushed and went into her room. She hated any reference to the way her family arrived in Black Valley. Her father, on the other hand, loved talking about it in public and he always put her to shame with his talk. And the people mocked him about it. They liked to get him to talk and make him excited, in order to amuse themselves with him. Being a conceited fellow, he was indifferent to this mockery, as long as he got an opportunity of discoursing about the great event in his past.

Exhausted by the events of the day, Mary threw herself down on her bed. She heard her father say:

"There was nothing else for it but death from hunger. From place to place we went with the loom on the cart with the children. Many a time we were that weak from hunger that I wanted to sell the loom, but I held on to it all the same. Then one day, outside the village below, we met Mr. Coburn, God lighten the darkness on his soul, he's a good man for a Protestant minister. He took pity on us."

Mary began to pray to the Blessed Virgin.

"Take Martin and me away from here," she prayed. "I want to go away far, where nobody will know us.".

"He's a good man, sure enough," said Timoney, the fiddler. "He'll send no hungry person from his door. It's seldom, though, you'll find one like him, for they are a cursed mean lot, the same bloody Protestants."

"It was him gave me a plot of land to build a house and garden," said Gleeson, "on the edge of his bog, after many a fine gentleman of my own holy persuasion had turned me from his door with an empty hand and a sick heart."

"Oh! Why doesn't he stop shouting and Michael sick in there?" Mary whispered.

"It's easy for him to be generous," said Patch Hernon fiercely, "on the money he steals from the people with his tithes."

"Pooh!" said Gleeson. "It would be as easy for him to be mean like the rest of them as to be generous. Don't they all rob the people? Who is a greater robber than the Catholic gombeen man, as soon as he gets his foot on the neck of his own flesh and blood? We have an example down there in Crom, Johnny Hynes, that got rich on account of the Repeal Movement, with the Repealers boycotting the Protestant shopkeepers. I remember when O'Connell and Richard Lalor Shiel started the Catholic Association in 1828, they promised us Heaven an' all when Emancipation would be won. We got it and in the following year the landlords, seeing the poor Catholic tenants were voting for them no longer, started the clearances and whole villages were thrown out on the roads. To hell or to Connaught, Cromwell the murderer used to say. Nowadays, begob, the gentry are clearing the people out of Connaught itself, into the grave or the workhouse, or the emigrant ship. It's America now, instead of Connaught, to die of hunger in the New York dives, or to be thrown to the wild Indians on the plains of the west."

Mary began to fall asleep. The mention of America by her father roused a thought in her mind. America? There was a means of escape from the horror of this life.

"Where did all the money go," continued Gleeson, "that was collected for the Catholic Rent? Into the pockets of the leaders. Nothing was done with it, except to make the leaders rich and powerful. It was the Whig Government started the schools in '31. They started the workhouses, too. I know my history. O'Connell started the Precursor Society in '39 to help the Whigs, when their yellow gold was coming into the pockets of the leaders. Then in '41 he started the Repeal Association when the Tories came into power, but when it got strong and swept the country, he turned tail at Clontarf, with the victory in his grasp. What have the people got now, as a result of all their struggling in the last years? How can they improve the land when it's not belonging to them? They have to give everything that grows on it to the landlords and the ministers except the few miserable potatoes they eat to keep them alive. Their rents are raised if they improve the sod that belonged to their ancestors, or if their houses, or their clothes begin to look decent, as the Lord ordained them to look. They have to live in dirt, for fear the drivers would report them to have money and raise their exactions."

Mary began to dream. It seemed to her that an angel came to her and told her to rise up and follow him. She arose and went with the angel to a great ship with white sails, on which they embarked. They went over the western sea to a rich land where the corn grew taller than a man's head and there were no masters. She asked the angel where she was and the angel said: "This is America. Make a home here and God will bless you." Then she awoke with a start to hear her father's voice:

"I'm telling you that O'Connell was put in jail to save his face. He is up there in Dublin now, at Conciliation Hall, talking about freeing the American negroes. It's not talk we want, but powder and ball to drive the tyrants from our holy soil. We should bare our breasts to the bullets and the grape-shot and die like men, instead of dying like sheep in a windy ditch."

Mary lay on her bed, staring at the roof, thinking of her vision.

CHAPTER VII

BY NEXT MORNING, Michael's condition had greatly improved and he was able to take some nourishment. Work continued in the potato gardens. Mary now helped with the picking, leaving the old woman to attend to Michael. It was ominous that there were more potatoes affected by the rot than on the previous day. As they continued to dig, this rot increased. However, the Kilmartin family was not greatly worried, as the rot among their crop was far less than among the neighbours. And Michael seemed to be making constant improvement.

According as each garden was dug, a long shallow pit was made. Dry ferns were strewn along the bottom of this pit, over which the potatoes were piled in a tapering heap. The pile was thatched with more ferns and withered stalks. Then earth was pitched on to the top of the mound and battened down with spades until it was air-tight. Great care was taken not to allow any diseased potato into the heap.

When Kilmartin's four little gardens had been dug and pitted, he judged that he had lost about four bushels, or one tenth of the whole. That was not at all serious. The rot was worst in the garden that O'Hanlon had share-cropped. Normally yielding about seven bushels, this year it yielded no more than five, after the diseased tubers had been discarded. So that the poor man and his family could look forward to a year of acute distress, with only two and a half bushels of potatoes as their sole means of nourishment.

"God is powerful," Sally said, nothing daunted by this prospect. "In any case, the Queen is going to give out pay to the people, they say."

Indeed, a feeling of confidence was general among the

people, even though some had lost one third of their potatoes, while in Glenaree many had lost nearly the whole amount.

"The Queen is going to give out pay," they said.

This idea came about, owing to the fact that a sergeant of constabulary from Crom came around with two men, all carrying carbines and notebooks, to make an inventory of what potatoes had been lost.

"What did I tell you?" the people said. "The Queen is going to make the landlord pay for every pratie that is lost."

And so, with light hearts, as soon as the potatoes were pitted, they began to thatch their cabins and to get their stock ready for the October fair. The summer's shearing had also been woven into frieze by Gleeson, and Tony Derrane, the tailor, was going around the Valley turning the frieze cloth into garments. As a rule, it was the gayest time of the year and the blight did not seriously detract from the general gaiety this year, owing to the people's confidence that action would be taken by the Government to relieve the damage. For the very poor are unable to see far into the future. If they can make provision for their immediate wants, they are not greatly troubled by a remote disaster, whose shadow is only beginning to assume shape on the horizon.

In Kilmartin's house, of course, the shadow of Michael's illness was more than a spot on the horizon. He now spent the days sitting in the corner of the hearth in a straw armchair, covered up to the ears. He hardly ever spoke and made life very unpleasant in the house. Curiously enough, his malady did not interfere with his appetite and in an effort to help him get better, the old woman kept slaughtering the fowl, one after the other, as chicken broth was understood to be the best remedy for ailments of the lungs.

A rumour had got about that the landlord was going to remit that half year's rent. People were saying:

"We can eat our own oats this winter. The price of the pigs is going to remain in our purses too."

A week before the fair day, on which the rent was habitually paid, the bailiff came around to dispel this idea. The Kilmartins were busy putting the finishing touches to a fresh coat of thatch on their house when he appeared late in the afternoon.

"Hey, there," he called from the lane, not even troubling to enter the yard. "I want you, Brian."

Brian was perched on the north side of the roof, tying quoins across the new thatch. He put his hand to his hat and immediately came down off the ladder. He was almost as deferential to the bailiff as he had been to the doctor. That was only natural, as the bailiff was held in greater fear by the people than any other agent of the class that governed them. They called him a "driver", since it was part of his duty to drive the cattle of defaulting tenants into the pound, where they were sold for auction. He served notices and acted as general detective as well, carrying all manner of information to Mr. Chadwick, the land agent. Although he was feared and detested by the people, they each paid him an annual fee, for the purpose of "keeping in with him." And woe betide the tenant that failed to do so, as the bailiff's word was law with Mr. Chadwick, who was generally too drunk to take any active part in looking after the estate, except to receive the rents.

This fellow's name was Simon Hegarty. He was small, with very bowed legs and a high-bridged, pointed nose. There was a whitish rash on his lower lip, which curved outwards. He had prominent upper teeth. This gave his countenance rather an idiotic expression, which he strove to cultivate, as it disarmed suspicion. His foxy, blue eyes seemed to drill holes into everything they regarded.

"Good day to you, Kilmartin," he said as he handed Brian a notice he stripped from a bundle. "Thatching, I see. How are the potatoes with ye?"

"Good day, sir," said Brian, wiping his hand on his trousers. "They are fair enough. The rent, is it?"

Hegarty handed him the notice, put the others back in his

pocket and began to beat his legs with his ashplant.

"Yes," he said, "it's the rent. This notice was made out special. Do ye want me to read it to ye? Give it here."

He began to read:

> "The tenantry on Major Thompson's estate, residing in the manor of Crom, are requested to pay into my office on the 22nd of October all rent and arrears of rent due up to the 25th of September, otherwise the most summary steps will be taken to recover same.
>
> "(*Signed*), JOCELYN CHADWICK.
> "10th *October*, 1845."

He handed the notice back to Brian, spat out a straw which he had between his teeth, bent his ash-plant between his two hands, leaned back on his heels and looked at Brian closely, his head to one side.

"There's more to that now than meets the eye," he said, "and what do you suppose it is, Kilmartin? I'm asking you, as one man to another."

" 'Faith, I don't know," said Brian, "unless it is that people were saying..."

"And now," said Hegarty, "do ye mind me asking you what the people were saying?"

"On account of the blight," stammered Brian, "they thought that the arrears, them that are in arrears..."

"Say no more," cried Hegarty, pointing his stick at Brian in a menacing fashion. "There are people going about, and I may tell you we know them all, saying the rent should be held back on account of this blight. Well! Don't you pay no heed to them, Kilmartin, if you know what's good for you. Sell your oats and whatever else you have to sell. Pay up and you're safe. Otherwise it's the road for you. Good day to you now."

With that he walked away up the Valley, whistling and swinging his ash-plant.

"What did he say, father?" said Martin, when Brian returned.

Brian told him.

"Poor Patch Hernon," Martin said, "what's he going to do? The cow died on him and he has no pigs either. What's more, he is six months in arrears. It's the road for them, surely."

That evening, Mrs. Hernon came over to Kilmartin's house. As soon as she got into the kitchen, she threw her apron over her head, sat down by the wall near the door and wailed aloud.

"It's the road for us, surely," she wailed.

They did their best to comfort her and promised that if there was anything left over of the price of their pigs and their oats, after paying their own rent, they would help her.

"I won't see my own flesh and blood thrown on the road," the old man said.

CHAPTER VIII

ON FAIR DAY, the Kilmartins were up before dawn. Martin brought the mare from the field and straddled her, while the two women scrubbed the pigs with soap and warm water. After snatching a hurried meal, they all put on their best clothes, except Maggie, who had to stay at home with the sick man.

Mary wore her marriage dress. It was really a handsome costume. Beneath a scarlet cloak, she wore a blue gown with a dark velvet flounce. She left the house with her shoes and stockings under her arm, in order to save them from the dung in the lane. The old man looked equally well dressed in his grey frieze coat and black stock over a white linen shirt, with his white beard trimmed and his long, narrow head surmounted by a grey stove-pipe hat. Martin was dressed like his father, except that he had no stock and he wore a Canadian hat as it was called, low crowned and wide-brimmed, made of soft, black felt. Unlike his father, he lost dignity in his finery and it seemed that his muscles were bursting through his clothes. Thomsy was as disreputable as usual, except that he wore Michael's grey coat and black hat. He tried to put on Michael's shoes, also, but they were too large for him; so he had to set forth with his feet covered in sacking.

"My soul from the devil," Martin said, as he eyed Thomsy's outfit, "when Tony Derrane gets round to us, you'll have first call on the frieze. The look of you would drive a hungry crow from a carcass."

Brandishing a hazel switch, Thomsy set off with the old man to drive the pigs. Michael followed with the mare, which carried the oats in her panniers. Mary came last. The old woman followed them out into the lane, calling after them not to forget this and that. It was very exciting.

All along the Valley, the lane was thronged with people and with animals. There were pigs, cows, yearling heifers and bullocks, mares with foals at foot. Although there were only about two hundred and fifty people in the Valley at that time, it seemed this morning that there were thousands on the march. The morning was grey, with a cloud-flecked sky and a shrill wind from the north, but it seemed that this was in keeping with the time of year and that it suited the grim contours of the Valley. Now all the tilled earth was shorn of its fruits and the little cabins had on their new, pale-golden coats of straw, all snug and puffed out stiff against the lashing gales of the coming winter.

The lane was very narrow and covered with loose stones. Briars ran across it in places, so that it made unpleasant walking. By the time Mary reached her father's cottage, half a mile away, her bare feet were scratched and covered with mud. The cottage stood at the mouth of the Valley, at the junction of three roads; the road going up the Valley, the one going right to Crom around a spur of mountain and the third going left to Glenaree, skirting the demesne wall of Crom House.

It was the prettiest little house in the Valley and Mary felt a thrill of pride when she reached it. There was a little flower garden in front of it, with a gravelled path down the centre. The path was lined with round stones, whitened like the walls of the house. The garden was bound by a trimmed hedge. It had a wooden gate, painted green, surmounted by a Celtic cross, which her brother Patrick had fashioned. The three rooms of the cottage faced south, but there was an additional room, built at right angles to the eastern gable, running north. In the angle made by this room there was another garden, where different kinds of vegetables grew, much to the envy and wonder of the Black Valley people, who knew only one vegetable, the potato. There were even a few gooseberry and black currant bushes.

She entered the cottage, to find her mother getting ready

for the fair. Her father and her brother Patrick had already gone with the pig. Even though the weaver had no land, he reared a pig on the potatoes that some people gave him in payment for the exercise of his craft. However, the kitchen did not smell of pig like Kilmartin's kitchen. The weaver had made a sty for the animal, unlike Kilmartin, who believed that a pig would die of cold without the warmth of the hearth fire. There was, however, an almost equally unpleasant smell in the place. It came from the loom room, owing to the fact that urine was necessary in the process of weaving. Apart from this slightly unpleasant odour, the kitchen was a delightful place, dazzlingly clean.

Mother and daughter embraced one another fervently and shed tears. It was the first time that they had seen one another since Mary's marriage, according to the rule that a bride must not see or speak to her mother for the first months of her honeymoon. Having embraced, Mary sat down to the hearth and began to wash her feet in a basin of water that her mother set before her.

There was a great likeness between Ellen Gleeson and her daughter. The mother was fifty-two and already white-haired, but she was so tall and slim that the whiteness of her hair merely added dignity to her carriage, without detracting from her mature beauty. Like Mary, she had a long face and a narrow, low forehead, with rosy cheeks and long-lashed blue eyes. In repose, her eyes had the same hard expression as her daughter, a fixed and rather harsh stare, born of that dreadful tramp from the county Sligo with her husband and children, two of whom had died on the road. The shock of that journey it was that turned the woman's hair white. When she smiled, or when moved to tenderness, as at this moment, the hardness melted from her eyes. Her lips opened in a most charming manner, showing her immaculate white teeth. A rare creature she was, restrained and dignified, so unlike her squat, loud-voiced husband. Her maiden name was Crampton and she was the daughter of an English sailor, who deserted her mother shortly before she was born. One could see the different racial strain in her face.

"And how are you getting on, alannah?" she said.

"Musha, I don't know," Mary said. "It's a queer house and it's hard to get used to it. It's like being in a prison up there in the middle of the Valley. I feel lonely for the fun we used to have here in the evenings. Nobody ever comes into that house, except the evening Michael got sick. And that's awful, too, that man sitting there the whole day by the fire, without a word out of him."

"Poor boy!" said her mother. "It's a great pity, such a fine strong lad he was, too."

"I pity him," said Mary, speaking in an angry tone and yet obviously ashamed of her anger. "But what's going to happen to us, to Martin and me, in that house? Everything is given to Michael, not that I begrudge him what he is getting, mother, but they never think of the future. Every hen in the place will shortly be killed. The pound of butter that could be saved and sold for good money is spent on him. And I know it will do him no good, for death is written on his face. Then the potatoes are rotting on us and there's nothing else. You'd be surprised, mother, but although they have land, they have saved hardly anything. There's no more than a few sovereigns in the house and what'll be got to-day for the pigs and the oats is owed already, to the landlord and the shop. So I worry and no wonder."

"God is good, alannah," said her mother.

"God helps them that help themselves," said Mary. "They are queer people. They wouldn't sow a head of cabbage or an onion, for fear the other people would make fun of them. Nor would they try to catch a fish in the stream. Nor would they hunt a rabbit either. Everything like that counts, but they wouldn't do it. The old man nearly ate me when I talked about making a pigsty, or putting the hens in the barn. 'A custom is a custom,' he always says. But I ask myself what is going to happen if this blight gets worse. The potatoes is all they have to live on. If only Martin would take charge in the house, but he won't. The old man rules him with a rod of iron."

"Isn't he kind to you, asthore?"

"He is," said Mary, still more angrily, "but what is the good of being kind? He should show his power against the old man and take charge. If he did, I'd soon arrange things so we could save a few shillings against a rainy day. What's the good of having land if you can't make money out of it? People always looked down on us because we had no land, but we lived better than they do. I won't stand for it, mother. If things don't change I'll say to Martin: 'Take charge here, or take me to America.'"

"To America!" cried Mrs. Gleeson in horror. "What put that awful thought into your head?"

"And why not?" cried Mary, pulling on her stockings. "There's money to be made there."

The mother said nothing. When Mary had laced her boots they went into the bedroom. Mary arranged her hair before the mirror. In her new home there was no mirror. Then, indeed, she looked so beautiful that her mother burst into tears of pride. She took a big comb from her box and gave it to her daughter.

"You keep it, alannah," she said. "It's fitter for you than for me. It is a comb my father brought from a place in Spain to my mother. God bless you, asthore, and may the Virgin look down on you and protect you."

Mary had done up her hair in Spanish fashion and with the big, high comb stuck at the back of the radiant pile, she looked quite like a great lady.

"Oh! Mother, I can't take it from you," she said.

Hearing her mother sob behind her, she whirled round and said:

"What is it, mother?"

"Nothing, treasure," said her mother, "only...I'm so glad to see you looking so well and lovely. I wish Ellie were settled down like you."

"Ellie?" said Mary, and her face lost its radiant happiness. "What ails her?"

"I don't know," said the mother. "I'm beginning to get worried about her. She seems to be a changed girl since she went to that house."

"In what way?"

"You remember how airy she was, always laughing and joking with everything, as happy as a bird in May. Now you can't get a word out of her. She was here last Sunday and she flew at me when I began to question her about what people are saying."

"And what would they be saying?"

"About her and Mr. Chadwick."

"So that's what it is. Does my father or Patrick know about it?"

"Patrick does, but sure your father is only interested in politics, bad cess to them. My only fear is that Patrick might fly at her to-day and make things worse, if he meets her at the fair. He has a terrible will that would drive him to raise a hand against Mr. Chadwick himself. I wish she was out of that house."

"So that's what it is," said Mary. "I'll see to that."

"Take care, child," said the mother. "Anger will get you nowhere. We like in queer times and Mr. Chadwick is as queer as they make them. God forgive me for letting her go to that house."

She sat down on the bed and wailed aloud. Mary put her arms about her and said:

"Don't worry yourself, mother. I'll talk to her. Maybe what you heard is only the back-biting of jealous people. Come on, get your cloak and we'll go."

They made a fine couple as they set forth together, both

of the same height, the mother's white hair contrasting as
vividly with her black cloak as the daughter's dark hair
contrasted with her scarlet one.

It was nearly a mile to the village. From the narrow defile
between two mountain peaks, which formed the Valley's
mouth, the land spread out in a widening arc, descending
slowly to the lowlands, beyond which lay the distant sea. There
were clusters of little cabins strewn over this lowland, with a
big house at intervals standing on a patch of land more fertile
than the rest. Close at hand, to the south of the road, stood
Crom House, a squat, gloomy building beside a little lake, in
the centre of a demesne. The whole grounds were practically
naked of trees. Both the house and land looked bedraggled
and unkempt. Even the wall that bound it was practically in
ruins and covered with briars.

CHAPTER IX

THE ENTRANCE TO the demesne adjoined the beginning of the village street. As they were passing the entrance gates, they met Mr. Coburn, the Protestant parson.

"Good morning, sir," Mrs. Gleeson said.

The parson smiled vaguely, muttered something and passed in through the gates. He was in a brown study and had not recognised them, even though he and his wife had been very kind to the Gleesons since their arrival in the parish; first of all giving them a strip of bog on which to make a house and afterwards helping them with clothes, food and even money. The parson, who was of a peculiar mentality, took a liking to the gruff, sturdy weaver. This morning, however, he was too intent on his thoughts even to recognise such old friends.

He was a thin, frail little man of sixty-five, with a pale face and extremely sensitive features. Born in Dublin of English parents, he had got this living on his ordination and he had spent all his life ever since in Crom, except for occasional visits to London, where his sole remaining relatives now lived. As there had never been more than about fifty Protestants in his parish, out of a population which numbered over five thousand at the present time, his duties as a clergyman had been very slight. In spite of this paucity of members of his church, he was maintained by tithes, levied on the Catholic masses, who consequently loathed him as a member of the oppressing class. A consciousness of their hatred and of his unjust mode of life had eaten into his soul, giving his naturally simple and honest countenance the furtive expression of a criminal. Cut off from human intercourse with educated people, since most of the neighbouring gentry and officials were crude, senseless fellows, and being unable to associate with the masses of the people, owing to their distrust and hatred of his religion, he had become a recluse and a "village intellectual," a neurotic, half-mad creature.

A letter, which he had just received by the mail car from Clogher, had roused him this morning to a desire for social activity and he was on his way to interview Mr. Chadwick about the matter. This determination to "do his duty as a Christian gentleman" was occasional with him; but the fit never lasted long. This morning, however, the question of the potato blight, with which the letter dealt, appeared to him the most important public duty with which he had hitherto been confronted.

Waving his arms like an idiot, the letter fluttering in his right hand, he trotted along, muttering to himself. The harsh wind whistled among the leafless branches of the sparse trees that lined the grass-grown, rutted drive. When the parson came to the end of it, he halted and gazed at the house, tapping his forehead, as if he were trying to remember something. Then he shrugged his shoulders, drew in his breath through his teeth and cried aloud:

"Dear me! What a shame! What gross habits of life!"

The house seemed to be practically a ruin. It was an ugly, square, stone building, as grey and bleak as if it stood on the ocean's edge, to be buffeted and bleached by wild seas and raging storms. Not a curtain was visible on any of the windows. The door had lost most of its paint and stood ajar. One of the columns of the porch had a large, wide crack in it. The lawn was like an ill-kept meadow, covered with hummocks of grass and the dung of animals, of which there were several at the moment browsing on it. To the left there was a group of people standing by the edge of a lake, around which a horse, ridden by a wild person whose coat-tails were flapping in the wind, was galloping. There were fences at intervals round the edge of the lake and as the animal leaped these fences the group of watchers set up a cheer and the rider swung his hat about his head.

"Dear, dear!" cried the parson, as he trotted up to the door. "It's all so very disorderly."

He entered the hall, after making an attempt, which he knew to be quite useless from previous experience, to ring the bell. There was a musty smell in the hall, which was practically empty of furniture. A large room, seen through an open door on the right, also looked empty. A man came running along a flagged passage that led to the kitchen. His steps sounded hollow. He appeared in the hallway pulling on his coat. Mr. Coburn enquired if the master was about.

"He's in bed, sir," said the man in an insolent tone. "His breakfast was just sent up."

Then he dashed along the hall, saying as he disappeared out the door:

"You can go on up."

With a wild yell, he headed for the Lake, where the horse was being ridden over fences.

"Dear, dear!" said the parson, as he proceeded up the wide stairway. "What a disorderly house!"

Until the passage of the Act of Union with England in 1800, the Thompsons had lived here in considerable style. In common with a great number of the Irish gentry, they moved to London in that year. Since then, they had rarely visited Crom House, except before an election, when they helped to drive their tenants to the poll to vote for them. After the rise of O'Connell's movement, when the peasants began to vote for their own nationalist candidates, the Thompsons deserted the place altogether. So it began to fall into ruins. During the past thirty years, the estate had been in charge of agents who had little interest in it and did not stay long. They used this house as their residence.

On the first landing, the parson trotted down to the end of a gloomy corridor and knocked on a door.

"How did he go, Reilly?" cried a loud voice from within. "Come in, you fool."

The parson entered. A loud laugh greeted him.

"Bless my soul, I thought you were Reilly. Good morning, Coburn."

"Dear, dear," muttered the parson, as he closed the door behind him.

Mr. Chadwick was sitting up in a big, four-poster bed, that was surmounted by an ornate canopy. He had his legs crossed under him like a Turk, his back being supported by a number of pillows. On a table beside the bed, there was a fowl, some bread and a jug of steaming punch. He had a glass of punch in his hand. The gentleman looked rather oddly dressed in a blue night-cap, with a long red tassel, the same colour as his hair. His face was quite as red as his hair and very freckled. He had brown eyes, with greyish spots in them, like a lark's eggs. His eyes had a very malign expression. His eyebrows were white. Altogether, rather an odd-looking fellow and yet fascinating.

The room was large and windy, with very little furniture. The window had a hole in it and the hole was stuffed with paper.

"Bah!" said Mr. Chadwick, putting down his glass and blowing on to his cupped hands. "Do you feel it cold here? I'm damn glad to see you. Tell you the honest truth I was longing for someone to come in. I was expecting Reilly as a matter of fact, but I'm glad it's you just the same. Have a glass of punch? What? Curse this hole. Another winter. Good God! I'll never survive it. Never mind. As soon as the rent is raked in, I can get away for a bit. Sit down, won't you?"

The only chair in the room was a close-stool made in the shape of an armchair. The parson gently declined the seat. Chadwick reached for a bell-rope that hung by the bedside, missed it and swore.

"Damn this rope," he said. "Another glass. Do you mind giving it a pull, Coburn?"

The parson pulled at the rope gingerly.

"Give it a good pull," said Chadwick. "That's it. Sit down, won't you? What's the news? There's a queer smell in this room. What? I warn you that if you came here to collect for the poor, that I haven't a..."

"I've not come about money," said Coburn with some heat. "It's about something else. I detest money."

"So do I," said Chadwick, laughing uproariously and curling up in bed. "A Scotchman made a good remark at the County Club the other day. 'Money talks,' he said, 'but it only says good-bye to a fool.' Do you know him? Man called Anderson. It never bothers even to say goodbye to me."

He suddenly sprang up in bed, seized his glass of punch, drained it and re-filled the glass from the jug.

"May I offer you a glass?" he said. "Why, of course...drat the girl. Why doesn't she come? Another glass....Give it another pull. It's probably broken in any case. I wish I had never undertaken to look after this property. Look at me, Coburn. How old do you think I am? Come now. No flattery."

"Still in your prime," said the parson acidly, "if you took proper care of yourself."

Chadwick smiled maliciously. Then he slowly sipped his punch, gave his shoulders the little nervous shrug of the habitual drunkard and then suddenly looked very glum.

"Nonsense," he said. "I'm a wreck at forty-five. This is the devil of a life. I've changed out of all recognition since I came here five years ago. Now I can't go. There's nowhere else to go. Mark Thompson is the best of fellows and he meant well, of course, when I lost my property, years together in the regiment and jolly good years they were, Coburn, the two of us. Damn it! He gave me this agency out of pity. Think of it! What has it done to me? Answer me, Coburn. I've just become a sot. This is no place for an Englishman. Why don't you sit down on the side of the bed and have a glass of punch? I'm a sot. I know it. Cut off here among a lot of howling savages. You wouldn't have the courage to face it, Coburn. No wife, no children, no prospects. Own up now. What would you do? Cut your throat or go to the colonies?"

"I should certainly not commit suicide by drinking myself to death," said the parson.

Chadwick glared at the parson for a moment with manifest hatred and then he incontinently burst out laughing. Turning over on his side, he stretched out his legs, yawned and closed his eyes. Then he suddenly opened his eyes once more, drained his glass and tried to belch.

"Wind," he said. "I'm a martyr to it. What's that you've got in your hand? Come in."

There had been a knock at the door and as the parson held out the letter, about to disclose the object of his visit, Ellie Gleeson came into the room in answer to Mr. Chadwick's shout. Chadwick's eyes glittered when he saw the girl. They became fixed and he thrust his head forward, exactly like an animal sighting a mate. Ellie was quite as beautiful as her sister, but in a more coarse and sensual way. She was a year older and her face already looked somewhat used. It was beginning to lose its freshness. There was a discontented look about her full, red lips and her big eyes had the rather cross, mean expression of the sensual girl. She had beautiful golden hair and a finely moulded body, except that her breasts were rather too big. Like her sister, she walked with an elegant grace.

"You want me, sir?" she said, standing midway between the door and the bed and facing her employer boldly.

It was obvious that there was something intimate in their relationship from the bold, confident way she looked him in the eyes.

"Fetch a glass for Mr. Coburn," said Chadwick.

Without a word she turned on her heel and left the room. The parson's eyes followed her.

"Well!" said Chadwick. "I see you have a letter. From a lady?"

"It's from Mr. Campbell Foster," said the parson rather severely.

"What about?"

"The potato blight. May I read it?"

"Potatoes!" said Chadwick. "I hate the vegetable. Why not? Read it. What has he got to say?"

The parson coughed and began to read. It was difficult to understand him as he mumbled his words and failed utterly, now and again, to decipher the script. The gist of the document was that Mr. Foster maintained that the potatoes were rotting in the pits and that this rot could only be prevented by making an air passage under the whole length of the pit and by having two vent holes, or chimneys, on the surface of it. To guard against frost, a sod was to be placed over the vent hole at night, or when there was heavy rain. To save seed for the coming year, the tops of the potatoes, where all the eyes were clustered, should be cut, thus leaving the majority of the edible portion for consumption.

Ellie entered the room with a glass. The parson looked at her and then continued to read with feeling.

"I suggest," he read, "that a nominal subscription be entered into by each county and that a committee of all the leading men of each county should be formed, having the subscription at their disposal..."

Chadwick leant from the bed and tried to grip Ellie's breast. She glared at him and left the room hurriedly. He stared after her greedily and then lay back, drawing the clothes about his ears.

"These committees should buy, as they think fit," continued the parson, "each, one thousand tons of oatmeal at the lowest possible price, holding the oatmeal over in stores until the next spring or summer, when it should be retailed, under proper supervision, by a store-keeper for cash, at a moderate profit. The committee should raise money to buy the oatmeal with their joint notes, which the banks would at once discount..."

He paused and looked at Chadwick.

"Are you listening?" he said angrily.

Chadwick sat up and stared with open mouth.

"What's that?" he said. "Oh! Your letter? Who is it from? What is it about?"

The parson got furious.

"It's about famine," he cried.

"Famine?" said Chadwick. "What do you mean? Are you having a joke? Have some punch."

"It's not a joke," cried the parson. "Mr. Campbell Foster is an authority on the matter. He says here... Will you please listen?"

"Go ahead. I'm listening. Damned busybody!"

The parson continued to read:

"I am as firmly convinced as that I am now writing to you, such is the general apathy, want of exertion and feeling of hostility among the people, that unless the government steps forward to carry out these or similar plans for the national welfare, nothing will be done. Such is the character of the people that they will do nothing till starvation faces them."

"Very well!" said Chadwick. "Let the government step forward, as he says. What has it got to do with me?"

"You could explain to them about the ventilation of pits," said Coburn. "Get Hegarty to go around and make them follow out Mr. Foster's instructions."

"I'll see them damned first," said Chadwick. "Filthy wretches. Chard, the solicitor, was in here the other day about the property, mortgaged to the hilt, you know, and I had a long talk with him. He knows this blasted country inside out. He tells me there have been famines here periodically since 1741 and you know the cause of it is that the lazy wretches live entirely on the potato."

"But that is no reason..." began Coburn.

"Nonsense," said Chadwick, handing him a glass of punch. "Your health. Don't you see the point? Bulky vegetable. Not very nourishing. Can't be stored from one season to another.

Brilliant fellow Chard. As he said, Ireland is essentially a grazing country. Then they put a bounty on corn, in 1783 I think it was, but it doesn't matter. Peasants sprang up on all sides. Instead of growing corn they grow potatoes. So you see, Coburn, you can't blame me if they die of hunger. It's none of my business. Mark Thompson's father let his whole estate become covered by these wretches. Squatters, ruffians of the worst kind, multiplying like rabbits. Priests encourage them to get married and breed, so that they can get more money out of them. Doesn't concern me, as long as they pay their rent. I've gone into the whole thing with Chard. They should be transported to the colonies."

"But they are at least human beings," said the parson. "It would not be too much trouble to ask your bailiff to explain about this ventilation."

"Why don't you do it yourself?" said Chadwick angrily. "You speak as if I were to blame for anything that may happen to them. I'm just a servant of the proprietor. My business is just to collect the rents and evict them if they don't pay. But you live on them. They pay you tithes. You get your living out of the rent. Why don't you do it?"

The parson waved his hands and got excited.

"If I had the authority I would do it willingly," he cried. "But what can I do? If I go around among the people, the priests will accuse me of trying to proselytise. I have trouble enough on account of the little charities I manage. It's not through laziness that I come to you."

"Very well, then," said Chadwick. "You miss the point, though. I won't have you lecturing me about famines and about my duty to these disgusting peasants. Let them starve. Good riddance, I say. They hate us and you know it. Would shoot us if they dared. Why should we help them? Let them die. There are three millions more than enough of them in the country. They got these little bits of land to enable them to vote and then they voted for O'Connell. Now they are trying to use this blight as an excuse for not paying their rent. Who is there?"

There was another knock at the door.

"It's me, Reilly, your honour."

"Come in."

A lean man entered the room and approached the bed on tip-toe. He was in a state of great excitement. He frothed slightly at the mouth. Beads of perspiration stood out on his forehead. His eyes glittered. He twisted his hat about in his hands. His nose was broken and he had a large scar across his right temple. His legs were bowed.

"He's a wonder, your honour," he whispered, as he reached the bed. "He leps like a bird and he can keep it up till the cows come home. I never seen anything like it."

A gleam of pleasure came into Chadwick's eyes. He breathed excitedly and he whispered:

"Is he really a good one?"

"He can leave any animal in the province standing," cried Reilly, his voice suddenly rising to a screech.

"God's blood!" cried Chadwick, leaping from the bed. "I'm going down to ride him. He stays all right?"

"I took him two rounds of the lake," cried Reilly, "and he lepped them all, one after the other, a real natural quick jumper, sir, without an effort either, like stepping over a puddle."

"If he's not what you say," said Chadwick delightedly, as he stood by the bed in his long, soiled nightshirt, "I'll castrate you. Hand me my breeches. Help yourself to some punch, Coburn."

"Might I remind you again," said Coburn, "to ask Hegarty..."

"Not now, Coburn," said Chadwick, pulling on his breeches. "No time now to talk about potatoes."

The parson sipped his glass of punch and thought:

"Contact with others corrupts the ideal. I had better wash my hands of them all. What I can do is little, but I had better attempt it alone."

CHAPTER X

THE FAIR WAS at its height. The long, ramshackle main street of Crom was crowded with people and with animals. In spite of the crisp wind that blew from the mountains, which rose sheer above the village to the north, there was a foul smell everywhere and the pock-marked roadway was a reeking mass of dung and urine. Although the street was wide, there was hardly room to move. Hucksters had set up their booths on either side of the street, thus congesting the space that was already insufficient. Some people had even set up shelters on the fair green, mostly beggars and tinkers. Cattle darted into houses. Pigs squealed and fought one another. Jobbers shouted and cursed, brandishing their sticks. Timoney the fiddler was playing in front of a shop and a few men, already drunk, were jigging near by. In front of the police barracks, a three-storeyed building, with loopholes like a fortress, a crowd of policemen stood watching the tumult in a hostile manner.

The centre of activity was the shop of Mr. John Hynes and the hotel that adjoined it. The two houses were really one, divided by an arch that led into a cobbled courtyard. They were two storeys high, with yellow walls. Formerly they belonged to a Protestant called Ryder, who had been ruined by O'Connell's Repeal Movement. This was how Hynes got hold of them.

He was born in Black Valley, where his grandfather had been one of the first settlers, following the "Act For Reclaiming Unprofitable Bogs" being passed by the Parliament of George II in 1742. This Act permitted Catholics to lease fifty acres, plantation measure, of bog, together with one half acre of arable land for the site of a house. The dispossessed Catholic peasantry swarmed into the bogs and on to the mountain-sides as a result of this Act, became landholders and multiplied, so that the population of Ireland rose from under four millions at the passage of the Act to eight millions at the period dealt with in this narrative. With the rapid increase in population the struggle for possession of the "unprofitable bogs" became intense, giving rise to all manner of secret society, that sometimes verged on civil war. Hynes's father got murdered in 1799 by one of these secret societies, because he gave some information to the authorities about people that were annoying him. Two men were hanged at Clogher for the murder and the widow had to leave Black Valley with her three children, owing to the public feeling against her. The people considered that her husband richly deserved his death for being an informer and the hanging of two men added to her husband's guilt. Therefore she must pay the penalty by being ostracised.

Old Mark Thompson, the present landowner's father, was then in residence on the estate and he was one of the bench of magistrates that tried the murderers. He took pity on the widow and gave her a cabin in the Catholic part of Crom, together with a sum of money to set up as a huckster. At that time, the village was divided into two parts, called English-town and Irish-town. English-town, or the eastern part, adjoined the entrance to Crom House and it was inhabited by Protestants exclusively, all of English origin, petty officials, tradespeople and retainers of the proprietor. Irish-town, to the west, was inhabited by the native Catholics. These latter were miserably poor and lived in wretched hovels, while the Protestants had respectable two-storeyed houses with slate roofs.

In one of these hovels the widow set up her little huckster's shop. John was then thirteen and he was a precocious lad, without whom the widow's undertaking would have been doomed to failure, since people had a horror of setting foot under the roof of an informer's widow. The lad bought a donkey with what remained of the landlord's money after the shop had been stocked. Then he took his sister Julia, aged fourteen, with him. They roamed the country with their donkey, in whose panniers they carried needles, thread, clay pipes and other small articles for sale. They exchanged these for eggs, butter and such old clothes as the rag-man at Clogher might buy for a small sum. He had a withered hand from infancy and he used this as a protection against the horror aroused in the good people by the idea of trading with an informer's get. "Poor orphan!" the kind people said. "The curse of God lies heavy on him. It isn't right to turn a crippled orphan from a Christian door, even though his blood is cursed." So they traded with the children.

The widow died when John was eighteen and his young brother emigrated to America in the following year. The ship on which the youth sailed was detained in mid-ocean by a man o' war. He was pressed into the Navy, where he was killed fighting against Napoleon Bonaparte. Left alone in the world, John and Julia pursued the task of amassing wealth with the industry of labouring ants. At the age of thirty, John married Louisa Hegarty, the sister of the man who was now bailiff. She had come into a legacy from a relative in America and with this money he expanded his business. He got better premises and procured a licence for the sale of wine, spirits and ale. Things went well with him and he wore down the hostility of the people by taking an active part in the nationalist movement under O'Connell. In this, of course, he was guided by self-interest rather than by patriotism. For it was the purpose of this movement, which was really economic although it was religious on the surface, to support the rising Catholic petty middle-class traders against their Protestant competitors. So the people took their trade from Ryder and gave it to Hynes.

During the thirty years that had elapsed since his marriage, his power and his prosperity had kept pace with that of his class all over Ireland, under the leadership of the great demagogue O'Connell. During that time, in the village of

Crom, the Catholics of the west had gradually encroached on the preserves of the Protestants in the east and Hynes was now installed in Ryder's two houses. His younger son was the local doctor. One of his daughters was a nun. His elder son worked with him in the shop. His other daughter managed the hotel, where his sister Julia, who had begun life with him, looked after the cooking. In a word, he had made himself, next to the landlord, the most powerful man in the parish.

·He was now standing behind the counter in his shop, reading out from a list what was due to each person for the oats he had bought and which were now stacked in his shed at the rear. His wife stood beside him, handing over the money from the till. The people crowded up on the other side of the counter.

Hynes had now reached his sixtieth year and he looked much older, owing to the hardships he had suffered as a child. He was tall, lean and very stooped. He had the face of a miser. He wore a black, slouch hat, with a low crown and a wide brim. It was drawn down over his brow, concealing his eyes, except when he raised his head suddenly to look at the person with whom he was dealing. Then two small grey eyes appeared, hostile, foxy and suspicious. His thin lips turned inwards. He had sallow cheeks and a hooked nose. Except for his white starched shirt and his black cravat, his clothes were very shabby, made of grey frieze. He held his withered right hand close to his side like a man carrying a parcel. It was curious the way he started spasmodically when anybody raised his voice to argue with him, as if he expected a blow or an insult. This was undoubtedly a relic of his youth, when the country children used to follow his donkey through the lane, pelting him with stones and crying: "Ho! Look at the informers. The curse of God is on them."

At the moment, Hernon and his wife were being paid for their oats and Hernon was arguing about the price, claiming that he should receive more. His wife, Kitty, was related in a remote way to Hynes on her mother's side. For this reason, Hernon, who was always eager to find cause for dissatisfaction with life and had the mania of persecution, thought that he should get preferential treatment in the shop.

"How could I pay you that price?" Hynes was saying, as he glared furtively at Hernon from under the rim of his hat. "Sure the meal itself is only eleven and ninepence a hundred. Is it asking the same for the grain you are? Can't you be satisfied with what everybody else is getting?"

"They're satisfied, are they?" shouted Hernon, jabbing with his elbows at the crowd on either side. "I'll tell you one thing, John Hynes, and it's no lie either. It's robbery, the price you're giving."

"You're only making a show of yourself, Patch," said Kitty. "Give us the money, Mrs. Hynes."

"I'm afraid of no man," said Hernon, spitting between his chest and the edge of the counter. "If the people had courage same as I have, they wouldn't be robbed. But what can one man do? Take the damn oats and may they choke whoever eats them."

Brian Kilmartin, Thomsy Hynes and a man called Toomey, who was married to Brian's other daughter, Nappa, crowded round Hernon to pacify him. Ordinarily half-demented, Hernon was always quite beside himself when he had taken a little drink.

"I'll get my rights yet," he said, as they led him away to the drink counter at the other side of the shop. "The day'll come yet when the poor man'll come into his own. The landlords and the grabbers that are living on the people's backs will be laid low."

Mrs. Hernon stayed behind to take the money. There was very little for her to get, however, since they owed most of it already to the shop. In fact there was not enough to pay for a barrel of salt herrings she wanted to buy for the winter.

"There you are now," said Hynes, looking around at the

people. "With one side of their mouths people call me a robber, and then with the other side they want me to oblige them."

He had a whining voice like a beggar.

"For the love o' God," said Mrs. Hernon, "don't make big out of little and the terrible times that are on us. The cow died in the spring on us. We had no pigs. The few praties that we put in the ground are now cursed with the disease. Is it any wonder the poor are turning wild in their talk and forgetting what they say? Give us the barrel, for the love an' honour o' God, to stand between my children and the hunger during the long winter that's before them."

"I'll give you the barrel all right," said Hynes in his whining voice, "but we all know what it is to be poor and I'm telling you that when some of us were poor we kept a civil tongue in our heads."

Kitty Hernon left the counter, got her fish barrel, and sat on it, over against the back wall of the shop. Her sister Nappa came and sat with her on top of the barrel. Kitty was thirty, the first of Kilmartin's children to survive. She had seven children, three of whom were there with her, thin little boys that stood as still as ghosts against the wall. The mother was just as thin as the children. Her face had the horribly care-worn and frightened look that can only be seen in the faces of poor mothers, who are continually worrying about how to find food for their young. Nappa was two years younger. Her cheeks were rosy and she was quite plump. Her eyes had a contented look. The reason was that she had no children. Her husband lived in Glenaree, where he acted as the local blacksmith.

"You wouldn't think we were of the same blood atall as that miser," said Nappa, "the way he turned on you. Now what are ye going to do about the rent? Ye owe the last half year's, too, don't ye?"

"We do, 'faith," said Kitty plaintively. "We do, asthore. I haven't slept a wink for the last fortnight thinking of it. Himself is out of his mind, too. Everything is turning against us."

Each of them had a thigh on the barrel, whose upraised rim bore sharply into the slack flesh of their rumps. They both wore black shawls out far over their foreheads. In the gloom of the shop, their faces looked deadly pale, peeping from the cowls of their shawls. Just like masks, hanging in space and motionless, except for the movement of their lips.

"Did you speak to your father?" said Nappa. "He might help ye."

"I spoke to him," Kitty said. "But sure he has little beyond what he got for the pigs and the oats. We owe over ten pounds now. He said he'd do what he could."

"Now that the weaver's daughter is in his house," said Nappa viciously, "it's little anybody'll get out of him. Look at her over there. Look at the style of her. She's waiting for our Michael's death so that she can be cock o' the walk in the house. The shame of it! A weaver's daughter! Who sold the pigs for them?"

"It was my father," said Kitty. " 'Faith, he still has control of the purse. He won't loose hold of it as long as he can keep on his feet. He'd rather have Michael in the house than Martin. She has Martin under her thumb alright, but she'll have a job with the old man. 'I'd ask you for help,' I said to him, the evening I went over to the house, 'only I suppose you're only a lodger here now.' He flew at me. 'I have the power still,' he said, waving his stick, 'and I'll keep it as long as there's breath in my body.' 'The purse is in my box,' he said, 'and it will stay there, or my name isn't Brian.' 'Faith there's no love lost between him and the weaver's daughter. Ho! Here's her mother now. Rigged out like the Queen herself."

Mrs. Gleeson had now come into the shop and had joined Mary at the counter. Mother and daughter were outstanding in the sombre and rather sordid place. The two sisters were especially irritated by the way Mrs. Hynes gaped in open admiration at Mary, while she had not given themselves more then the fixed smile due to customers. In her youth Mrs. Hynes had herself been noted for her beauty. Although fifty, she was still a handsome woman, with plump, rosy cheeks, sea-blue eyes and dark hair. Like most women who have sensed the ecstasy of beauty in themselves, her life pulse quickened at the sight of beauty in others. Not so the two poor creatures into whose flabby thighs the upraised edge of the fish barrel was boring, as a harsh reminder of their unsatisfied hunger for everything beautiful in life that had passed them by without touching them.

"That gown Mary has on must have cost pounds," said Nappa. "I heard it was from the minister's wife she got the cloth. And a velvet flounce to it, too. And will you look at the comb?"

"That belongs to her mother," said Kitty. "The old witch! I believe she's half a jumper. Why wouldn't she be and her father an English sailor from God only knows where? They're as thick as thieves with Mr. Coburn. It was him got Ellie her place with Mr. Chadwick. Like fine ladies in gowns and cloaks, while honest people have only old shawls."

"From what I hear," said Nappa, "the same Ellie is no more than a whore in Mr. Chadwick's bed. Nice people to have in our father's house."

"Buying sweets they are now," said Kitty. "Ho! May they choke them."

"Look how thick they are with Louisa Hynes," said Nappa. "She's going down their throats like a thrush feeding her young."

"Whist! They see us," said Kitty. "Here they come, with a smile on them, the dirty hypocrites."

The vicious faces of the sisters became fawning as mother and daughter approached.

"Have ye sold the pigs?" Mrs. Gleeson said to Mrs. Toomey.

"We have, 'faith," said Mrs. Toomey. "But sure, it only

comes in one hand before it goes out the other. We have just enough to pay the landlord and to buy a grain of oatmeal."

Mary's face was flushed and she looked radiant. She was intoxicated by the attention she attracted in the crowd. The doctor had stopped to talk to her before she came into the shop and he had with him the member of parliament for the constituency and the editor of the *Clogher Vindicator*, both of them here to hold a meeting. All these important people had remarked on her beauty and said nice things to her. She held out the bag of sweets she had bought towards the three little boys, who hid their faces behind their sleeves with shyness.

"Fine boys! God bless them," said Mrs. Gleeson. "And how are the others, Kitty? You poor creature, you have a house full of mouths to feed."

"Ah! musha," said Kitty plaintively, "how would they be with the hunger? Since the cow died on us in spring it's little they've had. May the Lord look down on us. Now this disease has taken nearly all our praties. God only knows what's going to happen to us, unless the Divine Saviour takes pity on us."

"Amen!" said Mrs. Gleeson. "The poor have only to pray and hope that God in His Almighty kindness will harken to them."

"Take them, then," Nappa Toomey said to the little boys. "Why don't ye have manners and say 'God spare your health' to the fine lady? Take them and don't disgrace your mother."

She laid a bitter stress on the words "fine lady".

"Musha, it's little chance they have of seeing a fine lady at the head of the Valley," said Kitty. "Up there, it's no fine clothes they see, only rags and dirt."

Mary's eyes hardened as she caught the malice in the tone of the two sisters. She thrust the sweets sharply towards the children.

"Take them," she said angrily, "they won't poison you."

The three little boys, the eldest of whom was eight, snuffled and edged about nervously, like three lambs herded in a corner and trying to hide their heads under one another's bellies. They stared at the proffered sweets. Then the eldest suddenly snatched at the bag and took a few. The others followed suit. Then Mary offered the bag to the sisters. After refusing politely several times, each greedily dipped her hand into the bag. The children packed all the sweets into their mouths at once. Then they stood still as before, their cheeks swollen, their eyes distended, glaring in a startled fashion all round the shop and chewing a little, timidly, once in a while. They kept shifting from one foot to another and wiping their runny noses on their sleeves. Like geese, they would raise their bare feet, one each, and hide them under their red petticoats for a few moments.

"I hope there's no trouble at the meeting to-day," Mrs. Gleeson said. "I hear a lot of wild talk about the rent going to be held back."

"And why wouldn't it?" said Mrs. Hernon, suddenly speaking in an angry tone. It seemed as if she had been holding back her anger until then and that it had suddenly got the better of her. "It's easy for some people, who have no rent to pay, to talk about not wanting trouble. People that have no land like you don't have to be afraid of the road."

"No," said Mary, also losing her temper, "she has only to be afraid of the tongues of the wicked. Come on, mother."

They both marched out of the shop.

"You shouldn't have turned on them like that, Mary," Mrs. Gleeson said.

"Why not?" Mary said. "You'd let everybody walk on you."

"There's Ellie now," said the mother, pointing across the street.

"I'll go and talk to her, mother," Mary said. "You stay here. I want to have a word with her alone."

She marched across the street, determined to vent her anger on her sister.

Chapter XI

ELLIE WAS STANDING outside the wall of a house, talking to her brother Patrick. He had obviously forestalled Mary, as Ellie had her face hidden in a corner of her cloak and she was sobbing. Patrick, a tall, consumptive-looking man of twenty-two, was whispering excitedly to her.

"What's going on here?" Mary said. "What are you saying to her, Paddy?"

Patrick turned towards Mary and said angrily:

"I'm just telling her what I think of her. I won't have her drag my name in the ditch."

"You mind your own business," said Mary. "Come on up the road a bit, Ellie."

They walked away together towards the western end of the village. Ellie was still sobbing.

"Wipe your eyes," said Mary to her sharply. "Don't shame me in the middle of the fair."

Ellie snuffled.

"Hold your head up," Mary continued. "Walk on quickly out of this crowd."

Here in the west of the village some of the cabins had a patch of potatoes growing in their front yards. Others were just surrounded by dung and weeds. They turned down a lane, where the hovels were still more wretched, belonging to squatters that had been evicted from the neighbouring countryside. At the end of the lane there was a hill, on which formerly stood the monastery of Crom. Now there were only fragments of its walls remaining, together with a round tower, from whose tapering summit the monks of old had kept a look out for marauding Norsemen. Weeds now grew out of the tiny watch-holes at the top of the tower. The grounds of

the old monastery had been turned into a Catholic cemetery
and the gravestones lay thick among the ruins. Right on the
edge of the hill, which overlooked the lowland country,
spreading immediately below, there was a grassy mound, where
villagers were wont to sit and chat on Sundays. Here the two
sisters seated themselves.

"Well!" Mary said, "what did he say to you?"

Ellie burst into tears once more.

"I can't tell you," she sobbed.

"Why so?"

"Because it isn't true."

"What isn't true?"

"Oh! nothing, only I'm so lonely in that house and
everybody has turned against me."

"And why would they turn against you?" said Mary fiercely.
"Why would you be lonely? Aren't there six of you there
altogether? Reilly, the groom, and John Flanagan and Mary
Halloran from the Valley and Sally Hynes and..."

"They don't speak to me no more," Ellie sobbed.

"So that's what it is," Mary said. "And why not?"

Now she hated her sister. At first she had meant just to
vent her anger on her, but now she hated her. Ellie had always
been a lazy creature, mean and selfish. She had always tried to
avoid any work there was to be done. Even when she was
only fifteen, but already fully developed, men had begun to
paw at her. Her father had often taken the rod to her, lest she
might bring disgrace on his roof. And now she smelt of
perfume. It was this smell of perfume, giving the lie to her
humble tears, that made Mary hate her.

"It's the master," Ellie blubbered. "He does be at me."

"Well! Why do you let him?"

"But I don't."

"Stop crying and talk to me like a sensible person," shouted
Mary. "Has he done anything to you? Speak up."

"He hasn't, but..."

"But what?"

"I'm so afraid, Mary," Ellie said. "If my father hears of it, he'll kill me. But it's not my fault."

Ellie looked at her with such a forlorn expression on her pouting face that Mary's anger suddenly vanished, giving way to pity and tenderness. She put her arms around Ellie and whispered:

"You poor creature! Why can't you talk to me? Then maybe I could help you."

Now Ellie wept freely in Mary's arms. Then, after a while, she began to talk rapidly.

"I was only two days in the house," she said, "when he caught sight of me one day in the hall and he coming in from hunting. 'What's your name?' says he and I told him. Then he asked me how old I was and where I came from. 'Come along,' says he, 'and pull off my boots.' I followed him upstairs and I was that much ashamed with the shyness that I was hardly able to pull the boots off him. But he kept joking with me and then he threw me on the bed and started playing with me. What could I do? The tongue was still in my mouth with fright and shyness. But he didn't have his way with me all the same. Then he says, 'I'll have you wait on me,' and that was how it started. He lets no one come near him only me and that's what makes the others jealous, so they won't talk to me, although they pretend it's on account of me carrying on with him. He makes me wash him all over in a big tub with warm water and soap and he's put me in a room near his own, so that he would have me handy any hour during the night, for he sometimes wakes up with the horrors from drinking too much. Then he shouts and he sees things, something he did when he was with the soldiers in India. I do be terrified out of my life, the things he orders me to do, strip off all my clothes and get into bed with him and then he not laying a hand on me, only clutching me like I was his mother and he pretending to be a baby at breast. Then I have to sing to him, same as to a baby and pretend to rock him and he babbles there in a way to put the heart crosswise in me, thinking he is mad. For mad he is when he has the drink taken. And then again, when he is sober, and he can be merry enough when he is sober and in his right mind, he keeps warning me that one of these days, that's what he says, one of these days he is going to pluck the ripe apple from the bough, them are his very words, whatever he means. He is kind, sure enough, but he sometimes is cruel, too, and in a way he takes joy out of terrifying me, the way he comes at me sometimes with a whip, maybe, or just any weapon he finds handy, and the way he roars, threatening to have my life, and then when I screech with fright, he laughs fit to burst his sides. He'd make you split your sides laughing sometimes at the things he says. But when he is in drink and pretends he is a baby, then it's awful and I feel I'm putting an immortal sin on my soul, although he lays no hand on me that I could tell the priest about."

"Was it he gave you that scent?" said Mary sullenly.

For some reason, her sister's speech had made her feel jealous, instead of feeling pity or disapproval.

"You think I gave in to him, don't you?" said Ellie passionately.

The recitation had effected a change in her also. She recovered her self-possession and now looked at her sister in the bold way she had looked at Chadwick when she came into his room that morning. Now it was obvious that she had been acting to some extent, when she was crying. Not really acting, because she felt in an obscure way that she was committing sin and she was afraid that some evil might come of her conduct. But the cunning and selfish qualities in her nature made her incapable of deep feeling, except about things that ministered to her desires and pleasures.

"This scent he gives me to sprinkle on myself," she continued. "He says he can't stand the smell the people do have. He makes me wash myself in the big tub as well. What harm is there in that? Some people hate to see anybody getting on in the world."

"So that's what it is," cried Mary, flaring up into a passion. "You think I envy you. Well! Then, put that thought out of your head. God forgive you, Ellie. And may God help you, too, when your father gets to hear of your goings on."

"You'll run to him and tell him, I suppose," cried Ellie, now in an equal fury. "Alright, then, but he won't get me under his roof again. I'd rather go to America. If that's all the love you have for me, you and Patrick scolding me for nothing, I'm better off away from ye. My mother as well, last Sunday she kept picking at me. Ye all hate me."

"Nobody hates you, you fool," Mary cried. "Oh! There's no use talking to you. You were always the same. Why don't you go to America then and not be bringing shame on us?"

Ellie jumped to her feet, stamped her foot and cried:

"I'll do what I please."

With that she hurried off back towards the village. Mary again felt tender towards her and wanted to run after her, but a great cheer rose at that moment in the village street and she made no move towards her sister.

CHAPTER XII

THE MEETING HAD now begun. It was held in the chapel yard to the west of Hynes's shop. The chapel stood on an eminence, with a grassy slope leading down to the street. There was a cross to the west of the gate and the parish priest now stood by the cross opening the meeting. The people crowded in the street and in the chapel yard, some kneeling, others lying on the grass.

Father Roche, the parish priest, was a fussy little man with a bald head and a very red, round face. He was a poor speaker, as he stuttered when he got excited. But he made up for his lack of eloquence by waving his arms and speaking at such a high pitch that his speech sounded like a prolonged scream.

"You are relapsing," he said, "into drunken and rowdy habits, after those splendid years in the recent past, when your temperance and your obedience to the constituted authority of your national leaders was the marvel of the world."

He paused, wiped his face with a big red handkerchief, which he whipped from the tail of his coat with the speed of a conjuror and then repeated several times:

"You were the marvel of the world."

The people cheered him enthusiastically, in spite of the way he denounced them for their vices. Poor people! Their principal vice was their poverty. In any case, they all knew that Father Roche's bark was worse than his bite. There was no kindlier, more diligent, nor more charitable man in the country than the fussy and rather ridiculous little Father Roche. As the people said: "He would tear the hide of you with his stuttering tongue and then give you his own breakfast and go hungry."

"And now," said Father Roche, "in this crisis of the nation's history, I have the great honour and pleasure of introducing to you here to-day, our distinguished representative in parliament and the trusted lieutenant of our immortal liberator Dan O'Connell..."

He paused as a great cheer burst forth at the mention of Daniel O'Connell's name. Then he said, pointing to a man that sat on a chair behind him:

"Mr. McCarthy Lalor."

Mr. Lalor got to his feet amid renewed cheering. At a time when big men were the rule rather than the exception, Mr. Lalor was beyond the ordinary in size; one of those rapacious giants, unknown in our puny generation, who could devour a leg of mutton at a sitting. Still on the right side of fifty, he would be in his prime if he were not so fat. His fat, however, had not gone to his belly. It was evenly distributed, as on a mammoth bull, the neck, shoulders, chest and gullet offering a greater proof of his appetite than his abdomen. His full, florid countenance was scaled like a fish and his little eyes had that ferocious expression often seen in the eyes of fat men, who are by no means ferocious because of their fine condition. He exuded consciousness of his importance as a henchman of the great Daniel O'Connell and his dress imitated that of the liberator. He wore the great frieze cape of the leader and he carried it loose about his shoulders, as the leader had the habit of doing.

A mass of dark grey curls crowned this magnificence and as if in token of his strength, they ran straight across his lofty forehead, giving an aspect of terrific virility to his countenance. His voice rent the heavens as he boomed:

"Reverend chairman and fellow countrymen, I am here to-day..."

As if re-echoing the thunder of his voice there was a further outburst of cheering. It was an impressive scene. Behind Mr. Lalor stood the long, white-walled chapel, surmounting the grassy slope and further to the rear, the mountains rose, in a great irregular mass, their blue peaks rising higher and higher to the distant horizon. In front, beyond the ragged village street, the misty lowland stretched to the distant sea, on whose fringe the grey mass of the town of Clogher, surmounted by its steeples, was dimly visible. While in between stood the mass of the people, their rude faces upturned, their mouths open, waiting for "the word" that would lead them out of the bondage of poverty and oppression. The ruins of the round tower stood to the right. On the left stood the police barracks, with its ominous fortress holes and its crowd of men with carbines standing in the yard. The people, their rulers and the soothsayer speaking from a green mound! While carried on the bleak October wind came the lowing of cattle and the squealing of pigs, being driven away down into the lowlands towards the sea, by shouting drovers.

"Fellow country men and women," continued Mr. Lalor, when the cheering died down, "as your elected representative in parliament, I am here to-day in pursuance of a campaign to rouse the country from end to end, in order that the government may be forced to arrest the progress of a calamity, which is threatening our national extinction as a great and noble people. I refer to the blight that has fallen on the potato crop and the famine that will follow in its trail unless drastic measures are taken to prevent it. We, the people's representatives, realise that by a merciful Providence there is more than sufficient food in this country, as the result of a plentiful harvest of oats, to feed double the population, but this food is passing out of the country, at the rate of sixteen thousand quarters of oats per week, not to mention a vast number of cattle, sheep and pigs. There they go before my eyes."

With a great sweep of his arm he pointed down the road, which was dotted with animals being driven to the sea for export.

"We want the government immediately to prohibit the export of this food and to throw open the ports to foreign foods and to stop distilling. By the application of our own money, of which we are robbed year after year in excess taxation, the government must buy provisions for relief, the railroads must be built and the labourers paid in food. We want absentee landlords taxed fifty per cent and residents ten per cent to provide the capital for this railway building, which in England has reversed the condition of 1842, when one million and a half were on the rates, to the present one of comparative prosperity. As the representatives of an ancient and glorious nation, we are demanding justice, not charity."

Now the cheering was tumultuous and it was some time before he could proceed. A murmur passed through the crowd. Those that understood what he had said, and they were not many, were explaining to the others that railways were going to be built, that the landlords were going to pay for the destroyed potatoes, that the government was going to supply food and money.

"The Corporation of the City of Dublin," continued Mr. Lalor, "under the presidency of the Lord Mayor, John L. Arabin, has appointed a committee and at its meeting on the 28th of this month, the Right Honourable Daniel O'Connell is going to put forward the plan of the people's representatives for dealing with this catastrophe."

The remainder of his speech was drowned in wild cheering, while he called on the people to stand fast, in support of their elected representatives. The other speakers, a young barrister named Considine, and Dillon, the editor of the *Clogher Vindicator*, received scant attention, as they dwelt on the "historic struggle for freedom of this great and ancient people." The audience kept shouting "God bless you, Mr. Lalor," while Mr. Lalor kept waving his hand and raising his hat in smiling acceptance of their homage.

When the meeting was over, they surged forward and carried Mr. Lalor on their shoulders to his jaunting car and they followed the car some way on the road to Clogher, cheering and calling down God's blessing on his head. And then they all trooped meekly over to Mr. Chadwick's rent office with the money they had received for that food which was being driven down the road for export, together with the jaunting car of Mr. Lalor, the saviour of the people.

CHAPTER XIII

HERNON AND HIS wife took no part in the general rejoicing. No matter what the government did at the bidding of "the people's representatives" it would be too late to save them, unless they found something at once for the landlord. They waited outside the door of the rent office for the old man.

"Keep your mouth shut," Kitty said to her husband. "I'll talk to him."

Hernon was by now in such a state of excitement that his hands and feet were completely beyond control. The three little boys stood in a row by the wall with their hands joined, the one nearest to his mother clasping the end of her shawl. The whole family stood there against the wall of the rent office in a line, as if on parade for inspection, or else like a family of beggars making a forlorn appeal for help to the crowd.

At last the old man arrived, accompanied by Martin and Mary. He looked furtively at the Hernons, obviously not at all anxious to see them. Kitty came forward and said:

"For the honour of God, can you do anything for us?"

"What's that you say?" said the old man.

Now that the time had come to fulfil his promises of help, he regretted his generosity. He had the peasant's horror of parting needlessly with hard-earned money. He pulled a cloth purse from his bosom and tapped it with a gnarled fist.

"There'll be only four pounds, or maybe five, left in the purse," he said, "after I pay the rent. Is it asking me for that ye are and Michael sick on me? How do I know what moment the Lord will call him and he that sick with his chest? Is it wanting me to be without money for his funeral ye are?"

He lied about the money, as he would have over nine

sovereigns left after paying the rent. However, he had to consider the next half year's, which would have to be paid out of this, as he would have no pigs for sale in May and anything might happen to the yearling calf, which generally met that payment; not to mention the potato blight and Michael's illness. His caution was only natural under the circumstances. In any case, he knew Hernon to be a helpless fellow, who could not be relied on to repay anything.

"A pound itself might stay his mouth," said Kitty, wiping her eyes with a corner of her apron.

"Now you're talking," said the old man. "A pound is another thing altogether. I thought ye were asking for the ten pounds that ye owe."

"Don't be afraid, Kitty," said Martin. "If one pound isn't enough, we won't refuse you two of them."

"God bless you a mhac," said Patch Hernon.

" 'Faith, you're generous with our money," said Mary. "Some people are high and mighty with their talk, casting aspersions on people that have no land, but the same people are not ashamed to beg."

"I'm not begging from you," retorted Kitty savagely. "I'd rather die in a ditch."

"Can't you be easy, Mary?" Martin said gently.

"And why should I?" Mary cried. "Did you marry me, or did you marry everybody belonging to you down to the thirty-second cousin by the buttonhole? Charity begins at home. What are we going to do if the hard times come?"

"Didn't you hear the member say that the government…"

"The government, is it?" said Mary. "Depend on yourself and don't mind the government. It's little the government cares…"

"Silence," whispered the old man fiercely. "Not another word out of you. Come on, Kitty. Leave the talking to me, Patch. You're inclined to be hasty in your talk. Let me talk to Mr. Chadwick. He knows me for a good tenant and a man of my word."

They all pushed their way into the rent office. It was crowded with people. On one side there was a table, behind which Mr. Chadwick was sitting, together with his clerk and Hegarty the driver. The rent book lay open before Chadwick. Hegarty stood by his right shoulder. The clerk sat on the left, handling the money and giving receipts. There was a big chest of drawers and a safe against one wall. On the wall behind the table hung a picture of the Queen. There was a big black patch on the ceiling, from dampness. It was very cold and damp in the room, as the turf fire in the grate smoked without lighting properly.

Chadwick was dressed in a very slovenly manner. There was a hole in the sleeve of his coat and a patch over his right eye; both of which resulted from riding his new horse that morning. The animal proved not to be as good a fencer as Reilly had said, when the master got on its back. As a result of this fall he was in a devilish temper, which he vented on the tenants. He bellowed at them like a sergeant on parade with a squad of recruits.

"What the devil do you mean? Can't pay the full amount? Nonsense. What the devil do I care about your rotten potatoes? Pay up or take the consequences. What do you know about this fellow, Hegarty?"

The people grovelled before him, curtseying, their hats clutched against their bosoms. Mary watched all this in amazement. She found it hard to believe that this terrifying, red-haired man, with his lordly manner, was the same fellow who babbled at her sister's breasts. She was fascinated and at the same time she shuddered with horror. Now for the first time she realised the real meaning of what her sister had told her.

When the old man's turn came, Chadwick looked and saw Mary. His eyes became fixed, and he leaned his head forward a little on his bull neck, just like an animal sighting a mate. It was the same way that he had looked at Ellie when she came into his room. Paying no attention to the old man, he whispered to Hegarty, who whispered back an answer. Mary knew that he was asking Hegarty who she was. She drew back as far as she could and hid her face in her cloak.

"Begging your honour's pardon," said the old man, while the clerk was making out the receipt for his rent, "but Patch Hernon here, he's married to my daughter, your honour, and I'd like to say a word to you about him."

"What's that?" said Chadwick, with his gaze still fixed on Mary.

"So that's her sister," he thought. "Damn sight better. Much better. A real beauty, by God."

"He's in a bad way, your honour," said the old man.

He proceeded to give an account of Hernon's miserable condition and how impossible it was for him to meet the landlord's demands.

"What's that?" roared Chadwick, turning on the old man fiercely. "Who is he talking about, Hegarty?"

"They're badly off, sure enough," said Hegarty. "That man there, Patch Hernon, he means. His cow died on him last spring and he was a defaulter with the last half year. Now his crop has failed with the blight."

"Damn his crop," said Chadwick. "Why blame me? Pay up. You're hiding the money. I know you. You have it all hidden away. Out with it."

"Not a red copper has he got," said the old man. "I thought, maybe, I could give you a pound on account for him, until he gets a chance of earning something, and that you'd stay your hand with the writ."

"A pound?" cried Chadwick. "How much does the fellow owe, Simpson?"

"Ten pounds six and eightpence to date, Mr. Chadwick," said the clerk.

"What?" yelled Chadwick. "And you're suggesting…One pound! My God! Man, are you insane?"

Martin nudged the old man, who said:

"I could scrape two together for him. It will leave myself…"

With trembling hands he took two sovereigns from the purse and laid the two gold coins on the table, while Hegarty whispered an appeal for mercy in Mr. Chadwick's ear. Chadwick now again looked at Mary and he thought:

"Better not be too hard with them. She is certainly a beauty."

"Very well," he said aloud. "I'll give you a last chance… er…what is his name? Hernon? Very well. See that you have the full amount by…I'll give you three months. If you haven't got it by then, you may expect the consequences. By God! They are going to be serious for you. Dismiss.

He treated them exactly as if they were soldiers up before him for punishment. As they trooped out of the office, his eyes followed Mary.

"What relation is she to this fellow Hernon?" he whispered to Hegarty.

"Her sister-in-law," whispered Hegarty, "is married to him."

Outside in the street the weaver was in the centre of a little group. A man had him by the coat lapel, crying:

"Didn't you hear what Mr. Considine said about baring our breasts to the grape shot in defence of the country?"

"Devil damn the bit they'll do only talk," retorted the weaver. "They will do nothing. You mark my words."

"I should talk to him about Ellie," Mary thought, "but what's the good? He's only interested in things that don't concern him."

It was now bitterly cold with the fall of evening. There was a howling wind. They put the articles they had bought in the mare's creels and set off homewards. Martin halted the mare on the outskirts of the village and made Mary sit on the crupper behind the creels.

"You shouldn't have turned on Kitty like that," he said gently.

"If we set out to pay every poor creature's rent that's in need," Mary retorted, "all the gold of the leprechaun wouldn't be enough."

"But we can't be heathens all the same," Martin said.

They both felt cross and they continued in silence towards the Valley. Ominous dark clouds shut out the sky above the Valley, and the cries of the curlews, carried on the howling wind, re-echoed through the mountains. Even the singing of the homing crowd sounded drear and ominous.

CHAPTER XIV

IT BEGAN TO rain that night and for seven days the rain continued with such force that the Black Valley people were unable to haul their potato crop from the pits, as was their custom after the fair. This delay infuriated old Kilmartin.

He would not keep still for a moment, although there was positively nothing he could do about the crop, short of committing suicide by working in that perishing rain. For the cold was intense and the steady downpour was varied by lashing showers of hail. And yet, with an energy astounding in a man of his age, he was on his feet from cock-crow until he retired unwillingly each night, groaning about his rheumatism. With a sack about his shoulders, he ran back and forth from the house to the barn, examining the sky and shouting curses at the elements. Indoors he kept silent on account of Michael's illness; although his glaring eyes and the way he sat, leaning forward with a clenched fist on his knee, like a man ready to spring, were more disturbing than oaths and abuse.

This intense restlessness on his part was not altogether due to his fear that the rain might cause the complete destruction of the crop already affected by the blight. He was afraid that the young couple, awaking from the first ecstasy of their mating, would now begin to struggle for mastery in the house. He watched his eldest son, like an old buck watching a young rival in the herd.

As yet, however, Martin showed no sign of having any real interest in life beyond the joy of his beautiful bride's caresses. Each day he sat about the house with a dazed look in his eyes, smiling vaguely, starting when he was addressed, like a man in a dream. And when darkness fell, he retired once more, eagerly, to his bed, like a drunkard to his pot. Mary, too, was equally absorbed. Her eyes had lost their hardness. They had become vague and dreamy like those of her husband; as if this curtain of rain had shut out the world, for the moment, leaving only the cocoon of love in which she and her husband lay entwined.

Jealous of the young couple's rapture, the old man did everything he could to annoy them, particularly by nagging at Martin for his idleness.

"You might find a basket to mend," he would say, "instead of sitting there doing nothing. There's many a thing a willing man would find to do. Ah! God was unkind when he struck my best son with sickness."

And he showered attentions on the invalid. Although Michael had been steadily growing weaker since his loss of blood, the father now pretended to believe that he was making a rapid recovery. As long as Michael was alive in the house, he felt that Martin would not dare struggle for mastery. For this reason, he had every delicacy that the house possessed lavished on the sick man. The fowl were slaughtered one after the other, although Michael now barely tasted the broth and refused the meat altogether. Nevertheless, the meat was put aside religiously for him, in the hope that his appetite might turn towards it. In the same way, all the butter and eggs were put aside for use. If he coughed in the night, the old man would be out of bed like a shot, to ask how he was, to get him a drink, to tuck the clothes about him, to sit and amuse his wakefulness.

That Michael seemed to be indifferent to this attention did not disturb the old man in the least. He was guided in his conduct by something even stronger than his love for his son. He felt his old age coming on and he was using all his wit and strength to ward off the waning of his power.

When the rain ceased towards noon on the seventh day, he shouted with joy like a small boy released from confinement.

"Get the mare," he cried to Martin. "Straddle her while I go down to open the pit."

"Wait till after dinner," said Martin lazily. "We'd hardly be down there before dinner is ready."

The old man cursed and dashed out of the house. Thomsy rose from his seat in the hearth corner, stretched himself and said:

"Come on, Martin, we had better go with him."

They both followed the old man. He had already got his spade from the barn and he had begun to run across the fields towards the far garden by the river bank. The ground was so sodden with rain that the water splashed from his feet as he ran.

"Great God!" he yelled back at them. "The river is flooded."

The river had at this point overflowed its banks and the swirling water was half-way up the potato garden. The pit, however, was still beyond the flood. The old man at once dug into its end with the spade and laid bare the covering of ferns. These he hurriedly pulled aside with his hands. Then he slowly raised himself to his full height, some rotting ferns still in his hands. He stared, speechless, at the mass of corruption into which the potatoes had turned.

Then he drew back a pace and looked sideways up at the sky, his face wrinkled into a foolish grin, as if asking God for an explanation of this awful mischief. As he looked, he drew his hands slowly along his thighs until his arms were rigid. Then he opened his fists suddenly, dropped the ferns and rubbed his palms together, making an inarticulate noise in his throat like an enraged idiot. He got on his knees beside the hole that he had made in the pit and plunging his arms up to the elbows into the heap, he groped about among the mass of corruption, to find out if the centre also had rotted.

Thomsy arrived while the old man was groping in this way. He gaped and cried out:

"In the name of God, what is it?"

The old man started, drew back, rose slowly to his feet,

turned about and held out his arms towards Thomsy.

"That's all that's left of them," he stammered, holding out his arms, from which the corruption dripped to the ground.

"God have mercy on us," said Thomsy, taking off his hat and crossing himself.

The old man walked out of the garden, stooping, his arms hanging limply by his sides. He seemed to have got suddenly old and decrepit. At one blow, the spunk had oozed from his body. As he was climbing the fence from the garden into the neighbouring field, he paused and looked up the Valley.

It was a fearful sight. The sky had not cleared after the rain. It was dark and lowering, with a scant drizzle falling here and there from some shreds of cloud, that hung like floating rags across the sky. In this gloom, the mountains that encircled the Valley seemed to have thrust themselves forward, as if swollen by the rain; and the narrow crater in between, now barren of all growth, looked like a desolate shore from which the sea had been sucked by a monstrous moon. All along the mountain-sides, turbulent streams flowed down upon the sodden, blackened earth to cover its nakedness. The only sound was the roar of the falling water.

"It's a curse that has fallen on the land," muttered the old man as he continued towards the house.

Martin was straddling the mare outside the barn.

"You can spare yourself the trouble," the old man said to him. "They are all gone."

"What's that?" said Martin, pausing as he fixed the straw under the canvas on the mare's back.

The old man held out his foul arms and then continued towards the house. Martin ran down to the garden.

"What happened?" Maggie said when the old man entered the kitchen.

He made no answer, but pulled off his bawneen and went to the back door, to wash his hands in a bucket of water. Maggie had just slaughtered one of the fowl. She held the bird against her knee, the neck in her left hand. Blood dripped from the slit she had made in the comb with a knife. The bird was spasmodically shaking its wings, as its lifeblood drained from its quivering body. She looked at her husband and then dropped the expiring bird on the floor. She ran out into the yard. Mary followed her. The dog crept towards the fowl and reached out to lick the blood that had fallen, drawing back when the fowl quivered and shook its wings violently, as it plunged about on the floor in its death agony. Michael, who sat huddled in a blanket by the fire, threw a sod of turf at the dog. The dog yelped and rushed out into the yard. The fowl made a final effort with its wings. Then it opened its beak, stretched out its legs and lay still.

"Where are they gone?" Michael said in his whining tone. "What's happened?"

"The potatoes rotted in the pits," the old man said quietly as he came down to the fire.

Suddenly Michael's gloomy face became suffused with a wild gleam of merriment.

"Rotten?" he said. "Are they, though? Like me."

Then he burst into a peal of horrid laughter. The old man looked at him with open mouth.

"God forgive you," he said.

Then he went into his room, stripped off his clothes and got into bed. Maggie came back into the kitchen.

"Where's your father?" she said.

The sick man shrugged his shoulders and pointed to the bedroom. She entered and started when she saw the old man lying on his back in bed.

"What ails you?" she said.

Lying still on his back, with his hands crossed on his bosom under the clothes, just like a corpse, with his white beard lying along the quilt, he stared at her in silence. Then again she questioned him.

He sat up, menaced the window with his clenched fist and cried in fury:

"All my life I've struggled with it. Now it's got the best of me. Well! Let the devil do his worst. Let the curse fall."

Then he lay back again, folded his hands on his bosom and lay still.

CHAPTER XV

THE DAMAGE WAS not so serious as the old man said. One other pit was completely destroyed; but the remaining two, including the one of which O'Hanlon received half, were practically intact. There were just a few potatoes here and there affected in these two pits. However, the Kilmartins were now able to haul only fifteen bushels into their barn, instead of the original forty.

"We may give up the idea of rearing any pigs the coming year," Martin said. "There won't be enough for us to eat, after keeping seeds, not to mind feeding any pigs. We have to tighten our belts now and no doubt about it."

This disaster had put him on his mettle, which proved to be a fine one, beneath his placid exterior. During the three days they spent hauling the remnant of their crop into the barn, Mary's love for him took a deep root, in that feeling of pride which alone makes a woman's love for her man healthy and durable.

Suddenly he had become as dominating as his father. On that first day at dinner, when the old woman began to wail about the rot, he silenced her angrily and glared just as his father was in the habit of doing. And he looked exactly like his father at that moment, the same hawk-like countenance and blazing eyes.

Lying on his back in bed, the old man heard this outburst and took comfort.

"Ha!" he said to himself. "He has it in him all right."

The old rascal was only pretending to be overwhelmed by the disaster. He took to his bed and pretended to be "near his end," so that he might hand over control to his son without loss of dignity. He lay there for the three days they were working at the potatoes, carefully separating the affected from the healthy ones and storing them in the barn. Then he called Martin into his room.

"Here," he said, handing Martin the cloth purse which held the household money. "Take this now and look after the house and land and may God bless you. Your mother and I are near our end and it's time for us to lie back and save our souls before we go to meet our God."

His hand trembled as he handed over the purse and there were tears in his eyes. Then he suddenly stuck out his beard and added fiercely:

"But remember this. The curse of God falls on any son that is cruel to the couple that bore him."

"Have no fear of that," said Martin quietly. "The two of you can now take your ease in God's name. You may be sure that Mary and I won't let idleness take a seat by your hearth."

"God bless you, Martin," said the old man, "and may you always remember only what is good of me."

On the following morning, having made this capitulation, he was up with the dawn, his voice as loud and fierce as it ever was, rousing the household. But he no longer milked the cow, nor did he give orders in the house. As soon as he had eaten breakfast, he set out with his stick, walking hurriedly as usual. He wandered all over his little plot of land, every inch of which was as familiar and dear to him as his own right hand. He visited the cow, the calf, the mare, the sheep, drove them before him and spoke to them, just as he would to human beings. Then, having seen that everything was as it should be on his share, having picked up any stones that had fallen off the fences and scattered the dung of the animals to manure the soil, he went along the lane and spent the day chatting with other old people, who like himself were taking the only holiday of the peasant, the furlough of approaching death.

The conversations he had with these old people were not, however, the customary pleasant discussions of old times, delightful arguments about relationships and boundaries and giving in marriage and feats of strength. The rotting of the potatoes and the menace of hunger made every person's speech bitter and foreboding. For the rot in the pits had been general and some people were already depending for potatoes on the charity of their neighbours. The poorest among them, the squatters and those tenants who had no stock, were merely clinging to their homes in expectation of help from the government. The dreaded journey to the workhouse would have to be made if this help were not forthcoming. They all sat about in their cabins, dazed and helpless.

In contrast with this general apathy, the young couple in Kilmartin's house were working like honey bees. As soon as Mary got the reins of authority in her hands, she determined that there was going to be a great change in the mode of life of the household. First of all she got Martin working on the patch of rocky, waste land at the back of the house. There was about a quarter of an acre of ground there that had never been put to any use and there she decided to have a vegetable garden.

"It's far better than the ground my father made his garden on," she said, "and look what he has now growing there at his door. Onions, turnips and cabbage, the finest food in the world. No person need be hungry that has an inch of ground atall. If one crop fails another won't. Let you make the ground ready for spring and we'll put seeds in it. Let the people say what they like, but we'll have the laugh on them and we eating what grows in our garden."

She inspired Martin with her enthusiasm and he set to work with Thomsy, smashing and digging the rocks, clearing the ground and hauling soil in baskets on his back from a pit below the barn. The old man sneered at this work and took no part in it, considering it revolutionary and dangerous.

"They'll only raise the rent," he said, "if they see any improvement made."

"I'll see that they don't, said Mary, "if I have to strangle the agent with the hands God gave me."

There was no end to her energy and to the new ideas she had about everything. She scoured the house from end to end, so that even poor Maggie rebelled, seeing the habits of her life so startlingly changed.

"There's no use trying to get rid of dirt in this house, asthore," she said. "The poor were born to be dirty."

"Well! I mean to get rich," said Mary. "And this dirt is the first thing that I find in the way."

Thomsy made the most violent struggle against this campaign for cleanliness. Mary insisted on his having a new suit from that year's frieze. When the tailor had finished his work in the house and gone, Thomsy went to put on the new clothes over his rags, but Mary grabbed them from him.

"You'll wash yourself first," she said, "before you put these clothes against your dirty pelt."

"Ga! Sister," said Thomsy, "is it my death of cold you're after?"

"Never you mind," she said. "From now on you have to live like a Christian."

She got a barrel and half filled it with hot water in her own bedroom. Then she ordered Thomsy into the room.

"Go in there," she said. "Strip off your dirty rags and scour yourself. You go in, Martin, and scrub him with this soap and brush."

"Is it out of your mind you are?" cried Thomsy, looking at her in amazement.

Martin roared with laughter, looking at the poor fellow's horror. Maggie got indignant.

"It's not fair to be making fun of the poor man," she said.

"I'm not making fun," said Mary. "I'm for his good. It's a shame the state he has been left to live in all these years. He'll be a different man when I'm finished with him."

"Never," cried Thomsy, stamping on the floor. "You'll never wash me. By the blood of the Divine Saviour! I'd rather be hung, drawn and quartered."

Martin, still laughing wildly, seized the unfortunate Thomsy and carried him bodily into the room.

"Let me go, you devil," screamed Thomsy.

"Throw me out his rags when you have taken them off him," said Mary.

Thomsy's screams could be heard half a mile away as Martin stripped him to the skin and then plunged him into the hot water. Then he threw the rags out into the kitchen and began to use the brush and soap with no gentle hand. Mary took the rags out into the yard on a shovel and set fire to them. Then she took up more soap and water to the loft, threw down all the rags that formed Thomsy's bedding and scrubbed that place clean. When she came down off the loft, Thomsy was dressed once more. He now wore a clean shirt and his new suit.

"Don't you feel better now?" said Mary.

Thomsy pretended to be shivering with the cold and he was rattling his teeth together.

"Ga! Sister," he stammered, "my death be on your head."

He crouched over the fire, shivering, as if the loss of his dirt had really given him a chill. However, after spending the night on the new bed that Mary made down for him, he was man enough to thank her the following morning.

"Ga! Sister," he grumbled as he came down the ladder to his breakfast, "a change of masters is not as bad as the proverb says it is."

And so the household settled down to the new kind of life that Mary had introduced among them, timidly allowing themselves to become inoculated with the germs of civilisation which her weaver father had brought with him to Black Valley. And Mary herself was so happy moulding her new home to her liking that she had no thought of the calamity that loomed on the horizon.

That calamity, however, suddenly grew larger and its shadow spread over the Valley. A rumour came that the government had refused to help the people. Immediately, the destitute began to wander into the village.

CHAPTER XVI

FATHER ROCHE WAS reading aloud from a Dublin newspaper in his sitting-room. Dr. Hynes and the curate, Father Thomas Geelan, sat by the fire listening to him. The parish priest was very excited.

"There will be no hope of contributions from England," he read, "for the mitigation of this calamity. Monster meetings, the ungrateful return for past kindness, the subscriptions in Ireland to repeal rent and O'Connell tribute, will have disinclined the charitable here to make exertions for Irish relief."

He crumpled the paper savagely in his right hand, took off his spectacles and shook them with his left hand at his listeners. His chubby, round face was livid with rage. As he leant forward, the blaze of the turf caught his bald pate and made it shine like ivory.

"That's what Sir Robert Peel tells his cabinet," he cried. "The greatest scoundrel in the history of man. Think of it. Charity! Did you ever hear the like of it?"

He held out both arms towards his listeners as he continued:

"England takes five million pounds from us every year in rent alone. As rent for land she robbed and holds by the law of the brigand, by the law of the bayonet and of the grape-shot. In rent alone she takes five million pounds a year. Not to mention taxes. She takes three million quarters of grain every year. She takes one million head of cattle, sheep and swine. And now, when the poor Irish people, who supply her with this wealth, year after year, have lost the potato crop on which she forces them to live, she talks of charity. We want justice. Justice! We want our own."

"Justice!" said the curate gloomily, as he spread out his hands to the blaze. "There is no danger of getting that by asking for it with outstretched empty hands. With empty hands we'll only get a wooden horse from England."

He laughed dryly and added:

"Timeo Danaos et dona ferentes."

The doctor looked at the curate in a startled way. He had not a very quick intelligence and the curate's remarks always disturbed him. At the same time, he was strongly attracted by Father Geelan. Since his return to Crom as medical officer, he was becoming more and more influenced by this sombre, scholarly man.

Father Geelan was indeed a strange person. He had been a brilliant student at Maynooth, but somehow his life had been a failure since his ordination, judging it from the point of view of the average person. He was now approaching sixty and yet he was merely a curate in an obscure parish, while younger and far less able men had become his superiors. He was undoubtedly more fitted to be a monk than a secular priest; but his political views, rather than his sanctity and his incapacity for intrigue and flattery, were responsible for his failure to advance in his profession. He was of the type of that gallant priest, who led the Wexford insurgents in arms during the rebellion of 1798. This belief in the use of arms, rather than "outstretched empty hands," as a means of attaining freedom from oppression, was responsible for his remaining a curate in a place like Crom, wasting his erudition on parables for ignorant ears.

His appearance was odd. His hair had gone grey in a ring all round the base of his skull, leaving the crown still black and luxuriant. His figure was shapeless and although he was a big, heavy man, his shabby black clothes hung loosely about him. He had enormous shoulders, hands, feet, and head. His face was square, dark and emaciated. Although he was clean-shaven, he appeared to have a growth of beard, owing to the sallow darkness of his complexion. His eyes were deeply sunk and full of a wise sorrow; the sorrow of the deep-thinking man who has looked a long time on the sufferings of his fellow creatures in a brutal form of society.

"What is O'Connell going to do?" said the doctor to Father Roche.

The curate laughed once more in a mocking fashion. Father Roche put on his spectacles and said:

"It's not much use for him going on deputations to the Lord Lieutenant. Lord Heytesbury'll do nothing except at the crack of Peel's whip and we all know what that will be. The shame of it! There they go, the Duke of Leinster, Lord Cloncurry, Lord Mayor Arabin, Dan O'Connell, Henry Grattan, John Augustus O'Neill, a galaxy of great names, to beg for consideration from a Jack in office like Lord Heytesbury."

He straightened out the newspaper and read:

"The Lord Mayor read to the Lord Lieutenant resolutions drawn up by the committee by which the deputation was appointed, stating, that famine and pestilence were immediately imminent unless the government took proper measures to prevent them, that this could best be done by employing the people on works of national utility, that the ports ought to be closed against the exportation of corn, that public granaries should be established in various parts of the country and the corn sold to the people at moderate prices and finally, that the use of grain for distilling should be abolished."

Father Roche paused, and the doctor remarked:

"Very reasonable proposals."

"All the more reason why they should be rejected," said the curate, "by a government eager to destroy us as a race."

The parish priest continued to read:

" 'The state of the potato crop,' replied his excellency, 'is receiving the anxious consideration of the government.

Scientific men have been sent from England to co-operate
with those of this country, in endeavouring to investigate the
nature of the disease and, if possible, to devise means of
arresting its progress. They have not yet finished their enquiries,
but two reports have already been received from them and
communicated to the public.'"

The curate laughed harshly and said:

"They asked for bread and were given the report of
Professor Playfair."

" 'The government,'" read Father Roche, "'is also
furnished with constant reports from the stipendiary
magistrates and inspectors of constabulary, who are charged
to watch the state of the potato disease and the progress of the
harvest. They vary from day to day and are often contradictory.
It is therefore impossible to form an accurate opinion on the
whole extent of the evil. There is reason to hope that the failure
is only partial in some places. There is no immediate pressure.
I will submit your proposals to the cabinet, but a greater part
of them can only be enforced by legislative enactment and
they will all require to be maturely weighed before they can be
adopted. No decision can be taken before reference to the
responsible advisors of the Crown.'"

The parish priest looked at his listeners over his spectacles
and added:

"You heard what the responsible advisors of the Crown
said about these proposals? Now listen to this. This puts it all
in a nutshell. Listen to this editorial."

Again he quoted from the newspaper:

"They may starve! Such in spirit, if not in words, was the
reply given by the English viceroy to the memorial of the
deputation, which, in the name of the Lords and Commons
of Ireland, prayed that the food of the country should be
preserved, lest the people thereof perish."

The curate got to his feet, stretched himself, and said:

"But surely, Father John, you didn't expect the government
to help."

The parish priest threw the newspaper on the table and began to pace the room with his hands clasping and unclasping behind his back.

"I don't know what I expected," he said. "I haven't slept a wink since the poor people began to crowd into the village a few days ago. What am I to do? The cries of the poor creatures are like knives stabbing me in the heart. They come to me, but I don't know what to tell them."

"It's too late now," growled the curate. "The people's grain and their pigs and their oats are gone over the sea, to fill broad English bellies. But there was something to be done and something to be said to the people on fair day. They should have been told to put their meat and their grain in their own good stomachs."

The parish priest turned on him suddenly and said in an angry tone:

"What's that you're saying, Tom? Are you out of your mind?"

Father Geelan shrugged his shoulders and said:

"I'm not, then," he said quietly, "out of my mind atall, Father John, but it's the people's leaders that are out of their minds, for letting the people's food go out of the country and then begging for some of it back. Ha! Ha! It's the most foolish thing I ever heard. There isn't enough food in England to feed the English, so Ireland is kept as a granary and a butchery next door. Isn't that their policy?"

"You're talking through your hat," said Father Roche. "If the rent was kept back, that would give the government the excuse they were waiting for, to send their soldiers to massacre the poor defenceless people and clear them off the land at one sweep."

"More fools the people are if they are defenceless," said the curate.

"I know all that talk," said the parish priest, getting angry. "Armed rebellion like we had in Ninety-Eight…"

"Hear, hear," said the curate.

They continued to argue while the doctor listened excitedly. He felt in a curious way responsible for the threatened calamity. Ever since his childhood two mutually antagonistic influences had been working on his nature. One influence drew him towards the people whose blood ran in his veins. On the other hand, he felt hostile towards the people, owing to their treatment of his grandfather and the way his father had suffered in his early struggles. Then again, the ambition of his parents had brought him up to be a "gentleman". For that reason, even as a little boy, he was not allowed to play with the poorer village children, and in school he learned in his primer "what a pleasure to be born a happy British child as I have been." So he was a solitary boy, when he was home on holidays from his school in Clogher, for the children of the gentry and petty officials, with whom he would be allowed to associate, regarded him as a peasant boy and would not speak to him. Nowadays it is hard to imagine the degree of snobbery prevalent in those days, or the manner in which the painful feeling of belonging to a subject race affected the character of ambitious young Catholics who were struggling to improve their position in society. By the time he had finished his medical studies in Dublin, he had come to despise the masses of the Irish people, as an inferior race, a species of amiable buffoon, from whom he should do everything in his power to dissociate himself, in ideas, in manners, in language, in allegiance.

However, immediately after he had taken up his appointment as dispensary doctor at Crom, his conscience began to affect him. The call of the blood became stronger than the gibberish he had assimilated at school and in Dublin. His journey to Black Valley and his meeting with Mary Kilmartin had roused in him a feeling of shame. That beautiful creature, with the gracious dignity of a queen, had shown him the folly and emptiness of his ideas. Ever since then, the condition of the people horrified him and he even began to regard his own father as a kind of thief, who was striving to enrich himself at the people's expense. That is why he now felt in some way responsible for the impending calamity.

"But can't we do something?" he said to Father Roche. "Couldn't we get together and open a subscription or something?"

Father Geelan turned out his pockets in answer to this suggestion. The doctor nodded.

"I know," he said, "but Mr. Coburn is getting up a committee and..."

"To proselytise," cried Father Roche. "That's what he's after. He's appealing to his friends to subscribe to a fund that's going to be used to proselytise the people. He'll give them soup if they turn Protestant. He'll put their children in homes and raise them enemies of their holy faith."

"I know," said the doctor, "but it's awful to be able to do nothing."

"Now there's nothing left to us but to do our duty," said Father Geelan.

Old Julia Mullins, the parish priest's housekeeper, came into the room with a cloth under her arm.

"Are you ready for your supper, Father John?" she said.

" 'Faith, then, I am, Julia," said Father Roche, "but I'm ashamed to eat it and people starving in the street."

"Prut!" she said, going to the table with the cloth. "What nonsense you do be talking!"

The curate and the doctor went to take their leave. Father Roche followed them to the door, saying:

"We mustn't lose heart. The government must be forced to act."

It was pitch dark outside. The doctor felt annoyed with Father Roche for failing to give him a plan of action.

"If there's anything I can do, Father John," he said, "I wish you'd call on me."

"Thanks, Joe," said Father Roche. "God bless you."

The two men strode up the street. They found their way with difficulty, guided solely by a lanthorn which the curate held aloft. The long, thatched house of one storey, in which the parish priest lived, was at the western end of the village, adjoining the ruins of the old monastery and the graveyard. The curate had lodgings in a cottage near the chapel.

"What do you think will happen, Father Tom?" said the doctor as they walked along.

The curate gripped the doctor by the arm and halted in the road.

"I am afraid to think," he said gloomily.

The hand that gripped the doctor's arm trembled.

"Maybe you and I won't live to tell the tale of all that's going to happen," he continued. "I'm afraid that something is going to happen in Ireland that will make our race wanderers on the face of the earth like the ancient Jews. I dream of many things. And in my dreams I see woeful destruction coming. But I dream, too, of a resurrection and a homecoming. Remember that, son. Look round you. Listen to the wind."

The doctor listened to the great, full-bodied breeze that swept down from the mountains and across the village.

"Learn to love this Irish earth, as your real mother," whispered the curate. "Then it will speak to you and tell you deep, deep things and beautiful things that are stronger than any misfortune. Listening to the wind, I dream. Come on, now."

The doctor felt strangely exalted as he walked along beside the clumsy bulk of the curate, whose lungs wheezed as he walked. Then a voice hailed them suddenly from the darkness, crying:

"For the love and honour of God and of the Saviour, help a starving mother and her child."

The curate held out his lanthorn towards the voice. In its dim light, the gaunt face of a woman became visible. The face of the little child could also be seen, peering from its mother's ragged shawl. The curate automatically put his hand in his pocket and then he said gloomily:

"Come with me, good woman. I have nothing to give you but my supper."

"God bless your reverence," said the woman, "and indeed I wouldn't take the bite out of your mouth and you needing it yourself, but I'm on my way to the workhouse this night and it's ten miles to Clogher. I'm afraid for the child and we with nowhere to stay."

The doctor gave her some coppers, then he bid the curate good night and hurried forward towards the lights of the hotel that glimmered in the distance. He shuddered as if he had caught a chill.

A small carriage was drawn up outside the hotel and a voice hailed him as he approached:

"Come with me quickly, sir. The master has cut himself."

It was Reilly, Mr. Chadwick's groom. The doctor questioned him and then hurried indoors for his bag.

CHAPTER XVII

HE RAN OUT with the bag and mounted the little carriage. Reilly lashed the horse into a gallop.

"It's the drink," he shouted in his sing-song, high-pitched voice. "He went away after taking the rent and then he came back in a mortal state of drunk and disorderly conduct. Young Mr. Broderick came to-day and they started playing cards. The master lost at the cards. The next thing we knew, he had his throat cut. The blood was pouring out of him like a stuck pig, saving the comparison. Gee up, there."

The horse tore down the drive at a headlong gallop, with the carriage bumping dangerously against the loose branches that strewed the rutted way.

"I drew the skin to either side," yelled Reilly, "and then we tied it up with knots and lashed towels around the gash. There was only a little drip and I leaving the house. Begob, I'd swear he's still alive."

They drew up before the door of the house so furiously that the near wheel of the carriage almost smashed against the steps. The doctor hurried into the hall, where he was met by a slovenly grey-haired woman.

"Hurry, sir," she said, wringing her hands. "It's beginning to pour out of him again. We can't keep him quiet and he that afraid of dying. This way, sir."

The doctor and Reilly followed her upstairs into Chadwick's room. There they found Ellie Gleeson and two other women struggling with Chadwick on the bed, which was as gory as a battlefield. There was blood on Chadwick's face above the towels, that encircled his neck like a clumsy strangler's knot. There was more blood scattered on the bedclothes and all over the women. The man had an idea that they were trying to kill him and he cried out for help when he saw the doctor.

"Save me from them," he yelled.

The doctor had only to glance at the wound in order to discover that it was not at all serious. Chadwick had simply drawn the blade hurriedly across his throat, making a long gash in the thick layer of flesh that covered his gullet. Neither the windpipe nor the arteries had been touched. The bleeding, however, was profuse.

"Pull yourself together," said the doctor. "This is just a slight flesh wound. You'll be alright."

Chadwick was now sobbing and gurgling like a child, while his eyes rolled about in his head and he trembled all over. The doctor set to work. With the help of the women he soon had the wound stitched and bandaged. Chadwick bore the stitching with unexpected courage; just as if he were impervious to physical pain, but in mortal terror of something that troubled his mind. When the doctor had finished, he stepped back and said:

"There you are. Now you're as right as rain."

Chadwick lay back exhausted, shuddering spasmodically. He closed his eyes and presently he fell into an uneasy sleep, almost before the doctor had finished washing his hands.

"You'll have to keep a good watch on him," whispered the doctor to the women. "Who's in charge here?"

Mary Halloran, the slovenly woman with grey hair, pointed at Ellie Gleeson and said in a hostile tone:

"She does look after him, sir."

The doctor started, recognising at once Ellie's resemblance to her sister, pronounced at the moment owing to her intense excitement. In fact, she looked distraught. There was a daub of blood on her right cheek. Her lower lip trembled. Her nostrils expanded and contracted as if she were exhausted from running.

"Are you ill?" said the doctor.

"Could I talk to you outside?" she said, shaking her head in answer to his question.

He followed her out of the room. She brought him into her own bedroom next door and closed the door behind them. It was pitch dark there. She clutched the doctor by the coat excitedly and began to speak at once.

"I'd be obliged to you, sir," she said, 'if you'd say nothing of this. If my father came to hear of it there would be trouble and I'd have to leave here. I don't want to go. He has only me to look after him. The others don't care if he destroyed himself. It's only the drink that puts harm in him. For the love of God, sir, give out it was an accident. Will you, sir?"

"I don't understand," the doctor said in amazement. "Have you a light here?"

"No, no," she said, getting still more excited and coming so close that he could feel her firm breasts against him. "Promise me you won't say anything."

"I don't know what you mean," said the doctor. "Why should I? What happened?"

"Will you promise?" she insisted.

"Who are you, in any case?" said the doctor.

"I'm Barney Gleeson's daughter, Ellie."

"Oh! I thought you were. Let's hear all about it."

"It's a long story," she said, drawing away a little and clasping her hands against her bosom. "Mr. Broderick came this morning and they began to play cards. They played all day and drank as well. Then Mr. Broderick went away and the master said to me: 'That rogue has cheated me.' True or not, them were his words. He was mad because Mr. Broderick won the horse off him, the one he bought from Colonel Bodkin. So I says to him he should lie down and rest. He's been routing for days. I had his boots off and his coat. I thought I had him nice and quiet, with him sitting there on the side of the bed, half crying and talking about his father. When he's that way, sir, he always talks about his father and how he brought disgrace on his father's name. Them are his words. 'I have him nice and comfortable now,' I said to myself and I began to pull off his breeches when he suddenly turned on me. 'Out of my sight,' says he, 'you slut!' I lost my temper with that and I answered him back. 'Devil take you,' says I. Lord save us! He roared at me and then he ran for his razor case that was lying there. He outs with the razor and then he makes for me. I froze with the fright, thinking I was done for this time. For he's mad when he has the drink taken. Then he bursts out laughing. 'Take it,' says he, handing me the razor. 'Take it and put an end to me. I'm no use for God or man.' I begged him not to talk nonsense. Then again he shouted: 'How dare you doubt my word?' With that he gave his throat a welt of the blade and out poured the blood.'

"Good God!" cried the doctor. "Why do you want to stay here? This man is mad. I'll have to report him."

"Oh! No, sir. You don't know what you're saying. He's not mad. It's only the drink. Can't you wait till morning in any case and talk to him. Then you'll see. If there's any rumour about it, I'd have to go."

"But why do you want to stay here?" said the doctor, beginning to get annoyed with her.

"Because I do," she said sulkily, "that's why."

"I can't make head or tail of it," said the doctor.

"Promise me before you go not to tell," she cried again, throwing her arms around his neck and pressing herself against him. "Promise me that."

Suddenly the doctor felt overcome by a delicious intoxication that dulled his senses.

"I promise," he said thickly.

Now he trembled more than the girl herself.

"Thank you, sir," she said happily. "God bless you."

Then she opened the door. They went back into Chadwick's room. Reilly and the other women were whispering in a group. Chadwick was still sleeping fitfully.

The doctor whispered instructions about how to deal with the patient and then beckoned Reilly, who followed him downstairs.

"There's no harm done after all," whispered Reilly cheerfully on the way down. "Mary Halloran was telling me it was on account of losing the horse. But sure he needn't have put his hand to all that trouble. Mr. Broderick is not the man to take advantage of a friend in drink. Ah! the drink! It's a man's worst enemy."

A shower of rain was falling as they set off for the hotel. As soon as they got out of ear-shot of the house, Reilly leaned back from the driver's seat and whispered:

"It's that misfortunate girl is the cause of all the trouble. Since she came to the house, the master is out of his mind. He wasn't like that before. Oh! No! People can say what they like about him, but he has always treated us like a proper gentleman. I wouldn't believe a word she says, if I were you, sir."

"How do you mean?" said the doctor.

"She has a hold over him," whispered Reilly, in the confidential tone of the scandalmonger. "All the years he's been here I haven't known him look at a woman until she came into the house. Only the bottle. By the powers! Since she came, he's a danger to himself and to everybody near him."

"Then why do you stay with him?" said the doctor. "A man like that should be put into a mad-house."

"Oh no, sir," said Reilly. "Don't make a report about him. It's her. That girl should be made go. There's no harm in Mr. Chadwick. There isn't a grander man when he's in his senses. I wouldn't report him, sir, for he'd only lose his situation and the people would get a worse agent in his place."

"Funny," thought the doctor, "how they all like that awful-looking drunkard."

"Will you be wanting me in the morning?" Reilly said when they reached the hotel.

"No," said the doctor. "I'll come on foot. Wake me up

during the night if anything happens. Good night."

He felt terribly nervous and discontented. His mother met him in the hall and began to fuss about his wet clothes.

"Go on upstairs and strip off at once," she said.

"Oh! don't bother me," he said angrily, "you'd think I was made of china."

He went into the parlour at the rear of the hall. This had formerly been the family sitting- and dining-room, but now it was put aside exclusively for the doctor's use, except that the father still kept his money and documents there in an iron safe. It was a long, narrow room, with a table in the middle. One end of the table was laid for supper. A turf fire blazed in the grate. It was very cosy in the room. He sat down before the fire and put his hands to the blaze.

"What's coming over me?" he thought. "Why did I turn on my mother like that?"

He put his head in his hands and said aloud:

"Good God! I'll go mad in this place. I should never have come back here."

He shuddered and again held out his hands to the blaze. His sister came into the room with his supper on a tray. She did not speak to him. She approached the table slowly, with her eyes on the ground, walking with a sort of little hop and keeping her body rigid above the waist. She was made very like her brother, with a fine crop of golden hair, a rather short and podgy figure and small features. She had, also, his rather furtive expression and his painful self-consciousness: even more marked in her case, as a delicate stomach since childhood had increased her tendency towards morose brooding and for taking offence from imaginary slights. The people said that she "was not all there," owing to her silence and the way she sometimes laughed when alone, for no apparent reason.

"Who's making that row in the kitchen, Bridget?" said the doctor.

She said something in a mumbling, inarticulate whisper

and then, having put the food clumsily on the table, she stole out of the room, just like a ghost might go. The doctor looked after her sourly and then listened to the wild laughter in the kitchen. He recognised Reilly's voice and became very angry.

"Instead of going back to look after his master," he thought, "he'll stay there now the whole evening, having fun for himself. They have no real feeling."

He began his supper, brooding on the misery of his life as he ate. The dreary, bare mountains and the gloomy valleys, the bogs, the village itself, all terrified him in this mood. Love the earth as a mother, indeed! what nonsense! He was appalled by the thought of having to spend his whole life among this squalor and general discontent, without any social life, connected with the outside world solely by the mail car that came twice a week from Clogher. And what was Clogher? What was to be had there by anybody whose demands on life were even slightly removed from those of an animal? Nothing but a larger and more discontented Crom.

Now he cursed his family for having tried to turn him into a "gentleman," giving him appetites which he could not satisfy, showing him the joy of brightness and then thrusting him back into the darkness of his native village. They pretended to sacrifice themselves for his sake, sending him to school and college and now even living in the kitchen, so that he might have a room to himself. A private room for the gentleman of the family! What advantage was there in his sitting here miserably alone, while they were having fun in the kitchen, listening to Reilly's account of a steeple-chase? A gentleman! They watched him as if he were still a little boy on apron strings. He couldn't take a drink like any other man, or have fun with girls.

Ha! There was the rub. He put down his knife and fork and stared at the table, as the memory of Ellie Gleeson came into his mind. He could feel her throbbing, firm breasts against him and a choking feeling in his throat made him swallow his breath. He left the table and went back to the fire. Now he did not think, but he kept trembling.

His father came into the room, carrying a ledger and the day's takings in a little satchel. He peered at his son from under the rim of his black hat, as he walked stooping to the iron safe.

"You were down at the Big House?" he said in his whining tone. "Mr. Chadwick is sick, Reilly the groom was saying. What ails him? Reilly said he fell and cut himself. Is it the drink? Where did he cut himself? How did he do it?"

The old man uttered this string of questions without seeming to have any interest in getting an answer to them. The doctor did not trouble to answer. The relationship between him and his father was a curious one. He despised and disliked his father, but at the same time he feared him. The old man was despised and disliked by everybody, but he "had the power" as the people said and for that reason he was feared. And the doctor's attitude towards him was the same as that of the people at large. There was nothing personal between them. John Hynes had never taken the trouble to establish personal relations with anybody. He never had the time or the inclination. All he thought of was getting power, so that he might have "satisfaction" for those contumelies he had suffered as a child. His son being a doctor, for instance, was part of the "satisfaction".

"Heh!" he continued, as he drew a chair over in front of the safe and sat down on it. "Bad cess to him! Fitter for him to pay me what he owes."

The doctor looked angrily at the old man, who now transferred the satchel to his withered hand and took a key from his pocket.

"If I say nothing," he thought, "he'll feel obliged to me. Then I can have fun in his house. I'll have somewhere to pass the time."

And again the memory of Ellie's breasts passed like a warm

cloud through his mind. Intoxicating! The old man fumbled with the key in the lock. It did not fit properly.

"He owes me more than eighty pounds now," he whined. "I have a poor chance of ever getting a penny of it. Times have changed. There is little honesty left among the gentry now."

The safe door swung open. The old man opened the satchel and thrust his good hand into it. He counted the money lovingly as he put it into the safe. Then he put in the ledger and locked the safe once more. He stood up, swinging the big key on his finger, and looked at his son.

"What did Father Roche say about the deputation to the Lord Lieutenant?" he said. "Are they going to give the people work? Or did they get no satisfaction? I suppose they didn't. The government are a lot of grabbers. The people are no better. Why don't they go into the workhouse? Don't me and my like pay for the workhouse? But they come begging instead of going there. Heh! There is no honesty left."

The doctor made no answer. The old man put the empty satchel into his coat pocket and walked stooping to the door, his withered hand held close to his side like a man carrying a parcel.

"Mr. Chadwick!" he mumbled. "A fine specimen! I have a poor chance of getting what he…"

He was gone. The doctor again put his head in his hands and brooded about his father almost with hatred. For he could recall nothing that inspired tenderness; only that loathsome, furtive look, that constant mumbling about money, that constant whining about "the waste that goes on in this house."

Bridget came and cleared the table in silence. The doctor tried to read a dog-eared old story book called *The Battle of Aughrim*. After a few minutes he threw it aside and got to his feet. Holding his clenched hands in front of him, he cried out suddenly:

"I've had enough of this. I'm going to live as I please."

Later, when he got into bed, he could not sleep for a long time, for the memory of the girl's breasts attacked him whenever he closed his eyes. Finally, when he did fall asleep, he soon awakened in terror. And then he lay in the darkness of his room, thinking of a night in Dublin, when he paid a visit with some other students to a street where there were illicit drinking shops and loose women. He fled, on entering the street, followed by the mocking cries of his comrades. But he returned alone a little later, pretending that he came looking for his comrades. Although he did not heed the sluts who accosted him, as he wandered up and down the street, peering into the open doorways of the rowdy shops, he had revelled in the same intoxication that had possessed his body just now in sleep. And although, in his sleep, his conscience had revolted against this intoxication, he submitted to it when awake. So that he stared into the darkness and willed to rid himself of that which irked him, should the opportunity be offered.

When he arose in the morning he felt elated, as if he were about to embark on a thrilling adventure. As soon as he had finished breakfast, he set out towards Crom House. The day was bright and sunny. Already in the main street there were groups of people who had wandered in from the countryside in search of help. At the distance of their homes, the village had seemed a place of refuge and of plenty. Now that they had arrived, however, they stood about helplessly, feeding their empty bellies on the warmth of the wintry sun.

For the past few days, this spectacle of hungry and despairing people had unnerved the doctor and made him feel ashamed of not being able to help. This morning he took no notice. From the moment that he had surrendered during the night, the fate of the poor no longer concerned him.

His heart began to beat wildly when he came in sight of Crom House. One of the men-servants was working on the lawn with a rake. He leaned on the rake and eyed the doctor in a curious fashion. The doctor flushed, as if he had been spied by this man entering the street where there were sheebeens and bawdy houses.

"He's better, sir," said the man, touching his hat with the end of the rake handle.

The doctor entered the hall. He halted uncertainly. There was nobody there. Suddenly he began to tremble and wanted to run madly away from the house. Then he looked about him furtively and made the sign of the Cross on his forehead.

CHAPTER XVIII

DURING THE RAINY spell that followed the fair, a neighbour woman began to barge Kitty Hernon, one of whose children had thrown a stone at the neighbour's hens. Mrs. Hernon accepted the wordy battle and the two women screamed at one another over the fence that separated their yards.

"Some people are high and mighty," said the neighbour woman, when the battle was going against her, "but they are not ashamed to beg."

Recognising the words that Mary Kilmartin had uttered outside the rent office on fair day, Mrs. Hernon became inarticulate with shame and rage. She burst into tears, retired indoors and sat down on the earthen floor, where she wailed with her face covered. Patch, who had been out visiting during the argument, now came and challenged the neighbour woman's husband. He stripped to his shirt in the lane and stood there, indifferent to the rain, with a large stone in his right hand, calling his neighbour foul names. The neighbour, a man called Halloran, was a mild fellow. He came out of his house and tried to pacify Hernon.

"It is only a fool," he said, "would take part in a war of women's tongues."

Hernon hurled the stone in answer. It stuck Halloran on the chest and he fell with a hollow groan. Hernon fled to the mountains, thinking he had done murder. The neighbours came and took Halloran into his house, where it was found that he was only winded by the stone. But Hernon, ignorant of this, kept running up the mountain.

At the head of the Valley, the houses were not scattered, but huddled together, to the number of ten, in a kind of hamlet.

The mountain rose immediately above this hamlet and nobody else lived farther to the north, for a distance of twenty miles. All that mountain country, reaching as far north as the county Mayo, was uninhabited and without boundaries. For that reason, the people at the head of the Valley reared sheep, which they grazed in common on the slopes. They had no other cattle in the place, except a few asses and Patch Hernon's young heifer. Their land at the foot of the mountains was barely enough to produce potatoes for their sustenance. As a result of this they were very morbid, wandering over the wild, misty mountains after their sheep. As we have seen, Hernon had been, in fact, for a long time bordering on insanity.

As he ran up the mountain path, in flight from what he had done, his mind finally gave way completely. After he had run about half a mile he halted, panting. Now he was surrounded by the empty wilderness. There was only the rain and the dark, heathered earth, bellying all round him. And suddenly, in this awful wilderness he saw the Evil Eye. His own eyes grew large and his lips were smitten with a palsy. He stood still, glancing furtively from side to side, seeing the Eye everywhere. And he thought of how his cow had died in spring and how his potato crop had been destroyed, and he heard the voice of Mr. Chadwick threatening that he had only three months to pay his arrears of rent. Then finally he heard the word beggar whispered in his ear. This was the final insult of the Eye. He sprang forward with a smothered shout.

He moved in sudden, irregular spurts along the wild path, darting from side to side, as if to avoid enemies, panting. The Eye followed him, glaring at him through the rain. It glared at him from rocks and from ravines. He began to pray aloud, not to God, but to the mountain devils, asking for mercy. His panic increased with his progress, until at last he reached the Black Lake, perched high among the silence of the mountain peaks. He hid in a cave that overlooked the lake and there was no sound there, except the droning fall of the rain and an occasional bleat from a sheep that cried out in its terror of the cold rain.

He crouched at the mouth of the cave, not daring to look inwards at the pitch darkness, where he knew the Evil Eye was glaring; but even though he did not look, he knew that it was urging him to leap down into the black waters of the lake below. So he stared at the water hypnotised. The lake was almost circular in shape and its rocky sides, sloping outwards, were like the sides of a half-filled bowl in which some liquid is boiling; so was the surface of this black lake disturbed by the countless drops of falling rain. There was no other motion and no other sound above the droning of the raindrops falling; until presently, after a loud wailing cry, Hernon began to babble inarticulately.

Then he stripped off his clothes and going on his knees, he reached down with his right hand into the lake and made the sign of the Cross upon himself. He was about to plunge into it when he was hailed from the rising ground to the rear. He looked and saw his wife waving to him and shouting. Then his suicidal madness passed and he became ashamed. Picking up his clothes, he hid in the cave and dressed himself. He was dressed when she arrived, almost as distraught as himself.

"What's on you, fool?" she cried. "Is it out of your mind you are? Did you think you killed Mike Halloran, or why else did you run? I came after you, for fear you'd never turn your head before you got to Mayo and you that cowardly."

"Is he dead?" said Hernon.

"There's nothing on him," she said. "Come on home, you fool."

Then Hernon began to laugh and said in a strange tone: "The Evil Eye was wrong after all."

"What are you talking about, man?" she said in amazement.

He laughed again, hysterically, and said:

"I saw it, following me. It was everywhere. I'll get aunt Kate to put the charm on me against it. I'll get her to-night. Hurry. There is no time."

His wife, terrified, made the sign of the Cross on him and then they hurried homewards. They met the eldest of their children on the path and the boy, seeing his father, burst out crying. His father's eyes terrified him and he had to be soothed by his mother before he would leave the rock behind which he hid in his terror of those eyes. The people of the hamlet, those who had come out to look for the runaway, also saw Hernon's eyes and knew that he had seen the eye of the Evil One. For it was thus that they construed insanity.

"Send for the wise woman," they whispered to Kitty Hernon, as she brought her husband to the house.

As soon as she had lodged her husband by the hearth, attended by some neighbours, Kitty herself went to fetch Kate Hernon, the wise woman of the Valley. This Kate Hernon was Patch's aunt and she lived a short distance towards the south, alone in a small hut. Her kind was common enough in those days, a relic of old pagan times, when under Druidic law medicine had reached a high degree of perfection among us. Through centuries of degeneration, the ancient art had become a species of black magic among the people. And so this old woman cast spells, to lend importance to the herbal cures she concocted. Even so, she had talent and she was marvellously efficient as a midwife.

She came after nightfall, wearing a black shawl that covered her from head to foot. She was tall and thin, of a great age, with ragged white hair which streamed about her face. In her countenance there lurked the phantom of a ravaged beauty when it was in repose. But when she opened her lips to speak, her face became horrid like that of an evil witch; for the practise of her buffoonery had got her into the habit of speaking in an exaggerated manner, rolling her eyes and twisting her lips. There were only a few teeth left in her gums.

This old hag spat on to the floor when she entered the house and then she raised two claw-like hands to the roof and intoned:

"Peace to you, spirit of the mountains. Close your eye and let the sick have peace."

Hernon's dwelling was only half a cabin, as the Hallorans next door occupied the other half. Really only one room, it had been cut in two by a narrow wall that did not reach much above a man's height. Behind this partition was the family sleeping place. All the children had been put away there before the hag's arrival, lest they might get terrified by her raving. This was a useless procedure, as they could hear everything above the top of the partition. The living-room was in a very sordid state, which was only natural on account of all those children romping about in a chamber that was only ten feet by eight, with a great deal of that space occupied by the furniture, cooking utensils and farming tools. There was even some oat straw and a little heap of potatoes, all that was left of the year's crop. The floor was an amazing sight. The earth had nearly all been dug up by the children and made into mud pies. The naked rock was exposed and it was quite difficult to walk from the door to the hearth, in the gloom which the light from a tallow wick could not dispel. There was hardly any light from the fire, which smoked badly. Hernon, although he had his share of a turf bank in the common bog, had cut no turf that summer owing to a fight he had with the neighbour who cut with him. So he had now to rely on dried cow-dung for fuel. The dung had not dried properly and it smoked without giving light.

Hernon began to tremble violently when he saw his aunt. Sitting in the hearth corner, he was as motionless as a statue, except for the movement of his eyes and lips. He was deadly pale. His head was slightly lowered and thrust forward, like a man shrinking from a blow. The old woman took no notice of him, but seemed to address herself to the fire, or to some spirit which she affected to see in it. Her words were no longer intelligible to those who heard her, but they were all the more impressive. Indeed, three neighbour women, who had come in to watch the affair, threw themselves on their knees and began to pray. Kitty stood in the doorway of the sleeping apartment, to keep the children quiet.

Suddenly the hag got very excited and made deep, groaning sounds in her throat. Then she began to struggle with an invisible enemy, which must have risen to attack her from the smoking fire of cow-dung. Now she writhed backwards and forwards, gasped and made the gurgling sounds of a person being strangled. The children screamed and Kitty ran into their room to quieten them. Hernon, obviously hypnotised, mimed his aunt's movements and sounds. The three other women threw themselves prone on the floor.

Then the hag suddenly delivered a counter-attack against her invisible enemy, crying "Ha" in a ferocious whisper. She drew her great shawl forward before her face and then made an encircling movement with her arms, which she folded slowly on her bosom, with a great effort apparently, as if crushing something that struggled. At length she uttered another "Ha" of triumph and then she became limp and silent. She dropped her invisible burden to the floor and stamped on it.

"You are dead now," she cried, "and take care you stay dead."

Then she took a large sea-shell from the pocket of her skirt, scooped some ashes into it from the hearth and poured the ashes slowly, mumbling the while, over Patch Hernon's head. Then she put the sea-shell smartly back into her pocket and drifted from the house like a ghost, without saying a word. Hernon jumped to his feet and began to laugh.

"It's gone," he whispered excitedly. "I can't see it. The Eye is gone. I'm cured."

"Praised be God," the neighbour women said.

Kitty came from the room and embraced her husband, weeping loudly. There was joy in the house. In the morning, however, Patch had a fever, having caught a chill naked on the mountain. But the women said that it was the departing evil spirit that had tried to maim him. And Kate Hernon sent a potion made from purging herbs, which he drank, while hot stones were placed against the soles of his feet. And so the fever passed after a few days and he was able to be about once more.

However, even though he no longer saw the Evil Eye, his frenzy remained with him. The evil had now gone into his feet, making them itch, so that he could not keep still. And in his head, there was always a hammer beating. He thought this hammer was reminding him that in three months he would be evicted, unless he could pay his arrears. It also told him that all the people were in league against him for his destruction. Now, however, he was on his guard and cunning. He became silent, watching for an opportunity to take revenge.

His wife, his children and all the people thereabouts were now afraid of him and kept out of his way as much as possible. Halloran next door, being more afraid than any, offered him a rabbit which his dog had caught on the mountain; but Hernon hurled it back across the fence.

"I'll take no meat of yours," he shouted. "I have herrings in my barrel and sheep on the mountain. I have a heifer, too, and an ass to fill my belly. No bailiff will take my stock to the pound."

After that, people got out of his way when they saw him coming. And he himself was no more eager to meet them, until one morning, he said to his wife:

"I'm going to Crom to keep an eye on them."

"Who are they?" said Kitty.

"The driver and the Peelers," he said.

Then he took his ass and set off towards the village. When he was passing Kilmartin's house, Martin and Thomsy, who were working on the new garden, shouted a salutation. He did not answer. The Kilmartins were now allied with his enemies in his mind, since it was they, by giving Mr. Chadwick two pounds towards his rent, put him in the way of being called a beggar by the people. In the same way, when he was passing the weaver's cottage, he spat and vowed vengeance, remembering that Mary had said:

"Some people are high and mighty, but they are not ashamed to beg."

He was just entering the village on his ass, when the doctor was going in the gate of Crom House. The poor wretch at once became full of hope.

"Praised be God," he thought, "maybe Mr. Chadwick is dying. Then I might get relief from the new man that takes his place."

He spurred his donkey with his heels in order to enquire from the doctor, but when he drew level with the gate, the doctor had already disappeared around a corner of the drive. He was afraid to follow, so he went into the village and spoke to mountain people he met lounging there, asking them why the doctor had gone to Crom House with his little bag. But nobody could give him any information. Towards noon, he saw the doctor coming from Crom House to the hotel. He went up and smoke to him.

"God bless your honour," he said, "is there sickness at the Big House?"

The doctor halted and looked at him, swaying slightly. There was a strong smell of whisky from him. His eyes were bloodshot. He curled up his lip and then passed on without speaking. Hernon got terrified. He mounted his donkey and rode home from the village. That evening he went up on the mountain, caught one of his sheep and slit its throat. He brought home the carcass and when his wife asked him in terror why he had done this, he answered her wildly:

"Up at the Big House they are drinking the share of money I gave them on rent day. Mr. Chadwick has called in the gentry to help him drink it. I saw the doctor coming out of the House and he drunk with whisky. Oho! By the divine blood of the Saviour! When they send their bailiff and their Peelers, it's little they'll find that I won't have eaten."

That night and next day, they feasted on the carcass of the little mountain sheep. When it was eaten, Hernon again mounted his ass and went into the village. Made bold by this scheme for outwitting his enemies and also by the good meat he had in his belly, he no longer kept silent, but went about everywhere in an arrogant fashion, boasting of his cleverness and threatening his enemies.

Hegarty the driver soon heard that Hernon was slaughtering his sheep and why he was doing so. Indeed, it was impossible for him not to hear, for Hernon now shouted in the village street, like a prophet of evil, to the crowd of people that gathered to listen to his ravings.

"Good people," he said, "it is written in the book of Saint Columcille that the army of the tyrant will come out of the east and they'll strip the land. Whatever is on four feet will be taken and they'll put a curse on the ground, so that nothing will grow. And they'll leave a plague after them. So let ye be ready for them and eat everything ye have, so when they come there'll be nothing for them and they'll grow weak with hunger and then the honest poor can fall on them and put them to death. Then the land will be free. There is sin among us."

Hegarty went to Chadwick and told him what Hernon was saying.

"Your honour," he said, "unless you put a stop to his talk and show the people your power, they'll be all slaughtering their sheep and cattle. Then there'll be no rent paid in spring."

So Chadwick got a writ against Hernon and one morning, about a week before Christmas, Hegarty marched up the Valley with an escort of four armed policemen. They took Hernon's heifer and the four sheep that remained. They drove these animals away, to be sold in Clogher to make up for Hernon's arrears of rent.

Hernon hid on the mountain while the seizure was being effected. That evening, however, he ran naked all the way into the village, armed with a reaping hook, to hill Hegarty. He was captured by the police, certified as insane and lodged in the mad-house at Clogher.

In that way, Kitty Hernon and her seven children were left destitute and dependent on the Kilmartin family.

CHAPTER XIX

ON CHRISTMAS EVE, while the Kilmartins were having supper, Kitty Hernon entered the kitchen. After saluting the family, she sat down by the wall near the door. She sat on the floor like a beggar, her face almost hidden within her shawl. She rocked herself gently to and fro, as a token of grief and humility.

The Kilmartins were all very embarrassed, owing to the way Patch Hernon had been barging them during the past month. Kitty herself had also spoken ill of Mary, together with spreading scandal about Ellie's conduct at Crom House. And now she was sitting on the floor like a beggar.

On Christmas Eve, however, it is considered a mortal sin to bear enmity for past offences, on the anniversary of the night when the Blessed Virgin, big with the Saviour, was forced to take refuge in a stable. Every door is thrown open and everything in the house is shared willingly with whoever enters, to ask for shelter or refreshment. So Mary went to Kitty and took her by the hands and raised her from the floor.

"In God's name," she said, "come and sit down to the board with us. It's not much we are having, just a bit of dried ling and butter with our potatoes, but you are welcome to it."

Kitty burst into tears and threw her arms around Mary, who hugged her. The poor woman looked so ill and miserable that Mary felt pity and forgiveness. Yet, strangely enough, as soon as their bodies touched, each felt as spiteful as ever. As they embraced, Kitty felt that Mary was already with child and she became furious at the thought.

"Life is bitter," she said, "but my shame for what has been said is more bitter than the misfortune that has fallen on me."

"That's all forgotten, Kitty," said Martin. "Sit down with us."

"God bless ye," said Kitty, taking a seat at the form. "Blood is thicker than water, they say."

As she uttered this last sentence, she cast a quick, sidelong glance at Mary, as much as to say, "It's not your blood I'm talking about." Then she looked all round the house and said with a sigh:

"I hardly know my own father's house, it has changed so much. It's like the house of a rich person now, all polished and covered with ornaments, without a pig or a hen to dirty its glory."

"Musha! It's poverty keeps it without anything to dirty it," said Maggie. "We have no potatoes to feed any pigs and the hens are all killed for Michael. Sure, if you call a bit of holly an ornament, you are welcome."

"It's fine to be getting rich," said Kitty in a bitter tone.

It seemed that the devil had possessed her since she touched Mary in the embrace. She had come to the house genuinely humble and anxious for sympathy in her misery. Now, however, she was aflame with spite and with a desire to hurt these people to whom she had come for comfort.

"It's fine to be getting rich," she said again, "while other people are without bite or sup. There isn't even the workhouse for some of us. It's already full."

Her face was emaciated and over-wrought. She seemed to have contracted her husband's nervous twitching of the eyes and lips. The veins stood out clear under her skin. Furthermore, she spoke exactly as her husband used to speak, in a loud tone, arrogantly, without looking at those whom she addressed. Without a doubt, that was part of her scheme of spitefulness, to give them the idea that she was going mad like her husband.

She now fell on her food ravenously, although she was not at all hungry. Indeed, she had just had supper before leaving her house and she had eaten a far better meal than what the Kilmartins had, for there was still something left of the last sheep which had been slaughtered. It had been salted and put down in a tub. However, she had scarcely swallowed more than two mouthfuls, when she was struck with remorse for her unseemly conduct. She threw down her knife and burst once more into tears.

"I'm glad the end has come now," she said, "for me and my children. While there was hope there was misery, waiting for the messenger of salvation who never came, cocking an eye along the empty road and hearing the lies of the wind at night. Now there is only the peaceful coffin and a cold, silent hole in the earth's belly."

She suddenly jumped to her feet and hurried into the room where Michael lay. He was no longer able to sit by the fire. She threw herself on her knees by his bed, clutched the quilt and moaned:

"Ah! Brother, we're comrades, one of us eaten by worms and the other by the serpent of hunger."

The sick man was terrified by her words. He burst into a loud wail which ended in a fit of coughing. Maggie came and dragged Kitty back into the kitchen.

"Be easy now," she said. "There's no sense in giving way to your trouble. Have courage, daughter."

"To-morrow," wailed Kitty, "I can't go to Mass and I not having a shilling for the priest. Now when the children die of hunger, I can't expect the priest to come with the holy oils. I'll be treated like a pagan."

The whole family had now to gather round her in order to pacify her hysterical outburst. However, when Martin brought her a shilling from the purse, she immediately grew calm and grabbed the shilling without a word of thanks. Drawing her shawl far out over her forehead she said angrily:

"I'll go now. I only came because I didn't want to let Christmas pass with bitterness between us."

Martin followed her into the yard and asked her if her potatoes were all gone. She said they were. Then he took a

large basket of potatoes on his back up to her house. Although
Mary knew what he was doing, she said nothing until he had
gone. Then she said to the old man:

"There must be an end to this. You should speak to him.
What next? With the way the potatoes are rotting in the barn,
there won't be enough for the spring sowing, not to mind
giving them to people that won't stint themselves. It would
be easy for us, too, to eat our sheep and live like the gentry,
with meat for every meal."

"Sure, if they didn't eat their sheep," said Maggie, "they'd
be taken on them."

"While they were eating them," said Mary, "they might
ask us did we have a mouth."

"True for you," said the old man. "Let you speak to him,
though. He's your husband more than he is my son. Begob, I
think it's you has my blood in you. You have fine sense for a
woman."

Of late he always took sides with Mary in any discussion
that arose. He liked the way she managed things and he was
now as enthusiastically on her side as he had formerly been
hostile. He found her thrifty and hard like a true peasant. She
loved the earth.

So, when Martin came back, it was the old man who
attacked him for his extravagance.

"We have Sally O'Hanlon beside us," he said, "she and
her family of scavengers. We can't afford to feed the Valley."

"Is it comparing your own daughter to Sally O'Hanlon
you are?" said Martin. "Surely you wouldn't let your daughter
starve for want of a potato."

"You have to remember," said Mary, "that you'll soon be a
father. Are you going to let your child be born with nothing
to feed on?"

Martin looked at her sheepishly. There was wonder in his
eyes, as if she had become a stranger to him. She was, indeed,
altogether a different person from the girl he had courted and

who had won his love. And yet, somehow, she was nearer to him now, in this harsh character she had assumed of late, than she had been formerly. Formerly, when she smiled on him, or looked up into his face with a rapt expression when they were united in love, it seemed that she was in some way remote and unattainable; as if she were watching him and did not altogether trust him. Now, however, even though she had become cruel and intolerant, in the privacy of their bed she had become tender like a mother, ravishing him with her caresses.

Panting with the effort of thought, he cried out in an angry tone:

"I don't know what's come over you, Mary. You're harder than my father himself. Have you no charity in you? Devil take it! While there is a bite in this house I'll see nobody go hungry, relation or neighbour or stranger or whatever it may be. I trust in God. His help is nearer than the door."

He worked himself into a fury, and the old man, pleased with his son's ferocity, whispered:

"Silence. We have a tyrant in the house."

Later, when Martin and Mary had retired, as if to make amends for her harsh words, she almost smothered him with her embraces. And then, when they were about to fall asleep, both feeling pain through excess of tenderness, she whispered:

"Life is going to be hard, Martin. So we have to stint ourselves. The house terrifies me without a pig or a hen in it. And then, these hungry mouths all round us. And meal three shillings a stone now."

CHAPTER XX

NEXT MORNING MARY called at her father's house going to Mass. The weaver and his wife were having an argument, which ceased when Mary entered.

"What's the matter?" said Mary. "Are you having a fight on Christmas Day? Nice way to be going on."

Patrick scowled at her and said:

"I suppose we're not good enough for you now, since you became a landholder. You're ashamed of us, are you?"

Then he rushed out of the house, calling to his father.

"What ails him?" said Mary.

"He's worried about what should be worrying you, if you had any care for your own flesh and blood," said the weaver.

He took his stick from the back door, spat on it and marched out the door like a soldier.

"You see how it is with them," said Mrs. Gleeson, who was sobbing on a stool in the hearth corner.

"I see nothing at all only foolishness," said Mary. "Is it madness has come on them all of a sudden?"

"It's not, then," said her mother. "It's Ellie."

Mary sat down opposite her mother and said:

"What has she done now?"

"How can you ask?" said her mother. "Even the children are shouting it after us now."

"I don't hear them," said Mary. "I wish people would mind their own business."

"You've got hard," said her mother.

"I'm not hard," said Mary, "but I've got sense. If she's doing what's wrong, why doesn't her father take her to task?"

"He tried to, but she wouldn't listen to him, so he went to the priest and now, as likely as not, we'll be denounced from the altar."

"From the altar?" said Mary in horror. "Why should we be denounced from the altar?"

"Father Roche was inclined to put the blame on us for the way we brought her up. And sure it's a disgrace entirely, with the Big House no more than a bawdy place, since your sister went to live in it, as the woman for everybody's pleasure. Drinking and rowdy conduct going on there every evening. Card-playing and singing. Every rake from here to Clogher. And the doctor worse than any of them. It appears that Mr. Hynes went to the priest as well, asking him to put a stop to his son ruining himself. I went to her, but she turned on me. 'I'm finished with ye,' says she. 'Well, then,' says I to her, 'I wash my hands of you, now that you've turned your sinful eyes against the face of God Himself.'"

"Well, then, I'll not turn against her," said Mary. "Come on, mother. You should be ashamed of yourself, deserting your own daughter in her hour of need."

"I'll not stir an inch," said Mrs. Gleeson. "I couldn't face that altar to-day, with my daughter being denounced from it. I went to the curate's Mass in Glenaree."

"Stay, then," said Mary. "It's no wonder she's gone astray, like the lamb of a cowardly sheep."

She dashed out of the house and hurried towards the village. Now she had forgotten all her irritation with her sister. She only knew that the poor girl needed her help.

"I must get her away from here," she said to herself. "She can go to our cousin Julia in Liverpool. She can find something to do there and earn her passage to America. Shame on them for the way they are treating her."

She found Ellie waiting for her at the gate of Crom House. Ellie was in tears. Mary rushed to her, drew her within the gate where people passing could not see them and there they embraced. Now Ellie wept aloud, with her head on Mary's shoulder.

"There now," said Mary. "Hold your head up like a good

girl and don't let people see you haven't courage. Come on with me. Mass'll soon be starting."

"I haven't the courage to face it," said Ellie, "with Father Roche going to call my name from the altar. Only for it's Christmas Day I'd…"

"Come on," said Mary. "Don't be foolish. From now on, you'll do what I'll tell you. I wish you had listened to me long ago."

"Thank God for you, Mary," said Ellie.

They walked towards the chapel. There was still a large crowd of people outside in the yard and every eye was turned towards the two sisters. The crowd was whispering in a hostile manner. The two sisters, however, walked erect through the yard. They looked extremely beautiful in their scarlet cloaks and dark blue gowns. The chapel was already nearly full, so they knelt within the door by the Holy Water font and began their prayers. Presently, the bell rang, people crowded into the church and Father Roche, accompanied by his serving boys, came on to the altar to say Mass. Mary noticed that his face looked angry.

"My God," she thought, "he's going to denounce her."

At last the time came for the sermon. Coughing nervously, Father Roche read a passage from the Scriptures and then, hiding his hands under his vestment, he began his sermon. His voice was shrill with passion.

"There are outrages being committed in this district," he said. "Thank God that most of them are committed outside this parish. There were stones flung at a bailiff at Torlough the other day. A bullock was stolen off Colonel Bodkin's demesne and eaten while it was half alive. These are un-Christian acts, but there might be some excuse for them on account of the idleness of the government, not giving the people work and they starving. At the same time, the people who commit these outrages should be horse-whipped through the parish, for giving the government an excuse to bring in coercion acts. But there is conduct going on in this village that cries out to God for vengeance. Ye all know to whom I am referring. Have these people no shame in them, to be carrying on like that while poor creatures are dying of the hunger? It's got to stop. And let the scarlet woman that's the cause of it clear out of this parish before I have to lay hands on her."

Here he completely lost control of himself, raised his fist and cried out:

"I'll curse her by bell, book and candlelight, that whore of Babylon that's responsible for a debauch of fornication and drunkenness among us. I'll curse others, too, that should be an example to the poor, unless they give up their bad ways in time."

He continued in the same strain for some time, with such ferocity that certain fanatics among the congregation threw themselves on the ground and writhed with exalted rage. Ellie got to her feet and ran out the door. Mary followed her. She caught up with her at the chapel gate and took her by the arm. Ellie was again sobbing.

"This is no time for crying," said Mary angrily. She was not angry with her sister, but with the priest and all these people, who seemed to her unjust. "I'll settle everything for you. You go to the house now and pack your things and meet me at the gate with them as soon as you can. I'm going to the house for a minute."

Ellie agreed humbly. She was beside herself with fear of what the priest might do to her. They parted at the gate of Crom House and Mary ran all the way to the weaver's cottage. Her mother was surprised to see her.

"What happened, Mary, alannah?" said Mrs. Gleeson.

"Never you mind," said Mary. "Where is the purse?"

"What purse?" said the mother.

"Ye should be ashamed of yerselves," cried Mary, "for bringing children into the world and then not looking after them as ye should. What she has done is more yer fault than her own. She's going now. I'll get a cart and put her on it. Where is the purse? The least ye can do is pay her way to Liverpool."

Wailing aloud, the mother got the purse and Mary took three pounds from it.

Chapter XXI

IT WAS AFTER dark when Mary returned. The old couple and Patrick were alone in the house, sitting by the fire in silence. As a rule, on Sunday evenings, there was a crowd of visitors at the weaver's cottage. On account of the priest's sermon nobody came this evening.

"She's gone now," Mary said, as soon as she entered the house. "No thanks to ye, either. I got a cart and put her on it. I took her across the fields beyond the village and put her on the cart, so that the people wouldn't see her go. Tommy Cook's cart I got. The Dublin coach will leave in the morning. She's staying the night at Sheila Toner's house in Clogher. I'd stay with her only Martin might be anxious. God help her. It's little she has to thank you for, father, you with your rod and your shouting. You made the girl grow up into what she is, instead of being kind to her."

With that she left the house. Nobody tried to stop her going. Then there was silence. Gleeson felt that both his wife and his son agreed with what Mary had said. He got to his feet and went out into the yard. There he leaned against the fence and meditated.

"Never again will I be able to hold up my head," he thought. "No man'll listen to me with respect."

His thick lower lip caressed his upper lip and the back of his neck hardened. A wild desire for vengeance entered his mind. A sound like the ticking of a clock began in his head. This exalted him and he felt a melancholy happiness, as if he were going to give his life for a cause. He went back into the house and they said the rosary. He led the recitation in an arrogant fashion and while he prayed he felt conscious of the glorious vengeance he was about to take. And then, when his wife and son had retired, he went once more into the yard and stood for a long time, with his arms folded, leaning against the gable of the house.

"He ruined her," he thought. "Let the tyrant pay for it now."

Without thinking, he moved over to the pigsty behind the weaving-room. He groped about among the thatch of the sty and touched an old pike that was hidden there. He had found it a long time ago in the bog, where it had been dropped by some revolutionary fugitive during the rebellion of 1798. On touching the pike handle a tremor passed through his body. He hurriedly rearranged the thatch, entered the house, and went to bed.

He did not sleep. The ticking of the clock continued. His wife wept quietly for a long time in the bed beside him. Then she spoke to him gently and suggested that they should bear this new cross that God had asked them to carry in a Christian spirit. He did not reply. However, the clock stopped ticking while she spoke and he felt a maudlin love for his daughter who was now gone from him. But when his wife, despairing of establishing contact with him, turned towards the wall, crossed herself, and went to sleep, the weaver hardened. The clock started ticking once more.

Now and again his wife started in her sleep and began to mumble. At these moments the ticking of the clock became articulate. It said:

"Kill the tyrant. Kill the tyrant."

At length, the weaver drew in a deep breath, nodded his head several times, and said, half-aloud:

"It will be done."

CHAPTER XXII

FROM THE MOMENT that he had made the sign of the cross of his forehead, entering Crom House on the morning after Chadwick had tried to cut his throat, the doctor had felt that he was a damned soul. Yet, if he were asked what he had done that was damnable, he could not answer. The rumours that had got abroad about Ellie's whorish conduct were quite untrue. Mr. Chadwick himself may have plucked the ripe apple from the bough, but he was careful not to allow his guests to share the fruit with him. And there was nothing very damnable, after all, in drinking and card-playing. It was only what every young man of his position was doing in the district. There was no other form of amusement.

It was not what he did that persuaded the doctor he was damned, but the company in which he did it. Conceptions of sin are all, more or less, determined by the society in which one lives, or the class to which one belongs. To drink and play cards with people of his own class and religion would not have made the doctor feel damned. To drink with Mr. Chadwick and his friends did make him feel damned. Of course there was Ellie, whom the cunning Chadwick held out as a bait; and the doctor sinned in thought whenever he looked at her. But it was Chadwick that kept him awake at night, tossing on his bed and accusing himself of being a damned soul. It was Chadwick that had cut him off from the people. And it was that which damned him. He had allowed himself to become an outcast from his people.

Chadwick had disappeared at the same time as Ellie, and the doctor's visits to Crom House came to an end for that reason. A fortnight after her disappearance, he was attending patients at his dispensary, when Captain Mordaunt, the district inspector of police, stopped on his way to the police barracks and began a friendly conversation. This fellow Mordaunt had been one of those who frequented Chadwick's house, and the doctor had become rather intimate with him. Now, however, as he stood outside the dispensary, chatting with the inspector, the doctor felt ashamed of this intimacy. He was conscious of the hostile looks cast in his direction by the crowd of poor people who waited there. Their eyes said: "There's John Hynes's son hobnobbing with one of the tyrants. He's sold to the enemy." The inspector told a funny story, and while the doctor was laughing at it politely a young man in the crowd fell down in an epileptic fit. The inspector finished his story and then, without a glance at the stricken creature, he went on his way to the barracks. As the doctor bent down to help the sick man, he heard the growls and curses of the people all round him.

"And why shouldn't he be on the side of the tyrants?" said a woman at the back of the crowd. "Hasn't he got informer's blood in him?"

The doctor blushed and trembled, but he kept silent. That evening he could not eat his supper, but sat over the fire burning with hatred of everybody. He hated himself most of all for having been fooled by Chadwick.

"He only pretended to be friends with me and to treat me as an equal because he owed money to my father and wanted more credit. Also to have me around to look after him when he was bad from drink."

So he thought. And the others? Now he realised that they also had despised him as "a native." He recalled all their contemptuous references to "the natives." Then, of course, he had thought that he himself was not included by them among "the natives." Now he realised that he had been. In particular, he remembered an incident which occurred while he was playing cards with Chadwick and a young man called Burke. The doctor had been winning. In his excitement, he had pushed his chair back from the table and sat on the very edge of it, concentrating on the choice of his next card. Annoyed by his losses, Chadwick suddenly remarked to Burke in a very insolent tone:

"He sits like a native. Curious thing that, Burke. I've always noticed that natives sit like that in one's presence. As if they were apologising for taking a liberty. Have you noticed it, Burke?"

"Rather," Burke said. "Come along, Hynes. Get going."

"Have you noticed, too," continued Chadwick, who was very drunk, "how deliberate they are? I mean, they take such a long time to make up their minds, when it's a question of money, no matter how small the amount. It's the wretched poverty to which they are accustomed, you know. What?"

"I should imagine so, Jocelyn," Burke said. "For God's sake, Hynes, are you ever going to play?"

The doctor had sat there, unable to move through humiliation. And now, as he thought about it, the humiliation was even greater. He put his head in his hands, groaned, and gnashed his teeth. And then, suddenly there was a knock at the door. Startled, he jumped to his feet and cried out:

"Who is that?"

The door opened and the curate came into the room. He closed the door and then stood looking at the doctor in silence. The doctor did not speak, either. He flushed and began to tremble slightly through embarrassment. He had avoided the curate ever since that night when they had walked together from the parish priest's house. The curate's face was indistinct in the lamplight. The grey ring around his black skull, and his dark face, made him look menacing in the gloom. The doctor felt afraid of him. But when the man approached finally and his expression became discernible, the doctor no longer felt afraid. The priest's eyes, deep and far-seeing, were soft with pity. The wheezing of the priest's lungs and the faint, acrid smell of peat smoke from his shabby clothes, which had got wet from rain on the way to the hotel, also comforted the doctor, as he held out his hand to greet his visitor. The curate sat down to the fire and held his hands out to the blaze.

"What weather!" he said. "Dirty, dreary, and unreliable. But should we complain in times like these? God help the poor people that have to sleep out in it, on empty stomachs."

He looked at the doctor, who had sat down opposite him.

"To struggle towards perfection," said the curate dreamily, "is the purpose of civilised man. To struggle towards perfection. God help us, it's a long way from perfection we are."

He smiled sadly and then groped about in the back pocket of his coat. He pulled out a large red handkerchief with white spots. A number of things came out with the handkerchief, including three buttons and a tiny book, which fell to the floor. The doctor picked it up and handed it back. The curate took it, opened it and flicked over the pages of manuscript, of which it was composed.

"I have a poor memory," he said, "so I write down all the most beautiful things I read, the gems, to carry around with me like this in my pocket. Then, when I am rambling along on the mountains, I can read. The poets and the saints are the only people that reach perfection. Trying to reach Heaven. That's it. They forget everything in the struggle to reach that loveliness. The ecstasy. They suffer for it, but that kind of suffering can be the greatest happiness. People are too much afraid of suffering. Look at the country and the way it is now. There is nothing holier than to fight in defence of liberty, to die for it, for the freedom of the earth that bore you and the happiness and prosperity of those you love. But that brings suffering; and the cowardly are afraid of suffering. And yet the cowardly can't escape suffering by shirking the fight. Famine. That's what's coming. Famine and death, because the people shirked the fight. Ah! Yes. Everything that is noble and beautiful comes out of the pursuit of holiness; freedom and the joy of living a pure life."

He caressed the book with his fingers, as he went on talking in this irrelevant and confused way. Then he put the book back in his pocket and blew his nose violently. A sound of laughter came from the kitchen. The curate also laughed and held out his hands to the blaze.

"The tear and the smile," he said. "Some day mankind in general will reach perfection. They will love their neighbours as themselves. But before that time comes there is a great deal of weeding to be done. Pulling weeds. That's beautiful work, too. Not as beautiful as the work of the poets and the saints. They show the way. But you and I, who are neither poets nor saints, but humble workmen in the garden, we have to do the weeding."

Suddenly he frowned and looked at the doctor.

"No chain is stronger than its weakest link," he said in a menacing tone. "The poorest tenant, the squatter, the day labourer, the beggar, they and only they are the chosen of the poets and the saints. And it's not by turning our backs on the chosen of the poets and the saints that the rest of us can reach the heavenly heights of perfection, the shining glory of eternal beauty and the joy of a clean conscience. Take care, son. We are a house divided against itself. We are a house on a hill, threatened with a hurricane. A brigand had taken up his abode in our house. He has enslaved us with the help of his marauders. We have read the signs in the heavens, but we are unable to make our dwelling place secure. The tyrant has stripped us of all power and devoured our substance. He has set us one against the other and made us helpless. So the weak among us try to escape by fawning on the tyrant, by clothing themselves in his raiment and imitating his speech. But they cannot change the blood in their veins."

He leaned over close to the doctor and whispered fiercely:

"You can't change the blood in your veins. It will cry out in the darkness of night against your foolishness. I told you before to love this Irish earth as your mother. How? Ask the people. They know. It's in their veins. Listen to them. Feel with them. Bow down before them. It's only when we deny our instincts, through greed or cowardice, that we sin. So humble yourself. Not in words, with the tongue, but down in your soul. The future is still pure and holy. Let people cast stones if they wish. The people are always right in the mass. For a moment they may be wrong or for a generation. A generation is only a moment in history. In the long run they are right. Turn your back on the marauders and your face to the people. They'll accept you with open arms. You've been chosen from many and trained at the people's expense to gain proficiency in the art of healing. At the people's expense. The pennies your father collected from the poor. The spades of poor land slaves dug those pennies out of the earth. The people's pence. We are all one family and each person in the family has his duties towards the rest. This house that shelters you and the chair you sit on are gifts to you from the people. The clothes on your back. Give them what you can in return."

He went on talking and the doctor listened to him, exalted. And suddenly, all that had been mysterious in life became manifest to him. He felt happy and wise and courageous.

Chapter XXIII

NEXT MORNING, WHLE the doctor was having breakfast, Reilly came into the parlour and said that Chadwick was back and wished to see him urgently. The doctor started.

"Is he sick?" he muttered.

"He's a bit queer, sir," Reilly said, "but he's not what you'd call sick. It's loneliness, I think, more than anything else. There's only two of us in the house now. The others is gone."

"How do you mean?" said the doctor.

Reilly looked around him furtively, although they were alone in the room and there was no possibility of their being overheard. Then he leaned forward, cocked his head to one side and whispered:

"They were warned. I was warned as well, but I'm standing by him. Mary Halloran stayed with me. The others is gone."

As he spoke, his lips curled sideways, like a man imparting secret information. The doctor felt angry that he should be addressed in this way, as if he were expected "to stand by" Chadwick.

"I'm too busy this morning," he said.

"He said to bring you back with me," said Reilly in a crestfallen tone.

"I told you I'm busy," shouted the doctor.

"Alright, sir," said Reilly, touching his hat.

The doctor went out on a sick call and returned home about noon. He found a note from Chadwick awaiting him. It ran as follows:

"DEAR HYNES,

"No doubt you realise that you are implicated in

the recent, shall we say unfortunate, events, that have made Crom House the centre of a somewhat lurid fame, to the same extent as myself. In the circumstances, apart from all considerations of good fellowship, I think some mutual collaboration is to the point, to put it mildly. Damn it! Let us face the facts like men, Hynes. This is no time to behave in a childish way. I am referring to rumours. Although I am practically invested and to some extent cut off, if I may say so, damn fools, they have all left except Reilly and an old woman, still, I keep well informed. God's blood! Trot along, Hynes. You can depend on me to behave like a gentleman. I can assure you there are going to be no recriminations as far as I am concerned.

"Trusting that you will receive this communication in the same spirit as that in which it was written, I have the honour to sign myself,

"Yours faithfully,
"JOCELYN CHADWICK (Capt. – Hussars)."

The doctor burst out laughing when he had finished reading this extraordinary document. Then he threw it in the fire and set out for Crom House, determined, as he told himself "to get done with the monster once and for all." Not wishing to be seen by the people entering Crom demesne, he went around a back way, through the bailiff's yard and then through a wicket gate that led into the stables. He found Chadwick waiting for him in the big reception room, which opened off the hall.

This was the only room downstairs that was even partially furnished, so that it served as a sort of general living-room. In the old days it had been a pretentious apartment, abundantly furnished in the atrocious taste of the late eighteenth century.

The process of decay, which had reached a climax during Chadwick's residence, made it look like an abandoned museum. A saddle and a pair of riding-boots lay on a very ornate French chair. A mass of fishing tackle lay on a writing-table. Paintings of the Thompsons and primitive weapons from Africa decorated the walls. The floor was partly in mosaic and in the centre of it was a large table, on which there was a cloth. Some dishes, fragments of bread, a bowl of butter and a plate, on which there was a fork stuck in a piece of sausage, still remained on the cloth. There was a dank smell in the room.

Chadwick was marching up and down when the doctor entered, one hand clenched behind his back, the other in the bosom of his greatcoat. He also wore his hat and he had a large muffler wound several times round his throat. The muffler, by the way, was to hide the scar caused by his attempted suicide. He had worn it ever since, giving a cold as an excuse. This was ridiculous, as all his friends knew about the affair of the razor. Even he himself delighted to enlarge on it when he was drunk.

"I didn't notice you coming up the drive," he said as he shook hands eagerly with the doctor. "I've been watching through the window. What? Nerves, you know. How did you get here?"

"I came around by the wicket gate," said the doctor.

"Ha!" said Chadwick. "It's come to that. What?"

Chadwick scratched his back violently between the shoulder blades. It was now over two weeks since he had put on clean linen. Ever since Ellie's departure he had been wandering around the county on a debauch and he had hardly slept in a bed. On his return, old Mary Halloran had tried to make him change, but he wouldn't even take off his greatcoat. He was really in a wretched state.

"So they've intimidated you?" he continued in a very insolent tone. "I thought you had more spunk in you than that, Hynes. Or was I mistaken? What? Damn it, do you want to cut and run like the rest?"

"I don't know what you're talking about," said the doctor.

In Chadwick's presence, the doctor found it difficult to conquer the feeling of being an inferior. Nor could Chadwick overcome the urge to be insolent and to show his real attitude towards the doctor. Before the arrival of the latter, the former captain of hussars had been very humble indeed, owing to his need for medical attendance. He was on the verge of delirium tremens. But the doctor's attitude had infuriated him. He no longer felt any need for help. He was at least four inches taller than stumpy little Hynes. With his chest and his heavy jaw thrust forward and his powerful rump sticking out a little to the rear, he stood over the doctor in a threatening fashion.

"Never mind," he said. "We'll go into that later. The important thing is that you are here. We may as well start at once. This affair must be threshed out to the full."

He went to the fireplace and kicked the peat sods into a blaze.

"What is there to discuss?" said the doctor.

"God's blood!" cried Chadwick furiously as he whirled around. He took two smart, short-legged paces towards the doctor and then halted with his heels together. "Nothing to discuss? Do you call this nothing?"

The doctor shrugged his shoulder and went to the mantelpiece against which he leaned his shoulder.

"Nothing that I know anything about," he said in a quiet tone.

"What the devil do you mean?" said Chadwick, following him aggressively. "I've made you welcome to my house. You've had your fling here."

"I've paid for whatever I've had here," snapped the doctor.

"I see," said Chadwick in a low tone, full of menace. "You adopt that attitude, do you?"

"I'll adopt whatever attitude I like," cried the doctor pettishly.

His voice was almost a scream, like that of an angry child.

He felt ashamed of himself for being over-awed, but he could do nothing to control his voice, or his features, which quivered. Chadwick laughed. Clapping his hands together and giving his shoulder the nervous twitch of the drunkard, he went towards the door.

"All this is buffoonery," he said jovially. "Let's have a drink, Reilly. Where the hell is that fellow? Halloran. Where are you, foolish woman?"

He pounded out of the room. The doctor, leaning against the mantelpiece, strove to regain control of himself.

"Speak out," he kept saying to himself, "and don't be afraid. Why should you be afraid of that drunken swine?"

Yet when he heard Chadwick yell out in the hall he trembled once more. Chadwick returned with a decanter and two glasses. He poured two drinks on the mantelpiece. He handed one to the doctor, who refused it with a shake of his head.

"What?" said Chadwick. "Won't drink, eh?"

"Thanks," said the doctor. "I've given that up."

Chadwick looked at him with hatred and then tossed off his own drink.

"Sit down," he said.

They both sat down facing one another. Chadwick's face became a bright red colour after drinking the whisky. He also seemed to have gone faint, as if his heart were giving him trouble. He drew in a sudden breath and covered his face with his hands. The backs of his hands were freckled like his cheeks. They had a reddish growth of hair on them. When he took away his hands his mood had changed. He looked pathetic.

"What's that proverb they have in the local lingo?" he said. "Reilly keeps coming out with bits of the gibberish. Drink with success and kick failure. Something like that. You must know it, Hynes. You've got the bog in your blood. What? Won't admit it. Gentleman, new style. Well! Here's to the end of a gentleman, old style. Here goes."

He took the other glass and drained it. Then he belched

violently and spread himself out on his chair. With his hands on his rather corpulent stomach, he continued in a pathetic tone, which was, however, insolent at the same time.

"She was my sheet anchor," he said. "I don't mind telling you. I was attached to the wench. Sounds maudlin, but it's true. Why should I tell you this? Damned if I know why I sent for you. Well! Roast me, if I don't believe that the feeling was mutual. Gad! I feel certain of it. The swine made her leave. Roche denounced her from his silly altar and then her sister whisked her away. If I had been here I'd have horse-whipped the bitch. I mean the sister, what's her name, Mary something. Mumbo jumbo. They persuaded her that horns were going to grow on her. What do they want? Eh? You knew her, Hynes. You came here with the rest of them, smelling around. Deny it? Ha! At the first sign of trouble you took to your heels."

Hynes jumped to his feet and cried in a loud voice:

"Look here, Chadwick…"

"Captain Chadwick to you, my good fellow," said Chadwick, leaning forward arrogantly.

The doctor stared at him for several moments, trembling violently. Then he sat down without saying anything further. Chadwick leaned back and cleared his throat arrogantly. He stretched out his glass towards Hynes and said insolently:

"Fill my glass, will you, Hynes."

The doctor rose and filled the glass obediently. Chadwick never even thanked him, but sipped, ruminating. Presently he said, as if waking from a brown study:

"It was idyllic in a way. Time and again I said to myself: 'Here you are, Jocelyn, old boy, cut off in this hole. Make the best of a bad job, old boy. Here is this little peasant girl. Darned lucky to have her, in a way.' And she helped me make the best of it. And yet she cleared out. Wouldn't hear of coming back. I followed her to Clogher, you know. I almost went on my knees to her in Athenry. Galloped after the Dublin coach. Tried to persuade her to leave it. Still, I feel certain she had a soft spot in her heart for me. Only for you fellows spoiling everything. A lot of howling savages. Sot that I am, I once carried Her Majesty's commission. Chew that, sir."

He had now worked himself into an alcoholic rage. He snuffled slightly and his speckled eyes had become very bloodshot. His lower lip was protruding. Now he sprawled in the chair, sagging in the middle, as if he were dissolving into some slippery substance. The doctor now looked him fiercely in the eyes. Hynes kept drawing in his breath and he was obviously getting ready to say something very important. His lips moved, as if he were rehearsing his speech. Chadwick continued.

"There is one person I shan't forgive in a hurry," he said through his teeth. "I may forgive you, Burke and the rest of them, but not the sister. I'll cure her insolence. She made some remarks to the servants. By God! I'll make them all rue it. Tyrant, am I?" I'll show them what tyranny really means. I've been too kind to the dogs. Now I'm going to show my hand."

He staggered to his feet, smoothed down his greatcoat and glared all round him. Then he reached for the bottle, poured out another drink, raised his glass and said in a quite different tone:

"Well! Here's good luck to her in any case. She had a barrel full of courage."

He swallowed the drink, belched, sat down again and continued:

"I offered her money when she wouldn't leave the coach. Wouldn't have it. Damn lot of peasants there, and a sailor who wanted to fight me. She had chummed up with him, I suppose. Damn these women. One man out of sight, another in bed. Hell take it. In the lodging-house, at Clogher I mean, where Reilly told me she was, I mean before I galloped after her, gloomy place, talking gibberish, they are all murderers. Nothing else to be done. A worthy soul. She can have her sailor. But as for the rest…They've asked for it and they're going to get it. There's still law in the land. Famine! I'm going to root them out like a nest of rats. You wait, Hynes. You're going to see some good hunting around these bogs of yours, old boy."

He leaned back and chuckled drunkenly. Then Hynes suddenly found voice.

"You call it fun?" he cried. "People dying of hunger? Is that your idea of fun?"

"What people?" said Chadwick in a surprised tone. "What are you…eh?"

"You are responsible," cried the doctor, shaking from head to foot. "You and your kind have ruined and degraded this country. Now the people are beginning to die of hunger. You have tried to ruin me. Because you owe money to my father and wanted to get more credit you had me around here. I know all about your friendship. I don't want it."

He had got to his feet while he was speaking. Now Chadwick also rose and faced him.

"I have horse-whipped men for this," growled Chadwick.

"That was before you became a sot," snapped Hynes viciously.

There was a note of exaltation in his voice. It was the first time in his life that he had felt a free man.

"You common, low…" began Chadwick, in a voice that was scarcely audible. He took a pace forward and raised his fist. "You dog!"

The doctor laughed in his face. It was a womanish and slightly hysterical laugh, but it astonished Chadwick, who drew back slightly. Then the doctor, with a curious smile on his face, walked towards the door, almost sideways, as if to guard himself against a surprise attack. As he was leaving the room he paused for a moment.

"You can drink yourself to death now," he cried. "Don't expect any help from me the next time you get the horrors. Don't be so cowardly either. Use a gun next time. It's surer than a razor."

He closed the door gently after him and then ran down the hallway on tiptoe for some reason. Chadwick made no move to follow him.

"Good Lord!" he said aloud. "What next?"

He stood still for a long time, his face black with anger. Then he nodded several times and sat down. He covered his face with his hands. He remained perfectly still for several moments with his face hidden. Then he rose abruptly and reached for the whisky bottle. He withdrew his hand without touching it and stared at the ceiling, with his mouth open. Then he closed his mouth smartly, thrust out his jaw, stiffened, reached for the bottle, held it out in front of him and then smashed it against the mantelpiece. He threw the neck into the fire. After a moment's pause, he seized the glasses also and smashed them against the fire-place. Then he rubbed his palms together.

An extraordinary smile slowly spread over his speckled face. He began to chuckle. Then he strode towards the door with long, rigid strides and cried out:

"Reilly? You clown, where are you? Get my horse."

CHAPTER XXIV

AFTER HIS ENCOUNTER with Chadwick, Dr. Hynes returned to the active pursuit of his profession with fanatical fervour. He and the curate became almost inseparable. Old Hynes was delighted. He had suffered terribly during the period that his son was "debauching" at Crom House, afraid that his whole scheme of life was going to fail through the doctor's misdemeanours and that he would never reach the final manifestation of his power; that obscure and undefined goal towards which he had been struggling all his life. The following incident will show how deeply he had felt.

Shortly before Christmas, on the day that Patch Hernon was taken to the lunatic asylum, old Hynes went to Clogher to lodge money in the bank and replenish his supply of goods, as he was in the habit of doing once a month. On this occasion, having completed his business, he drove in his jaunting car to the residence of Canon Herlihy, to whom he offered ten sovereigns for a Mass.

"One Mass, your reverence," he said, "but a very special one it must be. I could get ten Masses from Father Roche back home for a tenth of the money, but I want the best there's to be had and I'm willing to pay. It must be said by yourself, and sure you're nearly as powerful as the bishop himself. It's a special intention I have. Here's the money. Ten gold sovereigns."

Knowing the man's character, Canon Herlihy was more astonished than he was scandalised by the grossness of the request and the way Hynes stood, sucking in his lips, while he clutched the sovereigns in a little bag like the covering of a scapular. However, the canon took the money and promised to say a special Mass. Hynes went home happily, certain that he had bought Heaven by his extravagance. But he soon began to regret his money, as the doctor continued to frequent Crom House. He even suspected that Herlihy had pocketed the money and had not said the Mass. Then came Father Roche's sermon and the doctor, even though he went no more to Crom House, became a greater problem than ever, owing to his gloom and his savage attitude towards the family. The old man went to the curate.

"Father Tom," he said, "for the love of God, go to him. His mother and myself are only poor ignorant people. We don't know how to talk to him and he that full of learning. As it is, he's sitting there, all by himself, with a scowl on his face."

So the curate came, as we have seen already and everything suddenly changed for the better. The old man was so pleased that he gave the curate five pounds "for a new suit, and it's yourself that has earned it." The curate gave the five pounds to the relief committee that had just been started.

Deeply superstitious, Hynes was now convinced that God had finally approved of him. Even though he had always been scrupulous in the fulfilment of his religious duties, he had been haunted since childhood by a suspicion that God disapproved of him as a usurer. He had the peasant's conception of God, as the defender of the poor and the down-trodden. Now that God had been brought over to his side by a bribe of fifteen sovereigns, a wonderful change was noticed in the old man's appearance. All the people of the village remarked on it. He seemed to regain his youth. He walked almost straight and he was not afraid to look people boldly in the eyes. He assumed an arrogance of manner that was astonishing to those who had known him as a furtive, prowling sort of fellow.

However, it would not be quite true to say that his son's conversion was solely responsible for this change. The starting of the relief works had a great deal to do with it; for it was about this time that the government finally decided to take action about the threatened famine. The old man realised that these works might mean a fortune for him, if he could handle the affair properly. As we shall see, his cunning was equal to the opportunity presented. First of all, we must explain the nature of the opportunity.

The Mansion House Committee, whose visit to the Lord Lieutenant we have already mentioned, met on November 19th and sent an address to the Queen. The address was never presented, as the Peel cabinet resigned on December 5th. On the tenth, the Corporation of Dublin sent a further address, begging for relief works. After the failure of Lord John Russell to form a government, Peel returned to power on the twentieth. In her reply to the Dublin request, the Queen said the welfare of her Irish subjects was the object of her constant care. And yet, when Peel's cabinet met parliament on January 22nd, 1846, the only reference to Ireland in Her Majesty's address was regret for the frequent assassinations that occurred there. This regret occasioned the introduction of a Coercion Bill on February 22nd. In the meantime, in order to deal with the threatened famine, Peel brought in the Labour Rate Act.

Under this Act public works were to be started in Ireland, on money lent to the Irish by the Treasury at five per cent interest. The government expressly stipulated that no useful work was to be performed for this borrowed money (at five per cent). There was to be no reclamation. No industries could be established, lest they might interfere with the young English industries. Government inspectors were to keep a sharp eye on every activity, lest any of it might be useful or productive. But these useless works, executed on borrowed money (at five per cent) were hailed with delight by the starving people, but especially by Hynes. Like a vulture, that soars in ecstasy over a battlefield, he took delight in the people's misery, since that misery was going to put money into his pocket. All the money the people got from the relief works would cross the counters of his shop. His hotel would be crowded with officials.

"God bless this famine!" thought Hynes.

At first he was worried by rumours that were afoot. For instance, an article in the *Clogher Vindicator* suggested that the government was going to establish depots, from which food was to be distributed at cost price, that the workers were going to be paid in kind, including clothing, "in order to save the populace from the usury of gombeen men." The government, however, hastened to dispel this idea, asserting that it had no intention of interfering with "legitimate trade". The depots for sale of food were not to operate, where there was a tradesman capable of supplying the needs of the community. The workmen were to be paid in coin of the realm, at the rate of eightpence farthing a day. Finally, Indian corn was being imported from the United States, to be sold to the people as cheap food.

"God bless the government!" thought Hynes.

He became as active as a ferret in a warren on receipt of this cheerful news. At this time of year, as a rule, he received no great demand for meal. He had only two or three sacks of it in his shop. He must get a plentiful supply, or else the government might open a depot in the village. He thought of a wonderful plan, a daring plan, but at the same time one with magnificent possibilities. The idea came to him one morning when people rushed into his shop with money in their hands, crying for meal, biscuits and salt fish. They were all people who had been hanging around the streets, begging, for weeks.

"What's this?" said Hynes.

"It's Mr. Coburn, God bless him," they said. "He threw it to us in handfuls."

"Yes, be Jabers," they said. "He has loads of it. Long life to him."

The parson had received by the mail car that morning a packet of silver from a group of charitable ladies in England. They had adopted Mr. Coburn's parish and in his own words "had denied themselves sweetmeats and perfumes, in order to help the starving peasantry." On receiving this packet – it was the first of many – Mr. Coburn, as a protest against the lassitude and bureaucracy of the government and in order to show how an individual "Christian gentleman," acting on his own account, could hasten the work of relief, ran into the street and scattered the silver like manna among the crowd of beggars. "Ask and you shall receive," he shouted exultantly. They picked up the coins and rushed with them into Hynes's shop.

• "Could you believe that now if you saw it written?" said Hynes as he served them. "Wonderful are the ways of God."

The parson's windfall nearly exhausted his stock of biscuits and meal. So he brooded all day over a plan for getting a huge supply of food, ready for any eventuality. Then he broached the plan that night to his wife in bed. He attached no importance to her opinion, but he wanted to hear himself speak aloud about it. A thing sounded one way, very often, in one's mind and quite another way when it was spoken aloud.

"Do you think it's time for Tony to get married?" he said. "Have you anyone in mind for him? Do you know anyone in Clogher? Is this a time to take a chance with new business? Would a man be wise or foolish to take money out of the bank at times like these and lay in a big stock for the works? Will the people eat this yellow meal that's going to come from America? Will the Government fix a retail price for it?"

His wife knew that he expected no answer to these apparently irrelevant questions, but the matter of her son's marriage interested her. He was now over twenty-eight and it was time for him to settle down.

"He'll have to be driven to the altar," she said. "He'd no more think of courting a girl than turning Protestant. And sure I know you have Rabbit's daughter in mind for him."

"Who said so?" cried her husband angrily. "Why should I? Aren't there a score of women with fortunes he could marry, him with a brother a doctor and a sister a nun? Sure the highest in the land isn't good enough for him."

"But I was only saying…" began his wife.

"Silence," said the old man.

He had made up his mind. His sleep, however, was uneasy. Several times during the night he muttered, "Fifteen hundred dry. Fifteen hundred dry." He was in the habit of sleeping with his healthy hand hanging down by the bed. When he muttered, the fingers of this hand bent over the palm, like the tentacles of an upturned crab. He was awake earlier than usual, long before dawn. Contrary to custom, he did not rouse his wife, by hitting her in the ribs with his elbow. He sneaked out of the room on tiptoe, carrying his boots in his hand. He roused his son Tony in the room next door. Telling his son to make no noise and to put on his Sunday clothes, the father crept down to the kitchen, where he lit a candle and put it on the table. Then he took half an oaten loaf from the cupboard, together with a jug of milk. He sat down, broke the bread in two and poured milk into a mug. He soaked his piece of bread in the milk and began to chew. Even so, he found it difficult to chew, as the bread was as hard as metal and the old man's teeth were loose. His son arrived, yawning and grumbling.

"Not a cock has crowed yet," said Tony. "It's pitch dark. What ails you this morning?"

"Be quiet," said the father. "Eat. You'll soon know. Hurry."

He threw the other piece of bread across the table. It made a metallic sound on the board.

"I don't want us to be seen leaving the village," he said. "We have business."

The son looked across at his father's face, which he could see only dimly in the candlelight. Tony was not intelligent, but he was cunning. He knew at once that the old man was after big prey. He chuckled. Unlike his father and the doctor, Tony was a great hulk of a man, tall, loose, heavy, with large feet and hands and a bony head, whose ugliness was completely exposed by his habit of keeping his hair clipped to the bone. His ears stood out nearly at right angles to his skull. His nose did not curve inwards like his father's nose. The tip was bulbous, with widespread nostrils. His jaws were heavy. His mouth was wide and thin-lipped. His mouth and eyes were like his father's. His lips had already begun to suck inwards and his eyes were grey and furtive. His size, however, and his great strength prevented him from having that feeling of inferiority and the feeling of being alien from the herd, which persecuted both his father and the other children. Tony felt at one with the people. In fact, he copied the characteristics of the country people, even to the extent of pretending to be a clown and an illiterate fellow. Yet, when he had to give evidence some time previously in a lawsuit which his father had brought against a debtor, a dispute about land, the fellow showed a remarkable grasp of the law, completely outwitting the barrister who cross-examined him.

"Huh, huh," he said, as he rapidly crunched the hard bread with his strong young teeth, "you have something in mind? Huh?"

The father swept up the crumbs from the table on to his palm and swallowed them. He got to his feet.

"I'll warn Julia," he said.

His sister slept in a tiny room off the kitchen. She was the same Julia who had tramped the lanes with him in childhood with a donkey. He had still more confidence in her than in his wife, whom he considered a frivolous person, owing to the way she laughed merrily at times. Julia was a real slave to the vice of avarice, though of a peculiar type. She never received a penny reward for her services. Yet, in her old age, she still worked, cooking for the household and the boarders, lest there might be any waste. There she lay, in the miserable, damp room, on a pallet, covered with ragged blankets, her grey hair lying loose on the dirty pillow. When he touched her lightly on the shoulder, she sat up at once, crossed herself and reached for her skirt. He gave her a number of instructions to which she made no reply, continuing to dress while he spoke. Then he went back to the kitchen to see his wife coming downstairs in her bare feet. Her skirt was thrown like a cloak over her shoulders. She had on a white petticoat over her shift. In her right hand she carried a lighted candle.

"What got you up?" said Hynes angrily.

His wife approached him, holding out her left hand in which she had a little bottle of holy water.

"I couldn't let ye go without a blessing," she said excitedly.

"Huh?" Hynes said. "And where would we be going?"

His wife sprinkled some of the water on him. He took off his hat and crossed himself, making a funny sort of curtsey which was meant to be a genuflection. She went over to Tony and sprinkled some of the water on him also.

"God bless your journey, asthore," she said.

Tony crossed himself carelessly with one hand while he wiped his mouth with the other.

"So that's what it is," he said.

The mother bent down impulsively and kissed him on the cheek.

"Tcha!" said Hynes angrily. "None o' your capers now. Hurry, Tony."

He left the kitchen, followed by his son, who paid no attention to his mother. The mother looked after him with loving pride. Giving birth to him had nearly killed her and she was ill for two years afterwards. The greedy fellow had to have two wet-nurses. Perhaps it was the alien pap that turned him into a giant.

Still moving with great secrecy, father and son harnessed a grey mare to a jaunting car and drove out of the village. It was dreadfully cold. They turned up the collars of their greatcoats and kept slapping their hands together. There had been a light fall of snow during the night, so that the mare's hooves and the wheels of the car hardly made a sound. Dawn was now breaking. As yet the earth was perfectly still.

"It's like this…" Hynes began, when they were out of the village.

He explained the plan in great detail. Although his eyes glittered, his tone was gloomy, as if he expected disaster to result from his daring. Tony listened in silence, flicking the mare about the ears with the whip. They descended a steep hill that bore sharply to the left. Here the road was lined with bushes from which the snow dripped in little blobs. The mare slithered as she descended at a walk. She kept making rumbling sounds in her throat and she arched her tail from time to time against the well of the car, as if inclined to mire. But when she reached the bottom of the hill, she shook her head, cleared her nostrils lustily, pulled at the reins and broke into a sharp trot, from which Tony broke her with a sudden jerk. Her rapid movement disturbed his train of thought. Hynes stopped speaking and slapped his mittened hands under his armpits. There was silence for a long time, as the mare advanced at a hard walk, jerking at the reins. She was cold and she wanted to run. Then Tony sighed, eased the reins, cracked the whip along her flank and she was off, high-stepping, in a gorgeous trot, her wide-open nostrils flashing in the risen sun.

"I'm satisfied," Tony said. "The veins in her legs give her trouble, I'm told, but the place is good. Her sight is bad, but she is healthy enough to carry children. The place is very good. I'm satisfied, father."

Hynes leaned across the well of the swaying car and whispered:

"And the risk? Our money? Is this the hour to risk it?"

Again Tony was silent for some time, as the mare trotted furiously, with tail upraised, breaking wind, leaving clear deep prints of her hooves in the smooth, fresh snow.

"There is little or no risk," he said at last, in a solemn tone, "as the government is behind it. No risk except the hand of God."

The risen sun now shone brilliantly on the pure, soft snow that lay like the milky seed of spring's concupiscence, on the rough fields, on the fences and on the winding, narrow road.

The air was crisp. Now they were in the lowlands, where the earth was rich compared to the barren heights, on whose edge the village stood against a background of serried, snowy mountains. All was ennobled by the sunlit snow. But the two gloomy men were not aware of this beauty, or of this nobility. Like two wolves, they trotted down from their mountain lair towards the town, huddled in their cloaks, leaving deep tracks in the pure fresh snow, of steel-shod hooves and of wheels.

They halted once at a tavern, where each took a glass of ale. They warmed the ale with a hot poker and waited there, sipping, for an hour, before they continued their journey. Then they drove on to the outskirts of Clogher, past the workhouse and the military barracks and then along the seashore, until they entered Main Street, which ran right across the town. Clogher was then a town of twenty thousand souls, but judging by the throng in its main street at that hour, one would have thought it held twenty times that number. There was something inhuman about the mass of hungry vagabonds that slouched on the pavements; rather like a horde of ants which had lost contact with their labyrinthine heap, where there had been order, work and sustenance. Now they waited for an unknown government to restore order for them. These loafers watched the trotting mare and the sombre men, who sat huddled in their coats on the car, with beseeching eyes. But the two men were just as indifferent to the eyes as they had been to the glory of the risen sun on the fresh, white snow.

There was snow here, too, but it lay like a rash on the rotting pavement and on the foul street. Here everything looked foul. Even the foundations of the shabby houses seemed to be rotting and rising up at the base, like the cracked skin around the edges of a sore.

They debouched into the fish market, beyond which, to the east, behind a slash wall, the mouth of the Ghost River poured its mountain water into the salty ocean. Here, also, there was beauty, with the red-skirted and bare-footed fishwives, beside their booths, crying merrily: "Herrings alive. Herrings alive with their two eyes open. Who'll buy the fine fresh herrings?" A flock of snow-white sea-gulls soared above the market and the river. On the sea, rolling majestically abroad, there were the sails and the dark hulls of ships.

They turned to the left along the quays and halted before a gloomy, two-storeyed house that adjoined a warehouse, in front of which there was a heap of planks. Ships were moored to the quays, their spars swaying slightly and creaking. There was a strong smell of tar, of bark, of hides, timber, and of fish. Over the low door of the house at which they halted was written: "James Rabbit & Son, Importers and Brandy Merchants." Tony gave the reins to a lad, and they entered the house.

"God save all here," Hynes said.

Stone steps led down to the floor of the shop, which looked, for that reason, like a cave. There were lights burning there. The room looked tiny on account of the amount of goods stacked there, principally bags of meal. Several peasants, men and women, crouched in a corner. A young woman stood behind a counter.

"God save you kindly," she said in answer to their salutation.

The two men went up to her and shook her by the hand. She was Mary Anne Rabbit, granddaughter of the proprietor, through his only son, now deceased. She wore spectacles and she was horribly ugly, owing to a strawberry coloured birthmark on her forehead and left cheek. Her legs were swollen, so that she seemed to be dragging loose, heavy clogs when she moved. Otherwise she was well built and quite capable, as Tony said, of carrying children. And she had a charming smile.

"Is James up?" Hynes said to her in a whisper.

"Himself is having his breakfast upstairs," she answered. "Let ye go on up."

The father moved out of the shop by a little door at the back of the counter. Tony paused for a few moments, as if intending to say something to the girl; but he said nothing, and then followed his father. They climbed a narrow stairway to the next floor and knocked on a door. A gruff voice bade them enter, which they did. They found old Rabbit seated at a small table by a window that overlooked the harbour. He was eating. His face looked healthy and he had lost none of his curly grey hair, although he was seventy-five years of age. He had lost his left leg in the naval battle of Aboukir Bay. He wore golden ear-rings. This gave him a piratical appearance, which was not lessened by his ferocious old face.

"Top o' the morning to ye," he growled. "Sit down and have a drop of coffee with me. It's a cold morning."

"I have what'll warm it," said Hynes, pulling a small bottle from the tail of his coat. "It's early to be breaking in on you, James, but we have business that won't wait."

"Devil take you," said Rabbit. "You have always something in your mind that can't wait. What is it now? How are you, Tony? As ugly as ever, God forgive you. Sit down."

"God help us all," said Hynes, sitting down and putting the bottle on the table, "but you're holding out well, James."

"And what would ail me?" said Rabbit, stumping over to a cupboard to get some glasses. "Huh! If God keeps the cholera and swine fever from me, I'll see you buried, Johnny. Aye! And dance at your wake, you old codger."

" 'Faith, you're a great and powerful man, sure," said Hynes in a whining tone, "all alone here with only Mary Anne to help you and you after leaving half yourself in foreign parts, in bloody, woeful war, not to mind the swelling of the rest of you."

"Hell to your soul, man," said Rabbit putting the glasses on the table; "will you open that bottle and stop talking? I suppose it's the cheapest you could find, you miser?"

"Indeed and indeed, then, it isn't," said Hynes, opening

the bottle, "but a drop of the best. Hold out your glass, James."

They all drank. Rabbit banged his empty glass on the table and said:

"Up here I can keep an eye on everything without moving a foot. I'm well situated here."

Hynes looked out the window at the boats.

"The day comes," he said mournfully, "when even the hawk on high can't tell the difference between a mouse and a stone. It's coming on myself, James, the crawling weakness of old age. Thanks be to God, I can depend on my son here."

"He's big enough surely," said Rabbit. "Another drop out of that, Johnny a ghradh. What brought you out so early, if it's no harm my asking?"

Hynes filled the glasses once more.

"I suppose it's Mary Anne you're after again?" said Rabbit.

"You've hit it on the head, James," said Hynes. "This time, though, I have a bargain in my fist that'll make your mouth water."

"Your health," said Rabbit. They drank. "What bargain would that be?"

His tongue loosened by the brandy, Hynes became eloquent. He quickly detailed the government plans for relief, especially the importing of cheap Indian corn from America. Then he sat forward and continued with vigour.

"There's a fortune in this, James," he said. "I heard of a shipload due shortly in Liverpool that can be bought for six pounds a ton. The meal'll fetch half a crown a stone shortly at retail over the counter. Maybe three shillings a stone. It just needs the ready money to buy big, before the market smells a good thing and dives for it. The early bird again, James. The government is going to put money in the people's fists and them that is ready can take every penny of it at an interest on their outlay that would frighten you, man. It would frighten you, I'm telling you straight. Good solid silver waiting for this meal as soon as it is landed on the quay. Well then, James.

Tony and I have the ready money to put into this. To cut a long story short, we're willing to take you in with us on the deal."

He grasped Rabbit's hand, opened out the fingers, and struck the palm a violent blow.

"We lay down a thousand sovereigns as our share of the partnership," he said, "with Mary Anne thrown into the bargain, your half share to go to her on your death. Spit on your fist and shake with me."

Rabbit drew back and his manner changed. The hearty expression of the old sailor gave way to the shrinking cunning of the merchant.

"Easy there, Johnny," he said. "I thought of that myself, this Indian meal, but will the people eat it?"

"Why wouldn't they?" said Hynes eagerly. "A hungry mouth doesn't pick and choose."

"It's a big risk all the same," said Rabbit. "It was tried before, this same yellow meal. The people wouldn't have it, for fear it would turn them into black heathens."

"Arrah! What hunger was there on them at that time compared to now?" said Hynes. "Have sense, man?"

"I have and plenty," said Rabbit. "Only for the risk, it's not for your thousand sovereigns I'd be waiting."

"Have another drop?" said Hynes.

"You can't soften me with brandy," said Rabbit.

Hynes smiled subtly as he poured out the fresh drink. He knew that Rabbit did not have a thousand sovereigns, or anything near that sum. Indeed, it was doubtful, Hynes thought, if he could scrape together one hundred sovereigns, even by exhausting his credit.

When Rabbit had gone into this business at first, after retiring from the navy with his prize money, trade was flourishing. It continued to flourish until the end of the Napoleonic wars. Ever since then it had declined. During the past ten years, since his son's death, he had just managed to keep his head above water. Hynes knew all this. He had been a long time weighing up the advantages of making a match between Tony and Mary Anne. He knew that the longer he waited the better the bargain. However, the time had come to stretch a point. There was not a moment to waste.

"Maybe you're right about the risk, James," he said, suddenly assuming a despondent look. "You're a wise man. 'Faith, I hadn't thought of that. Maybe we better forget what's been said. Your health, James."

Rabbit went pale. He leaned forward and said:

"What ails you, man?" he cried angrily. "What brought you here atall if you're not prepared to talk business?"

Hynes looked surprised and indignant.

"Me not prepared to talk business," he said. "Lord! Hear the talk of him, when it was himself..."

"It wasn't me," cried Rabbit. "It was you."

At last Tony moved in his chair and said:

"That's enough now, the two of ye. James, is it a bargain or not? A thousand sovereigns for half the business and Mary Anne's hand? Yes or no. There are others waiting for an offer."

Rabbit looked at the young man and then suddenly stretched out his hand.

"Put it there," he said to Tony. "I'll do business with you, when I won't do it with your lying miser of a father. It's agreed. Spit on it."

They both spat on their palms and then clasped hands. Old Hynes burst into an astonishing peal of laughter and slapped his thigh. He was beginning to get slightly drunk.

"Be the powers!" he cried. "It's signed and sealed at last. Rise up, Tony, you big lump. Go and bring her here, 'till I see is she male or female. What class of man are you?"

Tony got to his feet and said gloomily:

"I'm the class of man that's able to do what's needed in bed or out of it."

He marched out of the room. The two old men leaned

across the board, until their noses almost touched. For a few moments they showered compliments on one another and then they began to argue furiously about the marriage settlement.

CHAPTER XXV

HYNES HAD BEEN unduly optimistic about the "flood of money" which the government intended to pour into the district. It proved to be no more than a drop. At the opening session of the relief committee, there were more than a thousand men outside the courthouse, where the committee was in session, waiting to be employed on the works. Mr. Swan, the government representative, had to be escorted by six policemen through this howling mob on his way to the courthouse. The experience terrified and angered him, so he begged Father Roche to ask the crowd to leave. The priest got angry in turn.

"Why should I ask them to leave?" said he. "Aren't they here to employed?"

"Not all of them," said the inspector. "There is a vast horde there. We can only employ three hundred at a time on the works. In any case, each person must be examined carefully, to make sure that his credentials are such as would warrant his employment."

Then he explained to Father Roche what these credentials were. The priest listened in silence. Then he lost his temper and ran out to address the crowd, which greeted his appearance with a wild cheer.

"The government goose," cried Father Roche, from the top of a cart, "has only laid a wren's egg and a mangy one at that. A wren's egg, stuffed with yellow meal. Any of ye, men, that are hard-working and honest, that have a roof over yer head, that have a cow, or a horse, or a pig, or even a lame donkey, ye can go home. There's nothing for ye. Only the squatters and the beggars and the loafers are to be helped. There's only work for three hundred altogether. The people's own money, borrowed at five per cent, is going to be put to no good use, but to feed people that never tried to help themselves, only living as an outrage on the parish. Let only the worst in the parish stay. May God look down on the rest of ye."

This speech created the worst kind of an impression and the whole force of constabulary, led by Captain Mordaunt, had to be brought into action in order to quell a riot. In fact, nothing was done at all that day, for the row within the courthouse itself was almost as violent as outside. The committee was composed of Mr. Swan, Mr. Coburn, Colonel Bodkin, the resident magistrate, John Hynes and three farmers, selected because they were the highest ratepayers of their class in the district. I may add that none of these three farmers could either read or write. That did not prevent them from opposing whatever scheme was brought forward, on the ground that it was not "within the meaning of the act". Father Roche opposed any suggestion made by Mr. Coburn, owing to his suspicion of the parson's proselytising tendencies. Colonel Bodkin was bored with the whole business and kept shouting in a senseless way: "For God's sake, let's get the wretched business finished." Four days were wasted in this manner before a mode of procedure was finally adopted and candidates for employment were begun to be examined. By that time, the enthusiasm of the people had changed to deadly apathy and only the most wretched presented themselves. Among these was Thomsy Hynes.

It was Mary insisted on his coming, much against his will.

"It would be the making of us," she said, "if you got a ticket for the works. Sure Martin would go like a shot, only they're not taking men with land. Go on with you."

So Thomsy had presented himself every morning at the courthouse, until at last his turn came to be examined. As soon as his name was called, Mr. Swan consulted a list and said to Colonel Bodkin, the chairman:

"I'm afraid this man is ineligible. He has served a term of imprisonment, for disloyalty and attacking a servant of Her Majesty."

"Upon my soul!" cried Bodkin. "Disloyalty! What next? Why, sir, I know this man. I gave him a month's hard labour once for being drunk and disorderly and assaulting a constable."

"Begob, your honour," said Thomsy, "you did that, in this same courthouse, and a hot day it was, too. You were asleep on the bench, your honour, when you suddenly woke up and said: 'A month hard.' Well I remember it."

A roar of laughter greeted these remarks. Thomsy smiled, delighted at the attention he was receiving. He always got great pleasure from causing laughter by his rather buffoonish wit.

"It wasn't me struck the first blow, though," he continued. "It was the peeler struck it. He was a long string of a man called Townshend, we used to call him Fireball on account of his ginger hair, an Orangeman from Belfast he was. A bad one, by the powers. A papish tub o' guts he called me. He had it in for me on account of it being me that nicknamed him Fireball."

A further burst of laughter followed these remarks.

"Does he look like a rebel?" said Colonel Bodkin to Mr. Swan.

"Sorry, Colonel," said Mr. Swan. "I must follow the regulation. This man is ineligible."

"Damn your regulations," said the Colonel. "Well, Hynes, it seems you can't work here, damn it. Go and get drunk, but take care you don't hit any policemen.

He threw a half-crown to Thomsy, who thanked him and left the courthouse. The crowd outside shouted at him:

"Did you get the ticket?"

"Devil a bit of me," said Thomsy.

He sneaked over to the hotel and went in by a back way,

lest the crowd might follow him and demand to be treated. He bought a half pint of whisky and a bag of sweets to pacify Mary. Then he went by a lane across the mountains towards Black Valley. When he was in a secluded spot, he sat down, opened the bottle and began to drink. It did not take him long to finish it. Then he went his way homewards, staggering and singing. As he debouched from the mountain path on to the lane going up Black Valley, he met Patsy O'Hanlon, who was hurrying home from the village.

"Blood an ouns!" cried Thomsy. "Where did you get the tobacco?"

O'Hanlon walked very erect, swinging his arms, blowing clouds of smoke from a new clay pipe. He answered Thomsy in a very lordly manner.

"In a shop," he said. "Where else?"

And he marched past Thomsy, who scratched his head in astonishment.

"Arrah! What ails you, man?" he shouted after O'Hanlon. "Don't you know your neighbour?"

"I'm in a hurry," cried O'Hanlon. "I got a ticket for the works. They start in the morning. I have to be up with the dawn. Three hundred of us. I'm the only one out of Black Valley that was taken."

His voice already grew dim in the distance.

"So that's what it is," shouted Thomsy angrily, impotently trying to run after O'Hanlon. "You're big in the world now, huh? Well! Who would have believed it? Patsy O'Hanlon! Devil roast your dirty hide!"

He stood in the road and shook his fist at O'Hanlon. Tears of rage came into his bleary eyes. When he passed O'Hanlon's shack, he shouted "souper" several times, so that Sally came out and barged him.

"You're envious," she said, "you shameless drunkard, to see a bit of food slipping towards the empty mouths of the poor."

"Soupers," yelled Thomsy, as he staggered home.

He stalked into the kitchen and began at once:

"They had me marked down as a rebel. The government man had it written in a book. Then Colonel Bodkin…But what ails ye all?"

He realised suddenly that everybody in the kitchen was strangely silent. Maggie was weeping in the hearth corner.

"Hush," said Mary. "Michael is dying."

CHAPTER XXVI

THE SICK MAN, WHO had been wasting to a skeleton for the past month, had at last reached his end. Even so, he found it hard to die. After the last rites of the church had been administered and he had resigned himself to his fate, he struggled on through the night, fighting grimly. Dawn was breaking before he died. Then copper coins were placed on his eyelids and the death wail began in the house. Kate Hernon took charge of the mourning.

She led Maggie from the death-bed to the hearth and put her sitting on a stool in the chimney corner. Then she herself squatted on the floor before the fire, surrounded by a group of neighbour women, who drew their skirts over their heads. Kate sprinkled ashes on the women's heads and began to recite the death chant. She bent forward until she was almost prone, with her hands stretched towards the fire. Her body, forward from the hips, then broke into movement, miming the tortures of the human soul, as it struggles to break free from its prison in the human body. Her back twisted slowly, like an animal with a broken hip dragging itself along the ground. Her hands and arms also twisted, as if she were kneading bread in the air. She raised her shoulders as her hands reached outwards, urging forth the spirit, miming the act of birth.

Her chant was mostly an inarticulate cadence, while the other women, rocking themselves, now and again uttered prayers to God, begging him to accept the departing soul. At times, the old woman's voice imitated the death rattle. At times it rose to a wild shriek of triumph, during which she plunged forward, seized ashes in her hands and scattered them towards the open door, as was customary, to exorcise evil spirits that barred the soul's flight to Paradise. At last she stood up straight from her knees, paused for a moment as if listening and then thrust her arms above her head, crying with great fervour:

"God of Glory! Have mercy now and open your gates."

"Amen!" said the other women.

Thereupon they all lay prone on the ground for some time with their heads covered, until Kate Hernon rose and said in a normal tone:

"We'll go now and lay out the corpse."

The old man took Martin out into the yard and said:

"You better go to Crom for boards to make the coffin. Warn the cooper as well to come and start working."

On this occasion he was again master in the house according to custom.

"What about poitheen for the wake and the funeral?" Martin said.

"Heh!" said the old man. "I was forgetting that. Thomsy can go for it."

"I suppose ten gallons would be enough," said Martin.

"Pooh!" said the old man. "Sure ten gallons wouldn't bury a child. Ten wouldn't make the sign of the cross on the crowd that will be here. Twenty."

"Twenty?" said Martin. "It would be madness to get twenty, father, with the price it is now. We can't leave ourselves empty with the way the times are. Thomsy was refused a ticket for the works, too, and Mr. Chadwick won't give us any relief with the rent, on account of how he has it in for Mary taking Ellie away."

"Who cares?" said the old man. "Is it stingy you're turning! I have always lived as the customs of the people say I should live and I'll die that way. There's no going against custom."

"You know best," said Martin. "Father Roche won't like it, either, though, if there are people bad from drink. Last year he gave out from the altar on account of that funeral in Glenaree…"

"Let him mind his own business," cried the old man. "He's

God's messenger, but he has no right to interfere with the customs of the people. They were ordained by God Himself."

"Alright, father," said Martin. "Let it be what you say. You know best. I'll get the pipes and tobacco as well, when I'm in the village. We'll want candles, too. God save us! This will take a power of money. Well! I must be going. The people will be coming shortly."

"Take the purse," said the old man. "Pay on the nail. At the shop and at the sheebeen, too."

Maggie was prostrated by her son's death. Mary had to take all the responsibility of getting the house ready for the wake. Sally O'Hanlon, Kitty Hernon and Nappa Toomey came to help her. The corpse was laid out in the corner of the kitchen where the pigs' bed had been. For that an extra table had to be borrowed from a neighbour, together with forms for seating the visitors. By the time all had been prepared, Martin returned from the village with the pipes and tobacco. The old man sat near the head of the corpse and filled the pipes, which he passed around among the mourners. The wake had begun. As people entered the kitchen, they blessed the house in a whisper, knelt before the corpse in prayer and then sat down for a while. The men smoked a little. They talked in low voices about ordinary things. It was contrary to etiquette to refer to the cause of their presence. When leaving, however, they waited in the yard until they met one of the family, when they tendered regret in a formal manner. It was all very ceremonious. In the afternoon, Tom Gill, the cooper, began to make the coffin on the rock where the oats had been threshed. Then the keg of whisky was broached and the wake became livelier. By nightfall the house was crowded and there was even an atmosphere of gaiety. That also was proper and according to custom. Mary's mother came after supper-time. Mary retired with her into the bedroom.

"Why didn't father come?" she said after they had closed the door.

Mrs. Gleeson burst into tears. The two of them sat on the side of the bed.

"I don't know what ails him ever since Ellie went away," said the mother. "I can't get a word out of him and Patrick is no better. He has something on his mind. He won't stir out of the house."

"No news from Ellie?" Mary said.

"Not a word, child. She never went near her cousin Julia. God forgive her. I know the worst has happened to her."

"Isn't God cruel?" Mary said. "All these torments one after the other."

She lay down on the bed and closed her eyes, with her hands clasped under her head.

"We haven't a penny now," Mrs. Gleeson continued. "I went to Mr. Chadwick about Ellie's wages. 'What wages?' he said. 'Let the wench that took her away come for them. On her knees.' That's what he said. What's going to happen to us?"

"I'm so tired," Mary said. "I'm glad Michael is gone, God forgive me. He was like a worm eating us out of house and home. Now there isn't a pig, or a hen, or a duck left. And my baby coming."

The mother looked at her. The curve of the child was already quite pronounced. The mother bent down and smoothed her daughter's forehead. Mary threw out her arms, turned her head to one side and whispered:

"What did you say about father and about Patrick?"

"Nothing, darling. Rest yourself. I'll put a cover over you. Have a sleep. I'll attend to everything. You must take care of yourself from now on, with your first child."

"Doesn't he say anything?"

"Don't you worry about him."

"Why can't you tell me what he says?"

"Musha, alannah, anything to please you. 'Faith, he says nothing, him that used to be so talkative. Yesterday he got into a state, jumping up and walking about the floor in his bare feet and then sitting down again and grinding his teeth."

"Why does Mr. Chadwick want me to go to him? He had his knife in us."

Suddenly she clutched at her mother and whispered:

"Mother, I'm afraid. I'm afraid of that man. Pray for me."

The mother hugged her. Mary relaxed and then the mother drew a quilt over her. Mary kept shuddering and then she fell into a deep sleep from exhaustion. She was awakened by voices whispering in the room. She lay still and listened. Over by the window, Maggie and her two daughters were talking with their heads together.

"It's a terrible thing, surely," Nappa was saying, "to rise up and leave the sod we were raised on, to cross the ocean to a foreign land and be buried alive there, without a voice that we know, or a face, or even a kindly old stone with the nature of our country in it. But what else is there? Dan is no coward, as everybody knows, but sure nobody comes to the forge any more and we got nothing out of the land this year. The few pounds we have would soon go, so it's better to pay our passage with them to a land where they say there's plenty."

"If ye could only take me and the children," said Kitty. "I'm worse off than ye are and I with little mouths to feed."

"We would and welcome, Kitty, a chroidhe," said Nappa, "but how could we? The little we have left after paying our passage will be needed in New York. We can't land empty. They say it's terrible to be left empty there, with the sharks, too, that does come down to meet the ships and drag the people into their dives and rip them open. There are robbers, too, that does be selling tickets for the steamboats going into the middle of the land, up the river. So they said at the ticket office. 'Keep a tight hold on your bundles and on your money,' the ticket man said."

"If ye could take two of the children itself," Kitty said.

" 'Faith, it would be a help to you, asthore," Maggie said, "if they could take two of them, although it would be a torment to lose the little angels."

"I'll talk to Dan," Nappa said. "We might be able to rummage around for enough to take the eldest."

"The second eldest," said Kitty. "I wouldn't part with the eldest. That little Brian is already a help to me."

Mary turned over again and went to sleep. She didn't awake until the priest's attendant came in the morning to arrange an altar for Mass on the site of the hen coop. The parish priest came and said Mass. Afterwards Mary gave him breakfast in the bedroom. Then they prepared to take a collection as was customary, but Father Roche stopped them.

"There'll be no offerings," he said. "Ye need all ye have, good people. It's I that should be able to give to ye, instead of ye giving to me. God bless ye."

The people followed him into the lane asking God to bless him. Old Kilmartin, however, was displeased because there had been no offerings taken. It was going against tradition and, therefore, revolutionary. No good would come of it.

"Hech!" he said. "What are the times coming to? Burying a man without offerings. It's not right."

After the priest's departure the ceremony of burial turned into a kind of macabre feast. Martin and Thomsy went among the men outside with whisky in jars. Indoors, the women drank punch and lamented the dead in loud voices. In the yard men boasted about his strength and beauty. They recounted his deeds in heroic language. Then the finished coffin was brought into the kitchen and the family gathered round to pay their last respects to the corpse before it was enclosed. At this point, Kate Hernon and her chorus of women again took charge, chanting while the lid of the coffin was nailed down. Then the coffin was brought out and hoisted on the shoulders of four men. The funeral procession followed it. Old Brian led it on horseback, with his wife sitting on the crupper behind him.

Mary stayed at home to set the house in order. Sally O'Hanlon stayed with her.

"Sit down in the corner and rest yourself," Sally said. "I'll have everything done before you could say toso rap."

She prepared a big tub of hot water on the kitchen floor and set to washing the dead man's clothes. She was in great spirits, owing to her husband working on the relief scheme.

"People are going to begrudge us," she said, "on account of Patsy being the only man in the Valley to get a ticket, and sure it's a fine change in the world, when the poorest are put before the richest, before them that have a cow and a horse. The work will be hard. They are going to dig up the hill that turns south there beyond the village, as you go to Clogher. They'll dig it all away, according to Patsy. With that power of men, sure they could dig away a mountain. It's good money, eightpence farthing a day. We can have full and plenty now. But we're not people to turn proud on account of our riches. Now you have a neighbour, Mary, that won't forget your kindness. While there's a penny coming into my house, Mary, my treasure, I'll not see you in want."

Mary had to laugh in spite of her misery at the idea of Sally O'Hanlon being able to distribute bounty on eightpence farthing a day, after feeding seven mouths. And with oatmeal three shillings a stone already!

"You're a grand person, Sally," she said. "May God love you!"

When Sally went out to the drying fence at the back of the house with the washed clothes, Mary thought:

"God forgive me, I'm so glad poor Michael is dead. He was like a worm devouring everything and him wasting away."

By the time people returned from the funeral there was no trace of the dead man in the house, except his wrinkled old brogues that still remained in their nook by the chimney place.

Chapter XXVII

NAPPA TOOMEY AND her husband finally agreed to take the second and third of Kitty Hernon's children with them to America. They sailed in the middle of March on an emigrant ship from Clogher to New York. Three families from Black Valley also sailed. Indeed, nearly half of the ship's passengers came from the Crom district. Eighty-four of the poor wretches died of fever during the crossing.

Kitty found it a difficult matter to feed the five that were left to her. She had been living on charity since the beginning of the new year and charity was no longer available. With all the will in the world, the poor could not give to the poor, since they had nothing to give. At the head of the Valley, many of the sheep were slaughtered by now and all the potatoes were gone, all over the Valley, except those reserved for seed. People had begun to eat nettles. The Kilmartins still managed to give the poor woman a little, but even they had begun to get tired of her querulous visits. In any case, they were spending their last few shillings on meal. The expense of Michael's funeral had brought them very close to destitution.

"Why don't you go before the Relief Committee?" Mary said to her at last. "Maybe they'd help you."

"Sure they're giving out no money," Kitty said. "Only the Protestant minister and that would damn my soul. They'll take no woman at the works. I could do it if I got it. I'm strong though I'm skinny. If I could only get somebody to take the two youngest, I could forage something."

"You could try them in any case," Mary said. "It wouldn't harm you."

"Maybe you're right, asthore," Kitty said. "They might find a place on a ship's deck for me. If I could get to Liverpool I'd find work."

And she decided to go before the committee. She could not have chosen a worse day for her appearance. It was a blustering day towards the end of the month and the weather increased the tension among the committee men, if that was possible. Instead of developing into an efficient organisation for controlling relief, that institution had gone rapidly from bad to worse. The bickering between Father Roche and Mr. Coburn had now developed into open warfare. Colonel Bodkin sided with Mr. Coburn. The three illiterate farmers sided with Father Roche. Mr. Hynes remained neutral and was disliked by the rest of the committee. The principal bone of contention was the issue of Indian meal. For some reason, Father Roche had struck up a friendship with Mr. Swan, the government representative, whom Colonel Bodkin described as "a Cockney fop and a damned impertinent little guttersnipe," simply because Mr. Swan had found fault with a grey mare of which the colonel thought a great deal. Terrified by the riot which resulted from his speech outside the courthouse, at the first meeting, the parish priest continually advised the people, from the altar and elsewhere, to have confidence in the government, to obey the law and not to listen to agitators, "Young Irelanders, Fenians and that criminal gang of physical force men, imported from abroad." At Mr. Swan's suggestion, he went around persuading the people to eat the yellow meal. "It's not Peel's brimstone," he said, "and it won't turn ye black. See here. I'll eat it myself." And with his own hands, he made porridge of it in the hovels and ate some of it, smacking his lips. So the people took to the disagreeable stuff at his bidding. Money poured into Hynes's iron safe as a result.

John Hynes's plan had been realised by them. The first ship load, bought by him and Rabbit in Liverpool, had arrived in Clogher. Tony was already installed in Rabbit's store, waiting for the end of Lent to marry Rabbit's granddaughter. The name of Hynes and the word limited had been added to Rabbit over the door. The meal was on sale at three shillings a stone in Hynes's shop at Crom. The wolves had begun to fatten on the starving herd. And this infuriated the parson.

"This meal should be distributed by the government at cost price," he cried at the committee meetings. "The hunger of the poor should not be used as a means of filling the coffers of usurers."

Furthermore, the parish priest had carried on a violent campaign against the parson's private relief organisation. Early in February, Mr. Coburn had rented a vacant cottage opposite the Catholic church, to act as the "Headquarters of Crom Parish Assistance League, under the patronage of the Crestview Needlework Society." Father Roche regarded the choice of a site as suspicious. "There it is," he said, "right in front of God's door, a devilish plot to ensnare souls by proselytising the hungry." In spite of police protection, the sign, which was painted on a board stuck in the thatch, was soon battered by small boys with stones. At first, the parson had distributed clothes and food to anybody who came for them: but he desisted on discovering that this was as bad a method as scattering silver in the street. In any case, the most fantastic garments were sent to him from England by ladies and gentlemen of the upper classes. The lads of Crom used to hold carnival in them. Only drunkards and outcasts dared come to the cottage, for fear of the priest. Then the parson decided to distribute seed and to start a model farm, on a patch of ground that went with the cottage. This he manured with the newly discovered guano, of which he procured two sacks. To encourage the cultivation of rye, which his friend Campbell Foster declared to be the best crop for that district, he planted some, as well as barley, oats and a few potatoes of a new kind unknown in the neighbourhood. "Guano," he said to the people, "will double the yield." By this sane conduct, he was at last beginning to make headway and people were coming to him for seed and instruction, much to Father Roche's horror.

This was the state of affairs when Kitty made her

appearance. That morning, there was a fresh quarrel among the members, as the men on road-work had received no wages for ten days, owing to mismanagement at Clogher. Under the circumstances, the committee was in no mood in incur further responsibilities. Kitty began to speak at once. As if inspired by an evil genius, she addressed her remarks to Mr. Coburn, because he sat nearest to her. This immediately antagonised Father Roche.

"Look at me," she said, "me and my five children. Come here, will ye, and show yourselves to the gentlemen."

She gathered her five children in front of her like a clutch of chicks.

"My husband is in the mad-house," she continued. "He's not dead, but they're orphans all the same. They're worse than orphans. If they were real orphans I could get another man. I have a piece of land and a man would come to it. But they're only half orphans. And sure God in Heaven said to pity the widow and her orphans. I have hands and I'm willing to work for whatever can fill mouths. Give me work on roads. I'll do it as well as any man. We have no stock, not a stick in the house, nothing atall, unless ye count a roving donkey that's gone away on the mountain. There are people working that are well-to-do, but they have powerful friends. I have no one. Look at these children. I sent two to America with my sister. All the rest are here. Five of them. All mine. If I could only find a kind doorstep I could leave the youngest on, I'd be free to forage. The wild pig can dig with his snout. I could burrow somewhere and find what's necessary."

She spoke in a distraught fashion and continued for a long time until Mr. Swan finally interrupted her.

"It's against the regulations to employ women," he said.

At this Mr. Coburn jumped to his feet and cried:

"This is outrageous."

Mr. Swan shrugged his shoulders and raised his eyebrows. This excited the parson still more and he cried, shaking his fist at Swan:

"Sir, you are a mountebank."

He had been very pale while Kitty spoke and his hands had nervously clutched his knees. Now his face was flushed and his eyes sparkled. He was evidently about to give vent to an outburst of passion, which had been a long time developing within him. Everybody except Mr. Swan was astonished at his insulting words. Swan merely smiled.

"I'm prepared to overlook your remark, Mr. Coburn," he said, "on receipt of a proper apology."

"Apologise?" cried Coburn. "Never for speaking the truth. I have managed thus far to control myself. The heartrending appeal of this poor woman has been too much for me. Too much, I say. There is a limit to all things. There comes a time when forbearance is a crime. These useless works, which the people do not want, but for which they have to pay, are conducted by a horde of incompetent officials, imported from England, with tons of paper to turn into useless documents. Yet the poor wretches cannot receive their pittance, earned for cutting down our hill and making our road impassable, for money we are borrowing at five per cent. Give us our money. Let us use it to succour such as this poor woman and her children, instead of mangling the face of our beloved country. Decent people...I exempt Colonel Bodkin from all complicity..."

"Complicity, sir?" cried Bodkin, rising to his feet.

Owing to the indistinct way in which the parson spoke, the colonel had misunderstood his words.

"I exempt you from this plot," continued the parson. "Bear with me. I shall soon have finished. It's usury, selling this meal at famine price, as if it were precious stuff. Three shillings a stone. Christians getting rich on famine. It's an outrage. We're all mountebanks, we who delude the people into the belief that Her Majesty's Government..."

"Take care, sir," shouted the colonel. "You are treading on dangerous ground."

"I repeat," shouted the parson in a shrill tone, "that Her Majesty is badly served. Let the people be employed on the land. Let them be lent the necessary capital. Inculcate them with the spirit of independence. In the words of the poet: 'Teach man he is a free agent, give but a slave his liberty, he'll shake off sloth, and build himself a hut and hedge a spot of ground; this he'll defend; 'tis his right by nature. Thus set in action he will move onward to plan conveniences, till glory fires his breast to enlarge his castle; while the poor slave drudges all day, in hope to rest at night.' Gentlemen, I resign. I refuse to be a party to this corruption. Come with me, my good woman. As a Christian and a gentleman, I shall do what I can for you. Come with me."

He was moving towards the door, followed by Kitty, when Father Roche screamed at the top of his voice:

"A Christian gentleman, did you say? I say a bigot and a proselytiser."

Coburn turned about and retorted in the same tone:

"And I denounce you as a sycophant and a disgrace to your cloth."

As the two men continued to shout insults at one another, shaking their fists, Kitty fled from the courthouse, horrified by the scene she had caused.

"Now I'm ruined entirely," she thought, "bringing the parish priest down on me."

She decided to get home as quickly as possible. She had, however, eaten nothing that day and the weight of the two babies she carried, one was seven months and the other eighteen months, soon exhausted her. Despair soon gave her courage.

"He told me to come with him," she thought. "Where? To his house?"

The elder children, trotting after her, began to howl with hunger and weariness. That decided her. She turned aside towards the parson's house. It was in a hollow on the eastern outskirts of the village. The gate was almost opposite the police barracks. She marched down the little winding drive and then went round to the kitchen door, where the servant, a native of the village and a Catholic, regarded her with surprise. It was rare that one of the people came to the parsonage. Kitty was unknown to this woman.

"Could I wait here until Mr. Coburn comes?" Kitty said.

"What would you want with him, good woman?" said the servant.

"He told me to come," Kitty said.

"Is that so?" said the servant. "The mistress is at home. Maybe she'd do you."

"Maybe she would," said Kitty. "I'm in a bad state. These children of mine are starving."

"I'll go find her," said the servant, giving Kitty a suspicious look. "And where would you be from, good woman?"

"Black Valley," said Kitty.

"Is that so?" said the servant, giving Kitty a still more hostile look.

Mrs. Coburn was an invalid, had been one for years, owing to some disease that affected her feet. It took her a long time to come downstairs and by then Mr. Coburn himself had arrived, flustered and angry from his argument with the priest. He and his wife received Kitty in a little room near the kitchen. It used to be the children's schoolroom. During the interview that followed, the servant listened at the keyhole and was thus able to report the whole affair to the parish priest afterwards; no doubt, a very garbled version. In any case, Kitty made astonishing statements and requests. The poor woman was now quite distraught.

"Take the two of them," she said, on coming into the couple's presence. "These two babies. Take them, sir, and you, ma'am, take them as well."

She offered them the two babies she held in her arms. The couple looked at her in astonishment. Mrs. Coburn then looked enquiringly at her husband, who said:

"I must tell you, my dear, that this poor woman…"

"Let me tell her, sir," said Kitty, interrupting him. "Who can tell it better than a poor mother? Answer me that. I can't ask you for the love of God to take them, sir, and I knowing it will damn their souls. All the same, take them, put them in a home, even if they are brought up as Protestants. I struggled all winter, sir, yes, ma'am, I struggled through the snow and the hailstones, but now it's beyond me. I tried the workhouse as well. It's full to the doors and a poor place it is to find shelter, with the creatures lying sick in their own dirt. Where could a poor mother go? God is against us, so let the devil have his due. You have a bird's nest in Clogher. Put the two youngest in it. They are too young to know what they are doing. Let the sin be on me. I wish it. I can bear it, ma'am. You'd do the same if you were me. You had children yourself. Look at him, ma'am, this little one. He's hardly bigger than the day he was born and he seven months old. Take him in your hands, ma'am, and feel the weesy weight of him, like a wren after breaking the egg. What's there to put in his beak? Sure, I went dry, saving your presence, sir, I went dry with the worry about the rent that we owed. Patch is now in the madhouse. Seven months this lad is and Joe isn't much bigger, although he's eighteen months. How would they grow? Let people say what they like, but it's the nature of a mother to feed her children, even if she has to walk the fiery roads of Hell for it. Weesy as they are and miserable, don't think I won't suffer parting with them. The two others are gone with my sister to America and I do reach out for them all of a sudden, twenty times a day, maybe, and at night as well, I do hear their voices calling me, like they were fallen in the fire. It's the ache in my heart that does it and I longing for the little creatures. God gave them to me but hunger took them away. I'll have three of them left, so I won't be empty like a stripper cow. Little Brian, the eldest here, hold your head up a mhac and smile on the gentry, he'll soon be a help to me. You'd be surprised, ma'am, the way he's beginning already. He's a caution with the wits he has in him. He says to me the other day, he says: 'Pity there isn't a good fall of snow.' 'Why so, angel?' I said to him. 'Because,' he says, he did, God bless him, 'because I could make a trap with a kish and a cord. I'd get a piece of boiled pratie and put it under the kish and then the thrushes and the starlings, starved with the hunger, they'd come under the kish and I'd pull the cord and we'd have a potful of birds to eat.' He said that, 'faith. You'd hardly believe it, ma'am, the genius that's in him, but it's the gospel truth, what I'm telling you."

Here she paused to wipe little Brian's nose with a corner of her apron. Mrs. Coburn was by now in tears. The pathetic appeal had reminded her of her own five children, all of whom had now left her, married and settled abroad, except one who had a position in a London counting-house. The parson, however, had been intimidated by the outrageous request.

"My good woman," he said, "you must realise that it's impossible for me to do what you ask."

"And why not, sir?" said Kitty.

"I have nothing to do with any children's home in Clogher," said the parson. "I'm not a proselytiser. You must keep your children."

"Arthur," said Mrs. Coburn, "you simply can't send the poor creature away."

"I have no intention of sending her away," said Mr. Coburn. "But I can't take her children, my dear. Otherwise…"

"But surely," said Mrs. Coburn, "a mother wouldn't want to make such a sacrifice unless her want were desperate. She's not a heartless creature. You can see that."

"That's right, ma'am," said Kitty. "It's only that I don't want to let them wither before my eyes."

"I can't take them," said the parson. "I'm determined to have nothing to do with such conduct, which I think is reprehensible. But I'm ready to help you. Just a moment."

He left the room and returned with five sovereigns, which he gave to Kitty. She went down on her knees and kissed his hands and asked God to bless him.

"I'm saved, sir," she kept repeating. "I'm saved. This will take me and my children to Liverpool."

The parson offered to send his coachman and the gig in to Clogher with her when she was ready to go.

"I'll be ready in a tick of the clock," said Kitty. "If I could leave the children here while I go and collect my bundle."

They allowed her to leave the children there in charge of the servant. She went home and returned early in the afternoon with a big bundle of clothes. Then she set off in the parson's gig to Clogher. Certain that she was never going to return and inflamed with hatred of the people at large, for not having succoured her, she barged loudly on her way through the village. She barged everybody, including the parish priest. The poor woman was conscious of having put herself beyond the pale and she was trying to justify her conduct. When the gig came to the public works it was forced to halt. Three hundred men had been destroying the road, never very good, at this point, for the past three weeks. They had rendered it almost impassable. A great pile of rocks and clay lay on either side, while an immense pile had been hurled down to the bottom of the ravine that lay on the south. The various gangs of men were now idling, discontented and weak with hunger owing to the fact that they had not been paid for nearly a fortnight, while the stewards and officials tried to make them work, to render the road still more impassable.

"Ho! Ye loafers," shouted Kitty, as the coachman led the horse by the head through the morass, "ye are the men that got work, while the honest poor are left without bite or sup. Look at Patsy O'Hanlon, that has been living on my father's charity these five years. Look at him. And me run out of the parish by the hunger, me that was brought up on cow's milk and butter, in a house that owned land. Mr. Coburn is the man for ye. He'd drive ye back to the dung, where ye belong and he'd put honest people in yer place. A lot of rowdies. Bribery that done it for ye."

They gaped at her in wonder, as she sat there in the parson's gig, gaunt and wild-eyed, gap-toothed, in her ragged, black shawl, with her ragged children within the fold of her gaunt arms, like starved chicks under the outstretched wings of their dam. As the gig went down the hill past the morass, her harsh voice came back to them, shrill and defiant, crying:

"If a curse falls on me for what I'm doing, let ye be responsible on the day of judgment. It was a mother's love for her little ones that drove me to it."

Some of the men began to whistle after her in derision. Later, however, when news came from Clogher of her later conduct, there was something far more serious than whistling.

CHAPTER XXVIII

THREE DAYS LATER, Chadwick was having breakfast when Hegarty burst into the room without knocking. Blood was streaming down the man's face.

"What the devil…?" began Chadwick.

"It's murder, sir," said Hegarty. "The people are up. For the love of God, give me a drink of water, sir."

Reilly and Mary Halloran came into the room and gave him water. He was in a bad state. The white rash on his lower lip had almost disappeared owing to the way the lip was drawn back, exposing his buck teeth, like a horse yawning. His knees were knocking against one another. While they were washing the cut on his face, he managed to tell his story.

It appeared that the population had got excited by the report of the parson's servant. Then came news from Clogher that Kitty Hernon had lodged her two babies in the Protestant home. This news leaked out, because the crazy woman repented after she had lodged them. She went around Clogher saying that the parson had persuaded her to surrender them. Her three remaining children, after eating too plentiful a meal, on the money she had received from the parson, got a severe attack of cramps and looked like dying in the lodging-house. This she interpreted as the vengeance of God, so that she went about, quite out of her senses, making the false accusation against Coburn, even while she was paying her passage, and that of the children, to Liverpool with the money he had given her. When this news reached Crom the people got out of bounds. At dead of night, they attacked the parson's relief headquarters, razed it with crowbars and even destroyed the little garden at the rear before the arrival of the police. A section of them rallied, made a detour, entered the parson's grounds, caught his cow and cut off the animal's tail. They were massing to rush the dwelling-house, when the police arrived in force and dispersed them. A small party went to Hegarty's house, which they searched, looking for the rent demand notes, just about to be distributed. They found them and burned them. Hegarty himself escaped, but a stone, thrown by a youth, struck him on the forehead. He made his way to the Big House by climbing over a wall at the far end of the demesne.

"They're up," he said. "The people are up. It's a rising."

"Get my horse, Reilly," said Chadwick. "A horse's hooves is what strikes terror into those dogs."

"In the name of God, sir," said Reilly, as Chadwick pulled a cavalry sword out of its scabbard on the wall, "what's in your mind?"

"My horse," said Chadwick, brandishing the sword. "Be quick."

Reilly ran to the stables.

"Take cover," said Chadwick to the other two. "Lock the doors and arm yourselves."

He strode out of the house. Reilly brought the horse, which Chadwick mounted at once, carrying the naked sword in his right hand.

"God save us!" said Mary Halloran. "He's broke out again and him not taking a drink these months. I thought he was cured."

Chadwick galloped into the village and drew up before the police barracks. The village street was empty, except for a patrol of policemen. The head constable, accompanied by a few men, stood in the barrack yard.

"Got the situation in hand, Edwards?" said Chadwick to the head constable.

The head constable smiled.

"You must have been misinformed, Mr. Chadwick," he said. "The village is normal."

Chadwick looked at him, furious because of the man's attitude.

"Damn them!" thought Chadwick. "They are beginning to treat me with contempt."

Glaring at the head constable, he turned his horse and galloped back to his house.

"Reilly," he said, throwing the reins to his groom, "gallop back to the hotel and get me some whisky. A dozen."

"Yes, sir," said Reilly.

Chadwick marched into the sitting-room, where Hegarty still crouched on a chair, trembling from head to foot.

"You'll get a fresh demand note printed at once," cried Chadwick. "Just a moment. I want to make a change or two."

He sat down and wrote out a new demand note, inserting the words *ordered to pay* instead of *requested to pay*. He underlined the new words several times. He still had the sword in his hand.

"I'll have to have police protection," said Hegarty.

"I'll see to that," cried Chadwick. "Get going."

Hegarty had just left the house when Reilly returned.

"Where's the whisky, damn it?" cried Chadwick.

"He refused it," said Reilly. "Not only that, but he threatened to take action unless you pay him what you owe. He's a changed man, the same Johnny Hynes, since his son went into Rabbit's house."

"He said that," cried Chadwick. He sat down, covered his face with his hands, sighed heavily and then added in a tired voice: "Dash off, Reilly. Get some whisky no matter how. I don't care where you get it, or how. But if you come back without, I'll run you through the body. Understand? Be quick."

Reilly was moving towards the door, when Chadwick recalled him.

"Have you got any of that damned stuff you drink yourself?" he cried.

"The poitheen, sir," said Reilly. "Is it that you mean?"

"Yes."

"I have a drop of it, but sure it nearly choked you the last time you tried it."

"Get it. I'm choking as it is."

Reilly went away and presently came back with a small jar. Chadwick put the jar to his head and swallowed some of the spirit. He laughed loudly.

"That's better," he said. "Extraordinary how…Let me see. Where did I tell you to go?"

"Nowhere in particular, sir. You only said…"

"Never mind. Take the new carriage and the greys. Turn them out smartly. Give the carriage a good polishing. You scoundrel, you haven't cleaned it since I took it over to Colonel Bodkin's house. I saw a scratch on one of the spokes yesterday. I'll go into that later. Cut a dash into Clogher like a good man. We have to make an impression, damn it, now that our credit is touch and go. Go to Wallace's. I owe the old fellow a barrel of money, but I'll write him a note. Why should I? The greys should do the trick. Pull up before the shop with a flourish. You might come up at a gallop and a shout. Spin him a yarn, a legacy, anything. You've done it before. The rent, damn it. By God! It's going to be collected. How much do I owe you in wages, Reilly? Never mind. We'll go into that later. Strike the iron. This is all into my lap in the long run. Don't stand there like a fool. Hurry."

After Reilly had left, Chadwick finished the jar of poitheen and then went fowling with a pair of dogs on the mountain. He was in great spirits. When he returned to the house, Reilly was out on the lawn to meet him, waving his arms, obviously bringing good news.

"Did you get it?" Chadwick asked from a distance.

"I did and plenty, your honour," shouted Reilly. "Wait till you hear the news I have for you."

As Chadwick strode along to the house, Reilly ran beside him talking excitedly.

"Just as I was drawing up in front of Wallace's," he said, "I had them in a fair lather, sir, just as you told me, a proper gentleman stepped up and he says: 'Who owns that pair of greys?'"

"Who said this? What gentleman?"

"Wait till you hear. I answers him, telling him they were yours, and he says: 'Not Captain Chadwick of the – Hussars?' 'The same, sir,' says I.

"Who the devil was he?"

"A friend of yours, sir."

"What friend?"

"A gentleman by the name of Crampton, sir. He's consulting engineer for all the country around here."

"Not Jack Crampton of the…?"

"The same, sir. Begob, he was surprised when I told him who owned the greys. You could have knocked him down with a feather. 'Give my compliments to Captain Chadwick,' says he, 'and tell him I'll give myself the pleasure of calling on him to-morrow noon.'"

"Good Lord!" said Chadwick. "Engineer, you say. Nonsense. He married a barrel of money. The man retired years ago."

"He's not a proper engineer, sir," said Reilly. "Only the boss of the relief works."

"A hussar officer an engineer!" cried Chadwick. "Nonsense. Can't be the same. What does he look like? Fellow of about fifty? Large? Inclined to fat?"

"That's his picture, sir," said Reilly.

"Astounding," said Chadwick. "To-morrow at noon, did you say?"

"That's right, sir. He'll be inspecting the works here to-morrow. I think he has a wish for the greys. If you'd want to part with them, he'd pay you a good price. I asked a question or two and I heard he's throwing money about the town with both fists."

"God's blood!" Chadwick said. "We'll have to clean up a bit. Polish up the place. What? Send Mary Halloran here."

Like a man stranded on a desert island, he regarded the coming of Crampton as a delivery. Of late he had been cut by the county, he was terribly in debt and completely demoralised. He was now thinking of making an escape if he could only get enough money to do so. "They've discovered gold in California," he kept telling himself recently. And Crampton could easily save him. He was a wealthy man. So he made a great effort to receive his former fellow officer in a proper manner. The lawn was mowed and cleaned of its dung. The broken steps leading up to the hall door were partly mended and the door itself was made to open and shut properly. The lower part of the house was scoured and dusted. All the presentable furniture in the house was dragged into the living-room. Reilly was put into a lackey's suit and a lunch was prepared. Chadwick went out with his gun and provided some game, which he helped Mary Halloran to prepare. Then he anxiously waited for Crampton's appearance.

No Crampton came, however. By two o'clock lunch was spoiled and Chadwick began to lose his temper. He sent Hegarty into the village and along the road to the works, looking for the expected visitor. There was no sign of the consulting engineer. When Hegarty returned, Chadwick went into a rage and sat down to a bottle of whisky. When Crampton finally arrived towards nightfall, his host was quite drunk. Even so, their meeting was enthusiastic in the extreme.

"Tubs, old man," cried Chadwick, as they shook hands before the door. "Can it be true? God's blood! It's good to see you."

"Grouch, you old devil," cried Crampton. "You haven't changed a bit. More neck, perhaps. Well! Do you remember…?"

As they went arm in arm to the living-room, they kept halting and slapping one another on the back, as they recalled incidents during their association in the Hussars. They both talked in the same disjointed manner, their words popping out like champagne corks. They laughed uproariously. Crampton was exactly as Chadwick had described him to Reilly, an extremely fat man of fifty, powerfully built, with a baldish head of grey hair and merry blue eyes. There were deep, vertical creases in his ruddy cheeks. When he laughed, these creases looked like deep pits. He perspired heavily and his clothes were soiled, as he had been all day on horseback and the roads were in a foul condition.

"Table set," he cried on entering the living-room. "That's what I like to see entering a house. I could eat a camel, Grouch. Must be rather fun, pigging it in this wilderness. Not a word, old son, until I take the fine edge off my appetite. Yes. Perhaps a noggin of whisky would do the trick of warming me up a bit. Devil take your roads, Grouch. Pooh!"

Lunch was warmed and served as dinner. It was by now in rather a bad condition, but Crampton did not seem to mind. He was a glutton without any trace of palate. He devoured everything that was offered to him voraciously, making a loud noise with his mouth and scattering food all over the cloth.

"How the deuce did you become an engineer?" said Chadwick, when Crampton showed signs of having exhausted his appetite. "Didn't know you had talent of that sort."

"Matter of duty, Grouch, old man," said Crampton, with his mouth full of food. "Patriotism, you know, at a time like this. I was always a bit of a sentimentalist. Women and children starving, somebody has got to step into the breach, the call of humanity. We English, you know, are the world's sentimentalists. In any case, since the wife died…"

"Good Lord!" said Chadwick. "You hadn't told me…"

"So much to tell, Grouch," said Crampton. "Here you are, one might say, buried alive, it's impossible of course, pass the whisky…She's been dead three years now. Leaves one without…" He belched… "Strong stuff, that. One thing I can't stand in this part of the country is the amount…" He belched again. "This used to be a great claret country, I've been told. Poverty, I suppose. Don't you think so?"

Chadwick flushed. He had sobered somewhat and got into

a good temper on Crampton's arrival, but the man's lordly attitude aggravated him. They drew chairs to the fire and sat down with their glasses and their pipes. Chadwick made an effort and listened deferentially to Crampton's chatter. There seemed to be no end to the latter's energy. With his booted legs stretched out and the stem of his glass resting on his stomach, he began to enlarge on his duties as a consulting engineer, a job he had undertaken, Chadwick gathered, to employ his idle time. He had married a rich widow in the West Indian colonies. She had died in England, being unable to stand the climate and had left Crampton childless, with a large fortune. Although he knew nothing about engineering, he had volunteered for service on the relief works in Ireland.

"These works are damned interesting," he said. "If well conducted, which, unfortunately, is not the case, they might be the salvation of the country. There's a great deal of jobbery going on among these committees. Relatives of committee men are given preference. Then this idea of not giving work to anybody with stock is not good. The industrious man, who has saved a pound or two, is penalised. So, you see, they are emigrating; I mean the better class of peasant."

"I wish I could get rid of some of my peasants," said Chadwick. "This estate is littered with the wretches. Now the property has got to pay for them. Half the money for these schemes is levied on the proprietors. Major Thompson is going to be beggared if this continues. Hordes of useless officials. No offence, Tubs; I know you don't need the money, but what the devil is the point of all this waste of money on useless works?"

"You take a wrong view of it, Grouch," said Crampton, to whom the relief works seemed to be as exciting as a new toy. "Let me explain the system to you, and then perhaps…A sheet of paper, will you?"

Chadwick cursed under his breath as he went to fetch the paper. He had been dosing Crampton liberally with whisky, but the man seemed impervious to the effects of alcohol. Chadwick himself, who had been forced to keep pace, was now quite groggy again. Crampton began to make lines like a pedigree on the sheet of paper.

"The whole thing rather reminds one of military organisation," he said. "Here you have, at the top, the government inspector; he has the management of work tickets; jointly with the relief committee. Lists, you see, are drawn up; amount of property, if any, applicants possess; all very complicated and it needs a peculiar talent which, I'm afraid, our friend, Mr. Swan, does not possess. I've pulled him out of one or two messes already. The Irish hate anything straightforward. They obtain tickets under false names. You have to be as smart as they are. They respect that. So many of the beggars are called by the same name, too; so many Pat Murphys and Mike Kellys and God only knows how many Flannerys and Finnigans. Then again their faces look alike, with those long upper lips. What should be done – I've sent forward a memorandum – is to employ all indiscriminately. That would do away with jobbery."

"Who'd pay for it?" said Chadwick angrily.

Crampton raised his eyebrows and gave his host a look of grave surprise and disapproval. He held forward his glass.

"Could I have some more whisky?" he said, as if politely turning aside an awkward remark.

As Chadwick rose to open another quart, the consulting engineer continued.

"Another change I want to introduce," he said, " – I incorporated the suggestion in my memorandum – is task work instead of ordinary day labour by the hour. The difficulty is to find a sufficient number of persons capable of measuring work. You see, here we have a hill, just like this. Two gangs are placed at equal distances from the top of the hill. This curve represents our hill. The men are to cut away twenty yards forward and one yard deep at sixpence a yard, the road being ten yards wide. On one side the men might earn two shillings a day, or even two-and-sixpence, while on the other side, owing to differences of stratification…"

"Differences of what?" cried Chadwick furiously, as he poured whisky into Crampton's glass. "Look here, Tubs, don't mind my saying so, but all that is a bit of a bore."

"Thanks, Grouch," said Crampton, again raising his eyebrows. He sipped, and continued: "The fairest way is to adopt a scale of prices according to the material, as I have recommended in my memorandum."

"But where does it all lead to?" cried Chadwick, determined to bring Crampton down from his supercilious heights.

"How do you mean?" said Crampton, in an offensively gentle tone.

"This cutting down hills," spluttered Chadwick. "Why is it necessary? If these wretches are to be pampered on the landowners' and the ratepayers' money, why not make them do some useful work? That road to Clogher is now impassable."

Crampton smiled in a very superior manner, swallowed some whisky, and said:

"Upon my soul, Grouch, you haven't changed a bit. I remember that old temper of yours, a natural pessimist. Always think the worst of human nature. You fail to grasp the underlying genius of this system. It's like this. The idea is to introduce the skeleton of a really magnificent social organisation into this backward country. Let's take it from the bottom. First comes the ganger, chosen by the stewards and overseers, from the most intelligent of the workmen, getting sixpence an hour more for keeping the time of each gang. Then the stewards have charge of the work in their locality. Then the check clerks, nearly all schoolmasters, teachers of writing, and reduced sons of the gentry. They also keep time, to check that kept by the gangers. You have to have checks of that kind, to avoid fraud. The check sheets are re-checked and revised, if need be, by the overseers. Then, of course, there's my own personal staff of office clerks…"

"God Almighty! This army of clerks, gangers, overseers, and engineers, who are not engineers, all destroying our road at our own expense. Ha! Ha!"

He burst into a peal of angry laughter. Crampton, surprisingly enough, laughed also. Chadwick stopped laughing when Crampton started. The situation was becoming tense.

"Are you trying to make fun of me?" said Chadwick aggressively.

"Not at all," said Crampton, after emptying his glass. "Some more whisky, may I? On the contrary, I was amused at myself. I'm afraid I've been carried away. No point in explaining the intricacies of this thing to you, Grouch, who never had any administrative ability. That's not all of it. There are storekeepers, draftsmen, surveyors, and valuators, for all of whom I am responsible, as well as returning presents of game, even sacks of potatoes – precious things they are these days – sent as bribes. It would be too much for you, Grouch. Just to give you an example, to-day I had to arrange about pay. I made no mention of pay-clerks, but they are important. The pay-clerk has to provide sureties and he has to have an escort of two policemen. It's a strain on the constabulary, but the excellent fellows are standing up to it well, I must say. There is great confusion at the moment, though it's not my fault. I've been only ten days on the ground and I've done a lot, but there are not enough pay-clerks."

"What?" cried Chadwick insolently. "Not enough generals, after all?"

Crampton's blue eyes looked vicious for a moment. Then he smiled once more, leaned back in his chair, and laced his fat fingers around his glass, which he held high on his stomach like a chalice.

"Here at Crom, when I arrived this morning," he said, "the men were in an ugly mood. They had received no pay for over a fortnight. I told them they would be paid to-day, even if it had to be out of my own pocket. I then galloped away ten miles to another section and found a pay-clerk about to pay the men there. I addressed those men and told them about the plight of the Crom people. I was worried, Jocelyn, on account of the recent outrages here. Bad spot, I feel. I persuaded those other men to forgo half their wages, in order to help their brothers of Crom."

"Why the devil couldn't you get it out of the bank in Clogher?" said Chadwick. "You might have drawn the money out of your own account. It couldn't have been much. They only get a few pence a head."

"That would be irregular, my dear fellow," said Crampton coldly. "In any case, when I came back with the money, little as it was, these poor souls nearly kissed my hands. I feel that I can rely on their gratitude in future. Sorry for not having been able to come at noon, but you will understand that, under the circumstances, the call of humanity…"

Here Chadwick felt that there was no use waiting any further for an opportunity to say what he had in mind. The garrulous Crampton might go on talking all night.

"Look here, Tubs," he interrupted suddenly, "could you lend me two hundred pounds for a month or so?"

"I beg your pardon," said Crampton, sitting forward and cocking his head to one side like a deaf person.

"It's like this," began Chadwick nervously.

He hurriedly explained his position, his debts and the effort he had made recently "to meet long-standing commitments." What these were and what he had done to meet them, it would be difficult to imagine. He wanted to make a good impression on Crampton. The latter, however, had curled up, during the recital, like a threatened snail going into its shell.

"What salary do you get, may I ask?" he said when Chadwick had finished.

Chadwick did not like the impertinent tone in which the

question was asked, but he answered in a fairly polite way:

"Five hundred a year. The property is really worth over four thousand, but I can never manage to rake in more than two and a half, when everything is paid. Under the circumstances, it's as much as Mark can afford to allow me."

"Liberal, I should call it," said Crampton unctuously. "Then you have this house, thrown in free, I imagine, together with the demesne. Am I right? I thought so. How many acres? Must be considerable. Tillage land, I'm told. Good pasture, I dare say, into the bargain. Some timber. Bog for fuel."

"There's about two hundred acres all told," said Chadwick, "but the expense of servants, repairs, that sort of thing, amounts to more than the place...It's a bugbear, in fact. I expect, however..."

"Chadwick, my dear fellow," said Crampton, stretching out his legs a little further, "you should make a good thing out of all this land."

He had reached the stage of calling his former companion in arms by his surname. That was ominous.

"Tillage, you know," he continued, "with this cheap local labour and a ready market, is a paying thing. There are some crops, rye for instance, that parson of yours was telling me about it, clever fellow, a lot could be done with rye it seems. But I'm told you don't till."

He emphasised this last sentence and looked at Chadwick as if the latter were a felon of some kind.

"Where the hell have you heard all this?" shouted Chadwick, completely losing control of himself. "You seem to have done a lot of ferreting about in the village."

"Shouldn't use that word if I were you, Chadwick," said Crampton. "One can't help hearing things in a place like Clogger."

He deliberately mispronounced the name of our town, in order to show how remote his position in the civilised world was from that of Chadwick. Then he sipped his drink in silence, while Chadwick watched him with clenched fists. At last Chadwick could no longer endure the tension.

"Out with it!" he shouted. "Are you going to lend the money?"

"Pardon me," said Crampton in a surprised and hurt tone, "but do you think this bullying tone and this rather peculiar demand is in keeping with a host's obligations towards a guest? Eh?"

"Devil take you!" cried Chadwick between his teeth.

He strode to the far corner of the room, clasping and unclasping his hands behind his back.

"Tut, tut, my good man," said Crampton imperturbably.

"Don't you dare call me your good man!" shouted Chadwick, halting and turning towards his guest. "Who the devil do you think I am?"

"Tell you what I'll do with you," said Crampton. "I like those greys of yours. I wouldn't mind making an offer for them. What are they?"

"What's that?" said Chadwick, his mouth watering at once.

"I said I'd buy the greys," said Crampton.

"I'm not selling the greys," said Chadwick. "I'm attached to them."

However, he came back and sat down by the fire and he looked much more calm.

"As you please," said Crampton. "Only, it seems to me, if you find yourself in a tight corner, instead of borrowing, which is always a bad policy – all my life I've made it a rule never to borrow – a little sacrifice is often the best way out of a hole, and really, what are horses these days? A drug on the market, Grouch. A drug, absolutely. In London, of course, those greys would cut rather a figure."

"Best pair in the country. Have you seen them step? They'll do anything, Tubs. Hunt, race, jump, stay for ever. Damn it, Tubs, I couldn't sell them."

"Have it your own way, Grouch. Let's have another drink, shall we?"

By some miracle, they had again got on intimate and very friendly terms. They clinked glasses and toasted the greys. In fact, both of them were now very intoxicated, although Crampton showed no signs of it.

"Better spend the night here, Tubs," Chadwick said. "I'll go into Clogher with you in the morning. I think I'll let you have the greys after all, for the sake of old times. I really don't need a pair of horses of that class in this dreadful hole. It makes a bad impression, you know, in debt and cutting a dash with those greys into Clogher. We'll hitch the two saddle horses to the carriage. Damn it, Tubs, I wouldn't let anybody else have them but yourself, as I'm very attached to them, but I know you're partial to a good bit of horse-flesh, so I'll let you have them for a song. I won't ask a penny more than two hundred, with the carriage, brand-new, into the bargain."

"Two hundred!" cried Crampton, raising his hands in horror. He whistled. "Good Lord! man, do you call that a fair offer?"

"Tubs, you devil, don't tell me you've become a miser," cried Chadwick. "Man alive, that pair would fetch four hundred guineas in Dublin, not to mention the carriage. It's brand-new, I tell you."

"You've been reading fairy tales," said Crampton. "I couldn't go a penny beyond one hundred and fifty. Life in Clogher is expensive, you know, Grouch. That County Club is a nest of thieves. I dropped a packet at cards the other night."

"Oh! Damn it!" cried Chadwick. "I hate bargaining. Let's split the difference."

"I named my limit," Crampton said. "Not a penny more."

"Devil take it," Chadwick said. "You can have them."

CHAPTER XXIX

THE SALE OF his horses and his carriage did not benefit Chadwick from any point of view. In fact, he did not return to Crom House until he had spent every penny of it in foolish roystering and drunkenness, which ruined whatever shreds of his reputation were still left. Although he had been anxious to get the money principally to pay Hynes, just to prove to the doctor that "a gentleman has his code of honour," the thought of paying the debt never entered his mind while he had the money. And by the time it was spent, he was too ill as a result of drinking to bother about such a trivial matter.

The news that greeted him on his return alarmed him. Hegarty had received another beating while distributing demand notes in Glenaree. By now the fellow was so intimidated that he refused information to the police as to the identity of those who assaulted him. "They came on me from behind a wall," he said, "and struck me unconscious from behind." The truth was that they seized him in the middle of the hamlet of Bohercam, in broad daylight, practically the whole population of the hamlet, men and women, stripped him naked and lashed him with sally rods. Then they threatened to assassinate him if he informed the police. As a result of this beating he had distributed no more of the demand notes and waited for Chadwick's return.

"They're going to refuse to pay the rent," Hegarty said. "It's that weaver, Gleeson, has stirred them up. There's a physical force man that was going about, too, a man by the name of Rafferty from Clogher. The police have been searching for him this last week while you were away. The people say they'll pay nothing. Twenty families are gone to America now off the estate, taking every living thing they had. They were certain payers, too. I doubt if we'll collect anything, sir, out of Black Valley or Glenaree except by force."

"Force, eh?" said Chadwick. "I'll let them have it. I'll round up every cat, rat and louse on the estate. I'll show those beggars what I can do."

Next day he had a fresh notice put up all over the parish, under police protection, announcing that the property of any tenant refusing to meet the payment of his rent would be confiscated, by order of the court. The parson came to him after this notice had been posted.

"You can't possibly mean this, Mr. Chadwick," said the parson.

Mr. Coburn showed remarkable forbearance. The harsh treatment he had received at the hands of the people had not embittered him in the least.

"In the Lord's name," he continued, "I beg of you to hold your hand at this juncture. They have just sown their potatoes. They have nothing left to them but weeds and scraps. Any that have a few shillings will need these until the crops are ripe."

"Look here, Coburn," said Chadwick. "I've had enough of your meddling."

"Meddling?" said the parson.

"That's what I said," cried Chadwick. "Major Thompson does not maintain this estate as a charitable institution."

"But a landowner has his duties as well as his rights," said the parson. "That is the basis on which property is held. It is not a rude struggle between two hostile groups, like rival hordes of wild animals. When it becomes such, the fabric of society collapses in the hurricane of revolution, as we have seen it do recently in France."

"Ha! Ha!" roared Chadwick. "Jacobin in Holy Orders! You damn fool. Look here, Coburn, I've no time for your sermons. It's war to the knife, as far as I'm concerned, between me and these ruffians. If I had the power I'd shoot them like dogs. Have you no self-respect? They burned down your cottage and cut off your cow's tail. You should be ashamed of yourself."

"I'm a Christian minister," said the parson.

"A what?" said Chadwick. "How the devil is law and order going to be respected in this country if people like you go about undermining authority with such silly cant? Damned if I don't report you to the authorities."

"Do what you please," said the parson.

He went away muttering. That was the last effort he made to do his duty.

CHAPTER XXX

ON THE FOLLOWING Sunday – it was the first Sunday in May – an extraordinary thing happened. During Mass, Father Roche preached a violent sermon, warning the people against being influenced "by agitators and physical force men," saying that nothing but disaster would result from violent conduct and that they must "give unto Cæsar" what was Cæsar's; meaning that the rent should be paid. This sermon produced exactly the opposite effect of what had been intended. The congregation, feeling that their leader, their parish priest, in whom they had implicit confidence, who had assured them that the government would grant a moratorium this spring, had deserted them, were roused to a frenzy.

In any case, what happened afterwards must have been due to some sort of previous organisation and not altogether due to the priest's sermon. There was practically double the usual number of people at Mass that day. Only a fraction of the crowd was able to get into the church, or to hear the sermon. It was significant, also, that there were fewer women than usual and that nearly all the men carried sticks. Even so, I am certain that, apart from whispered propaganda by a few militant republicans from the town, no definite organisation had been established in the parish. It was a spontaneous movement on the part of the people; one of those silent and sudden movements of rebellion that spring from the earth itself. The peasant can endure tyranny longer than any other class of the community; but when the moment arrives for him to revolt, he needs no outside force to rouse him. His rebellion is instinctive.

All the adult males, therefore, of the parish had gathered that day at Mass in Crom. After Mass, they loafed about in the village, conversing in groups, until the priest had gone back to his house. Then, without word of command, they moved in a vast crowd towards Crom House, sweeping past the police barracks, where half a dozen police on patrol duty tried to stop them. Chief Constable Edwards reported afterwards that the number of demonstrators was over a thousand. That, of course, was a gross exaggeration, as the number of adult males in the parish came far short of that figure. Half that number would be nearer the truth.

At first they moved in silence, but when they came to the gate of Crom House and those in front turned into the demesne, wild shouts arose from the rear. Sticks were brandished and small groups began to sing revolutionary songs. It was at this point that Gleeson appeared with his pike, at the head of the column. Nobody knew whence he had come. He had not been seen at Mass. He just rushed out with his pike from some brushwood and halted before the crowd, his right hand drawing back his coat from his bosom.

"Bare your breasts to the bullets," he shouted, as he brandished his pike with his other hand. "Quick march. Long live Ireland."

A great shout rose from the crowd at these remarks. The shout was followed by complete silence, except for Gleeson, who marched now at the head of the column, his pike on his shoulder in military fashion, swinging his right arm and calling out the step like a sergeant.

"Left, right," he cried. "Left, right, left. Down with the tyrants."

The people did their best to fall into step with him. At the same time, it was noticeable that their enthusiasm diminished after his appearance. Those in front slackened pace and advanced only under pressure from those behind. In this manner they debouched on to the lawn and came in sight of the house. At sight of the house, a small portion of the crowd took to flight. Others called on them to stand fast, but even some of those took to flight on their own account. Nearly a hundred men took to their heels in this way and then stood hidden among the trees at a distance to see what would happen. The sight of the lord's residence brought to their minds the consciousness of their serfdom and the power of the ruling class. The remainder of the column advanced at a steady pace until the head reached the patch of gravel in front of the steps leading to the door.

At this moment the door opened and Chadwick appeared. Gleeson halted at once and brought his pike down from his shoulder to a position of attack.

"Present arms," he cried as he did so.

He was about to rush up the steps towards Chadwick, with his pike levelled, when Martin Kilmartin seized him by the arms and held him.

"Let me go," shouted Gleeson. "Let me get at him. I'll stick my pike through his guts. There stands the tyrant that ruined my daughter. I'll take vengeance off him. Let me go, I say."

Now it was clear to everybody that the man was out of his mind. Four other men came to Martin's assistance and they managed to disarm Gleeson. They dragged him into the centre of the crowd, where he kept shouting and struggling to break loose. Then he suddenly collapsed, sank to the ground and lay on his side, trembling. Tears rolled down his cheeks. He was a pitiable sight.

Chadwick, in the meantime, had stood in silence before the door, watching the scene with a smile of contempt on his blotched face. One hand was in his breeches pocket. With the other hand he rapped his boot with a hunting crop. Young Kilmartin now came forward after Gleeson had been quietened.

"No harm was meant to you, sir," said Martin. "We only came to make a statement about the rent. He wasn't with us atall. He's not right in his mind, sir."

Martin spoke respectfully, yet he did not take off his hat in salute. This gesture of revolt was instinctive. All the others remained hatted also.

"And what about the rent?" said Chadwick quietly, taking a pace forward.

Martin became confused. He looked behind him at the crowd, with a questioning look on his face. He suddenly became ashamed of standing there in front, as if he were the chosen leader of the people. But he saw something in the faces of the people which stirred him deeply. There was a fierce look in their eyes. The hands that grasped the sticks were clenched firmly. And then Chadwick spoke again.

"Speak up, you dog!" he shouted. "What do you mean by coming here?"

Martin swung towards Chadwick and his eyes blazed. He drew in a deep breath and cried in a loud voice, through his teeth:

"We'll pay no rent. We can't pay. We don't want to die of hunger."

A loud murmur came from the crowd. It passed from end to end of the mass like a gust of wind. Then there was silence once more, except for Gleeson who was now weeping aloud, hysterically, as he lay on the ground. Chadwick looked all round, with his head thrust forward. Then he came down two steps, halted in front of Kilmartin and said, almost in a whisper:

"Off with your hat, you ruffian."

Martin stared him resolutely in the eyes and did not move. Chadwick then raised his voice and cried:

"Do you hear me? Uncover, I say."

Martin swelled out his chest and his eyes enlarged. Then they almost closed. He clenched his fists by his side. Chadwick began to tremble slightly.

"So you refuse to uncover?" he shouted.

He seemed on the point of raising his crop to strike Martin, when another man from the crowd came forward, a large man wearing a chimney-pot hat. This man cried:

"We couldn't pay without selling our stock, your honour, and that would be black ruin for us. If you could spare us until the bad times are over…In the autumn, maybe, we could pay."

"Don't you worry about your stock," cried Chadwick. "I'll sell it for you. You ruffians! You came here to intimidate me, did you? Get out of here, or I'll horse-whip the damn lot of you. And you may rest assured that the rent is going to be collected, every penny of it. Get off my property."

Then the big man in the chimney-pot hat cried out:

"Down on your knees, lads. Let's ask him once more on our knees."

Gripping his stick with both hands, he got on one knee, but did not uncover. First one, then another, then the whole crowd imitated his gesture. There they all knelt looking up towards Chadwick in silence, an expression of fierce hatred in their eyes. Chadwick was astonished and he drew back slightly. He had never seen anything like this. It enraged him still further. The big man, who had spoken before, now cried out:

"From our knees, we're asking you, in the name of God, not to take the rent till autumn."

"Clear out," bellowed Chadwick. "Get out."

Now he raised his crop and threatened the crowd with it. They began to rise from their knees. Then he looked at Kilmartin, who had not gone on his knee or made any movement at all. He took a pace forward and said:

"Take this, you ruffian."

He struck Martin with the crop. Martin jumped aside, struck at the crop with his blackthorn stick and then closed with Chadwick. The latter managed to get his left hand on Martin's throat. He threw back Martin's head, raised his crop once more and struck. The heavy crop cut into Martin's back.

"You son of a bitch," hissed Chadwick.

He had thrust Martin backwards with his left hand, as he struck with his right. Martin staggered and then, with an oath, he rushed at Chadwick, his hands held out like claws. He leaped into the air, seized Chadwick's face in his hands and brought his knees into Chadwick's stomach. With a grunt, Chadwick went down. Martin held on to him. The crowd closed in on them, as they rolled over and over on the ground. The great number of men that attacked him probably saved Chadwick's life at that moment. All the sticks that were raised and the press of bodies that lunged forward made it impossible for any single person to get at him.

Then somebody shouted:

"Don't kill him. Take him to the rent office and we'll make him sign receipts for the rent. To the rent office with him."

A wild shout greeted this suggestion. Martin was torn away from the prostrate Chadwick, who was hoisted to his feet, firmly held by four men. Other men held Martin, who was now fighting mad. Chadwick's face was bleeding and his clothes were torn almost to shreds. He had been struck heavily with sticks all over the body. He was, however, by no means cowed.

"I'll see you in Hell," he cried, "before I sign any receipts."

"We'll see, faith," they cried. "Off with him, boys."

And they began to drag him along with them, striking him with their sticks. Suddenly the police appeared, coming at a run, in extended formation, from the direction of the barracks. Chief Constable Edwards was at the head of them. There were about forty of them there, all with carbines.

"The peelers!" shouted the crowd. "God save us!"

Those on the outskirts began to run at once. Had the police advanced quietly, the whole crowd would have undoubtedly fled. However, as those who took to flight had to do so in the direction of the police, in order to regain their village, the police got nervous and fired their carbines in the air, in order to ward off what they supposed to be an attack. This terrified the people and drove back those who fled.

Then somebody yelled:

"Charge the tyrants. Forward in Erin's battle line."

It was Gleeson, who during the struggle with Chadwick had got to his feet and recovered his pike, become possessed by another access of frenzy. Holding his pike at the charge, he now rushed towards the line of police and transfixed a constable named McEllistrum in the right thigh with the weapon before anybody was aware of what had really happened. He was at once struck down by the butt of another constable's carbine, but his mad daring had in the meantime spurred the people to a similar effort. They rushed in on the police with their sticks. A fierce battle ensued, lasting for over twenty minutes, before the superior discipline of the police managed to put the crowd to flight. A score of men lay on the ground, including four policemen.

Martin was one of the last to abandon the struggle. When he did at last turn to save himself from capture he tried to drag the unconscious Gleeson with him. He had not gone far when two policemen closed with him. He dropped Gleeson and gave them battle. Managing to capture one policeman's carbine, he struck out fiercely with the butt and wounded the second man seriously in the head. Then he fled with his captured carbine to a clump of bushes. He was just disappearing among the bushes when somebody fired a pistol after him. The ball lodged in his arm, forcing him to drop the carbine. He staggered, but made a great effort and continued his flight.

Then the police took Gleeson and six other men with them to the barracks and lodged them in the black hole. Gleeson had by then recovered consciousness and asked for a drink of water. Instead of giving him a drink of water, they took him into another cell and beat him with their belts.

"Now, maybe, he won't be so quick again with his pike," one of them said, as the weaver became unconscious once more.

Then they locked the door and left him alone. When he awoke from his stupor it was pitch dark in the cell, except for a tiny streak of light that came in around the edges of the closed spy-hole. He struggled to his feet and groped his way to the spy-hole. Putting his lips to the crack, he began to call for water. The slide was pulled aside and one of the men who had beaten him put his face to the hole.

"What d'ye want, papish?" he said to Gleeson.

"Water," said Gleeson. "For the love of God, give me a drop of water."

The constable grinned and then walked over to a corner opposite the spy-hole. There was a water cock there, over a grating in the floor, where the police passed water. The constable turned on the cock and then began to pass water, grinning at Gleeson over his shoulder.

"How d'ye like that?" he said.

"Lord have mercy on me," Gleeson said.

CHAPTER XXXI

MARY HAD NOT gone to Mass, being now very near her confinement. Maggie had also stayed at home. Her legs had begun to swell recently and she no longer left the house. The old man had ridden over to Glenaree and attended Mass at the local chapel, as he wanted afterwards to examine a sick cow belonging to a relative. He was an authority on diseases of cattle. So the household knew nothing of the grave events in the village until Thomsy's return. He had marched into the demesne together with the people, but had been one of the first to take to his heels. Then he had climbed into a tree and watched everything that happened from a distance. When Martin got wounded, he passed close to the tree where Thomsy was hidden in his flight. It was then that Thomsy descended. He followed Martin for some distance up the mountain and then lost track of him. He descended to the lane that led up the valley and ran home as fast as he could.

"Martin is shot," he cried as soon as he entered the house, panting after his run. "Your father is taken, Mary, and Martin is shot. He's gone on his keeping up the mountain towards the north, and he wounded in the arm."

Mary was putting a bowl on the dressers when Thomsy began to speak. When he had finished, she fell down by the dressers on to the floor in a dead faint. Maggie rose from her seat by the hearth and went towards her, saying in a querulous tone:

"You bosthoon, you shouldn't have frightened her like that."

The old woman did not seem to realise the import of Thomsy's news. She and Thomsy took Mary into the bedroom and put her lying on her bed. They were bathing her forehead with cold water when Sally O'Hanlon arrived. She seemed disappointed at not being first with the news.

"I shouted at Thomsy," she said, "but he went past me without saying a word. 'Faith, Patsy wasn't far behind him. He's not as strong on his feet as he was, on account of the hard work on the roads. She got a weakness, did she, when she heard it? Small wonder, the poor creature, and she so near her time. You go down to the fire, Maggie. You're sick yourself. The few words were hardly out of Patsy's mouth when he fell down, just like herself there. Barney had a pike with him, Patsy said, so it will go hard with the poor man. Ha! She's opening her eyes. Mary, asthore, take it easy now, poor girl. We're all here with you."

Mary opened her eyes, looked at them and said:

"Where's Martin?"

"He's on the mountain," said Thomsy. "He got away. I saw him. He got away safe."

Mary fainted again. Sally began to moisten her forehead.

"Hope to God she didn't hurt herself with the fall," said Sally. "How near her time is she?"

At that moment the child leaped in the womb. Mary opened her eyes, gasped and then shrieked, as a violent pain struck her.

"Easy now, asthore," said Sally. "Thomsy, a mhic, come here to me."

She took Thomsy aside and whispered to him. He nodded and hurried from the house.

"She must have brought it on with the fall and the fright," Sally whispered to Maggie.

The latter suddenly seemed to realise what had happened. She began to shake at the middle. Her teeth chattered. She caught up the edge of her apron, stuffed it between her teeth and made her way down into the kitchen, where she flopped into the straw chair by the fire. As she shook, she made a noise through her teeth like the humming of a bee. The collie dog came into the kitchen at a trot, wagging his tail with his tongue hanging. At the same time a horse's hooves sounded in the distance and the old man's voice, saying: "Where's your hurry taking you, Thomsy?" "To Kate Hernon's," Thomsy answered. The dog gaped at Maggie for a few moments with his tongue hanging. Then he walked slowly towards her, sat on his haunches by her side and buried his snout under her arms. The old man entered.

"Huh!" he said, when he saw his wife.

He looked startled and his lips were pressed tight together. He had received news of what had happened from people who were running along the road to Glenaree. He went on tiptoe into Mary's bedroom. Mary shrieked again at that moment. Sally was tucking the clothes about her, after having undressed her.

"Where is Martin?" Mary cried, on seeing the old man. "Where is my treasure? What have they done to him?"

The old man went up to her and took her outstretched hand.

"Have courage, daughter," he said.

"He's hurt and I not near him," Mary cried. "Oh! Mother of God! Have pity on us. Go to him, old man, and help him. Find him on the mountain."

"I will, alannah," said the old man. "I'll go now. Take care of her, Sally."

Yet he stood there looking at Mary, with tears in his eyes, until Sally shouted at him:

"Why don't you go and find him? There's no damage done. If he's hurt, find the bonesetter. We'll do what's to be done. Go to Father Geelan. He's your best man. Go before the peelers come nosing around. They'll not let their prey escape them easily. Be off with you."

Brian hurried from the room.

"Oh! Sally, will he be dead?" Mary said. "Did I hurt him when I fell? Martin would never forgive me."

"Prut!" Sally said. "What nonsense is this? Hurt who? How do you know it's a boy? Did anyone ever hear the like? Be quiet now. Kate Hernon'll be here in a minute. Whist! Here's somebody coming."

It was Mary's mother who came, followed almost at once by Patsy O'Hanlon. Several neighbours also came. The kitchen began to get crowded. News was brought that the police were already searching on the mountain and that they were questioning the old man, whom they stopped on the road. At last Kate Hernon came.

"God's blessing on all here," she cried on entering the house. "You have taken one, O Lord! Now let the unborn come forth without blemish to take the place of the lost one."

"Amen!" everybody said.

The hag then drew her shawl about her and swept into the bedroom. Mary crouched under the clothes in fear when she saw the old woman, but the latter approached the bed, muttering, and then spread out her hands before Mary's face, lowering them gradually while she muttered, until they touched the forehead of the young woman in travail. Mary felt unaccountably calm at the touch of the old woman's hands. The latter then passed hands over Mary's body.

"Close your eyes now, child," she whispered, "and give yourself into the power of the Blessed Virgin, the Holy Mother of God, and all will be well with you. Close your eyes now and let what is to come shine out in all the glory of this life. Close your eyes, daughter."

Sally whispered to Ellen Gleeson:

"Attend to whatever Kate wants. I have a plan to get help to Martin. The peelers won't notice a woman going the road. I'll be off now. Don't say a word."

CHAPTER XXXII

HALF WAY UP the valley, on the left, there was a deep ravine, which ran down between two mountains to the cabin where Kate Hernon lived. After Thomsy had sent the old woman over to Kilmartin's house, he climbed this ravine, until he reached a stone hut, where poitheen used to be distilled in the old times. It was inaccessible, except by the ravine that led up from the Valley. There was a goat path leading north, over the mountains towards the County Mayo. Furthermore, it commanded a view of the Valley southwards, to where the road turned towards Crom. As he had expected, he found Martin hiding there, lying on a bed of ferns within the door. A young man from Glenaree, named Fahey, was there also.

"God love you!" cried Thomsy as he knelt beside Martin. "Are you dead or alive?"

"I'm alright," Martin said. "Did you tell them at home?"

Thomsy nodded. The young man from Glenaree was tying a piece of Martin's shirt around the wounded arm. It had bled profusely and Martin was pale from loss of blood.

"Is the arm broke?" Thomsy said.

"It isn't," said Martin. "Only the ball is inside. I was bleeding like a pig all the way, as I could only put a poor knot on the wound and I hurrying. Is there any sign of the peelers?"

Thomsy said that there was not, so far.

"But they are sure to be up looking for you," he said. "You had better go on up farther towards the County Mayo."

"If I could only get the ball out of my arm," Martin said. "It's hurting something terrible. Ugh! Be easy there, Mattie."

"Quiet, man," Fahey said. "I have to pull it tight, so it will stop the blood."

"Is Mary all right?" said Martin.

"I just sent Kate Hernon down to her," Thomsy muttered. "It's on her."

"What's that you're saying?" cried Martin, sitting up and dragging his arm away from Fahey. "Has her time come?"

"I think it has, in God's name," said Thomsy.

"Why didn't you tell me?" cried Martin, getting to his feet at once.

"Where are you going in the state you're in?" cried Thomsy. "The peelers'll be in the Valley at any minute now. Stay here, man, until we get the bonesetter or the doctor to you."

"What do I care about peelers and she in that state?" cried Martin. "Out of my way, will ye?"

He tore out of the hut in spite of their efforts to stop him and he began to run down the ravine. At that moment, Thomsy, peering towards Kilmartin's house, saw the old man being stopped by three policemen. He shouted at Martin.

"Stop, Martin. The peelers. Look at them, arresting your father over there. Look. They're pointing their carbines at him. Come back, asthore."

Martin halted, screened his eyes with his hand and looked.

"They are, 'faith. God's curse on them."

He climbed back towards the hut.

"I told you they'd be here," said Thomsy. "Take the advice of a fool now, the two of ye. Make off up the mountain towards the north. They'll not catch ye there. There are only three of them. Hide out somewhere until nightfall. I'll go back to the house and we'll manage somehow to get the doctor or the bonesetter up to this. Let ye be watching for a light in it. When ye see the light, come to it. Are ye agreed?"

Martin and Fahey said that was the best thing to do.

"Well! then," said Thomsy, "hurry off now, for they are likely to come this way. I'll make off back unknown to them along the side of the mountain. God bless ye."

The two of them hurried up the mountain path towards the north, crawling along among the heather, when they were in view of the Valley below, and running when they were hidden by rocks. They made off in the direction of the Black Lake. Thomsy lay on his belly and watched the policemen for a long time. He saw them take old Brian back to the house and enter with him. After about a quarter of an hour they came out again and proceeded up the Valley towards him. Several young men were now running up the Valley and climbing the mountain in the direction of the Black Lake. The policemen went into various houses and there was a great shouting of women along the road. The women were threatening the policemen, who became afraid and turned back when they had come half way up the Valley. They took nobody back with them as all the men had fled from the houses.

"It's safe now," said Thomsy. "They'll not come again until nightfall, the scoundrels."

He got to his feet and hurried down the ravine. It was now late in the afternoon and great black shadows had begun to form on the mountainsides.

Chapter XXXIII

MARY GAVE BIRTH to a son shortly after nightfall. It had come a little before its time, but it was strong and fully developed. Judging by the old man's behaviour, one would imagine that the infant boy was his own first born. He went about the house with his stick, his lips moving slightly, like a man about to impart happy news, but unable to utter the words owing to excess of emotion. His eyes glistened with tears of joy. He kept peering in at the bedroom door with a foolish grin on his face and made no protest when the women thumped him and sent him away. He seemed to take no interest in the fact that his son was wounded and hiding out on the mountain. Messengers kept coming and going, bringing news of Martin, to whom the doctor was being brought by Sally O'Hanlon, and to every bit of news the old man answered fiercely: "Huh! They'll know again it's dangerous to touch a son of mine. Huh! He gave them what was coming to them." Like an old war horse, he seemed to have regained his youth through the wild happenings of the day.

Nor did Mary seem to be aware of what had happened to her husband after she had been delivered of the child. The miracle of life, which she had created within her body and which now lay beside her in its swaddling clothes uttering its first cries, shut out all consciousness of the rest of the world. She devoured with her eyes the tiny face and the tiny fists, clenched as if for battle. It was not until the doctor arrived, a little before midnight, that she became aware once more of what had happened. The doctor, however, brought good news. He had extracted the ball from Martin's arm and the wound was not serious. Furthermore, he was going to hide Martin in the village until his wound was healed.

"You needn't worry, Mary," he said. "Father Geelan and myself will see to it that he's well cared for. I know a place to hide him. The last place they would look for him is in the village, right under the noses of the police. And I'll be around often to bring you news of him."

"Oh! God bless you, sir," Mary said. "Do you think he could come and have a look at his son?"

"It's not safe now," said the doctor. "The police are searching everywhere. The important thing is to get him cured first. Don't worry and leave it to me."

"God only knows why you are doing all this," said Mary. "But may God bless you for it."

"It's the least I could do," said the doctor seriously. "We all have to do our share. Everybody that's on the side of the people has his duty to do. It's us against the tyrants. The people against the government. I'm one of the people. That's all. Don't thank me. I wish I had your husband's courage."

"God bless you for those words," said Mary, reaching out for his hand and kissing it. "It's the people against the tyrants. And it's proud I am that my Martin has the courage to fight for the people's rights. I'll sleep in peace now, sir, after those words you said."

"So will I," said the doctor, "I have more peace of mind after talking to you. I thought you had a grudge against me on account of...on account of your sister."

"Indeed, no, sir," Mary said. "I have no grudge against you. And what you are doing now would wipe out all grudges that ever were."

The doctor left the house in an exalted state of mind. "This new life," as he called it in his own mind, which he had learned to live under the influence of Father Geelan, had made him very happy. He was experiencing, as he went home, the ecstasy of a zealot. And when Chief Constable Edwards called on him in the morning and warned him that, if he were called on to attend Kilmartin, who was known to be wounded, he was bound by law to notify the police, the doctor just shrugged his shoulders.

"I'm warning you," Edwards said, "that the district is going to be proclaimed."

"That's none of my business," said the doctor. "I have my duties to perform. Law or no law, I'll perform them to the best of my abilities."

The district was proclaimed, on application being made to the Lord Lieutenant by the local authorities. There had been disturbances on other estates, as well as on that of Major Thompson, and in the town there had been continual acts of violence recently, principally attacks on baker's shops. The people were commanded to stay indoors between sunset and sunrise. Even those who had no houses were compelled to hide in some hole. Rewards to informers and compensation to relatives of injured persons were included in this new ordinance. The penalty for breach of the curfew law was to be fifteen years penal servitude. The Royal Irish Constabulary, which had been raised at this time to twelve thousand men, fully armed and trained as part of the Regular Army, were placed on a war footing in the proclaimed district. Independent of night patrols, they were posted by day on hills commanding the houses of persons supposed to be disaffected. They were "to hang about ditches, plantations and above all to make domiciliary visits, always taking their telescopes with them on day patrol and rockets at night." In a word, the unfortunate people of Crom parish were treated as if they were in a state of criminal and armed insurrection, instead of their being on the point of destruction by famine.

The weaver was liable under another law, the Disarming Act, to penal servitude for seven years. In accordance with this Act, no person could have arms of any sort without a legal certificate, after which they were branded and registered by the police. To have a pike or a spear, or any weapon resembling a pike or a spear, was punishable by transportation to a penal settlement for seven years. All told, there were ten charges brought against him, including sedition, conspiracy, attempted murder and "assaulting and wounding a servant of Her Majesty in the discharge of his duties." If convicted on all counts, he was liable to serve one hundred and twenty years' penal servitude. The government made it known at once that he was going to be convicted. They decided to make an example of the poor man. All attempts to procure bail for him, or for the other twenty men arrested with him, failed utterly. He was lodged with them in the county jail to be tried at the Great Sessions.

His wild conduct made him a public hero. Within a few days, people were singing a ballad on the streets of Clogher, entitled "The Bould Barney Gleeson." And in spite of government terrorism, or because of it, the spirit of rebellion increased among the peasants instead of diminishing. The night patrols of policemen were continually being stoned, and supporters of the government and anybody suspected of being an informer were subjected to every possible kind of annoyance. This roused the police to a savage degree. A large contingent of them remained, practically day and night, in Black Valley, searching houses, interrogating the inhabitants. It infuriated them not to be able to find any trace of Martin. They arrested Patrick Gleeson, but released him when he proved that he had not been in Crom on the day of the riot. Even so, after his release, he was beaten badly at night by two policemen who met him near his house. Terrified, he took to his keeping on the mountains. There was now a large group of young men from the parish on their keeping in the mountains north of the Valley. The police even made Mary get out of her bed four days after her confinement, so that they could prod the mattress with their bayonets. Then they lined the whole family, except Mary, against the wall of the house in the yard and questioned them for an hour as to Martin's whereabouts.

"We'll get him, dead or alive," said the sergeant, when he was going away.

That evening, Mrs. Gleeson came over to the house and announced that Patrick had left for the mountains. She was completely overwhelmed by the disasters that had befallen her. She sat in the corner of the hearth and wept aloud for her husband, whom she said they were going to hang. Then Thomsy turned on her:

"Arrah! What ails you, woman?" he cried. "Isn't Barney a notorious man? And that's more than some of us will ever have the courage to be. The only thing they can do to him, and McEllistrum only wounded in the thigh, is to send him out to Australia for life. Over there, he can comfort himself and boast to everybody about the mighty blow he had the courage to strike. Lord save us, in this land of woe, it is a great thing to be related to a man that had the courage to strike a blow. Even to throw a stone at a barrack window would be a gorgeous thing. And many a poor man that will have to die of hunger in a windy ditch would die the better of that flung stone. But ech!...Devil roast me! I'll never have that courage. It's boasting of your husband you should be, Ellen, instead of crying, and he a notorious hero."

"Enough of that nonsense," the old man said to Thomsy. "You're a fine person to be talking about fighting. Go on up on the mountain and have a look at the sheep. There are a lot of ruffians out now that might be up to stealing them."

"Ruffians, do you call them?" said Thomsy. "Men out on their keeping?"

"Be off with you," said the old man.

Thomsy went away and the old man went into Mary's bedroom, where Mrs. Gleeson was crying on the bed.

"She had better stay here with us," said the old man, "now that Paddy has left her. What sort of a man is he, to leave his mother like that?"

"Sure they beat him badly," Mary said.

"That's no excuse," said the old man. "Let her stay here with us."

"I'm afraid it's not long any of us'll be here, old man," said Mary. "I'm afraid it's the end for all of us. Mr. Chadwick'll take everything and we'll have only a roof over an empty hearth and my man lying wounded in a stranger's house."

"Pooh!" said the old man. "What talk is this? We have the cow, that'll be having a calf any day now, and the horse and the sheep."

"We had better steal away with them and sell them before he takes them," Mary said. "By scraping everything together, we could get as far as Liverpool."

"What's that?" said the old man, terrified by the suggestion of leaving the land. "You're sick, woman, and cowardly with your troubles. In your right mind, you wouldn't say such things. Leave the land, is it, at the first sign of trouble? Where else would you get land, or the riches that comes out of it? It's foolishness and a temptation of the devil to dream of leaving it. Taking the good times with the bad, there's no more peaceful life on this earth. It's the life that God ordained, tilling the earth with the sweat of the brow. To be master of your own plot of ground and of your own hearth. And making things grow, like a miracle, out of the cold earth. Tyrants come and go, but the landsman goes on for ever, reaping and sowing, for all the generations of time, like the coming and going of the year, from father to son. To Liverpool, is it, you'd be inclined to take me? Where I'd die and leave my bones, with the deep sea between them and this earth? Huh! No tyrant will drive me from this plot of ground. I'll die here and be damned to them all."

And he hurried out to the paddock to examine his cow, which was now fifteen days beyond her time and on the point of having a calf. He drove her before him gently, admiring her distended black belly and her taut udder.

"What's keeping you, little hag," he said to her reprovingly, as he scratched her forehead. "Is it laziness or devilment is the matter with you? Answer me."

The cow drew away her forehead, lashed her jaws with her tongue and began to chew grass, as if to say that it was none of his business when she decided to drop her calf.

The old man, deeply superstitious, was disturbed by this movement. He kept getting up all night and going out to the paddock to examine her, fearing that something occult was afoot. There was none. However, shortly before dawn, he was startled by something far more sinister than the occult powers.

It was Chadwick and his men marching up the Valley.

Chapter XXXIV

CHADWICK HAD HAD no difficulty in getting an order of seizure and ejectment from the assistant barrister at Sessions, who made a decree, under the Ejectment Act of 1815, against all Major Thompson's tenants whose rent was under twenty pounds and who failed to meet their demand notes. The law was made so convenient for the landowners, that Mr. Chadwick's word sufficed to procure the decree. Forthwith, he had hired a gang of ruffians in Clogher, procured a large force of armed police and marched into Black Valley on horseback, accompanied by his bailiff, also mounted. I must remark at this point that Colonel Bodkin did everything in his power to dissuade Chadwick from this course, but Chadwick told the colonel to "go to Hell." Whereupon, the colonel said he was no better than a common ruffian and the two of them would have come to blows on the road from Clogher if they had not been prevented by some people who happened to be present at the altercation.

Chadwick divided his forces at the mouth of the Valley, sending one part into Glenaree, to prevent the inhabitants hiding their stock while he was engaged in Black Valley. Then he marched his men quickly up the Valley, planting sentries at various points, intending to begin operations among the sheep men at the far end. In spite of the early hour and the speed with which he moved, the people were warned of his approach by the barking of dogs. When he arrived at the hamlet of the sheep men, there was not a soul there other than women and children. All the males had fled into the mountains, to drive their sheep away to safety among the northern regions. They had often outwitted the landlord's men in this way; but Chadwick had no intention of being outwitted.

Halting before the first cabin in the hamlet, which happened to be that of Halloran, the man whom Patch Hernon had struck with a stone, he asked for the tenant.

"He's not in, sir," said Halloran's wife, who stood before the door with a child in her arms.

"Where is he?" said Chadwick.

The woman remained silent.

"What have they got?" said Chadwick to Hegarty.

"Five sheep, eight lambs and a goat with two kids," said the bailiff. "They had an ass, too, but he died on them this winter."

"They're lost, sir," said the woman in a sing-song voice. "The sheep and the goat are lost on the mountain. Himself is out to look for them. We have nothing else atall, sir. The praties rotted on us. We hadn't enough for the sowing, not to mind pigs."

"Can you produce those animals or not?" cried Chadwick.

"Sure, we have no animals," said the woman, "only the sheep and the goat that are lost on the mountain. I have five children, sir."

"You may keep the children," said Chadwick. "As you owe me some rent and you have nothing to pay it with, I'm going to evict you. Get your personal belongings out of this hut. Get going."

When the horrified woman realised that she was going to be evicted and that the rowdies with crowbars were advancing to demolish her hut, she uttered a wild shriek and threw herself at Chadwick's feet. The child began to wail. Chadwick moved away from her and shouted:

"Come along, you men. Make a quick job of it."

Another woman standing in a yard near by cried out:

"God have mercy on us! We're going to be evicted."

"Every blasted one of you," said Chadwick, "unless you produce those sheep."

As the rowdies began to batter down the walls of

Halloran's hut with their crowbars, the women of the hamlet gathered together in a distant yard and began to whisper. Chadwick smiled as he watched them and whispered to Hegarty:

"You just watch, Hegarty. I bet those sheep will appear in no time."

He was right. The women presently began to call out to their men on the mountain, uttering their peculiar mountain cry:

"Hooyah! Hooyah! Hooyah!"

Men appeared on the crags above. The women then changed their cry to a long-drawn wail, which resembled the bleating of sheep. They rocked themselves and scattered stones about the yard from the fences, to indicate that Chadwick was threatening to evict them. The men answered with a wild shout and then their voices could be heard calling their sheep up above.

"Chowen! Chowen! Chowen!"

The cry re-echoed through the mountain caverns.

"Hold your hand, sir," said Hegarty, running up to Chadwick. "They're going to bring the sheep."

"Carry on, men," said Chadwick to the rowdies, who had paused at Hegarty's words. "Down with the hovel. Swing those bars. I'll show those ruffians they can't fool me."

"Ma-ah!" came the bleating of sheep from the mountains.

A cry of horror rose from the assembled women as the doorway and a large part of the front wall of the cabin came down in a heap. The thatch sank in the middle. Then the chimney wall crumbled up and fell. Mrs. Halloran, foolish with misery, gathered her five children about her in the yard beside the miserable bed that had been thrown out. She tried to cover the children with a ragged blanket.

"Who owns that hovel in the next yard?" said Chadwick.

"Patch Hernon, sir," said Hegarty. "There's no one living in it. That share of land is idle."

"Down with it in any case," said Chadwick. "I'll clean out the vermin. Swing those bars."

As they attacked Patch Hernon's cabin, Halloran arrived on the scene, driving his sheep, his lambs and his goat with her kids.

"Take them, sir," he said to Chadwick. "It is how I went up to find them."

He was perspiring and panting on account of his haste in running back with his flock. But when he looked around and saw his wife, his children and his wrecked hut, he cried out:

"The curse of God light on you, your honour."

"Ha!" said Chadwick, coming at him with his riding crop. He was still on horseback. "So you want God to curse me, do you? Take that." He brought the crop violently down on Halloran's shoulder. "Now call on God, will you?" He struck again, sending Halloran to the ground. "God doesn't know ruffians like you, do you hear? How dare you call on God?"

He was in a wild rage. Standing up in the stirrups, he ordered Hegarty to drive away the sheep and the goat. Then he shouted:

"I'll teach them to hide their animals. I'll teach them to come to my house and try to murder me."

Halloran got to his feet, took off his hat and crossed himself.

"God's will be done," he said.

Now there was silence, except for the bleating of the goats and sheep and the pounding of the crowbars. Hernon's cabin began to fall. One by one, the other inhabitants of the hamlet came up and offered their stock. Hegarty went about checking the numbers with those he had in his book.

"Are they all there?" said Chadwick when Hegarty had finished.

"They are all here," said Hegarty, "except those that were ate."

"Very well, then," said Chadwick. "Mark them. Get going."

All the animals were now herded into one yard. A pail of tar was heated. Then the landlord's cross was put on each animal's side by Hegarty. The Halloran family was driven out on to the road in the meantime. The man carried his bedding on his back. His wife carried the cooking utensils and one of the children, who was too young to walk. The people stood apart in a group, whispering blessings on the departing family. When the Hallorans were a short distance up the road, both man and wife burst into a loud wail.

"All ready now, sir," said Hegarty. "They're all marked."

"Drive them," said Chadwick.

Driving the captured animals before them, they ransacked every holding southwards along the road, until they came to Kate Hernon's cabin, at the mouth of the ravine. The hag was standing in her doorway, holding a long staff. Her cabin had only one room. The remains of another room were attached to the gable end of the chimney. The tenant had been evicted and that room demolished. The gable end was still yellow and black, from the stains of the destroyed hearth fire.

"Who is that hag?" said Chadwick to Hegarty. "Does she owe anything?"

" 'Faith, then, she does owe for the house," said Hegarty, "but it's never collected off her, for she's a witch of a woman."

"A witch, eh?" said Chadwick. "Ha! We'll see. Down with that hut, you fellows."

As the rowdies advanced with their crowbars, the hag came out in front of her cabin and began to chant, with the staff raised over her head.

"You there on your horse," she cried, "the curse of Cromwell is written on your forehead. The ring for the rope is cut around your throat, but it's no rope will hang you. I see hands on your throat and the black-handled knife of vengeance stuck in your side. Your black blood is going to flow in the darkness of the night."

Then she spat and began to dance in front of the rowdies,

who halted before her in terror. Her fame was widespread. As superstitious as the rest, they did not want to bring her curses down on them. Furthermore, Chadwick himself was intimidated and he had put his hand to his throat and pulled at his muffler when she had referred to the ring. But he refused to show his feelings.

"Get on with it," he yelled at the rowdies. "Kick that old woman out of your way. I can't have useless vermin like this cluttering this estate. Look sharp."

The rowdies, more afraid of him than they were of the hag, swept past her and began to attack the hut. She screamed curses at them, but presently she dashed into the hut and began to collect her things. When she had done so, they quickly demolished the wretched building. The hag was now on her knees, casting spells on Chadwick. The latter affected to laugh at her, but he looked rather nervous as he rode away and he kept pulling at his muffler.

The morning was well advanced when he reached Kilmartin's house. The old man, Thomsy, Maggie and Mrs. Gleeson were gathered in the yard outside. The yearling calf was there also. When Chadwick rode into the yard on his black gelding, the old man swept off his hat, made a curtsey and pointed to the calf.

"There he is, sir," he said humbly. "It's the first time in my life I was behind with the rent, but the crop failed, sir, and my son died as well on me and…"

"Speak when you're asked to speak," Chadwick interrupted, thrusting his horse forward, so that Brian had to jump out of the way. "Is this the father of the ruffian who tried to murder me, Hegarty? Eh? What has he got here?"

As Hegarty read out the list of the animals in Kilmartin's possession, Brian drew himself up stiffly and the subservient expression of his face changed to one of savage defiance.

"Why haven't they got any lambs?" said Chadwick when Hegarty had finished.

"They sold them a while ago, sir," said Hegarty.

"We had no potatoes left after the sowing," cried the old man, "and there was nothing in the house after the funeral."

"Shut up," cried Chadwick. "Round everything up and mark it."

"For the love of God, sir," cried Maggie, "you're not going to take the cow that's just after having a calf?"

"You just wait and see," said Chadwick. "Come on. Round them all up."

The cow had, indeed, chosen that morning to give birth to her calf, while Chadwick was plundering the head of the Valley. Maggie threw her apron over her head and went into hysterics. The old man took her gently by the shoulders and led her indoors. Then he came out and ordered the two others indoors. When they had entered the house, he closed the door and barred it. Mary had come down from her bedroom, half dressed.

"What's happening?" she said to the old man.

Brian stood with his back to the door, staring fiercely in front of him.

"He's taking everything," he said.

"The cow, too?" said Mary.

"Everything," said Brian.

He seemed to be dazed and helpless.

"But he can't," said Mary. "He can't take the cow, and it was the only thing we have to…"

Suddenly she went hurriedly into the bedroom, snatched the infant from its cradle and returned with it.

"Open that door," she said fiercely.

The old man looked at her and shook his head.

"Go back to bed," he said quietly. "It's no use, Mary. You'll only put us all to shame, begging mercy from that heart of stone. Go back to bed for fear you'd catch cold and sour the milk in your breasts. It's all the child has left now."

Mary bowed her head and went back to her bedroom

shivering. She put the infant in his cradle and then looked out the window. The cow and her tiny calf, which was just barely able to stand, were now in the yard. The cow was still suffering from her birth pangs and she lowed savagely, terrified by all these strange people.

"Put the cross on her," said Chadwick.

When Hegarty approached with the pail of tar, the animal snorted and ran away to the far corner of the yard. The calf tried to follow her and fell. He uttered a little cry. The mother ran back to him. Then several men closed with her and held her. Hegarty put the cross on her side, over a white patch near her left hip. Then they collected the other animals and prepared to drive away.

"What about the calf?" said Hegarty. "It's not able to walk."

"Leave it," said Chadwick.

They drove away. Then the old man opened the door and came out into the yard, where the little calf was uttering plaintive cries. Mary, watching through the window, saw the old man take out his knife, open it, and wipe the blade on his trousers. She put her hands to her eyes and turned away.

CHAPTER XXXV

MARY WAS LYING in bed, half asleep, when she heard a light tap at the window. Immediately she became fully awake and her heart began to beat loudly. Was it the police? Night and day they had been making sudden raids on the house. Then she realised that the police would hammer on the door brutally and request admission in the Queen's name. It must be Martin. She leaped out of bed at once and ran to the window in her shift. She pulled aside the cover and saw him outside, distinct in the moonlight, his face wild and pale, his arm in a sling. He put a finger to his lips warning her to keep silent. She nodded and ran into the kitchen, where she opened the door. Martin entered on tiptoe and took her in his arms silently. The dog was with him, licking his legs and capering about in an ecstasy of joy. The dog was always left outside since the police searches began, to give warning of their approach. The clever animal had made no sound after Martin had whistled to him in a certain way, when he approached.

"Let's go into the room," Martin whispered, after they had embraced. "I don't want to wake mother. She might begin to cry and I couldn't bear that."

They went into the room and sat down on the window-sill, where they could see one another in the moonlight, after Mary had put a covering over her shift.

"Isn't it dangerous?" Mary whispered. "Oh! Martin, darling! Oh! My dear treasure!"

"It's not dangerous," said Martin. "I have three men watching. Stop crying, Mary. I haven't much time and I have a lot to say. Could I see him?"

"God forgive me," said Mary. "I forgot that you haven't seen him. Whist! I'll take him over to the window."

Snuffling and wiping her eyes, she went to the cradle by the bed and took the sleeping infant carefully in her arms. She brought him over to the window, where Martin gloated over the little face that peeped from the clothes. He trembled as he reached out to take the bundle in his arms. Neither of them spoke for a while, but Mary was weeping silently and she put her hands all over Martin's face and then down the back of his head and along his back, as if to make sure that he was real.

"I'm glad you gave him the name of Michael," Martin whispered. "It's a lovely name. Isn't he small?"

"He's not small," Mary said, "only he was a little before his time. It's the fright I got. Oh! Look at the way you're holding him. Give him here. He'll catch cold."

She grabbed the infant and rushed back to the cradle with him and tucked him under the clothes once more. Then they returned to the window-sill and sat down. Martin put his arms around her and she leaned her head on his bosom and wept quietly. Martin trembled and could say nothing. A marsh bird was squeaking in the distance. Then Mary raised her head and looked at him wildly.

"Did you leave the place they had you hid?" she said. "Why did you?"

"I did," Martin said.

He found it difficult to speak and he looked at her wildly. It seemed to Mary that his face had changed completely and that she hardly recognised him. His eyes were so fierce and hard. He looked older. He had lost the genial, reckless gaiety of youth.

"But why did you?" Mary said. "Your arm is not right yet."

"It's nearly alright," Martin said. "Don't ask me why."

"But they're still looking for you," Mary said. "You couldn't…"

"I'm not going to stay here," Martin said. "I have men with me. I'm going on the mountain. So he took everything?"

Mary's eyes wandered all over his face. She was not crying now. Her eyes had also got hard.

"I know what's in your mind," she said. "For God's sake, Martin, think of little Michael. Don't, Martin."

"Don't what?" Martin said gruffly.

Mary clutched at him and pressed him close to her.

"If we could only escape, the three of us."

"Don't you be afraid, Mary," he said. "We'll escape alright. I have it all planned out."

"What have you planned?" she said.

"Don't ask me, darling," Martin said. "I'm with men. Have you anything atall left now?"

"There's eighteen shillings still in the purse," she said. "You better take that."

"Arrah! What are you saying?" he cried. "I have men with me. We'll feed ourselves. I'll not see you in need either. They can't take us. How are the potatoes looking?"

"They are looking well," she said. "The loss of the cow is a terrible blow. Your father has hardly spoken a word for the last eight days since she was taken. My mother was here with me since Patrick left her, but she went back again. She couldn't stand it here. Old Kate Hernon is staying over at the house with her. But what men are you talking about, Martin?"

"Don't ask me any questions, Mary," he said. "There are a few things I want. I won't be far. There'll be men watching over you. Have no fear."

Suddenly he took her in his arms and kissed her hungrily, murmuring endearments in a broken voice. Then she wept freely in his arms. The infant began to whimper. They both ran to the cradle and rocked it, holding hands beside it and looking at one another. Then they suddenly became shy of one another and Martin said:

"There are a few things I want."

She got the things he named and rolled them in a bundle for him. She also offered him a piece of oaten bread, which he refused.

"We'll have plenty," he said.

Suddenly they heard a long-drawn cry, like the call of a curlew.

"It's them," Martin said. "I must be going, Mary. I'll come again soon, darling. Have no fear. I won't be far. Tell father I came, but don't tell the old woman. God look down on you."

After another embrace, he rushed from the house. Mary bolted the door and then stood looking out the bedroom window. She saw him disappear with another man up the mountain. Then a loud cry broke the silence of the night.

"Halt!"

She listened. There was the explosion of a carbine being fired. It was followed almost at once by another explosion. Then she saw policemen running. She trembled. A yell of defiance from the mountain rang out and then re-echoed. It was repeated several times and then there was silence. The old man came into the kitchen and said:

"Was that firing, Mary?"

"It's only the police," Mary said. "Go back to bed. They'll not come to-night."

She drew the covering over the window and went back to bed. Her heart was beating wildly. What did he have in his mind? His eyes were so strange and he had kept repeating that he had men with him on the mountain. She could not sleep a wink until morning. Indeed she had hardly slept since the child was born, for more than an hour at a time. Although her senses were numbed and she could not feel anything very acutely, there was a dull ache at the back of her consciousness, which prevented her being able to sleep.

"What is going to happen?"

This question repeated itself endlessly in her mind. In the morning, the old man looked at her angrily and said:

"Was Martin here?"

"He was," she said. "He told me to tell you, but not to tell Maggie."

He looked at her angrily once more and left the house without a word. Everything was strange now. Everybody had changed. Even Thomsy joked no more. What was going to happen?

All the morning the police were very active in the Valley. They had got reserves from Clogher and about fifty of them combed the slopes to the east, in the region of the ravine, but they came down again in the afternoon without achieving anything. They marched back to Crom. Shortly after they had gone, Mary was knitting in the yard, while she rocked the cradle with her foot, when she heard a voice calling her from the fence. It was a boy of about fifteen whom she did not recognise.

"What do you want?" she shouted at him.

He took off his cap, glanced up and down the lane nervously and beckoned to her. Thinking that it might be a message from Martin, she went over to the fence.

"I was told to give you this," said the boy, taking a note from the inside of his cap.

"Who owns you?" Mary said as she took the note.

"Barney Reilly is my name," said the lad, already moving away.

Mary reached out and caught him by the shoulder.

"Let me go," he said. "I don't want to be seen here."

"Are you related to Reilly, the groom?" she said.

"He's my uncle," said the lad.

"Then take this," cried Mary, throwing the note at him. "Be off with you."

"I was told to leave it with you," wailed the lad. "He'd kill me if I didn't. Take it."

He threw the note at her over the fence and took to his heels. Mary shuddered as she looked at the note lying in the yard at her feet. Then she picked it up and hurried with it into the house. She sat down in the hearth corner and read it. "If you want to save your husband from the arm of the law," it said, "come this evening after nightfall to the summer-house in Crom demesne, down by the river. Keep this secret." It was unsigned, but she knew at once who had written it. She crushed it in her fist and threw it in the fire. The fire had gone low and the paper only smoked. She picked up the tongs and struck at it.

"Burn, you devil!" she cried, overcome by a frenzy.

"What's that?" Maggie called to her from the small bedroom.

Since the seizure of the stock, the old woman had refused to leave her bed. She had lost the desire to go on living and yet she had become exceedingly querulous.

"It's nothing," Mary said, "only the fire that's going out."

And then, although there was nothing to cook and the day was hot, she began to build a fire with the heap of sods that were stacked in the corner. After she had built the fire, she took away all the sods once more and went into Maggie's room.

"Could Mr. Chadwick do anything for Martin?" she said to the old woman.

Maggie's unshapely body was like a mound beneath the bed-clothes. The rings around her sunken grey eyes had grown darker. The down on her upper lip had got thicker, although the hair of her skull was falling out. She seemed to have a moustache. She made no answer to Mary's question.

"Oh! God!" Mary said, as she turned to leave the room.

"Did they come back from the garden yet?" said the old woman.

"God have mercy on us!" said Mary as she went out into the yard.

Now it seemed to her that the idiocy which had fallen on the old woman was the worst misfortune of all. There was nobody even to give her a hand with the child. Otherwise, she thought, she might be able to forage some food, or do something for Martin. What?

"Could he do something?" she said aloud.

She picked up the sleeping child from the cradle and hurried down towards the potato garden, where the old man and Thomsy were working. The baby opened his eyes and began to bawl lustily. She opened her bodice and thrust her breast towards his mouth as she continued on her way. On account of there being so little to eat, her milk was not plentiful enough for the child. Aware that the eighteen shillings left in the purse was all that stood between the whole family and starvation, she disliked breaking into it. There was now luxuriant grass in the little field where the cow used to graze. Her bare feet made pale tracks through the lush grass.

Brian and Thomsy stood up when she leaned over the fence of their garden and blessed their work.

"You, too," the old man said. "They look well. They're well above ground. God sends famine to remind us of our sins, but He sends plenty to show His goodness. There's riches in the earth for them that has patience with it."

He put his foot on the spade and came over to the fence. Thomsy continued to dig fresh clay from the bottom of the furrows and to place it against the base of the stalks. The old man began to make funny faces at the child. One would think he did not have a care in the world. He was that way while he was working at his beloved earth, but in the house he was now silent.

"Listen, old man," Mary said to him, "do you think Mr. Chadwick could do anything for Martin?"

The old man looked at her savagely.

"Is it him?" he cried. "It's not thinking of asking him for anything you are, is it?"

"Could he put in a word, do you think?" Mary continued. "And if he did would they listen to him?"

"Put that out of your head," said the old man.

He went back to his work. She looked after him, with her lips pursed and her eyes almost closed. Then she walked slowly back to the house, making another pale road through the lush grass with her slow feet. As she walked, she recalled how Thomsy had remarked, while they were eating the little derelict calf: "A man was telling me at that fair that the labourers in Canada get meat every day and shop loaves. God Almighty! It's hard to believe there's a place in the world where a labourer gets white bread every day and meat and wages into the bargain." On hearing those words, a violent greed possessed her and like a flash the temptation to leave at once with her child and beg her way, by every means, even by sin, to that promised land, became garrulous in her mind. At once, however, she had a revulsion of feeling and she had to leave the house. On her return, the old woman had said she should have stayed in bed a few days longer. "That's what turned your stomach, getting up too early."

"Why am I thinking of that now?" she said aloud, as she put the baby back into his cradle.

She resumed her knitting and looking up the Valley she counted the houses from whose chimneys smoke was rising. The smoke rose straight from the cabins into the calm summer sky. It rose straight for a long way, like the stem of a palm tree and then, being caught in the upper currents, it curved on either side, finally branching out widely like the matted head of a thorn bush. Now there was smoke from only twenty-seven fires. Ten were already quenched. How long would the others last?

"The blight," Mary thought, "and then the worm that kept eating us all winter. The two pounds we had to give Patch Hernon. No pigs on account of the blight. Kitty Hernon eating our share. Ellie, and then my father. Thomsy not getting any work. All useless mouths. Then Martin wounded and on his keeping, with the police after him. Transportation for life if he's caught. The cow and all we had taken. Even if the crop is good, Lord save us, won't he take that for the winter rent? And yellow meal at three shillings a stone at Hynes's shop. In the madhouse, Patch Hernon is getting two pounds o' bread and a quart of milk a day. Isn't it Heaven for him?"

She dug three turnips from the garden that Martin and Thomsy had made at the back of the house and prepared them for supper. She boiled a little Indian meal with them. They had been practically living on this diet now for a week, except for a rabbit that the dog Oscar caught. After supper, she prepared the child, put on her marriage dress, and said to the old man.

"Will you look after little Michael a while, old man, until I tell Sally to come?"

"Where are you going in that dress?" said the old man.

"It's a message I'm going on for Martin," she said.

"Huh!" said the old man.

It was still daylight when she left the house. Sally's cabin was only a hundred yards down the road. It was just a mud hut, built on to the mountain side in a deep hollow. The mountain side formed three of its walls. The front had been built up with pressed mud. The roof was thatched with ferns. An old stove pipe acted as chimney. When Mary entered, the family was at supper. Their table was the flattened top of a rock that protruded from the mountain. Two pallets were stretched on a bed of dried heather. Except for the stools on which they sat, there was no other furniture in the place. The smouldering fire of cow-dung gave forth a very unpleasant smell.

"May God increase all ye have," Mary said.

Sally jumped to her feet at once and, with a charming smile, she brought Mary a little can.

"A drop of milk," she said. "I was just finishing my bite before running over with it to you. I got it in the village to-day, washing over at the minister's house. The woman took sick that does the washing for them. Take it and it's proud I am to be able to give it to you."

She had really stolen the milk, but it had come from the

parson's cow. She had sneaked into the parson's grounds with her three children and managed to milk the animal while the children kept watch.

"Musha, thanks, Sally," said Mary, "but it's how I came to ask you would you keep an eye on little Michael while I'm out. Maggie is ailing so much I'm afraid to trust her with him."

"Arrah! Why wouldn't I?" said Sally. "You pearl of beauty, isn't it an honour to help you?"

She was in great spirits owing to her successful theft. Her desperate poverty had turned her into a kleptomaniac. Mary embraced her fervently, much to the little woman's astonishment. It was rare that Mary showed any emotion. Sally followed her out of doors.

"Is anything wrong, treasure?" she said.

"No, darling," said Mary, "only I'm out of my mind about Martin."

"I know it," said Sally, "but you needn't worry. As long as he keeps on the mountain he's safe. Then, when the hue and cry dies down he can escape. And what's to stop you going with him? Answer me that. If you had to suffer all I have suffered in my life! You're young yet, and your bed won't be empty long, I'm telling you. Is it to the village you're going?"

"I won't be long," Mary said, hurrying away.

Now she began to get afraid and the whole idea of appealing to Chadwick appeared to her ridiculous. He could do nothing for Martin, she thought, and his motive for sending her a message must have been a foul one. Should she turn back? The idea of turning back, however, brought to her mind actively the hopelessness of the future and she decided to go on with it. But in order to rouse her courage she dropped into her mother's house as she passed. Here she was confronted with an extraordinary sight.

Mrs. Gleeson and Kate Hernon sat in opposite corners of the hearth, watching a pot that was hung over the fire. They did not speak to Mary when she entered and there was a furtive expression in their eyes, as if they were caught doing something which they wished to hide. Patrick was sitting by the far wall on a form. His arms were folded on his bosom. His head and shoulders were pressed against the wall. His eyes were downcast and half closed. On the ground between his outstretched feet there was a little pile of shavings. The long blade of a knife protruded from his left arm-pit. From the right arm-pit, the end of a little piece of wood, which he had been whittling, protruded. He did not speak either, or even look at Mary, as she stood a little within the door, examining the three of them in surprise.

"Patrick?" she said. "You here? When did you come back?"

He looked at her with a fixed stare, like a madman. He did not speak.

"He dropped in, asthore," said his mother. "It's alright. The peelers said they didn't want him any more."

Patrick glared at his mother and said:

"Maybe they'll soon want me."

"There's fourteen stations of the Cross," Mrs. Gleeson said, "but from Sligo town to here there's been many a score of them and each one an iron door bolted against the joy of life."

"They raised him up on their shoulders high," crooned the hag, "and they struck him down on the flag-stones of the street. Ochon! Ochon!"

"God save us!" thought Mary. "They're all mad."

"What ails ye all?" she said aloud. "What's in that pot? What knife is that you have, Patrick?"

Patrick grinned and held out the knife.

"It's a black-handled knife," he said, "that I got from a sailor in the town a while back. Ask her what it's for, the black-handled one."

He pointed to Kate Hernon. Mary ran towards him and threatened him with her upraised fist.

"Let me hear none of your nonsense," she cried. "You'll not put the rope around my Martin's neck. Now I know where I'm going and why I'm going there. I'd rather inform on ye than let him be a party to that black deed. Let the murder not be on us."

The hag suddenly jumped to her feet and made a deep noise in her throat, like a person choking.

"I dare you," she cried, "and I double dare you, go against the vengeance of God. I'll curse you with the curse of Columkille if you breathe a word."

She made the horrible rattling noise in her throat again and then sat down. Mary shuddered. She made for the door.

"Oh! Where are you going, alannah?" said her mother.

Mary went out without speaking. After a few moments Patrick got up and followed her. He caught up with her on the road.

"I'm warning you, too," he said. "Don't meddle in what doesn't concern you. There's one man that won't give no evidence against my father. I'm telling you."

Then he hurried away in the direction of the mountain.

CHAPTER XXXVI

A LAMP HUNG by a chain from the roof above the table at which Chadwick sat. His hands were joined, holding a thin-handled whip, whose lash tapered out to a great length. It rose stiffly from the handle for about eighteen inches and then fell, in a narrowing curve, until the tip dangled in the air just above the naked brown board. His eyes stared without movement at the tip of the lash, as if he were dreaming. He was wearing his hat, his greatcoat and his muffler. A gentle breeze swept through the open doorway from the river which murmured just outside the hut, making the light flicker. It was dark outside. When the light flickered, a tremor ran down Chadwick's spine and he moved his right shoulder slightly, as if it itched. He was listening intently.

At last he heard the sound of feet on the grass outside. He smiled and stopped breathing, but he did not look towards the door until he heard the sound of feet on the wooden floor. Then he looked.

"Come in," he said softly. "Close the door after you."

Mary stood within the door, holding her cloak close to her body, staring at him. He abruptly got to his feet, kicking back the high stool on which he had been sitting and moved towards her. She gasped and turned back to the door.

"Where are you going?" he shouted suddenly, as he plunged towards her, seized her by the arm and swung her round. "It's too late now."

"Let me go," she whispered.

He pushed her aside roughly. Then he closed the door and drew the bolt. Trembling, she made no further movement to escape. Now there was a look of terror in her eyes as she stared at him.

"Sit down," he said, pointing to another stool.

She obeyed. He returned to his own stool and again put his elbows on the table. Now he placed the whip between them. There was nothing else in the room, except a couch in the far corner.

"You needn't be afraid," Chadwick said to her softly. "I'm not going to touch you…against your will. See this whip?"

Mary looked at the whip. She nodded. Now she did not tremble.

"I have a proposal to make to you," Chadwick continued in the same gentle tone. "You love your husband?"

She stared at him wildly and swallowed her breath.

"You have a baby, I'm told," he continued. "You love your baby? What? Answer me. Wouldn't you like to get away from here with them both? What?"

Mary half rose to her feet, but sat down once more at a sign from Chadwick. In a broken voice she whispered:

"I don't understand, sir."

"Ha!" said Chadwick. "Then, I'll put it quite plainly. You were responsible for getting your sister to leave me. Confounded nuisance it caused. Your father and your husband tried to murder me. However, I partly squared my account by taking your animals. Well! I'm leaving here, so I can afford to be merciful. For your sister's sake, because I was fond of the wench, I'm going to do you a favour…with this whip" – he pointed to the whip – "…and this."

He took from within his coat a money belt and spread it out on the table, between him and the whip. The little pockets were full of sovereigns.

"What's in your mind, sir?" Mary now cried in a shrill tone as she looked at the gold.

"Now, now," Chadwick said, holding up his hand, "don't get excited. You'll have to earn it. I don't believe in charity. After all, it's my money, even though some of it came from the sale of your animals. Here is what I propose."

Now his face looked utterly insane as he leaned towards her and began to whisper, gloating over every word, what he wished of her. At first she listened in terror, and then, as she understood the meaning of what he said, a flush of shame mounted to her cheeks. She put her hands to her bosom and cried:

"Stop. God forgive you."

Then she burst into tears and rocked herself. Chadwick smiled.

"A sovereign for every lash," he whispered, picking up the whip and switching it in the air, so that its point dangled close to her head. "The more you can endure, the richer you'll be. But if you cry out before the tenth you get nothing. Is it a bargain?"

Then Mary looked up at him and whispered hoarsely:

"I came here to tell you they are going to kill you, but now I hope they do. You deserve it, for you're the devil himself. God between me and you. Your blood be on yourself."

She made the sign of the Cross between her and Chadwick, who was roused by her words from the evil ecstasy into which his strange passion had plunged him. He drew back, stiffened, and thrust out his jaw.

"What did you say, woman?" he barked. "Kill me? Who? Speak up, or I'll flay you. What do you know, you bitch? Speak. Tell me."

He held the whip over her, as he got to his feet. She looked up at him, no longer afraid. Now her teeth were bared, liked a cornered animal.

"Strike," she said. "Your whip won't save you. They'll get you. I'm not afraid of you."

"Then I'll make you speak," Chadwick cried.

He raised the whip and swung it, but he shuddered and let it drop when it was about to descend on her. He sat down and laughed. It was a queer laugh. Now he began to babble like an idiot and he trembled violently, pulling at his throat as he spoke.

"God's blood!" he said. "Clever dodge! I was taken in by it. How much did she tell you? Not about the whip. I warrant she didn't say anything about the whip. Kill me? They tried that. Now I'm beyond their... one thing, though. Do you hear me? You can go a long way with gold. It opens doors, I tell you. Every one has his price. What? It's a passport to the ends of the earth. As many of them as you can earn. On the other hand, what's to prevent me, for five of them, these are hard times, I tell you, you can do a lot with five sovereigns, there was a case in court a short time ago..." Here he began to cough violently and then continued: "A man was hired to commit a murder for thirty shillings. Did it, too, upon my soul. They can't get me, the dogs. Trying to frighten me, are you?"

Now they stared at one another for some time in silence and then Chadwick suddenly dropped his head on his arms and rolled over sideways on the table. He made a noise as if he were sobbing aloud. Then the noise ceased and he breathed deeply. Was he falling asleep? Mary watched him and then got to her feet. She was opening and closing her fists, biting her lips and blinking. Suddenly she ran to the door, gasped and pulled the bolt. The door flew open, letting in a fresh breeze and the loud noise of the river. Chadwick raised his head.

"What's that?" he said in a tired voice.

Now his eyes were very bloodshot and he seemed half asleep.

"She's gone," he said.

Then he laughed and shrugged his shoulders. He began to belch. He shook himself and got to his feet. He suddenly went rigid, bared his teeth and began to curse violently. Then he went limp once more and picked up the money belt, nodding his head slowly. He fixed it around his waist, buttoned his coat and took his whip. With one hand in his pocket, he stalked out of the hut, leaving the lamp lit. However, when he had gone a few yards, he turned back, entered the hut and struck the lamp a violent blow with the whip. The lash twisted around the lamp and got stuck. He hauled at it, cursing aloud and brought the whole thing, including the chain, to the floor. Immediately, the spilt oil blazed over the board. He cursed again and dropped the whip. Then he ran out of the place.

CHAPTER XXXVII

IT WAS VERY dark as he stumbled along the path that led from the summer hut by the river to Crom House. He fell several times in his haste, struck against trees and tore his clothes among bushes that lined the path in places. He took no notice, but went forward like a panic-stricken animal in flight from danger, now and again crying aloud: "I must get away. There is no time to lose."

Near the house, he met a man with a lanthorn. It was Reilly, who came forward at a run, panting loudly.

"I got scared, sir," Reilly said. "When I was coming back from the town just now on the cart, I was stopped by a man below the village and he asks me were you going away and when were you going. 'I saw you taking in stuff on the cart into Clogher,' says he. 'Is it how Mr. Chadwick is going away?' 'When is he going?' says he. I know the man, his name is Considine, and he's in with the moonlighters. Lord bless us, sir, I wouldn't go this night, sir, if I were you. They have something planned."

Chadwick put his hand on Reilly's shoulder and said:

"Hold up that light, will you, Reilly. That's right. Do I look afraid?"

Reilly stared at his master for some time before he said:

"Begging your honour's pardon, but you look a bit queer. Is it anything ails you, sir?"

"Do I look afraid, you fool?" said Chadwick sternly, but in a low voice.

"Oh! No, sir," said Reilly. "Not afraid, sir, but I beg of you, for the love of God, to wait until morning. Then the police could go with you."

"Come along, Reilly," said Chadwick. "Go in front with

the light. Is Rover saddled? Where did you leave my luggage?"

"I left them where you told me, sir, at Shelly's Hotel. Rover is saddled, sir."

"One moment," said Chadwick.

Reilly halted. Chadwick fumbled at his money belt and took out a handful of gold. He gave it to Reilly, who held it out in front of his face as if afraid of the precious metal.

"But you gave me my wages this morning, sir?" said Reilly.

"What of it?" said Chadwick. "You're a good sort. Drink my health. There's plenty of gold in California. A new life there, too. I might invite you to share it with me when the time is ripe. Now march. Hold up the light."

"Lord save us, sir," said Reilly, as he trotted forward, holding up the light and looking back sideways into the gloom, "is it of California you're talking now and that on the other side of the world altogether?"

"Never mind," said Chadwick. "She warned me, but that was done with a purpose. Who? Young Kilmartin and the Gleeson fellow, her brother, their revenge. I'll cheat them. Just for fun. Let them have it."

"What's that, sir?" said Reilly, getting more and more nervous.

Chadwick continued to mumble, but now his remarks had become quite unintelligible. Presently they heard the horse neigh and then the black hide of the animal gleamed in the light of the lanthorn. Old Mary Halloran was standing by the horse's head near the front door. Chadwick called her over and gave her also some gold. Now Reilly burst into tears and said:

"Your honour, sure it's not leaving us altogether you'd be thinking of doing? You told me you were only going to Dublin with the rent."

"Rent?" said Chadwick. "What rent? Well! Good people, take care of yourselves."

With that he mounted the horse and galloped away madly

up the drive towards the village, spurring the animal furiously with his heels. It was pitch dark among the trees, but the animal knew the road perfectly and he presently debouched into the village. A police patrol, returning to the barracks, cried halt and flashed their lights on the animal, which reared in front of the line of men.

"Don't you know me, you fools?" shouted Chadwick at the policemen.

"Sorry, sir," said the sergeant in charge. "We have to halt everybody under the curfew law. Make way there, men."

Chadwick rode ahead. Now the frightened animal refused to gallop. It kept rearing on its hind legs, snorting and leaping from side to side of the road. Chadwick lashed it furiously and finally it went forward at a spurt which carried it beyond the priest's house at the far end of the village. Here it planted its fore-feet firmly in the road, at the beginning of the short hill which rose directly beyond the priest's house. Chadwick was nearly thrown out over the horse's head. When he righted himself in the saddle, he again took the whip to the animal, cursing violently. Now, however, the horse took no notice of the whip. It edged over to the side of the road, groaning, trembling and raising its fore-feet one after the other, as if making its way through a bog. At last, Chadwick had to get down and lead it. The animal resisted violently, but finally went forward at a walk up the hill.

The government relief works were situated at the top of this short hill. The mountains began immediately on the right and on the left there was a steep cliff. On the far side, beyond the summit, the hill was very steep, curving left down towards the lowlands of Clogher. Great masses of earth and stone, torn from the summit of the hill by the workmen, lined the road on either side. There was only a solitary lanthorn, in front of the night watchman's hut, to warn the traffic of the danger.

"Hey, you, watchman," said Chadwick, when he came near the light, "hold up your lanthorn, you fool."

Nobody came out of the hut. Chadwick approached, dragging his horse by the head. Now the animal was still more frightened and began to rear once more. Losing his temper completely, he turned round and began to lash it. Then he heard a sound, the rushing of feet and a low growl and he dropped the reins. Men were rushing at him from all sides.

"At him, boys," came a low cry. "Give it to the bastard."

At that moment, the lanthorn was quenched and there was almost pitch darkness. Chadwick fumbled in his overcoat for his pistol as the men closed with him on either side. The horse neighed loudly and galloped madly back towards the village. A knife was plunged into Chadwick's right side. A club struck him on the head. Then a man clutched him by the throat. At that moment he managed to draw the pistol from his pocket and fired at the man who was trying to strangle him. Immediately there was a wild shriek of pain. Another blow from a club struck him on the base of the neck and he fell forward over the body of the man who was clutching his throat. The hands clutching his throat now began to tremble and loosened their hold.

"He's done for," said a voice. "To the mountain, in God's name."

There was a sound of running feet. Chadwick, lying prone over the trembling body of the man who clutched his throat, groped with his left hand for the knife that was stuck in him. With a great effort, he pulled it from his side, raised himself on his right hand and then struck with the knife at the man beneath him. The knife passed through the man's cheek and his right ear. Then Chadwick dropped his head and fell forward unconscious. Blood flowed from his side in a full stream. Now lights flashed and the sound of running feet came from the village. It was the police, roused by the pistol shot and the horse's neighing.

In a few minutes, ten of them were on the spot. When they turned Chadwick over on his back and raised up his head, he opened his eyes, looked at them and muttered:

"She warned me. Her husband and her brother. Young Kilmartin. They..."

Then he dropped back, shuddered and lay still. The other man was dead, with the black-handled knife transfixing his right cheek and his ear. There was a hole in his left chest, made by the pistol shot. In death, there was a rapt smile on his pale face.

"It's young Gleeson," a police sergeant said. "Quick, men. After the others! Kilmartin can't be far off."

Chapter XXXVIII

THE WEEKS THAT followed Chadwick's death was like a nightmare to the people of Crom parish. In addition to the large force of police already stationed in the village, a company of soldiers was drafted from the military barracks at Clogher, to aid in the search for the assassins and "to put down the insurrection." It was in these latter terms that a conservative newspaper described the conditions in the unfortunate district. The conduct of the police had been aggravating enough, but even Father Roche had to denounce the soldiery from the altar as "a licentious rabble." Nothing resulted from the activities of the government, from the point of view of apprehending those responsible for Chadwick's death. The only result was to intensify the apathy and terror of the community and to increase, if possible, the disunion already existing among those who were trying to alleviate the terrible distress. By the time the soldiers returned to their barracks and the police ceased scouring the mountains, the curate was able to report in a letter to a society in America, to whom he was appealing for funds, that he had not seen, during a tour of the parish, "a smile on a single face, among a people whose gaiety was a legend."

Mary was brought to the barracks at Crom on the morning after the assassination and severely questioned. She admitted that her brother had made threats. There was no point in denying it, since the unfortunate man's part in the affair was only too well known. His corpse was there in evidence against him. She also admitted having gone to meet Chadwick at the summer-house, but maintained that she had tried to warn him. Her statement about the frightful proposal made to her by the dead man was discredited, until Reilly gave evidence a little later. Overcome by grief at his master's death, the groom made an extraordinary statement.

"'God strike me dead," he cried to the district inspector, "if I say a word that might hurt him, dead and all as he is, but it all began when that girl came into the house. Until then it was only the drink and quiet he was, too, when he had his drop taken, the best value in the world, with the stories he used to tell about foreign parts and about his old father and how the sun got at him in India. The heathens got at him, too, sir, and he caught in an ambush, where they cut off half his shame, saving your presence, he let it out one night when he was drunk, though I never breathed a word of it to a living soul. He had trust in me, sir, which he needn't regret, but he's dead now, sir, and let there be an excuse, Lord have mercy on him, for any queerness. He had no right to take the people's stock, with the hard times, but he was driven to it, one way and another. It was from the day he set eyes on her that went away, bad cess to her, that he turned sour and cantankerous. The devil came in with her, and he not having it in him to be natural, same as a man would be, so he could get her out of his mind. So when her sister took her away, he swore vengeance on the sister, on her that's sitting in there, on Mary Kilmartin, the weaver's daughter. That's why he took the cattle and sold them out of the pound and he was going to fly to California with the money, when they felled him. 'Stay with me, Reilly,' he used to say, 'my star will rise again.' He did, 'faith, even the last word he said was, that he'd send for me. But devil a foot he'd stir, and he with the money in a belt, until he'd have vengeance on the sister. 'I'll make her kneel to me,' he says. So he sent me with a letter, what a lad took to her. No man in his senses would think of doing the like and he a gentleman born, stooping to a thing like that, taking revenge off a poor girl out of a bog. But sure I couldn't go and give information against my own master. It was while I was down in Clogher with his luggage he went there. And I hurried back, for fear he'd do some wickedness and his temper, these last days it was awful, the master of him. It was a whip he had that put the fear in me. He kept it locked in a cupboard and he used to take it out and sit with it in front of him. Once he gave it to me to sell, for there were pearls on the handle. It was a time when there wasn't a penny in the house to buy a drop of drink and our credit gone, but he followed me out of the house again and took it off me. He did, 'faith, and he gave me a cut of it across the back. 'I have use for that whip,' he said. So there can't be a word of a lie in what she says, for it was on her that he wanted to use it. May God rest his soul, although it's myself that says it, I'm not saying he was right, but I wouldn't put it past him and he told me, too, on the lawn, that she warned him. So help me God, that's nothing but the truth."

This rambling statement, made by the distraught groom, forced the authorities to desist from bringing any further action against Mary, but it also proved that Martin was involved in the murder. All over the district, notices were posted, offering a reward of five pounds for information leading to the arrest of Martin Kilmartin, Jeremiah Considine and Francis Fahey, "wanted for the murder of Captain Jocelyn Chadwick." The other two names belonged to young men known to be leaders among those out hiding on the mountains. However, it seemed that the earth had opened up and swallowed them all. They had disappeared without trace.

It can be easily imagined what agony Mary suffered under these circumstances. Yet she bore everything with wonderful courage. Even during her interrogation at the barracks, she impressed the district inspector by her dignified bearing. It was she that took charge of Patrick's burial. I must say that the old man was equally active and courageous. In spite of the desperate circumstances in which they found themselves, he insisted on the dead man being waked and buried according to custom. Mrs. Gleeson agreed with him and Mary was forced to submit. "Custom is custom," said the old man. He maintained that to bury anybody without a proper wake was tantamount to a sacrilege. As there was no money to do this, the household effects of the weaver's cottage had to be sold. Little as the expense was – it amounted altogether to seventeen and sixpence – it was hard to cover it. In the old days, if a person had something to sell, a dress, or a cloak, or a piece of furniture, there was always someone willing to offer a reasonable price. Now this market was glutted. Hynes had ceased altogether to engage in this sort of traffic, either through pride in his new exalted position, or because he realised it was now bad business. Even so, they managed to find a buyer for nearly everything in the house, except the loom and the bed, and there were a few shillings left after everything had been paid. Then the question arose as to what was to be done with the mother. Old Kate Hernon, completely out of her senses owing to her eviction and the excitement of Chadwick's death, wandered away one night and was found raving in a ditch near Clogher. She was taken to the asylum. Mrs. Gleeson could not be left alone.

"You better come and stay with me," Mary said to her after the funeral. "You can help me with the child, since Maggie is laid up. That'll give me a chance to go out and look for something."

Mrs. Gleeson refused at first.

"This is the end of my road," she said. "I'll wait my end here. They are all taken now. I won't bring the curse that's on me under another roof."

Then the old man reasoned with her.

"We have a hard fight before us," he said, "trying to hold on to the land and keeping a roof over our heads until the bad times are over. So rise up and come with us. Don't make Mary have two hearths to tend, going back and forth on one pair of feet. Rise up and give me your hand."

Finally they persuaded her to come with them. Then the old man and Thomsy undertook to sell the loom. It was difficult to find a buyer and they had to go as far as the village of Tubberlane, ten miles beyond Clogher, before they managed to dispose of it to a family of weavers. The expense of carting it there and luck-penny left them with only six shillings as the result of the deal.

When Mary's father, a week later, was sentenced to transportation for life, in the penal settlement of New South Wales, the verdict scarcely moved her. She had reached the limit of her sensibility.

"God save Ireland," cried the weaver in the dock when he was sentenced.

It soon became obvious that the Deity had no intention of answering favourably the weaver's prayer.

Chapter XXXIX

IN SPITE OF the previous year's blight and the scarcity of food, the quantity of potatoes planted that spring was even greater than usual. Now the crop showed signs of being a bumper one. The spring had been severe. There had been frost and snow even in the first part of April. But June brought a heat that was almost tropical. Under the urge of this heat, the potato plants grew to an enormous size and their luxuriant foliage, dotted with beautiful white and pink blossoms, made Black Valley look like a flower garden. The people began to hope that their hardships were nearly over and that God would again bless their labour.

On St. John's Eve, they made bonfires in accordance with the ancient custom. Then they took coals from the fires and carried them around the boundaries of their gardens, to ward off evil from the earth's fruit. Next morning, they went out and plucked a few stalks in each garden. Lo! the seed had increased abundantly. There was wild rejoicing everywhere. Old Kilmartin was exalted.

"What did I say?" he shouted, as he spilt a small kish of the new potatoes on the kitchen floor. "God doesn't send hunger for long. He sends it to remind us of our sins. But when we repent he sends riches. The earth is rich. God has blessed our earth."

At noon, on the feast of St. John, they sat down to a meal that was for them a real feast. Mary had got a few young onions from the plot at the back of the house. She chopped them up and mixed them with the new potatoes. There was a piece of salt fish which Sally O'Hanlon had given her, the result of another bit of thieving on the part of that generous neighbour. Although there was no milk to complete this favourite meal, hunger supplied its place as a savoury. They all gorged themselves. Even Maggie had left her bed and taken her place at table, excited by the wonderful news of the new crop. The dog had his dish by the back door and the poor animal ate so much that his stomach swelled out to a point on either side. Of late he had got thin.

It was at this moment, while they were happily eating their meal, that the destructive attitude of Divine Providence again manifested itself. All morning, the sky had been spotless and the sun shone in all the glory of its summer heat. And then, suddenly, the sky darkened. Lightning flashed. A torrent of rain began to fall. Thunder rolled across the firmament. It grew as cold as in the midst of winter. It was horrifying. It all happened within the space of a few minutes. They were struck with awe. They dropped their knives into the kish and stared at one another. They crossed themselves.

Thomsy was the first to speak.

"Has it come again?" he whispered. "That's how it started last year."

"Silence," said the old man, rising from his stool. "Do you know what you're saying?"

"Let's go on our knees," Mary said, "and ask God to have pity on us."

They all went on their knees and recited the rosary, begging God not to send the blight on their crop. When they had finished, it seemed that the Lord heard their prayer, for the storm ended as suddenly as it had begun. The sky did not clear, but the thunder and lightning ceased. A drizzling rain continued to fall and it became very hot. The old man then suggested that they should sprinkle holy water on the gardens. Mary took a bottle of holy water they had in the house and went with him. They visited all the gardens and sprinkled the water on the plants here and there, in the name of the Father, Son and Holy Ghost. A number of other families, seeing them so engaged, came forth and did likewise.

It was a strange sight, truly, in the drizzling rain, under a dark sky, to see all those simple people going around their gardens with holy water, asking pity of the Lord.

Next day, the sky cleared and the sun came forth. It had rained heavily during the night and the blossoms had been washed from the stalks by the downpour, but when the old man went out with his spade once more and dug, he found that the crop was still wholesome.

"Praised be God!" he said.

Mary and Thomsy had come out with him and when they saw that the potatoes he threw out with his spade were whole, they burst into tears with joy.

"Oh! Aren't they big?" Mary said, as she went on her knees to pick them carefully. "I never saw them so big at this time of year."

"True for you," said the old man, digging eagerly. "That proves to you how it pays people to stint themselves. There are fools over there in Glenaree that ate some of their seeds and now they'll only have half a crop in spite of the great harvest that's coming. Two extra gardens I sowed. We'll have seventy bushels this year instead of the usual forty, or my name isn't Brian. Don't be talking, woman, we'll soon be on our feet again. Never say die. If our stock is taken, we'll begin again little by little. While we have the land we have riches. Now that the tyrant is dead, we're safe from persecution. The new agent that will come to be over us might be a Christian man. He'll give us time over the rent and maybe the government might step in with a loan. It happened before in the time of the great hunger. Ah! If only Martin was here with us, to see this great crop. Poor man! Many a drop of his noble sweat he gave sowing them."

At the mention of Martin's name, Mary stopped picking. She felt a sharp pain in her bosom and then a terrible emptiness spread all over her body, as if she had been suddenly disembowelled by a monstrous hand that carried off at one scoop, her heart, her lungs, all her vital being. With a rush, the agony passed into her brain and a feeling of shame made her go weak, so that the colour left her cheeks and she rose to her feet trembling. The thought flashed through her head:

"For days I haven't thought of him."

Thomsy looked at her anxiously and said:

"What ails you, Mary?"

"Nothing," she said, laughing foolishly. "Only I got so excited and..."

"Go on into the house," said the old man, too intent on his own joy to notice that it was Martin's name which had disturbed her. "You've been doing too much lately. Rest yourself. Pick those potatoes, Thomsy."

Mary went towards the house. What heavy heat it was! The smell of the growing plants was still in her nostrils even after she had left the garden. It was sickening. Tears were now streaming down her cheeks.

"Oh! Darling," she muttered, "it wasn't for want of love of you that I didn't think of you this while. I was afraid to think of you. Oh! I'm afraid of the hunger, and the little milk I have for our Michael."

Indeed, such was the case. Every moment of the day and during most of the night, her mind was tortured by the terrible thought that soon now there would be nothing for the little child and that she would have to go out on the highways with him, begging. And this torture dulled all else, dulled even the torture of Martin's absence. Only once had she heard of him since Chadwick's death. A man brought news that he was with a band of men on an island off the coast, away to the west, and that he was safe there, at least for the present. But that was a poor consolation. What of the future? What prospect was there of ever being with him again, or of escaping from the country? It was this awful thought which made her afraid to think of him.

Another violent storm came on the last day of the month.

They did not trouble greatly about this one, since the first had done no damage. Even so, a rumour got abroad that the blight had struck in the County Cork. Would it come this far? Every day, they anxiously inspected the crop. But the days passed without any sign of the evil. The potatoes that were dug for food still remained wholesome. It promised to be a miraculous crop. Even Mary began to take courage. And then, on the fifteenth of July, the bolt fell from the heavens.

When old Kilmartin came into his yard shortly after dawn on that day, he looked up the Valley and saw a white cloud standing above the Black Lake. It was like a great mound of snow, hanging by an invisible chain, above the mountain peaks. It was dazzling white in the glare of the rising sun.

"Merciful God!" he said. "What can that be?"

The rest of the sky was as clear as crystal. The old man stared at it in awe for some time. Then he ran into the house and called out the family to look at it. Mary and Thomsy came out. They were as startled as the old man.

"Did you ever see anything like that?" the old man said.

"Never in my natural," said Thomsy. "It's like a…"

"Snow," Mary said. "It's like a big heap of snow."

"How could it be snow?" said the old man. "And this the middle of summer? It's a miracle."

"Or would it be a bad sign, God between us and harm?" said Thomsy.

Other people came from their cabins and stared at the cloud. There was a peculiar silence in the Valley. The air was as heavy as a drug. There was not a breath of wind. The birds did not sing. And then, as the people watched, the cloud began to move lazily down upon the Valley. It spread out on either side, lost its form and polluted the atmosphere, which became full of a whitish vapour, through which the sun's rays glistened; so that it seemed that a fine rain of tiny whitish particles of dust was gently falling from the sky. Gradually a sulphurous stench affected the senses of those who watched. It was like the smell of foul water in a sewer. Yet, there was no moisture and the stench left an arid feeling in the nostrils. Even the animals were affected by it. Dogs sat up on their haunches and howled. Not a bird was to be seen, although there had been flocks of crows and of starlings about on the previous day. Then, indeed, terror seized the people and a loud wailing broke out from the cabins, as the cloud overspread the whole Valley, shutting out the sun completely.

All this time, the whole Kilmartin family had remained in the yard. Mary clutched the baby in her arms. Nobody thought of preparing breakfast, although the morning was now well advanced. It was only when the wailing began and Maggie joined in it, that Mary came to her senses and said:

"Don't frighten the child with your whining. There's no harm done yet. Hold the baby, mother, while I get breakfast ready."

"True for you," said the old man. "There's no harm done yet. Into the house, all of you. Pooh! Afraid of a fog, is it?"

Maggie stopped crying, but she went back to bed and closed the door of her room. The others made an attempt to be cheerful. Like people who feel the oncoming panic of despair, they gave voice to expressions of optimism, which they knew to be false.

"I often saw fogs heavier than that," Ellen Gleeson said, as she rocked the baby in the hearth corner.

"As heavy as that?" said Thomsy. "Sure that's not a heavy fog. I saw a fog once that was as thick as night. You can see to the end of the yard in this one."

"You can see farther," said the old man. "On the south side there, you can see as far as Patsy O'Hanlon's house. It's not a thick fog. It's funny the smell that comes from fogs."

"I never smelt a fog before like that," said Mary. "It must be a new kind of fog. But a fog can do no harm in any case. If it was rain now, that would be a different story. Rain might rot the potatoes and they…"

"Nothing will rot the potatoes," said the old man. "God forgive you for saying such a thing."

Mary cooked some Indian meal and turnips, of which a few still remained. While they were eating, a further astonishing thing happened. The sky cleared almost instantaneously. The sun shone brilliantly. Yet this change, which should have cheered the watchers, only increased their awe, for the stench still remained. They all stopped eating. The old man got to his feet. He reached for his hat and fumbled with it, looking about him at the others with the expression of a small boy who has committed some offence of which he is ashamed.

"Blood an ouns!" Thomsy said, jumping to his feet.

With his mouth wide open, he stared at the old man. Then they both clapped their hats on their heads and rushed from the house. Mary ran to the cradle, picked up the child and pressed it to her bosom.

"What ails ye?" her mother said.

Maggie began to wail in the bedroom. All the colour had gone from Mary's cheeks and her eyes seemed to have enlarged. She handed the baby to her mother and whispered:

"I'm going out to look at the gardens."

Thomsy and the old man, one after the other and with their hands behind their backs, were walking slowly down towards the potato gardens. Mary ran until she reached them. Ahead she could see the gardens, still shining in all the glory of their dark-green foliage, under the radiant sun. But the stench was now terrible. In single file, they came to the first garden and leaned over the stone fence close together, staring at the plants.

"They're alright," said the old man. "There's nothing on them."

"Whist!" said Thomsy. "What's that I hear?"

Towards the north, in the direction towards which Thomsy pointed, Mary and the old man saw people looking over fences, just as they themselves were doing. These people had begun to wail. In this wailing there was a note of utter despair. There was no anger in it, no power, not even an appeal for mercy. It was just like the death groan of a mortally wounded person, groaning in horror of inevitable death.

"It's the blight," Mary whispered. "Oh! God in Heaven!"

"Look," gasped the old man through his teeth. "Look at it. It's the devil. It's the devil himself."

With outstretched hand, that trembled as if palsied, he pointed to a little hollow about ten yards within the fence. Here the growth was particularly luxuriant and the branches of the potato stalks were matted as thickly as a carpet. Mary and Thomsy followed the direction of his hand and while he babbled foolishly they saw the evil appear on the leaves. A group of little brown spots had appeared and they spread, as if by magic, while they watched. It was just like the movement of an incoming tide over a flat, sandy shore. It was a rain of spots, spreading rapidly in all directions.

"Oh! God Almighty!" Thomsy cried. "Save us, oh, Lord! Jesus! Mary and Joseph!"

Rubbing his short, fat arms against his sides as if he itched, with his round, bearded face turned towards the sky, he prayed for mercy. Mary felt the same emptiness within her as on that other day when the old man mentioned Martin's name. Now, however, she did not think of Martin. The whole world seemed to have become emptied. The hand had scooped out everything. There seemed to be weights at the back of her eyes and her forehead became deeply ridged by the labour of keeping them open. Then a violent sobbing shook her. She closed her pained eyes and covered them with her hands. She leaned against the fence and gave way to a fit of sobbing. Yet no tears came from her eyes.

"The devil," shouted the old man, "he's on us. He's on us."

Uttering shriek after shriek, he climbed over the fence, fumbling so much that he dislodged several stones. He strode through the stalks, that came up to his waist, across the ridges, until he came to the affected spot. The stench was now that of active corruption. The old man seized the stalks that were marked with spots and began to pull them. The leaves withered when he touched them and the stalks snapped like rotten wood. But the potatoes clinging to the uprooted stalks were whole. The old man dug into several of them with his nails.

"They're not rotten," he cried, laughing hysterically. "Come on, Thomsy. Pull the stalks that are rotten. We must stop it spreading. Mary, you come as well. Pull the stalks. Pull. Stop it spreading."

Excited by the old man's frenzy, Thomsy also climbed over the fence and waddled through the stalks, but he halted when he was a few yards from the old man, who was pulling feverishly and shouting. The old man was now surrounded by a widening lake of spots.

"Sure, it's flying all over the garden," said Thomsy. "Look, man. It's all round you. You can't stop it."

"What's that?" said the old man, raising his head.

He looked all round him pathetically. Then his mouth fell open and he stood up straight. His hands dropped to his sides.

"You're right," he said faintly. "It's the hand of God. God's will be done."

Thereupon he crossed himself and bowed his head. Not troubling even to collect the potatoes he had pulled up with the stalks, he marched slowly back to the fence, carelessly trampling over the stalks that were still untouched. Mary turned away from the fence as he approached. She began to walk back to the house.

The wailing was now general all over the Valley.

CHAPTER XL

BY THE FOLLOWING morning there was not a single potato stalk in Black Valley that had not rotted. The crop, in which the people had placed such confidence, the only thing that stood between them and starvation, was a mass of corruption.

Mary had lain awake nearly all night. Towards dawn she fell asleep through sheer exhaustion. She was roused by the wailing of the child. She got up hurriedly, half awake, and began to talk to the child, soothing him, as she went to the window to pull aside the curtain. She was startled to find that the sun was high in the heavens and that it must be an advanced hour of the morning. Coming back to the cradle, she looked at the bed and saw her mother, who now slept with her, lying on her back with her eyes wide open, perfectly still.

"What ails you, mother?" Mary said. "Why didn't you wake me?"

The mother did not look at her, but answered in an indifferent tone:

"Nothing ails me. Sure we're as well off in bed as out of it. What is there for us to do?"

"Oh! You'd break the heart in a stone," said Mary fretfully as she picked up the infant. "You're as bad as Maggie. Get out of bed and dress yourself."

She hurriedly changed the infant's clothes, pulled on her skirt and then gave the child the breast as she went down into the kitchen. It was still in darkness.

"Heavens above!" she thought. "What has happened?"

For the first time since she had come into the house, except when he had stayed in bed for three days, the old man had allowed the sun to rise before him. Something serious must have happened to him. She opened the door. The dog rushed into the yard. A stench entered the kitchen when the door was opened. The dog went some distance into the yard, smelt the air and then sat down to howl on his haunches.

"Is there nobody up here?" Mary called as she opened the door of the small bedroom.

It was light here, since there was no covering on the window. She saw the old couple lying in bed, both of them awake, exactly as her mother had been.

"Ho!" said the old man in a queer tone. " 'Faith, you're up before me this morning. Hech! Old age is coming on me."

"It must be," Mary said. "The day is half spent."

"It's easier to fight hunger in bed than out of it," Maggie grumbled. She was telling her rosary beads.

"You won't fight it by talking of it," Mary said, turning back into the kitchen.

"That's true," said the old man, dropping his lean shanks to the floor.

He picked up his trousers and walked down into the kitchen in his shirt. Almost naked as he was, his old man's body looked pitifully thin and bony; especially the shins, on which there was hardly a particle of flesh over the rude bones. His eyes had lost their fire. They were red around the rims and sunken, the result of a sleepless night.

"Hi! You devils," he shouted, with a trace of his old ferocity, as he looked into the yard. "Be off with ye."

He shook his trousers at the dog and the cat, which were quarrelling over by the dung-hill. The cat, grown quite wild of late, since it received no food in the house, had taken to hunting at night. For some reason, instead of devouring his prey where he found it, he always brought it to the dung-hill. Now he lay on his back, his claws in the air, his jaws bared, over the carcass of a bird, which the dog was anxious to take from him. The dog looked at the old man, wagged his tail, barked at the cat and then ran to his master. The cat glared savagely, seized the carcass and then walked away slowly, halting now and again and growling.

"Hi!" said the old man, striking the dog with his trousers. "Is it eating cat's dirt you are? Hi!"

The dog lay on the ground and accepted the light blows in good part. He and the old man were devoted to one another. He wagged his tail and let his tongue loll, knowing that his master did not mean to hurt him.

"Give Oscar a bit of something, Mary," said Brian, as he pulled on his trousers. "He's so hungry that he was trying to steal dirt from that devil of a cat, that picks up every rotten scrap. We can't have the poor dog bringing disease into the house. That's how the plague comes through dead things that have worms in them. It's well known."

"Let him go and catch a rabbit," said Mary. "We have little enough for ourselves."

"A rabbit?" cried Brian. "And where would he get a rabbit? I haven't seen a rabbit these months. 'Faith, you wouldn't find a wren around the place now, not to mind a rabbit. God only knows where the cat gets what he gets."

When he had pulled on his trousers and tied his belt, he went over to the fence, shaded his eyes with his hands, and looked all round the Valley. Where there had been luxuriant potato gardens the day before there was now desolation. All the potato gardens seemed to have been swept by fire. The naked stalks had all turned black. The old man began to sniff.

"Feuh! Feuh!" he cried. "Isn't that an awful smell?"

Then he stared again, with his lips drawn back. He seemed to be quite stunned and unable to realise what had happened. Or else he did not want to understand it. He wished to hide the reality from himself.

"There isn't a person to be seen," he said, coming back into the kitchen.

Mary was kindling the fire with one hand, while she held the infant to her breast with the other. The old man knelt to say his prayers. Thomsy threw down his ladder and descended from the loft. He looked out the door.

"Ah! God help us!" he cried, as he saw the desolation.

"Would you go down," Mary said, "and see are the potatoes that were pulled yesterday still there?"

The old man, saying his prayers, raised his head and said: "What potatoes?"

"The ones you were pulling when the blight came." ·

"Ho!" said the old man. "Fine chance you have of finding any of them."

"He can try," Mary said. "Take a basket with you, Thomsy, and see can you get a few for breakfast. The meal is all gone."

Such was their despair on the previous day that they had not even collected the whole potatoes which the old man pulled in his frenzy. They had fled from the garden leaving them on the ridges, overcome by the strange helplessness of defeat. It was this same nervous exhaustion which had kept them in bed all morning, a dumb submission to fate which killed all initiative. Mary was the only one that had any energy or will power left. The infant and her youth made her unwilling to surrender without an effort. At her bidding, Thomsy took a small basket and went down to the garden. The smell was so foul that he had to hold his nostrils when he approached. He searched in his pockets for a morsel of tobacco to chew. He found none. Indeed, it was a long time now since he had had a smoke of tobacco. Once a day he filled his pipe with peat dust and smoked that. Conquering his revulsion, he climbed over the fence into the garden.

"There they are, 'faith," he cried excitedly, "as sound as ever. Thanks be to God."

Encouraged by the prospect of having something for breakfast, he rushed towards the place, where the old man had pulled the stalks. The blighted stalks cracked and broke in his passage. He put down his basket and began to pick the ones lying on the ridge. Only those that had fallen from the roots were whole. Those that remained attached to the roots after being pulled had rotted. Altogether, he collected about a stone of them into his basket. Then he rooted with his hands under the blackened stalks that had not been pulled. The potatoes clinging to their roots were black and full of corruption. He shook his head.

"True enough," he said aloud. "There's no use digging them. They're all gone."

He swung his basket over his shoulder and set off to the house. When he entered the kitchen he threw it on the floor and said:

"Here you are. This is all the crop for you. It was easy enough to carry it. 'Faith, it was no heavy load."

He emptied the basket on the floor. The old man, who had sat down in the hearth corner after finishing his prayers, said in a timid voice:

"You didn't try any of the…"

"I did," said Thomsy. "And what did you expect?"

"They're gone?" said Mary.

Thomsy nodded.

"God's will be done," the old man said.

He folded his arms on his chest and stared at the fire which Mary had kindled. Both Maggie and Ellen Gleeson had now come into the kitchen. All sat around doing nothing, just gaping listlessly at the floor. Mary, who was getting a pot ready to cook the potatoes, suddenly turned on them angrily.

"What are ye all sitting there for?" she cried. "Is there nothing to be done? How are we going to live, with the hunger facing us, if ye won't try to do something? Get up and stir yerselves, all of ye. If ye don't, I'll take the child and leave ye to yer destruction."

God forgive you, child," said Mrs. Gleeson, "sure there's nothing to be done."

"Sweep the floor," said Mary. "Do something."

"And where would you take the child?" said the old man

in a startled tone. "Surely, you wouldn't have it in you to leave house and land."

"Well, then," cried Mary, "stir yourself if you want me to stay."

Her tone at last roused the old man from his lethargy. He jumped to his feet and cried:

"It could never be thrown in my face that I was lazy or cowardly. Say what you want done and I'll do it."

"Let you get ready, then," said Mary, "you and Thomsy. I'll go with ye into the village. If there's any help to come from the powers, it's got to come now, before the hunger begins to devour our strength. I'm going to fight for my child in any case. It's up to ye to help me. They must give us something or put us in jail. In jail they'd have to feed us."

Here Maggie began to cry, and she said:

"Don't let me hear you talk of ructions. Isn't enough done already? My Martin on his keeping with a price on his head. Oh, Lord! Forgive us, blessed mother of God, for our sins."

"She said what was right," said Thomsy. "The powers must be made help us. I always said the people should strike a blow. I wish I had the courage to strike a blow."

" 'Faith, there's never any harm in asking, anyway," said the old man. "I'll go with you, Mary. Though, it's poor chance we have of getting any of whatever is going, on account of the way they're down on us after what has happened."

"Get ready," said Mary. "There's one thing certain. We won't get anything sitting here on our backsides praying to God. God helps them that help themselves."

CHAPTER XLI

JUST THEN, DR. Hynes mounted his horse and set out to Glenaree on a sick call. The man who came for him said it was urgent, as his mother had "not stirred for two days." So the doctor galloped. He now had a horse of his own, the grey mare that had brought his father and brother to Clogher for the match-making. His father had made him a present of the mare, saying that "we all can take a step up now, thank God." The doctor's riding had improved and he managed the animal with ease.

His spirits, however, had again fallen as low as when he felt that he was an enemy of the people, during his relationship with Chadwick. The exaltation of leading a new life of social service, under the guidance of Father Geelan, had passed quickly. He still worked hard, but it was with increasing bitterness and with a feeling of defeat. The poor fellow was condemned by nature to be a coward. The repressive action of the government following the riots and especially after Chadwick's death had terrified him. Alas! His type is all too prevalent; those who grovel in the dust and hide in their cellars, or throw up their hands in horror, when tyranny shows its fangs. The first sign of the mailed fist makes them feel that it is better to live a slave than die a hero. Not that there was any question of the doctor ever having thought of dying a hero. Even the thought of others doing so was enough for him. He longed for peace at any price.

And yet he hated his father more than ever for giving voice to those sentiments of cowardice which he himself felt. Even the gift of the mare made him feel ashamed; just as if it had been bought on the profits made out of the increasing stress of the people. Indeed, he suffered so much of late that he had lost a great deal of his fat and his face assumed the hang-dog, furtive look that had formerly been peculiar to his father.

News of the blight had reached the village on the previous evening, but as yet nobody had paid much attention to it, simply because those who brought the news were so overwhelmed by the calamity that they did not emphasise its importance. And in any case, the people from the mountains were always bringing tales of terrible hardship, greatly exaggerated, in order to arouse pity. It was with a shock, therefore, that the doctor saw what really had happened when he crossed Black Valley on his road to Glenaree. All the gardens which had been green a few days previously, when he last passed this way, were now black and naked. And the people whom he passed, going their way to the village, walked slowly, in silence, without hardly giving him a glance. Not one of them tried to stop him in order to ask a favour, or to beg, as was usually the custom. That terrified him. And he spurred his horse, as if to escape from it, until it galloped at full speed.

The horse was forced to slow down to a walk after reaching the summit of the mountain that separated Black Valley from Glenaree. Beyond that, the road was little more than a goat path. Not even a cart had ever penetrated Glenaree, the valley of the kings, as some cynical person in ancient times had named it. It was much wider than Black Valley and on the east it was bound by a low ridge, beyond which the great central plain could be seen from this height. It was truly a majestic sight, the great rolling plain of central Ireland gilded by the brilliant sunlight. Near by, however, in the glen itself, there was nothing beautiful or majestic. All over the shallow bowl, great round lumps of granite lay strewn and the little mud-walled cabins with their faded thatch, peeped from behind these monstrous grey rocks, as if in terror. Even the patches of green potato gardens that usually did a little to brighten this desolate greyness at this time of year, had now turned black. It was just as if an army of giants had carried off the earth's rich surface, its fruit-bearing soil and its comeliness and left only the dried entrails and the mangled bones. And the great boulders with which they had squashed its life.

After he had descended about a quarter of a mile, past the graveyard and the little whitewashed chapel where the curate said Mass, a very ragged youth came running out from a fence with his hat in his hand.

"This way, your honour," he said. "It's over here."

He pointed to the left. There was a small hut at the far end of a very rocky and barren little field. Then he ran towards the hut, throwing up his bare feet behind, so that the doctor could see their black soles, as he walked his horse carefully among the loose rocks. There was a great deal of filth around the hut, which was quite tiny and had neither chimney nor window. Smoke came out the doorway. A stinking pool lay right in front of the doorway. The doctor dismounted.

"Are you the sick woman's son?" he said, handing the reins to the youth.

The youth nodded and grinned excitedly. He was undoubtedly half an idiot. There was a great boil on his neck. In his excitement he now put on his hat and it proved to have no crown, as his matted hair stood up through it, like a dusty black bush. Two long upper teeth stuck out over his lower lip as he grinned. A pitiable sight!

"Why don't you clear this away?" said the doctor, standing in front of the pool, which barred the entrance into the house. "This is a nice thing to have in front of a house where there is a sick woman. Why don't you remove it?"

The youth continued to grin. Then he scratched his shoulders against his clothes and said in a singsong voice: "That does be always there, sir. It's the dung-hill, only there's water in it on account of the rain last night. There was a shower in the glen. And she's not sick either, I don't think, sir, for she never moves, not since she ate a feed of nettles the night before last. Me and my brother Michael and she ate them. Devil another thing we ate for a week. No one lives near here now, sir, since Toomey the blacksmith went to America. The next house you'll find down the glen there belongs to Patch Feeney. We borrowed the ass from him that Michael brought to call you. Devil a move she made, sir, since she ate the nettles, so we got frightened, Michael and me. She's swollen up. I was afraid in the house with her, so I went out on the road to wait for you. There's no one else near here and it's lonely and terrible, with the graveyard over there."

Here the youth burst into tears, dropped the reins and sat down, hiding his face in his battered hat. The mare snorted and ran a little distance away from the house. The doctor uttered an exclamation of disgust and leaped across the pool. He landed in the doorway and banged his head against the lintel. He swore and entered the hut. The foul air almost drove him out again. He conquered his revulsion with an effort and looked around. It was quite dark there, as the place was full of peat smoke. Near the hearth, on a pile of brush, a woman lay on her back. Some rags covered part of her body. Her bare legs stuck out, swollen and stiff, from these rags. Her stomach was swollen to a great size. Her jaw had dropped.

"What's the trouble?" said the doctor.

He could not see her very well. As she made no reply, he approached and bent over her. Then he straightened himself at once.

"Good God!" he said.

The woman was stone dead and had been dead for some time. She was already in an advanced stage of corruption and it was obvious to him what had been the cause of her death. A spasm of fear swept through him. It was the first case of plague that he had experienced. He hurried out of the hut without even drawing a corner of the ragged cloth across her dead face. In his haste to get away from the hut, he splashed through the filthy pool. That made him still more afraid, for fear it might be infected. He shouted at the youth:

"How long has she been sick?"

"Is she sick?" said the youth.

"She's dead," said the doctor brutally. "What's her first name?"

"Dead?" cried the young man, throwing himself down on the ground.

He burst into a loud wail and the doctor could get no further information out of him for a long time. He was on the point of mounting his horse and hurrying back to the village, since it was imperative to report the appearance of contagious fever at once, when he realised that he should warn the youth not to go near the house.

"You'll be dead, too, if you go in there," he said.

The youth stopped wailing, looked at the doctor and said in an exhausted tone:

"I don't care. I'm hungry. It's the hunger we have, sir. It's been on us since winter."

"My God!" said the doctor, overcome by a terrible shame at the harsh way he had spoken to the lad. "Follow me. I'll give you something to eat. Make haste now. I'm in a hurry."

The lad looked up at him incredulously. And then, with a wild cry, he jumped to his feet and tried to embrace the doctor's knees. The doctor drew away.

"Run on," he said.

"Oh! I will, sir," said the lad. "God bless your honour. I'll run for my life. May the Lord increase everything your honour has. May the Virgin Mary bless you, sir."

The doctor mounted the mare and followed the lad, who had by now reached the road. For some distance he kept in front, spurred to a great effort by the hope of food; but his recent privations finally took effect on him. He slackened his pace to a walk and then came to a halt by the fence, panting loudly.

"I can go no farther, your honour," he said. "I feel sick."

The doctor shuddered. Had the lad also got the fever?

Conquering his fear, he got off his horse and examined him. There was no sign of the disease. It was just hunger that made him weak and sick at the stomach, which had already swollen considerably. He put the youth on the mare and then mounted behind. In that way he rode towards the village. It was evidence of the people's apathy that those whom he passed on the road took no notice of the lad slouching on the mare's back. They all walked in silence, their eyes on the road. At first the doctor did not remark their number. There were always people trooping into the village since the scarcity had begun. As he came nearer home, however, he realised that this was no ordinary procession of beggars and of people going to seek work. There were whole families in this procession and many of the older people carried bundles, as if they were leaving their homes. He even passed a very old woman, who was carried along on her son's back. At last, when he came in sight of the village street and saw that it was densely packed with people, he leaned towards a group whom he was then passing and questioned them.

"What's going on to-day?" he said. "Why are ye all going into Crom?"

A woman turned her pale face towards him and cried:

"The great hunger has come."

Then several voices cried out mournfully:

"Aye! The hunger has come. We are following our heads before us."

Not an eye glanced towards the youth who was now fallen over the saddle, with his eyes closed. Pity had died on hunger's approach.

CHAPTER XLII

IN THE ANGLE made by the road which descended, curving sharply, west of the parish priest's house towards Clogher, there was a small copse of pine-trees. The ruins of the old monastery and the graveyard lay to the east of this copse, perched on the highest point of Crom Hill. There were no more than a few dozen of these trees and the ground on which they stood was held sacred, although it did not really form part of the graveyard. But there was an old legend which said that each one of the trees was really a monk, who had died for the faith in ancient times. A stone fence surrounded the place and not even the small boys of the village ever ventured on to the holy ground, to play hide and seek, or to rummage for the nests of the vast multitude of birds that congregated in it. For it was truly a bird sanctuary, as a result of its sacred character. Indeed, if the tall old trees were really martyred monks, these latter had pleasant music to cheer their after life.

This morning, however, the music which came from the feathered throats of these birds was discordant and war-like. A great multitude of strangers from Black Valley and Glenaree had invaded the sanctuary during the night, flying from the stench of the blight; and the former inhabitants resented this intrusion. Crows, starlings, magpies, thrushes, sparrows, linnets, and even gentle robins took part in the quarrel. Some were driven away and flew southwards towards Clogher, but others kept arriving from the north to renew the tumult.

In the centre of this copse there was a little arbour, where Father Roche was in the habit of coming nearly every day to meditate and read his breviary. A path led to the arbour from his house and he was the only one to use it. He was now on his knees in the arbour, praying to God for help. The sunlight, coming through the pine-trees, shone on his bald head, which was bent over his clasped hands. His eyes were closed. Although his lips moved, uttering prayers, his mind was unable to concentrate on what he was asking the Lord. In fact, he was half asleep. It had rained during the night and now the warm sunshine was drawing up the moisture from the earth, making the air drowsy. The clamour of the birds, harsh as it was, also helped to numb his senses. Finally, he was ashamed to face God, "after the mess I have made of everything." So he had told himself that morning, when the people from Black Valley and Glenaree began to gather in the road in front of his house. He had fled from them to this copse, ashamed to face them since he had nothing to give them. And now he was ashamed to face God, after his first appeal for help. God had not answered, or given any inspiration. So he had closed his eyes and abandoned himself to this dumb reverie.

And then, suddenly, he heard a voice in the copse near by. He started, opened his eyes, raised his head, and listened. Again he heard the voice:

"De profundis clamavi at te dominum. Domine exaudi vocem meum."

"A miracle," cried the poor priest, crossing himself.

Half-awake, he thought at first that it was the voice of God, at last answering his prayer; but as he became fully conscious, he recognised the voice as that of Father Geelan. Then he flushed deeply and got to his feet.

"Nice state of affairs," he said aloud.

Anger was always his refuge in times of crisis. Now he hurried towards Father Geelan in a furious temper. He found the curate standing near the ruins of the old tower east of the copse, praying aloud. He coughed, and the curate turned round. He also flushed.

"Good morning, Tom," said Father Roche. "Nice state of affairs, the two of us like a pair of runaways. There they are out in the road. Well! We have to face them. There is no use running away from it any longer. It's here now. This is the end of them, unless something is done."

He fluttered his hands in front of the curate, as a fighting cock flutters his wings at an enemy. The curate looked exalted.

"I'm glad to hear you say that," he answered. "The hour has come. I didn't come here to run away, but to ask God for help in what is before me."

Father Roche's anger immediately changed to fear. In a whisper he said:

"And what would that be, if I might ask, as your ecclesiastical superior?"

"The hour has come to strike," cried the curate. "If we are to die, let us die a soldier's death."

Father Roche at once began to dance around the curate, no longer like a cock, but like a frightened hen.

"You're at it again," he cried. "I thought you were cured of that. So that's what you're up to. Rebellion? Physical force? Isn't there a clause laid down in the Repeal Association, ordering the total disclaimer of physical force, violence, or breach of the law, any violation of the laws of men, or the ordinances of the eternal God, whose holy name be blessed? Isn't there? And what's more, most dutiful and ever inviolate loyalty to our most gracious and ever-beloved sovereign, Queen Victoria?"

"There is no law of God or man," cried the curate, "that forbids the destitute to sustain life. Come what may, I have decided to call upon the people to fight for their rights."

"With what, you fool?" cried Father Roche. "With their fists against bayonets? You're mad. I forbid you to stir a hand, or foot, or to speak a word. I'll have you unfrocked."

The curate drew himself to his full height, stared at his superior fiercely, and then relaxed. He bowed his head, shook, and muttered:

"Maybe you're right. But if you are, this is the beginning of the end for the Church. If the Church can't lead her flock to battle in the cause of justice and liberty, then she must make room for those who can, for those who look upon the sword as a sacred weapon in defence of justice."

Then he raised his head and cried:

"We could at least help to feed the people. There is no law against our asking the authorities to open the food depots."

"I'm sorry, Tom," said Father Roche, "for the hasty words I spoke. This is no time for arguments. Let us go and do our duty."

Side by side, they returned to the parish priest's house. They entered by the back. In the kitchen, they met the housekeeper, who told them that the yard in front was full of people, asking for food.

"Give them everything there is in the house," said Father Roche. "Come on, Tom."

He and the curate opened the front door and came face to face with the people. The yard, the road outside and the whole street as far east as the chapel was crowded with the hungry. They had stood in silence until the two priests appeared. Then a great shout arose from the mob:

"The hunger is on us, father."

Tears suddenly ran down the parish priest's face as he heard this cry. Then he raised his hands above his head and answered:

"All I have I give to ye. Have patience now and I'll see what more can be done."

Here the curate stepped forward and cried out:

"We'll get them to open the food depots."

"God bless Father Tom," shouted the people.

Chapter XLIII

WHEN GOVERNMENT IS an expression of the people's will, a menace to any section of the community rouses the authorities to protective action. Under a tyranny, the only active forces of government are those of coercion. Unless the interests of the ruling class are threatened, authority remains indifferent. We have seen how the feudal government acted with brutal force when the interests of the landowner were threatened, even to the extent of plundering the poor people's property. Now it remains to be seen what that same government did when those poor lost, by the act of God, all that was left to them by the police and Mr. Chadwick – the potato crop which they had sown.

As the two priests marched at the head of their people towards the courthouse, a force of police emerged from the barracks with bayonets fixed to their carbines. The district inspector, assisted by the head constable and all the sergeants in the garrison, commanded this force. The district inspector had a drawn sword in his hand. He drew up his men in line across the street, from Hynes's shop to the courthouse. Another detachment had been drawn across the road to Glenaree, blocking approach to the village from that direction. All the people within the space guarded by the bayonets of the police had been driven back in either direction.

"Halt," said the district inspector, when he came within a few yards of the priests. "I forbid these people to advance."

The crowd behind the priests came to a halt. So did Father Roche. Father Geelan continued to advance, until he was close to the district inspector. Then he shook his fist in the inspector's face and cried:

"I've had enough of your threats, you hired murderer.

Neither you nor anybody else will stop these poor people from demanding justice."

Then he turned towards the people, waved his arm, and roared:

"Come on, men. Rush them. God save Ireland."

The inspector, astonished by this outburst, stepped aside when the curate rushed at him. The priest, beside himself with anger, ran forward wildly, still shouting. The police did not block his passage. Very cleverly, however, they closed ranks when he had passed through them, so that he now found himself cut off from the people, who had made no attempt to follow him. Father Roche had prevented them. Immediately after the curate had spoken, the parish priest faced the people, threw out his arms, and called on them to halt. He was jumping off the ground and waving his arms, like an angry woman shooing trespassing hens from a garden patch. His voice rose to a screech. When the people, who were only too eager to avoid contact with the bayonets, had drawn back in obedience, he turned to the district inspector.

"What is the meaning of this?" he stammered.

"Are you not aware," said the inspector insolently, "that this district is proclaimed? All assemblies liable to lead to a breach of the peace are forbidden."

"But these people were…" began Father Roche.

"Your curate has plainly told me what they were going to do," interrupted the inspector. "I have had complaints from Mr. Hynes that they were going to raid his shop."

"It's a lie," cried Father Roche. "They were just going to ask for help, to have the food depots opened."

"Let them do that through their proper representatives on the Relief Committee," said the inspector. "This crowd must disperse at once or take the consequences, and I hold you responsible if you interfere with the authorities in the execution of their duty. Are you aware that the plague has broken out in Glenaree and that some of these people may be carrying the pest?"

"The plague?" cried the priest, now completely crestfallen. "What plague?"

"Tell them to disperse," said the inspector. He raised his voice and addressed the people: "Every one of you must get back home at once. Anyone caught in the street in an hour's time will be arrested. Come along."

Then he turned to Father Roche once more and said:

"Do your duty, Father Roche. Tell them to disperse quietly."

The priest meekly obeyed. He called on the people to disperse. For a few moments nobody moved, but when the police began to advance with their bayonets pointed for attack the stampede began. Some ran into the lanes. Others fled down the road towards the relief works. Others turned north towards the mountains. The curate had by now come back through the line of police and he ran after the people, shouting: "Stand fast, men. They dare not fire. Come back." Nobody paid any heed to him and he finally came to a halt in the middle of the street, panting. Tears of fury were streaming down his cheeks. Father Roche ran over to him and threatened him with his fists, while the inspector smiled, amused at the scene.

"I'll report this to the bishop," cried Father Roche.

The curate looked at him and said:

"God forgive you."

Then he strode away, stooping, towards his lodgings. Father Roche ran back to the inspector.

"They're gone now," he stuttered. "Does that satisfy you? But where are they going to get fed? They can't die of hunger. I won't let them die of hunger."

The inspector shrugged his shoulders and said:

"That should be the business of the Relief Committee. My business is to keep the peace."

"Nice way to do it," said Father Roche, "with bayonets."

"It wasn't these bayonets that were responsible for the cowardly murder of Mr. Chadwick," said the inspector.

"What do I care about Mr. Chadwick?" cried Father Roche. "Why don't ye catch and punish whoever did it? That's no excuse to browbeat and threaten innocent people. I'll report you for this."

"You're at liberty to do so," said the inspector. "Forward."

He marched forward with his policemen, clearing the village. Father Roche now found himself alone in the middle of the street. A blind anger made him clench his fists and mutter aloud:

"Hired murderers they are. It's true for Tom Geelan. Maybe he's right after all, God forgive me."

And then he began to walk slowly towards the hotel, his hands behind his back, stooping, hot with angry shame, without purpose, beaten. His anger was not the triumphant ferocity of rebellion, which rushes to arms and battle against the enemy. It was rather the impotent rage of defeat and it brought with it one of those moments of intense lucidity, which come even to stupid and irrational people, when they find themselves at the end of their foolish resources in a crisis. Now he realised, as he walked, that it was the policy of "peace at any price," preached by him and by all the other priests and politicians in command of the great Repeal Association, that had produced this catastrophe, a disillusioned, disheartened, disorganised people at the mercy of the tyrannical government. A few short months ago, less than a year ago, if the bugles of war had been sounded, a million men would have been ready, armed with the frenzy of revolutionary faith, to crush the feudal robbers that oppressed them. But the demagogue O'Connell had professed himself a pacifist and a loyal subject of Her Majesty. The bishops also preached peace and obedience to the laws that gave them fat bellies and rich vestments and palaces. All those in command said that life must be spared and that no cause was worth the shedding of a single man's blood. Now that blood was going to rot in starved bodies; bodies that would pay for the sin of craven pacifism the punishment that has always been enforced by history.

Rotting blood! Corruption! The air smelt of it already. Down from the mountain glens, it had descended on the village over-night. The gardens had turned black before the cottage doors. All was still and hot and foul in the desolate village. Not a sound but the tramping of the policemen's feet and the distant cries of those that fled. All doors had been shut. Faces peered at windows. Silence! Could it have been here, on this sloping green lawn before the chapel, that Mr. McCarthy Lalor, "the saviour of the people," had spoken at last autumn's fair, proclaiming the might and the resolution of the people's representatives?

Father Roche walked over to the hotel and entered. John Hynes and a small group of people were in the hall, talking excitedly. They became silent when Father Roche appeared.

"What happened?" said Father Roche angrily to Hynes. "Why did you complain to the police?"

"Sure they were threatening me in my own shop," said Hynes. "I had to get help or they might tear me to pieces. In my own shop. Heh!"

Now his tone was arrogant. This famine had made a man of him. He was not even afraid of the parish priest, whom he had formerly regarded with the subservient awe of a slave.

"You might have come to me," said Father Roche. "There was no need to go to the police. Look what they have done now. Bayonets. It will be hard to get the government to act if they think we are a gang of rowdies."

"Huh!" said Hynes. "It's too much action we have and not enough of the right kind."

He looked around him for approval at the group of people who stood there. They were all in the nervous state of people hiding from a mob. They were government officials attached to the works, lodging at the hotel, all except Simms, the sanitary officer, and Mrs. Hynes. They nodded approval of Hynes's speech. Father Roche was impressed by their attitude. Being a timid man, in spite of his violent temper, he was always influenced in his ideas by his environment.

"But what happened?" he said mildly.

"I'll tell you, father," said Hynes. "Come on in and sit down."

The priest followed him into a small room off the hall. The other people also followed. The priest sat down. Then Hynes continued, in an excited fashion, making a curious and repeated gesture as he spoke. He held his withered right hand close to his side and his left hand, clenched, out in front. Then he bent down in the middle and struck at the ground with his clenched hand, like a man using a hammer.

"There are some people," he said, "that are a curse to themselves and to their neighbours. Who brought all the trouble on this parish? Who was the greatest agitator in this parish? Gleeson the weaver, him that's now transported to Australia, after he tried to murder the police with his pike. Who turned a certain house here into a bawdy house and dragged people's name in the gutter with the scandal she spread? Gleeson's daughter, her that's now gone God knows where. Who murdered Mr. Chadwick, Lord have mercy on him and he owing me money that was never paid? Gleeson's son that's now dead and the husband of his other daughter Mary and he out hiding now, with a price on his head. Them are the people that brought all the trouble, that same people, the riots and the proclamations and the taking of the people's stock, so that money is owed me that will never be paid. Never. And then, along with that, along comes this daughter of his to-day, Mary Kilmartin, with that rowdy Thomsy Hynes and old Kilmartin himself along with her. What did she do? Old Kilmartin used to be a decent man until she came into his house. Now he's as bad as herself in his old age. The three of them were there, with a crowd of people after them. She was talking as she came into the shop. Agitating she was outside, same as her father before her. Heh! He had the history of

Ireland on his finger-tips, but he's safe now where he can't agitate, him and his pike. Up she comes to the counter and she says: 'Three shillings for yellow meal is robbery.' Old Kilmartin stood beside her and the look of him would terrify you. So I says how could I afford to sell it for less and my son going to the expense of importing it from abroad and then carting it from the town, but would she listen? The shouting began and I slipped out the back way, pretending I was going to go for the meal and that it was out in the shed. I ran to the barracks and cried murder. Was I right or was I wrong?"

Here he turned for approval to his audience. The parish priest got up and said:

"But did she threaten you? Was it all she said that the price was too much? How did she threaten you?"

"Threaten me?" said Hynes. "Father Roche, am I an honest man? Have I worked the nails off my fingers all my life? Did I ever raise a hand to a neighbour? Have I failed in my religious duties? Have I, father?"

"You have not, John," said the priest, "but you had no right to call in the police all the same. You should have come to me."

"They were in an ugly mood," said Simms, the sanitary officer, a thin little man with drooping fair moustaches, a Protestant, who also acted as clerk to the petty sessions and sexton for the parson. "It's the plague very likely that excited them. The plague has arrived, Mr. Roche."

Father Roche became furious at being called mister and on finding this "Protestant" taking sides in an affair that should concern only "Catholics". Had it come to this? The "people" were being hunted by the bayonets of the police, while he was here parleying with supporters of the "government."

"What plague?" he shouted.

"An old woman died of it," said the sanitary officer, twitching his moustaches as he sniffed. "It's here alright, Mr. Roche. Up in Glenaree. I'm on my way up there, as soon as order is restored."

"That will be never," said Hynes, again making the gesture of threatening something on the floor with a hammer. "Lock them all up, every one of them, the agitators."

"Father, I want to speak to you," interrupted a voice at the door.

Everybody looked in astonishment towards the voice. The doctor stood in the doorway. He was very flushed and his little eyes looked angry.

"Is it me you want?" said Father Roche.

"Yes, I'd like to speak to you, too," said the doctor, "but it's father I want to speak to about something."

John Hynes became furtive as soon as he heard his son's voice. He hid his withered arm behind his back and dropped his head, so that his eyes now appeared from beneath the rim of his black hat. He followed Father Roche out of the room. The young men working on the relief scheme and the sanitary officer looked at one another and winked. Mrs. Hynes also left the room. The priest and her husband followed the doctor into the sitting-room. Mrs. Hynes was about to enter with them, but the doctor raised his hand and forbade her. Then he closed the door.

"I'm glad you're here," he said to Father Roche. "I don't want to be partly responsible any longer for my father's conduct and I want you to be a witness."

"What's this?" said Hynes. "What are you saying?"

"I say you are a robber," said the doctor.

"Easy now," said Father Roche, stepping between them and holding up his hands. "Don't lose your temper. What's troubling you?"

The doctor pointed with his forefinger at his father and cried in a shrill voice:

"He refused them credit. He'd rather let them die of hunger than give them a grain of yellow meal on credit."

"Son, son," cried Hynes, "sure I couldn't…"

"So that's what it was," said Father Roche, turning on

Hynes. "It's credit they were looking for, is it? You told me they…"

"Wasn't it the same thing," said Hynes, stepping back, until he got his rump against the table and looking at them with a fierce light in his foxy eyes, "as to give it to them for nothing? Would they ever pay me back? What have they got to pay with?"

"All we have we got from them," said the doctor. "Father Geelan said so. It was their pennies that…"

"So you're turning against your own father," snarled Hynes, "me that worked the skin off my back to raise you and to make you a doctor. Now you're turning against me."

"Easy now, John," said Father Roche. "Couldn't you give them credit until times are better?"

"When will they be better for them ruffians?" cried Hynes. "Where are they going to get the money to pay?"

"The government," said Father Roche, "will make another loan for works. They'll have to. And it's in your own interests to give credit. Otherwise the food depots will have to be opened."

"They can't open them," shouted Hynes. "There's a law against it, as long as there are merchants able to supply the needs of the people. The law can't let me risk my money to import meal and then cut the ground from under my feet."

"You're not speaking like a good Catholic," said Father Roche.

"It's my money," shouted Hynes, again threatening the floor with his imaginary hammer. "My money that I gathered together, penny by penny all these years, while the loafers that now want credit from me were pelting me with stones. And now my own flesh and blood is calling me a miser."

"And that's what you are," cried the doctor, "a miser. I hate you, you horrible old man. I hate you. I'm done with you. I'll leave your house. I won't be responsible for…"

Here he began to stammer, failing to find words for his

anger. Then he shook both his hands at his father and cried again:

"I hate you."

He turned to leave the room. Hynes rushed towards him, caught him by the tail of his coat and cried in a whining tone:

"Wait a minute, son. Where are you going?"

The doctor wheeled round and whispered:

"I'm going to leave this house. I'm going to find lodgings somewhere else, where I won't feel ashamed of myself."

"You can't do that, Tom," said Father Roche. "At this hour, we must stick together. And you, too, John, you must be reasonable. A bit of credit won't ruin you. You had no right to call in the police. The government will have to act. They must act. It's up to us…"

At that moment, loud and hearty laughter came from the hall outside, and then there was a knock at the door.

"Is Father Roche there?" cried a voice.

"Come in," said Father Roche.

Mr. Crampton entered the room. He looked the embodiment of health and good living. His ruddy cheeks were creased with a smile. His baldish head was covered with dots of perspiration. He was even fatter than when he had called on Mr. Chadwick.

"Good day, gentlemen," said this worthy. "Have I broken in on a private meeting? Apologies. Good day, Mr. Hynes. And you, doctor? By the way, Father Roche, could I have a word with you? No, no. It's nothing private. I must say I have enjoyed my stay here. Marvellous country. And I'll allow myself the pleasure of thinking that my visit may bear some fruit, what? The idea of social organisation, you know, always a valuable thing, as the politicians say, to inculcate…Never very good at speech-making. Fact is, Father Roche, that we're going to pack up. No more money in the bank. I'll be sorry to leave. Upon my word, I've enjoyed my stay here."

"What's that you say, sir?" said Hynes.

Father Roche went pale and said:

"Do you mean to say that…"

"The works are coming to an end," interrupted Crampton, rubbing his hands together and leaning back on his heels. "The government has come to the conclusion that, with the coming in of the harvest, they would only detract from work on the land, those that…"

The doctor was suddenly overcome with a nervous desire to laugh. He stuffed his handkerchief into his mouth and hurried over to the fire-place, as Father Roche went to Mr. Crampton and stammered:

"You…you…mean to say they…they're going to stop the…the…the relief works?"

"Going to stop the works?" said Hynes. "What about me? I have a stock of meal that…"

"Not at once," said Crampton. "Not at once. Another week or two. But the local committee appears to have overstepped the mark. There's a chance, of course, that money could be raised from the banks, ha, ha, by mortgaging the stones; there's quite a mountain of them, that have been broken, excellent material for road-making and…"

At this point, the doctor could control himself no longer. With his handkerchief stuffed in his mouth, he rushed to the door and left the room, as the priest said:

"But don't they know about the blight?"

"Oh! That," said Mr. Crampton, "is bound to be purely local. You might say, a spot left over from last year's failure. In the major part of the country…"

The doctor closed the door behind him and hurried along the hall. The sanitary officer, Mr. Simms, came up to him and said:

"We must go now, doctor."

The doctor halted and looked at Simms.

"What are you talking about?" he said. "Go where?"

"The old woman," said the sanitary officer. "Up in the Glen. The plague.

"Oh, yes. The plague," said the doctor.

Now he no longer wanted to laugh. Instead, tears rushed to his eyes and he felt chilly down his back. He walked out of the hotel with the sanitary officer. The pair of greys which had formerly belonged to Mr. Chadwick stood outside the door, attached to Chadwick's carriage, now painted a dark grey colour. They looked beautiful. Mr. Coburn came trotting from the courthouse, fluttering his hands in front of him and muttering. He waved his hand to the doctor. The doctor slipped in behind the carriage and then hurried away up the street as fast as he could. Suddenly he felt that he hated all humanity.

CHAPTER XLIV

"WELL!" THOMSY SAID. "We had little for our journey."

"Is a side of bacon nothing?" Mary said. "Along with the satisfaction of giving that miser a bit of my mind."

"I never thought it would come to this," said the old man. "That I'd be eating what was stolen in my own house."

They were, in fact, sitting down to a stolen meal. As Hynes had said truly enough, Mary had come into the shop, followed by the old man, Thomsy, and a crowd which had got furious because the Relief Committee was not in session that day. She had terrified Hynes by calling him a miser and demanding that he give her credit. When he went into the shed at the back of the shop, she edged over towards the wall where a side of bacon was hanging. Watching her chance, while the crowd was shouting for Hynes, she managed to slip the bacon under her cloak without being seen. Then she stole towards the door and was one of the first to get away when the police emerged from the barracks. The three of them had regained the village by following the mountain path without being apprehended. And now they were eating some of the bacon, together with potatoes that had been left over from breakfast.

"I didn't steal it," she said fiercely. "I took it. A person has a right to take things to keep alive. I have to feed him that God sent me."

" 'Faith," said Thomsy, "stolen or not, it tastes lovely."

"It does, then," said Maggie, "but all the same, it's not right to steal. If it was known you did it, Mary, it would go hard with you."

"Oh! Let ye be quiet," said Mary. "Aren't ye all eating it? Ye can't have it both ways. And I'd do it again, too, if I got the chance. I'm not going to die of hunger, nor my child either, while I have a pair of hands. Eat up quick, will ye, before anybody might come in."

Now she looked quite a virago. The imminence of famine had wrought a marked change in her countenance. She bore a strange resemblance to Kitty Hernon. There was no similarity of features and her beauty was still as radiant as ever. But there was a similarity in the expression of the mouth and of the eyes. Her mouth had gathered together, somehow, like the first movement of the mouth of a person going to whistle. Her eyes seemed to be searching for something. They were never still. They were fierce, on the alert, suspicious. Her hands, too, were shifty, and it was pitiful the way she now grabbed at her food, tore it greedily with her teeth and looked around in an uncouth fashion while she ate; just like the old man. Formerly, she used to be so dainty and so restful, as if she were in a delicious swoon of passion.

Indeed, all five of them ate as if this were their last meal and as if some enemy were coming, hotfoot, to pluck the food from their lips. The smell of the boiled bacon hovered on the air. It was such an unusual smell that even the cat had ventured to approach the house, hoping to find some benefit. He did not enter, however. He had become too wild for that. But he lay on his belly by the door, his whiskers on the doorstep, watching. The dog was licking and chewing the bone of the bacon by the back door. He suddenly dropped the bone and roamed around looking for water, as the bone was very salty. Not being able to find any within reach, he returned to his bone and carried it out into the yard. The cat fled on his approach. Presently they heard the dog bark outside.

"Quick," said Mary. "Somebody is coming. We must hide this."

She jumped to her feet and seized the kish. Thomsy grabbed the last bit of bacon from it. The old man took a potato. There was nothing else left. Mary ran into the small bedroom, telling Maggie to take the pot also.

"Devil mend whoever it is," said the old man, stuffing the potato into his mouth.

Maggie hurried into the room with the pot. She had barely done so when Sally O'Hanlon entered.

"It's Sally," said Mary, coming out of the bedroom and putting her hand on her heart. "You put the fear of God in us."

The old man made gestures to Mary behind Sally's back, giving her to understand that Sally was not to be told about the bacon. Mary laughed. Sally stared at them and then sniffed.

"What smell is this?" she said. "It wouldn't be meat?"

" 'Faith, it is," said Mary, "and you'll have some of it. It was a present I got from my cousin Julia in Liverpool."

"Lucky for you," said Sally, "to have a cousin in Liverpool. God help me, I have a cousin nowhere."

Then she sank down by the wall on her heels near the door, threw her skirt over her head and began to wail. They were all astonished. Never before had anyone seen this little woman give way to tears. Mary went on her knees beside her and said:

"Oh! Sally, what has happened? What ails you atall? You put the heart crosswise in me. You crying? Is it Patsy that got hurt?"

Sally dropped her skirt from her face and said in a low voice:

"True for you, asthore, and it's no wonder you're surprised to see me crying. Though it's myself that says it, I was never a whinger. I kept a bold, hard face to the hailstones of misfortune all my life. But there's a boundary to the courage of the human heart. They say in the Holy Book that Samson was a mighty man, him that slaughtered the Lord's enemies with the jawbone of an ass. But he met his end, poor man, when he least expected it. The strongest falls, when he's weakened with misery, under the swinging of a wooden sword in the hands of a child. And 'faith, it's no wooden sword but a murdering blunderbuss, powder and ball, burning brimstone and the evil eye of the devil in Hell that's now quenching the power of life in me, like you squeeze the guts out of a louse with the fingernail."

This flow of wild words poured from her little mouth like the flow of water in a rocky mountain gulch on a cold winter's day, when the angry wind is howling and the sky is patched with torn clouds and the ragged earth is dark and desolate. Her wrinkled, yellow face was puckered with anger and although she had now ceased to weep, the tears flowed down crookedly through the deep crevices in her thin cheeks. In her eyes was that dreadful famine look; the scared stare of an animal.

"But what is it?" the old man said. "What happened?"

"Patsy was laid off from the works," said Sally.

"He was?" said Thomsy. "Oh! Bloody woe!"

"Woe it is," said Sally, "and a hungry death for all of us. The plague is here, and let it come when it likes. There is an open door for it, and not a hand strong enough to chase the wolf of destruction from the hearth. He came back like a corpse walking. Weak enough he's been this last while, digging that hill on a half-filled belly. But he bore up, poor man, knowing that his children depended on him. Mr. Crampton came to-day and laid off two score of them. The others will go next week. There's no more money, unless they can raise it on the heap of stones they've broke. Who wants stones and mountains full of them all round? Is it mad the world has got, to let the poor die of hunger while there's so much riches? Tell me that, old man. How can God above hold back his thunder, when such things are happening? Didn't Christ die for us all? He didn't die for the rich alone. Oh! God have mercy on us."

Here she threw up her hands, clasped them above her head and then again she rocked herself in tears. Now Maggie and Mrs. Gleeson joined her. Mary hurried into her room with a knife, cut a piece off the stolen bacon and brought it to Sally.

"Take this, Sally," she said, "and don't lose heart. Oh! Sally, it was you was the brightness of our life in all the sorrow that came on us, so don't fail us now. Do you hear me? Take this bit of meat. It's little, but it will help. And it came to me in the same way as the milk you gave me a while back. Oh! Laugh, Sally, and let us face what is before us with a smile anyway."

And Mary, kneeling on the floor before Sally, burst into a peal of loud laughter; but there were tears in her eyes and her voice was tremulous. Sally took the meat and then threw her arms round Mary. They both wept softly.

"Stop whining, the two of you," said the old man to his wife and Mrs. Gleeson, who were still wailing by the hearth. "Mary is right. I declare to God, this house is getting to be like a wake house. A man can't think of what to do in it."

"This will be a great help, surely," said Sally, looking at Mary's gift. "We have a grain of meal left and Patsy has wages coming to him, whenever he gets it. The little they pay it's not regular they pay it. The rich are paid on the nail and it's jail for those that don't pay them, but the poor are left to whistle for their mite. Ah! The poor! Why did God ever pester the world with them? But you're right, Mary. 'Faith, from now on, the hands that God gave me are going to be as nimble as the paws of a trick-o'-the-loop. True for you, asthore."

"That's the talk," said Mary, getting to her feet. "Oh! Sally, you put new heart in me. What do you think is best to do?"

"I know what I'm going to do," said Sally. "As soon as we get Patsy's wages, we'll take to the road. There's nothing here, and there won't be anything, either."

"The road?" said the old man angrily. "What's to be got on the road? Isn't it crowded with the hungry following their faces?"

"It leads to where there's riches," said Sally. "We might get to Dublin itself before the cold of winter comes."

"Maybe you're right," said Mary. "Only for Martin…"

"None of that," said the old man. "This morning you were full of fight and now you're talking of running away again.

Fooh! Stand by the land. You married into this house and into this land. A son has been born to you in this house. And while the sod is there and this roof, the law of God is against you going."

He shouted in anger, stamping on the floor with every phrase.

"Don't deafen us with your shouting," said Mary. "Nobody is going yet."

"And nobody will go," said Brian. "I'll see to that."

"Begob," said Sally, getting to her feet, "you might soon have to go. There is a new agent coming, I hear, in Mr. Chadwick's place. Won't people be evicted that can't pay their rents? They'll clear out the mountains and half the village. It was done in other places."

The old man stared at her. His lips moved, but he could say nothing. This argument was too much for him.

"True for you, Sally," said Thomsy. "Didn't we see them to-day with their bayonets? It's the destruction of the country they're after, same as poor Barney Gleeson used to say."

At the mention of her husband's name, Mrs. Gleeson bent her head and crossed herself.

"I know nothing of that," shouted the old man, going towards the door. "But I'm staying here."

He threatened the air outside with his fist and added:

"Over my dead body they'll come into this house. Huh!"

"Lord save us!" Maggie moaned in the hearth corner. "If we are to die of hunger, couldn't we all die in peace and quietness without shouting and making God angry? Now is the time for us to save our souls with prayer."

Out in the yard, the old man stooped and peered angrily into the kitchen. His eyes were bloodshot. He looked at them in silence. Then he spat and moved away from the door. The dog ran up to him, wagged his tail and let his tongue loll. Then he barked and ran on in front, delighted because his master was going somewhere. The dog was heading for the stile leading to the paddock and down towards the river; but the old man went the other way, towards the road. The dog turned back, raced into the lane and then ran up the mountain through the heather. The old man followed him.

It was now after sunset. Darkness was falling over the earth. The old man followed a path through the heather halfway up the mountain and then sat down on a mossy hillock, where there was a great boulder of granite. He leaned his back against this rock, folded his arms, and looked down into the valley. Not a sound broke the stillness of the evening. There were no birds. No youngsters rollicked at their evening play. All was still as in a dead world. All round this boulder there were droppings of goats and sheep. On the heather and on the sides of the boulder there still remained little wisps of sheep wool and goat hairs. This used to be a meeting-place of animals; a look-out from which they regarded the valley below. There were rabbit-holes there too; but even these were beginning to be overgrown with grass. All life had fled. What awful silence! Even the river, shallow with the summer drought, was silent. All life had ceased. And with the fall of night, a dark shroud passed down from the heights into the valley's bed, as if returning this passing habitation of man to the womb of eternal death.

The dog trotted around for some time, nosing the ground, smelling, and then, finding no fresh scent, no sign of life, he returned to his master. He put his snout on the old man's knee and looked up into his face. The old man was now resting his chin on his hand and his knees were drawn up under him. Tears were flowing silently down his old face. The dog wagged his tail and made a whining noise, trying to attract the old man's attention. But the old man paid no heed. He sat as still as the death around him, weeping on the mountain.

Then the dog raised his snout and began to howl.

CHAPTER XLV

THAT NIGHT, AS she lay awake in bed, brooding over the events of the day, Mary decided to escape from the Valley with her child as soon as possible. She was now convinced that the government would let the people die of hunger. But how was she going to reach Martin and take him to America, with her and little Michael? If she went herself to his hiding-place the police would follow her. The search for him was still active. And even if she managed to join him, the ports were watched and they had no money to pay for passage on a ship.

However, the very thought of escape gave her courage to think it possible. Coming to a decision of any kind is always a great help in a crisis. And she recalled her vision, on the night Martin's brother had fallen sick. Her angel guardian had appeared to her in sleep and taken her to a great ship with white sails on which they embarked. They had gone over the western sea to a rich land, where the corn grew taller than a man's head and there were no masters. And the angel had said: "This is America. Make your home here and God will bless you." Now she was convinced that the angel had foreseen this famine and the dreadful events which had made her husband a hunted assassin. Therefore, he would help her to escape.

This conviction was so thrilling that she could no longer stay in bed. She rose, took the sleeping child from his cradle, and went over to the window. She drew aside the curtain and looked at his little face in the dim light of the moon. Oh! The dear one! In spite of the poor nourishment he was getting, he was fat and strong. Nature had been kind to this little being, even if she had blasted the earth which fed him. He was already quite as big as a child of six months. She fondled him and put him back in his cradle. Then she returned to bed and fell into a profound sleep. Her decision had given her peace.

She was up with the break of dawn. After dressing hurriedly, she went into the kitchen and climbed on to the loft where Thomsy slept. It was dark there. She groped about until she reached his pallet on the floor. She shook him.

"Hush!" she whispered, putting her hand on his mouth, as he began to utter a cry of fright. "Don't let the old man hear you. I want you to do something for me."

"Eh?" he whispered. "Is that Mary? What ails you?"

"Listen, darling," she said. "Rise up and do something for me."

"I'm only half-awake," said Thomsy. "Is it night or morning? What do you want off me?"

"I want you to take a message to Martin."

"To Martin? But…"

"Will you do it or won't you?"

"Sure I will, but are you forgetting that the lads asked us to make no attempt to get near them, for fear the police might get on their tracks?"

"I know that," said Mary, "but we have to take the chance, on account of the way things are now. Anyway, with the hungry going back and forth in crowds on the road, a single man won't be noticed going. And I have to get talking to Martin, so as to…Never mind. The way I have it planned there won't be much danger of them following you. The last word we got was that they're on the island of Inishgola. That's thirty miles west of Clogher by the shore road. If you go north here over the mountain as far as Clashcam and then west over the mountain country, keeping clear of all villages, there won't be a soul that will see you. Then you can creep down to the shore and get a safe person to row you out to the island."

"It will be an almighty journey on an empty belly," grumbled Thomsy, "and they, maybe, not there atall in the heel of the hunt."

"If they're not they'll leave tracks of their going among the safe people of that parish," said Mary. "Anyway, it will be no hungry belly you'll travel on, a mhic. Dress yourself and come down below. You'll go now into the village for meal and I'll make a cake for you."

"Ga!" said Thomsy. "You know best. Anyway, there's no going against you. He's your husband and you wouldn't put him in the way of any harm for a foolish reason. I'll do that, Mary."

"God bless you," said Mary, "and mind you don't mutter a word to a soul, not even to the old man. Swear on your soul you won't."

Thomsy swore, and then Mary climbed back into the kitchen. She went into her room, opened her marriage box, and emptied the contents of the cloth purse on to her palm. There were five shillings and six pennies left. She took one of the shillings and the six pennies, tied up the rest in the purse, stowed it in the box, and returned to the kitchen. Thomsy had now descended the ladder. She gave him the money and hustled him out into the yard with her.

"Get half a stone of meal," she whispered, as they walked to the fence, "and hurry back. It's this evening you'll go with the fall of night, so that no one can see you going over the mountain pass."

It was now broad daylight. When he had set off along the road to the village she turned back to the house. The old man was standing in the doorway dressed only in his shirt.

"Where is Thomsy going at this hour?" he said, scratching his thigh.

"I sent him into the village for something," Mary said.

"What would he be getting at this hour?" said he.

"Meal," she said. "There's none in the house."

He looked at her closely and then entered the kitchen. Later, when he came out of his room dressed and she was kindling the fire, he said to her:

"How much is left in the purse now?"

"Four shillings," she said without looking at him.

Now she felt ashamed of her plot to escape, since it would mean leaving these three old people to their doom. She realised that Brian suspected something.

"It's little enough," he said quietly, as he knelt to say his prayers.

There was no anger in his voice, but his eyes were suspicious.

"He's watching me," Mary thought. "I must be careful. He'd do anything to stop me going."

The two old women had become as suspicious as the old man. It may have been an instinct inherited from nomadic days, when the aged were sacrificed in time of need by the young and vigorous; just as Mary's decision to escape did not take into consideration her duty towards her mother. Under the pressure of hunger, as among soldiers in war, the mask of civilisation quickly slips from the human soul, showing the brute savage beneath, struggling to preserve life at all costs. Maggie and Ellen Gleeson came into the kitchen before the old man had finished his prayers, although of late they had kept to their beds far into the morning. As soon as they had prayed they complained of hunger.

"We must wait until Thomsy comes back," Mary said.

"That would be a fine wait," grumbled Maggie. "Did you ever see him go into the village and not meander there all day, hoping to get a snatch of poitheen?"

"It would be foolish to wait for him, " Ellen Gleeson said.

"Oh, all right," said Mary. "Aren't ye the greedy geese? I'll get ready what there is."

"Pooh!" said the old man. "Do you hear that, women? She thinks the old have no right to eat. Huh!"

Mary went to the back of the house, rummaged about in the garden patch and found three small turnips, one of which was half-eaten by rats. There was nothing else now left there.

These turnips had escaped detection so far, because they were hidden by a clump of nettles. On returning to the house, she found the three old people engaged in earnest conversation by the fire. That also appeared odd to her, since the Kilmartin couple had hitherto kept Mrs. Gleeson at a distance, resenting her presence in the house. In their common danger, the interloper was received into their confidence.

"Now what ails ye?" said Mary, as they stopped talking and looked at her.

"We think," said the old man after clearing his throat, "that you had no right to send Thomsy for meal without asking our advice. What's in the purse belongs to the whole house, so we have a right to say what should be done with it."

Mary threw the turnips on the floor and put her hands on her hips.

"Alright, then," she cried. "Ye can have what's in the purse, but if ye do, I'm leaving this house to-day with little Michael. Does that suit ye?"

This threat immediately quelled the revolt of the old people. Suddenly, they all looked decrepit and miserable, like three aged trees struck by a sudden storm, which cracks the branches, loosens the decaying roots and makes the once proud heads lean towards the collapse of eternal death. Their eyes became lifeless. Mary did not relent.

"Instead of complaining there by the fire," she said in the same angry tone, "ye will have to forage now. We got no satisfaction in the village yesterday, so we have to depend on the earth around us. After breakfast, let ye all go out and gather up what ye can. There's nourishment in nettles and dandelions. There are berries and sloes on the bushes. Old man, let you go down and fish in the river."

"Huh!" said the old man. "Sure, there isn't a fish the size of your thumb in the river and it fished clean these past few months by everybody in the Valley."

However, after they had finished eating the turnips they

set forth. The old women went together with a bag and a small can, to gather nettles and berries. The old man rigged up some fishing tackle. They were not long gone when Thomsy returned. He was excited.

"There's commotion in the village," he said.

"What happened?" said Mary, taking the meal from him.

"I don't rightly know," said Thomsy, "but there are strangers from the town there. They belong to a body of men in England that help the poor. Quakers they call them. I saw one of them and he had a gold time-piece. They are powerful people. It was how word was brought to Clogher about the hunger and the charge made by the police. So a man told me that was after listening to one of the drivers that brought them. The priests are there with them and the parson and another 'big person' from Clogher, him they call the 'big gun'; he's head over the Protestants. The driver from the town said there's lashings of money going to come from these Quakers."

"We heard that before," said Mary as she put some food on the kish for him. "What else did you hear? No peeler talked to you?"

He sat down and crossed himself.

"There was a power of poor people around the strangers," he said, "and the peelers, 'faith, weren't in the road atall. It was like a fair day. Everybody said that food was going to be given to the hungry and that it would come from Clogher on horseback, loaves of white bread. They say the peelers are going to go around to make a list of the people that are in need. The blight is driving all before it down to Clogher."

Mary had begun to get ready for baking the meal, which he had brought. She started on hearing that the police were going to come round.

"My God!" she said. "When are they coming?"

"I don't know," said Thomsy. "Why? What harm is there in it?"

"Never you mind," she said. "Hide yourself some place

beyond the river when you finish eating. Keep out of the way until you are ready to go. They mustn't see you if they come."

Thomsy shrugged his shoulders and said:

"Ga! Sure, what would be the good of them searching here or asking questions?"

"Never mind," she said. "The least thing often gives a plan away. Hurry up and be going."

Thomsy did as he was bid. She baked two cakes on the griddle. She put them out in the yard to cool and sat watching them with her baby. She had hardly done so, when a lad came running down the road from the direction of the village. As he approached, he shouted that the police were coming.

"Where are they?" she said, jumping to her feet.

He made no answer, but ran past towards the head of the Valley. Her heart began to pound. During the first weeks after Martin's disappearance, when there had been police searches day and night, she was not as much afraid as she was now. Her fear was now due to the fact that she had a plan which they might discover. She looked southwards along the road. As yet there was no sign of them. She could see all the way up to the end of the Valley, all except her father's cottage, which was hidden behind a spur of mountain. O'Hanlon's hut was the only house between here and the spur. The southern part of the Valley was all bog. Brown heaps of turf were stacked here and there among the white bog cotton. Over on the left, beyond the grey wall of Crom demesne, the road to Glenaree wound up the mountain, like a white snake creeping through the dark heather. All was still. And then, suddenly, she saw three policemen come around the spur of mountain. The sunlight glistened on their carbines. Four horsemen followed them. The pounding of her heart stopped when she saw the policemen.

"I must hide the cakes," she said.

She ran into the house with them and then hid them in her bed. She felt that they would arouse the suspicions of the police, if the latter searched the house. Then she hurried back to the fence with her child. All along the northern end of the Valley, people were running on to the mountains after hearing the lad's warning. These poor wretches fled from the police as from murderous invaders. Now the police and the horsemen had come to a halt outside O'Hanlon's hut. Sally was curtseying to them. Two of the horsemen dismounted and entered the hut. Just then, Maggie and Ellen Gleeson came into the yard with a bag of nettles and a can in which there were a few berries.

"Who are these 'big people' I see with the peelers?" Maggie said.

"Bad cess to ye," Mary said. "Why didn't ye stay away? Let ye not say a word if the peelers ask ye questions."

"Sure, what could we tell them that would be harmful?" said Ellen Gleeson. "We can only tell them that the hunger is on us."

"Tell them that, then," said Mary. "Start begging from them when they come. Then, maybe, they won't search the house."

"Here they come now," Maggie said.

The two strangers came out of O'Hanlon's hut and remounted their horses. Sally followed the party as it moved away. She was making the sign of the Cross over them.

"They must have given her something," Ellen Gleeson said. "Oh! Did you ever see the like, four men on horseback? It's like the opening of the assizes."

" 'Faith," said Maggie, "I never begged in my life, but with 'big people' like that, maybe it's a fine hansel a person would get."

"Let ye be ready," Mary said. "Say the hunger is on ye and then, maybe, they won't search the house, looking for information about Martin. Ha! Look at Sergeant Geraghty pointing to us. He's telling the strangers about us. Oh! Mother of God! Is it how they got information about Martin? Are they men of the law?"

The group was now quite close. Mr. Coburn and the doctor accompanied the two strangers. Their presence reassured Mary somewhat. Now the old man and Thomsy joined the watchers. His curiosity to see the "big people" had been too much for Thomsy, so he had disobeyed Mary's command to keep hidden. He sidled up behind the old man, who carried a tiny trout in his hand. The old man took off his hat.

"Who are these people, women?" he whispered.

"Whist!" said Mary in a whisper. "Beg off them, old man."

Nobody said a word, however, as the police and the horsemen halted in the road. They were made speechless by the kind of terror which serfs feel in the presence of the ruling class.

"Good day to ye," the parson said.

"God save your honour," they cried in answer.

They found tongue when the parson had broken the spell.

"The hunger is on us," they said. "Noble people, help us."

The two strangers on horseback looked in wonder at the strange group, barefooted and in rags, holding out their hands for help. These two men belonged to a group that had come down from Dublin to investigate conditions in the Congested Districts. They belonged to the Society of Friends. They looked rather alike, except that one had a very wide mouth and the other had a pointed nose. Both had solemn faces, side-whiskers and the sombre clothing of clergymen. But they were related to one another merely by a kinship of conviction; a kinship which often produces a similarity of appearance as marked as that of blood. The man with the pointed nose was called Potter and he belonged to a wealthy merchant family in Dublin. The man with wide mouth was an Englishman of the same class. His name was Broadbent.

"Who is the tenant here?" said Mr. Potter.

"That old man," said the police sergeant, pointing to Brian.

The old man stepped forward and held out the tiny fish.

"That's all I've been doing all morning," he said, "fishing

in the river like a little boy. It's foolish work for an old man. But the hunger is on us. Look at that bag of nettles my wife picked and the hansel of berries in the can. It's like beggars we are, rummaging in the bare fields."

While he spoke, in the garrulous manner he affected towards the gentry, the Quakers dismounted. As there were bags attached to the rear of their saddles, the police had to help them throw their legs over the necks of their horses. The doctor and the parson stayed mounted. The doctor seemed to be ashamed of his company and kept looking towards Mary, who watched the police with suspicion.

"How much land have you here?" said the sharp-nosed Mr. Potter, coming up to the fence. "You're rather too old to be a profitable tenant."

" 'Faith, I am," said Brian, "but it's in my name, although my son is married in the house. He's not here now, though. That's his wife. Your honour, there's ten acres in the share, but the crop failed and the stock was taken. If we get time, noble person, and help from the lord, we'll be on the pig's back again in no time. We are honest tenants, sir. I was always a man of my word. The lord knows that and his bailiff will tell you the same. I never failed a penny on the demand note until the hard times came. That slip of mountain up there before you, as far as the big rock and over to where the blackthorn bush is standing by a little stream, it used to feed five sheep. Never a year but I got in the region of nine lambs from them. A healthy breed, sir, but they're gone now. Down below here, all down to the river, where you see the big grass and the black dog scratching in a hole, all that is mine, too. There was feed for a horse on it as well as a cow and a yearling. God pity us, they are all gone. Forty bushels of praties we used to dig and I sowed more this year, as there was no seed for oats. I put down what would give me over sixty bushels. Not a one of them is left. It's worse than the year of the flood. On top of it all, sir, one son died on me and the other is gone away."

"Where is he gone?" said the wide-lipped Mr. Broadbent.

"That's what the police would like to know," said the sergeant in an undertone, winking at the two constables.

"Oh!" said Mr. Broadbent, after Mr. Potter had whispered in his ear. "This is the young man who…"

The two Quakers now regarded the people in the yard in a rather horrified manner.

"They were always a very respectable family," said the parson, who had now dismounted and was fluttering his lean hands in his usual nervous fashion. "I don't think that, according to law, a man can be judged to have committed a crime until he is convicted of it before a court of law. Even murder. Anything is conceivable under certain conditions, Mr. Broadbent. Do not judge us too harshly. There have been periods in England when deplorable conditions were the rule rather than the exception. Not that I condone outrages. Far from it. Both these families, I refer to the Gleesons, also concerned in this dreadful affair, were always law-abiding and a credit to the community."

Mr. Potter looked at the parson doubtfully and then turned to the doctor.

"Any case of fever here?" he said.

"Not in this Valley," said the doctor. "One in Glenaree."

"Typhus, you said?" said Mr. Broadbent. "That dung-hill, for instance…I dare say that sanitary conditions are…"

"Non-existent, my dear Henry," said Mr. Potter. "Even in the towns. And in outlying districts such as this…Dear me! It was extremely bad policy to allow these places to be tenanted."

"These people," said Mr. Broadbent, "don't seem to be so badly off, judging from their appearance. No sign of actual hunger. Your baby looks fat, my good woman. When have you eaten last?"

Although she had advised the old people to beg, it was with an outburst of passion and in the most insolent manner that Mary answered the gentleman's question. Indeed, his question and his mode of putting it were extremely insolent and not at all in keeping with the principles of conduct expounded by Jesus Christ, whom the worthy man regarded as his master. But Mary had a reason for her outburst other than anger with his manner. She wanted to antagonise these people, whom she now realised to be influenced by charitable intentions and thus prevent them from entering the house. If they entered the police might enter with them and find the cakes.

"If my baby is fat," she cried, "he can thank God for it. It's little thanks are due to the powers, that took our stock and refused us work on the roads. It's not charity we're asking for, sir, but justice. We are not murderers either, sir, but honest people as Mr. Coburn told you, and if my man is on his keeping, I tell you, fine gentlemen, that a man has a right to stand up for his wife and child. You have broad cloth to yer backs, so ye can look at our rags and our dirt. Ye are welcome to it. But maybe the day will come when the poor people of the world will make the tyrants pay with their blood for these rags and this dirt."

She drew back from the fence as she finished her speech, as if preparing a line of retreat from an attack. The two Quakers looked at one another and raised their foreheads in a deploring gesture.

"A pretty exhibition of the unchristian spirit of rebellion," said Mr. Potter.

"Irish temper, I should call it," said Mr. Broadbent. "However, there is nothing like kindness to turn away wrath. Let us give her some bread."

"I agree with you," said Mr. Potter. "We make no distinction, in our work of mercy, between the disloyal and faithful subjects of Her Majesty."

As Mr. Broadbent proceeded to take a loaf of bread from his bag, the parson fluttered his hands, looking at Mary with disapproval. He felt that she had disgraced him in the presence of these strangers. The doctor, on the other hand, looked pleased.

"This will help you for the present," said Mr. Broadbent, handing a small brown loaf to the old man. "Put your faith in God and in Her Majesty's watchful care over you. In due course, a food kitchen will be opened in the village and you will get a meal a day."

The old man tried to kiss the hand which gave him the loaf, but he failed to do so. Mr. Broadbent withdrew his hand hurriedly, fearing contact with old Kilmartin, who might have some contagious disease. Then they all mounted their horses and rode away.

"This is only the beginning of many blessings," Mr. Potter said to them. "God protect you."

The old people crowded to the fence and shouted blessings after the benefactors. Sally O'Hanlon joined them, followed by her children.

"Help has come at last, praised be God," she said. "They gave me a loaf as well. A baker's loaf. It's a miracle, 'faith, fine gentlemen giving bread to the poor in Black Valley. It must be the Queen herself that sent them."

"The riches of them would frighten you," Maggie said. "Did you see the gold chain he had?"

"And look at the people crowding down from the mountain," Ellen Gleeson said. "They ran from the police but they are running to the noble people. They must have smelt the hansel of bread."

"Let us follow after them," said Sally. "It's not every day the poor get a chance of seeing such noble gentry."

They all followed her up the road, except Mary and Thomsy. The latter was on the point of going, as eager as the rest to savour the excitement at close quarters, when Mary caught him by the sleeve.

"You stay here," she said.

Thomsy looked at her mournfully. Then he glanced up

the road at the procession and his mouth watered. It was the instinct of the destitute that made him lust to keep close to these benevolent strangers; the instinct which makes hungry loafers torture their stomachs on a cold winter's day, by standing outside the wall of some luxurious restaurant, sniffing at the rich smell of food that comes from the kitchens through the gratings in the pavement, listening to the clatter of dishes and watching the fur-clad, jewelled women, convoyed by uniformed lackeys and full-bellied escorts, enter between the columns of the doorway, mingling the scent of their perfumes with the odour of magnificent food.

"Why can't I go and watch them?" said he.

"Because now is your time to clear off over the mountain," said Mary.

"How can I go," said Thomsy, "with the peelers in the Valley?"

Mary dragged him back into the house.

"Now is your chance," she said, "while everybody is watching the strange gentlemen. They'll have no eye for a man making off with a bundle. I trust no one. If you were making off with the fall of night, people would wonder where you were going. One word dropped in the village would tell the police what they wanted to know. In a time of hunger like this, no one is to be trusted and money to be earned for informing on a wanted man."

"Very well, then," said Thomsy. "God help me, I'm treated like a dog that kills sheep."

She got the cakes, broke them into pieces and tied them in a cloth bundle. She put the crook of an ash-plant through the knot.

"There's your bundle," she said, "and this is what you are to tell Martin. Tell him I'll come to meet him in some safe place that he can name so as to make plans for his escape out of the country. Say the hunger is on us here and we can't hold out much longer. Tell him it's death or escape for us and we may as well die one way as another. If he can't come to me here, let him say where he could come to me. If he's willing to try to make his escape, tell him I have a plan that might work. Tell him little Michael is well and that I'm longing night and day for him. Give him a kiss for me and for little Michael. And may God reward you, treasure, for going on this journey."

Then she embraced Thomsy, cautioned him against talking to strangers and gave him the dead Michael's brogues.

"They'll save your feet from thorns and sharp stones on the mountains," she said. "Put them on you while I get a shilling for you out of the purse. He might need it where he is."

She went into her room for the shilling while Thomsy put on the old brogues. When she came out she said:

"I think you better say nothing about the hunger being on us. It might make him lose courage. Tell him, though, that an angel came to me in my sleep and told me how to escape to America. Tell him that. And hurry now."

They embraced once more and then Thomsy waddled from the house, with his bundle on his shoulder. He made poor progress across the yard in the old shoes, which were as hard as iron. He halted and said to her:

"Ga! I can't wear them."

"Go on with you," she said. "You'll get used to them. Be quick while they are away at the head of the Valley. God bless you."

Groaning and bent almost double, Thomsy went out into the lane and then up along the mountain-side. He was round as a barrel, climbing the steep mountain through the heather. He halted once, looked back, pointed to his shoes and shook his head. She shook her hands at him, urging him on. Then he disappeared behind the large boulder, turning north. She crossed herself and began to watch the strangers, who were now turning back from the head of the Valley. The whole population was following them. She hid indoors until they had passed.

Some time later, the old people returned. They were babbling excitedly. They had eaten half the brown loaf on the way back; not so much through hunger as through a desire to taste this miraculous bread which had come to them from the hands of the rich strangers. When their excitement died down, Brian asked where Thomsy had gone.

"He told me," Mary said, "that he heard of work he could get in the town. He's gone to look for it. He may be gone for a good while."

They paid no heed to this. Thomsy often went away like that for days at a time.

"Ha!" Maggie said. "It's not work he's after, but something he begged off the big people and he's gone to drink it. We won't see him now until it's all spent. The poor nature of him! Not to think of us that's empty."

Then again they went on babbling about the strangers. The three of them were very happy. Coming on towards the fall of night, however, the sudden appearance of Sally O'Hanlon disturbed this gaiety.

CHAPTER XLVI

SHE BURST INTO the kitchen and cried:

"For the love of God, Brian, come over and look at Patsy. His stomach is swelled out and his eyes are turned in his head. He keeps trying to sicken and he not able. The rumbling of him is terrifying the children. He's like to burst himself. Come quick, you that are handy with the sickness of cattle. Maybe it's the same thing he has."

The old man jumped to his feet on hearing her words. There was an eager light in his eyes. He was glad of having something to do, after the enforced idleness of the past few months.

"Ha!" he said. "Was it something he ate?"

"It was, 'faith," said Sally, "something he ate, sure enough. He ate a piece of the loaf that the strange gentlemen gave us."

"The loaf!" cried the old man.

He and the two old women looked at one another nervously. Could the strange bread have been poisoned? They also had eaten it.

"It wasn't the fault of the bread, I think," said Sally. "It was the long hunger that weakened him. But come over quick. I'd send the eldest for the doctor, but he's crying and he hasn't much gumption. I doubt if he'd know what to say in the village."

"Let us be on our way," said Brian. "Have you salt in the house?"

"I have a lump of it," said Sally. "Is it good?"

"There is no better cure for a colic," said Brian, as he followed her out of the kitchen.

They all went with her. On the way she continued to chatter.

"I knew it was coming over him," she said. "All the time that he was working on the road, he never had a full belly. The gangers drove him hard in spite of that and he not strong enough. But his spirit wouldn't let him surrender. He knew what was depending on him. All he ever took going to work in the morning was a drop of gruel. And the gruel from yellah meal hasn't the same nourishment in it as gruel from oatmeal. 'Sally,' he used to say to me, 'this yellah meal leaves a hole in my stomach that the wind does be whistling through when I stoop. There is nothing like a feed of praties to fill the belly.'"

"True for him," Maggie said. "A person does feel hungry after eating the yellah meal."

"And then again," said Sally, "at night when he came home, it's only a small bit he'd eat, trying to save it all for the children. He bore up well until they laid him off. That broke his heart. They haven't paid us yet the wages he's owed. He never set foot out of the house to-day, after the police driving him away yesterday from the hotel when he went to look for his wages. He was lying down when the strangers came. It was with him they left the loaf of bread. When I came back he had it half eaten. Finding it there alone with him in the house, such fine bread, too, straight from the baker, he couldn't keep from eating it and he that hungry. And then the furoo-furoo began in his guts. Lord preserve us!"

They found the children crying in the yard and within the hut Patsy lay on his pallet, belching violently. Brian went on one knee by the bed.

"Where do you feel it, Patsy?" he said.

The sick man rose to a sitting position, put out his hands and flapped the air with them, as if he were driving away smoke. His face was yellow and bathed in perspiration. The whites of his eyes seemed to have enlarged. He was trembling. He was on the point of answering Brian when he stooped forward suddenly and tried to sicken.

"Get the salt," Brian said to Sally.

After several vain attempts to sicken, Patsy relaxed. He sighed heavily and dropped back on the pallet. Then he smiled sadly at Brian.

"God bless you, old man," he said, "for coming to me. It keeps coming and going, this sickness. Ah! God help me! My heart stops and a lump comes into my throat."

"Get a can of water, too," Brian said to Sally, as she handed him a lump of salt.

He put the salt to Patsy's lips and told him to lick it.

"Then you'll drink the water," he said. "It's a certain cure."

Patsy began to lick, but he soon stopped and gripped his stomach.

"There's a pain there," he groaned, "like a rock swelling in me."

"I'll shift that rock," said Brian. "Go down to the house, Mary, and bring me the black bottle that's on the shelf over the chimney place. The purgoid I have for cattle. It will drive out of him whatever there is."

"Wouldn't it be better to send for the doctor," Mary said, "and the way his stomach is swollen? How do we know what he has?"

"Do as I say," shouted the old man in the fierce manner of old times. "I have seen stomachs in my day that were swollen twice that size. Run for the bottle."

After Patsy had eaten a large quantity of the rock salt, he began to drink water. Now his stomach swelled to a point. By the time Mary returned with the purgative he had begun to expel the gases from his stomach. Then the old man forced some of the purgative down his throat.

"Now," said Brian, "you may say to yourself that you're cured."

Sally kissed Brian's hand.

"God bless you," she said. "There is no end to your genius."

The sick man, now greatly relieved and smiling, also added his thanks. Brian was delighted with himself.

"Pooh," he said. "That's nothing. Let him not eat anything now until to-morrow, so that his stomach can settle."

The sick man composed himself and began to drop off into sleep. The Kilmartins went home, sure that he was in no danger. In the morning, Mary went over to see how he had spent the night. Sally was worried.

"It's strange the way he is sleeping," she said. "Saving your presence, he went out on his little business a short while after you left last night and then he fell asleep. He never moved since. It's little he sleeps and he snores to wake the dead, but last night there was not a sound out of him. He looks half-dead lying there."

The children were sitting by the hearth, watching their father in a curious fashion. They sat very still and their faces expressed no sympathy; and yet they were so interested that they sat motionless watching, as if wondering what was going to happen next. For them, their father lying there was a new game. Mary stooped over the sick man and spoke to him. He opened his eyes at once, but he neither moved nor spoke. His face was even yellower than on the previous day and his eyes had lost all expression. They were like the eyes of a corpse. His stomach was still swollen.

"How are you, Patsy?" Mary said.

He remained silent for some time and then he said: "I'm tired."

"I wonder could he eat a bit of the bacon I have?" Mary said to Sally.

At this remark, the three children became wildly interested.

"God bless you, asthore," Sally said. "We could try him with it. I'm going into the village to see could I get his wages."

"I'll give you a bit of it," Mary said. "Let one of the children come with me. Tell me when you are going into the village, so I can keep an eye on him for you."

All three of the children followed her for the bacon. She gave them half of what she had left. On the way back, the one who carried it, a boy called Paddy, began to eat it raw. The two girls fought to take it from him. Sally, hearing their cries, came and seized the meat.

"Ye little savages," she cried, whacking them, "is that the way to behave?"

The children, indifferent to her blows, followed her into the house, holding on to her skirt. They hovered over her while she put it in the pot to boil and even tried to steal it while it was cooking. The meat, to which they were unaccustomed, excited them as the smell of fish excites cats. Patsy was given some of the meat when it was boiled. He ate it greedily with a piece of the brown bread. When he had finished eating, he said that he felt much better.

"I'll rise now," he said, "and go into the village for my wages."

"Stay where you are," said Sally. "I'll go for them. You must take a rest or you'll get sick again."

The children also were roused to activity by the meat. They ran out to play on the mountain. Sally ran over to Mary.

"Thanks to you, darling," she said, "he's better now."

"Pooh!" said Brian. "It's not the bacon did it, but the salt and the purgoid."

"Ah! 'Faith," said Sally, "it was the meat put life in him. You needn't come to watch him, Mary. He's well again. I'm going for the wages. Mr. Coburn told me yesterday that he'd speak to the clerk at the hotel for me. I'll bring back what news there is."

It was her daughter Julia that brought news an hour later to Kilmartin's house. The old people had gone out again rummaging for nettles and berries. Mary was alone in the kitchen giving suck to her child. Julia, a girl of eleven, came silently into the kitchen and stood against the wall by the door, watching Mary and twisting her fingers in her rag of a dress. Mary was looking at the floor, brooding over Martin. The girl stood there in silence for fully a minute unnoticed, until Mary chanced to raise her eyes.

"Mother of mercy!" Mary cried. "You imp! You frightened me."

The little girl was as thin as a rake. There was hardly a trace of colour in her pinched face. Her blue eyes were sharp and cruel. Her black hair was matted on her narrow skull.

"It's my father," she said.

"What ails him?" said Mary, getting to her feet.

"He's dead up on the mountain," said Julia.

She made this announcement in a matter-of-fact tone, as if it were of no concern to her. Mary ran across the floor and stooped over her.

"What are you saying?" she whispered.

"We were doing 'little pigs' up on the mountain at the back of the house," the child continued in the same listless tone, "Paddy and Catta and me, when we heard a shout. We ran over to where it was, but we could see no one. Then Paddy looked down in the big hole beyond the bushes and there he was lying. Paddy said that it's dead he is, because there is no blood on him. Paddy said that if you fell like that and there was no blood on you, that you'd be dead, because the hurt couldn't run out of you. So he's dead. Paddy said to come and tell you, so you could come and carry him into the house for the wake. He said it wasn't right to leave him lying out on the mountain, but he would stay and watch him until you came, to keep the fairies from flying off with him."

Mary gaped at her and said:

"Musha! God help you."

"Oh! It's the truth I'm telling you," said Julia, raising her voice. "Paddy said that it's well known that the fairies steal dead people."

"Come on with me," said Mary.

At the stile she shouted to the old people, whom she saw in a field at a distance. She waved at them to follow her. Julia ran on in front, halting now and again, to scratch her right calf with her left toe and to make further strange remarks about fairies and dead people. They climbed a rough path by the side of the hut to a flat stretch of heathered ground, at the far end of which there was a clump of furze bushes. The other two children were lying on their stomachs near the bushes.

"Here he is," the boy said to Mary.

"It's in that hole he is," Julia said, as they ran across to the bushes. "It's deep, deep as hell."

Mary went on her knees beside the other two children and looked down.

"There he is," said Paddy, pointing to his father. "Not a move out of him."

There was a steep fall of about twelve feet, from the clump of furze bushes, to the bottom of a ravine that was partly overgrown with briars. Patsy was lying on his back at the bottom, his arms extended in the form of a cross. He had not fallen down from the bushes, but from a point to the left, where there was a narrow ledge under an over-hanging rock. This ledge was used as a privy by the family. His hat was lying on the edge of it and the piece of twine which he used as a belt was caught in some briars half-way down the slope. He must have fallen through a sudden weakness while he was crouching on the ledge, as his clothes were in disorder.

"Did ye go down to him?" Mary said.

"Oh, no," said Paddy. "We were afraid to go near him. He's dead."

"And you fifteen years of age," Mary said to him, "you should have more nature in you. Hold the baby for me and keep away from the edge here, you little fool."

The lad was no bigger than Julia, although he was four years older. He was even thinner than she was and his expression was that of an idiot. He took the baby and Mary climbed down from the ledge to where Patsy was lying. He was still breathing, but he was unconscious. She raised him by the armpits and began to drag him up the slope. That was not difficult as he was no heavier than a child; but it was horrid to feel the nakedness of his bones and to hear the hoarse gusts of his breathing after she had raised him. The old man arrived to help her when she reached the ledge. They carried him into the hut and put him lying on his pallet. Now the old women arrived.

"What happened to him?" Maggie said.

"Musha, a foolish thing happened to him," said Brian. "He fell and he doing his little business, down into a hole. Throw water on him, Mary."

Water did not revive him. Ellen Gleeson said that they should put hot stones to his stomach. The fire was out. Mary was going to go for fire but Brian stopped her.

"You'd be too late," he said. "See that? The shivers of death are starting in his feet. By the powers! Look how his legs are swelling up. That's strange. It must be a disease he has."

"You're right," Mary said. "The rattle of death is in his throat. And no priest to give him the Holy Oils. Shake him hard, old man, to see could we put enough sense in him to make an act of contrition."

The old man shook Patsy by the shoulders, but that only increased the death rattle.

"He's gone," said Brian. "Let us make an act of contrition for him." They went on their knees and began to say the act of contrition. The children, who had watched these proceedings with great interest in the doorway, moved away into the yard when they heard the prayer. Like dogs that howl when they hear music, the little ones raised their faces to the sky and howled for their mother. The dying man kicked violently, stretched, and lay still. Presently his lower jaw dropped.

"He's gone," said Maggie, as she made the sign of the Cross. "Poor man! It was a foolish end to a hard life, if it was the fall did it. Maybe, though, it was the bacon disagreed with him."

"More likely it was the salt," said Mary, as she stooped to close the dead man's eyes.

Liam O'Flaherty

"You're a liar, it wasn't the salt," said Brian angrily.

"Oh, Musha," said Ellen Gleeson, "don't ye argue in the house of the dead. Poor Sally! Where will she get a coffin?"

"Hey! There," said Brian to the children. "Stop whining and run into the village. Tell yer mother to come quickly. Run off with ye."

"Should we take him down to the house?" said Maggie. "There is no place to wake him here in this poocaun of a place. We could have him laid out before poor Sally comes."

"Don't touch him," said Mary. "Look at the way he is swollen. Mother of God! He keeps on swelling and he dead. What class of disease is that?"

They drew back from the corpse nervously. Two women from the head of the Valley came to the door at that moment.

"God save all here," one of them said. "We saw the children running up the road and they crying. What ails this house?"

"Patsy is dead," Brian said.

"Dead?" said the woman. "Poor man! He's well out of it. There is another woman dead this morning over in Glenaree, so I was told going the road. Oh! Bloody woe! We have nothing to do only wait our turn."

The two strange women came into the hut and looked at the corpse and crossed themselves. Then they all squatted outside the door and talked of the famine. It was odd how little attention they paid to the fact of Patsy's death, a fact that would have been so awe-inspiring under normal conditions. Mary was the only one who was really disturbed by it. Somehow, it made her feel that her plan for escape was endangered by this death. Some other people joined them. There was quite a crowd there when Sally came back with the children. She was wailing aloud.

"Ah! God help her," the people said.

The little woman swept into the hut, looked at her husband, and cried out:

"Good-bye to you, Patsy, and God rest your soul."

Then she came out and addressed the crowd of people, in a defiant tone that contrasted strangely with her tears.

"I told them all that the hunger killed him," she cried. "When the children came and told me – I was after getting his wages – I shouted to the village that he died of hunger. 'Faith, that put the fear of God in them. They were all there, the strange gentlemen and 'big people' from the town. They collected money for me on the spot. I have it here, twenty-four shillings, a power of money. And they are making a coffin for Patsy. What's more, there is going to be a piece in the paper about us, for there was a lad there from the town that took down what I said. I gave them a bit of my mind."

CHAPTER XLVII

PATSY O'HANLON WAS the first man in the parish of Crom, within living memory, to be buried without a wake or a funeral procession. A rude coffin was made in the village and he was hurried off to the cemetery on the very evening of his death. The authorities were afraid that he might have been the victim of some new disease, although the doctor was unable to diagnose the nature of it. Afterwards, that peculiar swelling was described as "famine fever". His death was reported at some length by the *Clogher Vindicator*. "O'Hanlon's death," said that journal, in the course of a leading article, "is an outrage against the Christian sentiments of the Irish people. The eyes of the world are now centred on the horrors that daily occur in the parish of Crom."

It was true that the state of Ireland was beginning to cause indignation in foreign countries, but Ireland itself was not roused to action. The Repeal Association, which comprised the most active and progressive elements of the population, was just then engaged at Dublin in a foolish quarrel about the advisability of accepting the doctrine of physical force to combat reaction. The wealthier classes shrugged their shoulders and said: "What can we do?" This latter attitude was joyfully adopted by the government as its code of conduct.

The Crom Relief Committee made two journeys to Clogher, in an attempt to get the food depots opened and to raise a loan on the heaps of stones broken by Mr. Crampton's gangs. The banks refused to make any loan, pointing out that the government was bringing the relief works to an end all over the country, that no more money was to come from the treasury and that a loan could not, on that account, be repaid. The government authorities, when broached on the subject of opening the food depots and continuing the relief works, said that the matter would have to be considered by the Lord Lieutenant and by Her Majesty's government before any action could be taken. With regard to the relief works, the present attitude of Her Majesty's government was that their continuance would produce a feeling of unrest and dislocation, by "removing large sections of the community from their ordinary and lucrative avocations in connection with the harvesting of their crops." When told that there were no crops to be harvested in the parish of Crom, the authorities pointed out that Her Majesty's government had to formulate its policies with reference to the best interests of the country as a whole and that, in the country as a whole, this year's harvest promised to be exceptionally good.

Nor would they open the food depots, offering the opposition of local traders as an excuse. It was a fact that the tradesmen of Clogher adopted the same attitude as John Hynes towards this proposal. They said that to open the food depots while there was a sufficient supply of food in the shops would impose an injustice on legitimate trade, "within the meaning of the Labour Rate Act." The authorities compromised by offering to sell, at cost price, to charitable organisations, supplies of food that had been stored by the military in view of a possible insurrection. Beyond that they would do nothing.

What can we do?" they said. "Our hands are tied. We are merely servants of Her Majesty's government."

Colonel Bodkin's Committee, already rent by faction, ceased to meet altogether after the failure at Clogher. The colonel decided to confine his relief activities to his own estate and to disregard Crom, saying in public that "Major Thompson should feed his own damned paupers." Major Thompson was travelling on the continent. A new agent had not yet been appointed. The firm of lawyers at Clogher, who administered the estate in the meantime, took no interest in the paupers. Everything was left to the Quakers, who now established a relief committee in the village. They were anxious to point out that it was entirely unofficial, as if some criminal taint were connected with anything related to the government. Father Roche and Mr. Coburn agreed to co-operate with them. Neither the three illiterate farmers, who had served on the former committee, nor Hynes, would have anything to do with the new one.

In fact, Hynes was violently opposed to the opening of the food kitchen, as likely to interfere with his business. They took the courthouse as their headquarters and Hynes said this annoyed his lodgers. Eight officials connected with the road scheme were still at his hotel, drawing their salaries and awaiting further orders. As the courthouse was opposite the hotel, Hynes said that "the gentlemen would be annoyed by a crowd of beggars every time they set foot out of the house." And he firmly believed that the Quakers were running the food kitchen for profit.

"I invested my hard-earned money," he said, "in meal to feed the poor. I bought ship loads of it. Now the government has closed the works and strangers are competing with me, before the door of my own shop, with stuff given to them for next to nothing by the government."

In the midst of this disunion and this dreadful confusion among all classes, the Quaker organisation was doomed from the very beginning to failure. A fortnight elapsed before they served the first meal. By that time, the blight had become general over the whole of Ireland. Famine had become widespread. The funds, which had been collected for Crom and a few other stricken districts in the congested areas of the south and west, now had to be distributed far and wide. In the same way the relief workers had to be scattered. The result was that the Crom Committee found itself in the position of an army that attacks without having any troops in reserve. It was reduced to impotence almost immediately. Two hundred families had been made destitute by the stoppage of the relief works. The Quakers were terrified by the vast horde that crowded round the courthouse on the first morning. After working all day, they were able to distribute one hundred and twenty-seven meals. Fifteen hundred people, at least, went away unsatisfied. Next day, the crowd was much less, as many of the poor decided to await their end in the mountain glens, while others wandered away to Clogher. It was only the village folk who came. Even so, the crowd was still too large for the means at the disposal of the Quakers. Within a week after the opening of the food kitchen, there were five deaths in the village.

"Send us more money," the committee wrote to their headquarters in Dublin.

"What can we do?" answered headquarters. "We are overwhelmed by the general disaster. The potato crop has entirely been destroyed this year. You must try to do the best you can."

The doctor reported at the inquest on the people who died that hunger had been mainly responsible for their demise.

"What can we do about it?" said the coroner. "I can't incorporate that in the verdict. It's death from natural causes."

The stupor of indifference had taken complete hold of the authorities. It was no less manifest among the people themselves; even among those who had formerly been the most energetic. Sally O'Hanlon was an example of this peculiar characteristic bred by famine. With the money that had been subscribed for her in the village, she fed herself and the children on all manner of dainties. She put aside all thought of leaving home, as she had previously threatened to do.

"I'm staying in the Valley," she told Mary. "I have money now, so I won't go short. It would be foolish to go on the road and to lose the shelter of a house with winter coming. It's an old story that the far-off hills are green."

She made this statement about a week after her husband's death, when she came over to Mary's house with a present of some currant crackers.

"Oh! Sally," Mary said to her, "you shouldn't spend money on titivated things like currant crackers. I'm ashamed to take them from you. The money you got won't last for ever. For the love of God, be careful with it."

"Devil take that for advice," said Sally angrily. "The best way to meet trouble is on a full stomach. I'm taking warning by what happened to Patsy."

Nor did she make any attempt to get food at the kitchen. On the day it opened, as Mary was going into the village, in the hope of getting something from it, she found Sally crouched on her heels on a grassy mound near her hut. She was staring fixedly towards the river, shading her eyes with her hand, as if she were watching something very interesting.

"What are you looking at, Sally?" Mary said to her.

"I'm just looking," said Sally in a listless tone. "What else is there to do?"

"Not much, 'faith," said Mary. "Aren't you going into the village?"

"I'm not, then," said Sally. "I'm not that hungry yet, that I'd go begging soup from Protestants."

Later, when Mary was coming back with a small can of porridge which she got at the kitchen, Sally was in the same position. She appeared to be having a conversation with some imaginary person, for she was making gestures and talking aloud. She barely answered Mary's salutation and after Mary had passed she continued to talk aloud and to make gestures.

"Virgin Mother!" Mary thought. "She's gone out of her mind. What next?"

This change in Sally, whose courage and resourcefulness had been a tower of strength, had a most depressing effect on Mary, so that she herself began to lose courage. The three old people were now constantly nagging at her, as if she were to blame for their misery. It was no longer possible to keep them occupied picking nettles and berries. Everything possible was already picked and gathered. The valley was a desert. They would not go to the food kitchen, not so much because they were ashamed to accept charity in public as because they now felt that Mary should provide for them. They just sat around the hearth all day and complained. Added to that, she was beginning to have trouble with her milk. The child hurt her when she gave him suck and he had taken to crying afterwards, as if her milk contained no nourishment.

And it was so lonely now in Black Valley. There was hardly a sound to be heard in it. Only fifty people were left in the whole Valley. And even they went the road in silence, like ghosts. There was nothing to do but stare into the distance and wait for Thomsy's return. Her eyes became fixed on the gap in the mountains towards the north, through which he would return with news of Martin. She became intimate with the most minute details of the landscape. It sometimes assumed fantastic shapes before her tired vision. And at night she would rise, go to the window and listen for his steps.

When she found herself looking into the distance without thought, like Sally, she always made an effort to rouse herself; just as a person lost in the icy wilderness of the Arctic fights against the fatal desire to sleep.

And so she waited, until he returned at last, twenty-two days after his departure.

CHAPTER XLVIII

TOWARDS MIDNIGHT SHE heard the dog bark outside. The animal was now allowed to stay abroad at night, since there were no sheep that he might attack. At first she paid no attention to his barking. The she noticed that he was whining with joy between barks.

"It's Thomsy," she cried.

She jumped out of bed, pulled on her skirt and hurried into the kitchen.

"Who's that?" said the old man from his room as she was opening the door.

"I don't know," she said. "The dog is barking at somebody. It might be Thomsy."

She ran out into the yard. The dog was nowhere to be seen. She went into the lane and called him. He came running towards her, leaped on her, whined and then ran up the lane towards the north. She followed him. The night was starry, but there was no moon and she did not see Thomsy until she was within a few feet of him. He was lying under the fence and the dog stood over him, licking his face. She went on her knees beside him.

"Oh! Thomsy, darling," she said, "what ails you?"

"Ga!" said Thomsy, "I wasn't able to come any farther. Be off, Oscar. Ga! You wouldn't believe a dog would have so much nature in him. I was staggering to the house when he jumped on me. I fell down and devil a rise I could get out of myself after that. Will ye bring me a drink of water, Mary, my treasure? I'm at death's door."

"Come on, darling," Mary said. "Rise now. I'll help you to the house."

With her help, he dragged himself to his feet and they staggered towards the house.

"What news have you got?" she whispered. "Did you see him?"

"I have lashings of news," he said, "but I didn't see him for all that."

"Oh, God!" Mary said, halting in the road. "Lord have mercy on me."

"Be easy now," said Thomsy. "I'll tell you all. I saw him and I didn't see him, but although I didn't clap eyes on him, I got tracks of him and he's with powerful men at this moment, or my name isn't Thomsy. It's a long and wonderful story I have to tell you, only I must get a drink of water first."

The old man came limping towards them in his bare feet as they entered the yard.

"Is that Martin?" he said.

"It's only me," said Thomsy, lurching towards Brian.

"Huh!" said Brian, thinking he was drunk. "Nice state you're in, indeed, at this hour of the night, barging in on us poor miserable people. You proper rowdy! And us with the hunger on us."

"Ga! brother," said Thomsy, "it's not drunk I am, but dying of the weakness. Your hunger couldn't hold a candle to the one I have, me that didn't taste food for three days."

"Eh?" said Brian. "Where were you?"

"Catch hold of him and stop talking," said Mary. "He's falling out of his standing."

In spite of his exhaustion, Thomsy could not resist the temptation to act the buffoon. So he pretended to be much weaker than he really was. He began to groan aloud and he let his knees go limp. Mary and the old man had to drag him into the house.

"Ho!" said Maggie, who had now come into the kitchen. "Look at the cut of him. And where were you all this time, you drunken man?"

Ellen Gleeson had lit a tallow wick. They put Thomsy in the straw chair in the hearth corner. Mary began to rake the fire. The old man brought a mug of water.

"Ah!" said Thomsy after swallowing the water. "No poitheen or ale ever tasted as good as that stream water."

"So that's where you were," said Maggie angrily. "Drinking poitheen. Shame on you."

"Ye all might as well know," said Mary as she kindled the fire, "that I sent him with a message to Martin. It was no poitheen he was after."

The old people now looked in awe at him and they became silent. Enjoying this attention, which the poor fellow rarely experienced in his life, he stretched out his legs, closed his eyes and groaned with pleasure. He was in a wretched state. Even his beard was covered with filth. It had become much greyer since he left. The skin beneath his eyes had gone white and there were other whitish patches on the mottled red of his cheeks. Beads of perspiration stood on his forehead. He was wearing a knitted cap when he left. Now he wore the remnants of a tattered black hat, held on to his skull by a piece of string, which passed under his chin. He had also lost Michael's brogues. His feet were covered with sacking. With his eyes closed, his face without expression and his short legs thrust out from his rotund belly, he looked more like a comic figure in a carnival procession than a man. At last he opened his eyes and looked all round him.

"It was a woeful journey," he said, addressing no one in particular. Then he turned to Mary and added: "I did my best, sister, but it's hard for the slow dog to catch the winter hare. He has gone out of the island."

"I'll get you a bit of bread," Mary said.

She seemed reluctant to hear his story now that he was here, even though she had waited so anxiously for his return. Nor did Thomsy show any eagerness to begin his tale, in spite of the old people trying to hurry him. It was only after eating a bit of the bread Mary brought him that he began. They all sat on stools about him, gaping at the story-teller. It was a great moment for the despised buffoon.

"I got to the island of Inishgola all right," he said, "although it took me a week to get to it. Don't be talking, but there is terrible country between here and there. The poorness of Black Valley is nothing compared to it. It would be a day's work for a goat to find a green leaf on those mountains. Ga! You'd find nothing but stones everywhere. The people are eating one another in the villages, after eating the cats and the dogs. I heard of a man that sold two loads of turf for an ass and then he killed the ass and ate a bit of it and the meat of the ass turned his stomach and he died with the pain. It was a thin old ass, the man said that told me. I came to a small house in the mountains and I going, near the village of Bearnaglas. There were three people dead in the house. Young people they were, by the same token. I went on into the village, there were no more than eight houses in it left with people, and I said to a man I met, 'I saw three dead people in a house on the mountain, brother.' 'There might well be three dead people in a house up there,' he said to me, 'for there is three slips of young people in a house there and their mother died on them a while back.' But devil a move he made to put the sign of the Cross on himself after I telling him about the three young dead people. They are used to dead people in that far country. I saw two more dead people on the road. One of them had his face half eaten off him, but that's neither here nor there. I'm coming to the story and a queer one it is, sure enough."

Here he paused to bite at his piece of bread.

"Bloody woes!" said Brian. "You are bringing us news, surely, of the end of the world. You are talking, man, like the prophecies of Saint Columkille."

"Arrah! Can't you make haste," said Maggie, "and tell us what news you have of my darling?"

"It's easy to see that he has no good news," said Mary. "Bad news can wait."

"Ga!" said Thomsy. "It's not bad, the news I have of him, only it's how I have no news atall of him, only rumours of news."

"Hell to your soul," said Brian. "Is it trying to make fun of the people you are?"

Thomsy looked at the old man reproachfully and said:

"How can I tell it if ye all keep shouting at me?"

"Musha, he's right," said Ellen Gleeson. "Can't ye leave him alone?"

"It's easy for you not to worry, Ellen," said Maggie, bursting into tears. "It's not your son is out there on his keeping."

"My son is in a worse place, old woman," said Ellen.

Afraid that he was losing the attention of his audience, Thomsy now continued his narrative.

"The village I told you about," he said, "where I talked to the man about the dead young people, a place called Bearnaglas, it was opposite the island of Inishgola. It was out there the lads were hidden and Martin the captain over them. It's a wild place, four miles from the land. The sea was rough when I came to it and it was two days before I got going in a boat with men from the island that came to Bearnaglas to sell fish. 'Faith, they were close people as well and it was a hard thing to get news of the lads from them, for the people of those parts don't like to be talking loud to strangers. It's how no rent was paid there for years and they think everybody strange is informing for the government. There's no barracks around there now, since a peeler got his head broken a few years back. So they are free enough, God save them, except for the hunger. It's only fish they have to eat and there's no turf on that island, so they have to cut the sod and burn it in their fires. The potatoes they used to buy on the big land with their fish are not there any more, so the hunger is on them in spite of their fish and a queer kind of moss they pick off the sea rocks by the low shore. Saving your presence, I ate some of it and it had me running for days. Well! Anyway, to make a long story short, these men rowed me out to their island in a little boat. That put the heart crosswise in me. A curragh, they call it, a class of a boat you could carry on your back, not like the heavy ones down at Frenchman's Quay in Clogher. These curraghs are made of thin slips of wood, like a sort of long basket with a point at one end, and they have a canvas cover over the frame and the canvas is coated with tar. It hops on the water, so I got as sick as a dog. We got to the island and they splitting their sides with laughing at me."

"Well! What did you hear about him?" said Mary, no longer able to control her desire to hear the worst.

"He was gone," said Thomsy. "He was gone the day before I came."

"Man alive, did they take him?" said Brian. "Is he taken?"

"He's not taken," said Thomsy. "There was a crowd of men on their keeping, with him at the head of them. He was well known there on the island and they spoke well of him. 'The hawk' was the nick-name they gave him, and indeed it's often I heard you called that same, Brian, on account of the fierce look in your eyes, but you needn't be ashamed of it, for the hawk is a swift bird, surely. More power to him. They got word that a gunboat was coming to look for the men, or maybe it was to look for the rent, or for no reason atall, only to let the people know that the Queen was there with her big gun, as a tyrant over Ireland. In any case, Martin and his men made off in boats to the big land, farther to the west. The gunboat came the day after I arrived and we all hid in caves away up in the cliffs. There's only one village on that island and then there is a big cliff behind the village and it full of caves, and you'd have to know the place or you'd fall into the sea below. We left the women down in the village and the old people. Sorra word the government men could get out of the women, so they made off again. Kind people they were, too, in that island. They have a fiddler there as well, a blind man that used to play a good hornpipe. There was a French ship wrecked in that place and I saw wonderful things they got in it. They had a bird there that could talk, but devil a one knew what he said, for it was French the bird spoke."

"And where did Martin go to?" said Brian. "Did you follow after him? Make haste, man."

"I'm coming to that," said Thomsy. "I followed after him right enough, to the western village where he landed, but he was gone out of it. In that small village, there were only three houses with people in them, for the rest of the people had made off to the town of Westport in the Mayo country. God only knows why it is, but misfortunes come together and the people of that village said there was no fish in the sea this year for them to catch. So the most of them made off with the hunger. I asked them did they see a body of men from the islands, and they said a body of men went north from the islands towards the Mayo country a short while back. 'It's them I'm after,' said I, so I bid good-bye to the island men that came with me, and made off north to the Mayo country. Devil a much information I could get out of the people I met on the road. They had lost all the gumption they ever had, on account of the hunger. Here and there, though, I got tidings of a body of men and I met several bodies of men, but they were all bodies of men wandering with hunger and not men on their keeping atall. And it was a terrible journey, surely, all that way north until I came to a bay, where there was scores of little islands, so near one another and they that small, that you could jump from one to the other."

"Was there track of him on the islands?" said Maggie, rocking herself. "Was there track of my darling on the small sea places?"

"I never went out among them," said Thomsy, "and I'll tell you why. I met a queer man in a big village there. I was sleeping in a class of a barn that I crawled into with the fall of night. I curled myself up like a dog in a heap of straw and I fell asleep, for I was tired with the walking. I woke all of a sudden and I saw a body of men sitting around a lamp, more than a dozen of men, listening to a powerful man that was talking and he on one knee, with his fist closed and he shaking it at them. A Young Irelander he was."

"What was he?" said Mary.

"A Young Irelander," said Thomsy. "I remember every word he said, for I was afraid of my life as I lay in the straw listening to him. He had a pistol with him and some of the men had carbines. Well, the big man with yellow hair said there were going to be clubs started all over the country, to fight for a republic in Ireland, to drive out the Queen's men and to get freedom for the poor people. Liberty, he said, was going to be made the law all over the world. He said that France would lead the way, same as she did before. He said talk was no good, and begob, I agree with him, for I always said the right thing to do was to strike a blow or die in the struggle. Oh! Don't be talking, but he had powerful talk. He said that the clubs would go about among the soldiers in the regiments and tell them why they should side with the people. He said the soldiers are the sons of the people, only they are led astray and that they would never fire on their own flesh and blood if they were told in the proper way what the fight was about. More power to that talk, I said to myself in the straw. Blood and thunder! He said the people were to be stirred up by these clubs and all joined into an army…"

"Oh! Murder!" said Maggie. "What class of talk was that?"

" 'Faith, it was fine talk," said Thomsy, "and it looked an easy job of work, the way he told it. He said there are millions of the poor and only a few of the rich, and if the poor got together and made themselves into a proper army, with a proper plan, same as an army, and knew what they wanted to do and stuck together, same as an army, they'd make short work of the tyrants. Then there would be liberty all over the world and no hunger on anybody. Landlords, he said, would be shot down like rabbits when the moment came. Begob, I could hold myself no longer in the straw, so I up and I cried: 'More power to you! That's the talk I like to hear.' Blood an ouns! They all jumped to their standing and they made a rush at me, and I thought I was going to be killed. But the powerful man with the yellow hair stopped them, and then he asked me the why and the wherefore of what brought me on the road into that western country. So I told him about Martin and…"

"You fool!" said Mary. "Didn't I warn you not to tell anybody? The curse of God on you for a proper idiot. It's likely that man was a government informer, for they all have fierce talk. Maybe Martin is arrested by now."

"Hold your whist, woman," said Thomsy. "That man with yellow hair was no informer, but a bold hero. And it's a power of help he's going to give Martin. Wait till I tell you. When I told him about the transactions in Crom and how Mr. Chadwick was sent on the road to hell by people we won't name, he was as friendly to me as a brother. 'This is no spy, lads,' he said to his men. 'He has too honest a face.' That's what he said, God bless him. 'Let you go home and tell her,' he said, 'that I'll find him for her in the small islands, and I'll help to get him and her out of the country to America and…'"

"What's that?" said the old man, looking fiercely at Mary. "Was that the plan you had? To desert us? Is that what you're up to?"

"You'd rather leave him on his keeping until they find him and hang him, I suppose," cried Mary, with equal passion. "Is that the kind of father you are? I want him to escape to America. What other chance is there for him? Tell me that. You only think of yourself, and you with only a few years to live. We are young. We have our lives before us."

The old man watched her as she spoke. Gradually, the light of anger died in his eyes. Then he sighed as she stopped speaking and he lowered his glance.

"God forgive me," he said. "I didn't think of it that way. You are right, daughter."

"I am," said Mary, "and it's time you knew it. What more did the man say, Thomsy?"

"He said a lot more," cried Thomsy, "the finest talk you ever heard. Listening to him, you would think the battle was won. The men that was wanted by the police, he said, would be sent out to America. That's where the army of freedom will be got together, he said, out in America. Then they'll come back and free Ireland. He'll send word, he said, when the time comes."

"But when will he come?" Mary said. "Don't you know any more? Did he find Martin?"

"I don't know," said Thomsy, suddenly getting weary and closing his eyes. "They gave me a bite to eat and then I went with them along the road, but a patrol of peelers came on us and we had to scatter on the mountain. I lost them in that place and I made my way home. Not a bit since did I eat. It was a great journey surely, and I saw a power of strange things."

Here he opened his eyes and smiled with pleasure.

"Ah! He was a powerful man," he said, "with yellow hair and a voice as clear as a bell. Lovely talk he had of fighting and killing the landlords."

Then his head dropped forward on his chest and he began to breathe loudly through his nose.

"But was he taken by the patrol of peelers?" Mary said. "For God's sake, man, tell us was he taken, or did he make his escape to the islands where Martin is?"

"I don't know, sister," Thomsy mumbled sleepily. "He said you were to wait for news. Lovely talk he had surely."

Once more he sighed deeply and then he continued to breathe loudly through his nose. His mouth opened and his head rolled to one side. He had fallen asleep through exhaustion.

"I don't know what to make of it all," said Brian.

Now Maggie cried out, as she rocked herself:

"He is gone from me like the rest of them. Now I have no one left of all that came out of my womb."

She did not seem to understand very well what Thomsy had said. She rose and went into her bedroom. Ellen Gleeson also went to bed, seemingly indifferent. Both the old women had, by now, practically lost their faculties of understanding. The stupor of indifference was closing in on them like a paralysis.

The old man continued to sit by the fire with Mary. He opened his mouth to speak several times but said nothing. At last he got to his feet, looked at Mary, drew in his lips and clenched his fists. She was staring into the fire with her hands clasped about her knees. He put his hand gently on her shoulder. She started violently and turned towards him. She looked up at him in anger, but on seeing the pity and softness in his eyes she relaxed and began to weep softly. He pressed her shoulder and then turned away. He walked towards his room. Half-way across the floor, he halted and said, without turning towards her:

"You will have my blessing when you go, daughter. It's not into the grave with me that I'd want to be dragging either you or him. God bless you, Mary."

"And you, too, old man," she said fervently, as he went into his room.

But she did not feel anything as she uttered these words. Although tears came running down her cheeks, she was not moved inwardly. These tears did not refresh the arid emptiness within her, caused by Thomsy's failure to see Martin. What had he brought back? Nothing but a tale told by a strange man in a barn at night.

Thomsy began to snore loudly. The fire was going out. Her eyes became dull. Her head dropped forward on her bosom.

"To-morrow," she whispered, "I must go and sell my dress. The only thing I can do is wait. God have mercy on me and my child."

CHAPTER XLIX

ALTHOUGH IT WAS after eleven o'clock in the morning, Dr. Hynes was still in bed. He had been lying awake for three hours. He did not feel definitely ill, but he had lost his appetite completely. He had refused the food his sister brought him and he kept drinking water. There seemed to be some sort of mist in his head, making it difficult to think. And yet strange images kept appearing before his mind. Lying there on his back, he contemplated these images with morose pleasure, making no effort either to examine their nature or to expel them from his consciousness. He was utterly indifferent to life. He just wanted to go on for ever lying still on his back and to keep drinking water.

His sister came into the room several times to say that he was wanted for sick calls. Each time he said to her:

"Say I'm gone out. I tell you I'm not going to see anybody. I know they're not sick. Let somebody feed them. It's not my business to feed them. Am I the only person in this parish to attend to them? And don't bother me again."

As we have seen already, there was a great deal of good in this little man. He was sensitive and kindly; even ambitious to be of service to his community. He belonged to that large class of timid and mediocre people, who lack the moral courage to obey by their own dynamic force the urge towards the ideal. They feel that urge, owing to their sensitiveness and a suspicion that they are missing something in life. A consciousness of being frustrated by a mysterious force beyond their control drives them to sporadic extremes of conviction; at one moment to action, at the next to cynicism. They crave to belong to an army marching towards a distant goal. Alone, or against opposition, they are helpless and prone to despair.

During the period he was under the curate's influence, when he had adhered to the doctrine of loving Ireland as a mother, he had been happy. But the vague mysticism of the curate failed to hold him, when he discovered that Father Geelan was a voice crying alone in the wilderness; a revolutionary soldier disarmed by the soutane which he wore and by the mitred felons to whom he had vowed obedience. And then came his visit to the old woman dead of typhus, followed by the bayonet charge of the police. He had seen the curate helpless before that attack and he had seen the people flying without a leader. That completed the evaporation in him of the urge towards the ideal. The attack which he made on his father was merely an expression of violent fear.

This fear was twofold. He was afraid of having contracted typhus from the old woman and of being arrested by the police as a revolutionary. As he had never taken any active part in politics, not even being a member of the moderate Repeal Association, this latter fear was groundless; but his distraught nerves made him even believe that he might be suspected of complicity in Chadwick's murder. So he avoided all possible contact with people, both as a precaution against infection and against arrest. True to type, he gradually began to blame the people for their wretched condition. He accused them in his own mind of laziness, dirt, inability to organise and to fight for their rights.

"If they won't fight, why should I fight for them?" he began to ask himself. "Why should I sacrifice my future for their sake? Why should I run the risk of catching the fever? The best thing to do is to get away from here before it is too late."

And then an opportunity for escape appeared, through the scheming of his brother Tony, whose business at Clogher had made fantastic progress owing to the famine. There was a practice to be had shortly in the town, through the retirement of a doctor called Lawton. Tony thought it should be secured for the family. His success had fanned his ambition, and he was already making plans to become master of Clogher. We know how admirably he succeeded and how it became a cant phrase in our district that "big Tony Hynes has Clogher in his big pocket." At the moment, however, he was still feeling his way with great care, in order to neutralise the opposition of the Clogher bourgeoisie, who were jealous of this rough giant from the mountains come into their midst. Tony felt that his educated brother, with his "Dublin manners," practising in the town, would add greatly to his prestige. So he broached the matter to his father. The old man consulted his wife. She agreed with her husband, as she always did.

"It would be a fine thing for him," she said. "Things are going from bad to worse here."

"You're right there," said Hynes. "I'm thinking it's not long until we all move into Clogher. There isn't much more to be got out of Crom."

This consultation occurred about a week after the doctor's quarrel with his father. The old couple were of opinion that the plan was a good way of ending the misunderstanding between him and them. So they went to him and said:

"We know this place doesn't agree with you, so we thought, maybe, that Dr. Lawton's place at Clogher would suit you better. Would you care to go into the town and talk to Tony about it?"

They were surprised at the readiness with which the doctor consented. And yet, although he consented at once, he showed no enthusiasm outwardly. This was in order to guard himself against remorse of conscience for deserting his post at this crisis. He could say to himself that the others were responsible. He saw Tony and negotiations were now almost completed. Any day now he would be free to leave the village and take up his residence in Clogher. It was very exciting, even though he was slightly ashamed of himself for going.

Here I must remark another peculiar thing about this

complex individual. The images that passed before his mind exercised a turgid influence on his blood and the most constant of them were connected with Ellie Gleeson, particularly the moment when he felt her stiff breasts against his chest. He had been free from these sensual thoughts since he had severed his connection with Chadwick. Now they had returned.

Once more he was roused from his lethargy by the appearance of his sister in the room. She did not knock or ask permission to enter. Like a peasant, she sneaked into the room and stood by the wall near the door, nervously pulling with her left hand at the fingers of her right hand. Now and again she managed to make the knuckles crack.

"Who is it now?" said the doctor dreamily.

"It's Mary Gleeson from the Valley," Bridget whispered.

According to the local custom, a woman retained her maiden name even after marriage.

"What does she want?" said the doctor.

"She wants you to look at her baby."

"What's the matter with it?"

"I don't know."

"Why didn't you tell her I'm out? I told you to tell everybody I'm out, unless it's serious. Say I'll be at the dispensary later on. She can take the baby over there."

"I couldn't tell her that," Bridget said, becoming very excited. "She gave me a comb for my hair."

The doctor now sat up in the bed, leaned on his elbows and looked at his sister for the first time. There was a queer mist before his eyes. In an extraordinary manner, his sister looked absolutely repulsive to him and he almost shouted at her:

"What did she give you?"

Bridget raised her eyes from the floor, looked at her brother and burst into a peculiar laugh. She often laughed in that way, for no apparent reason, even when alone. She did it through an excess of shame. Her toes would itch suddenly. She would feel an irritation at the centre of her spine, as if something hot were being drawn along the bone under the skin. Then she would burst into a shrill laugh. It lasted only for two seconds. Then she blushed deeply, dropped her eyes again to the floor and pulled at her fingers, making the knuckles crack. Her beautiful golden hair looked incongruous on her ugly head. She had got extremely fat recently and her stomach protruded like that of a pregnant woman. On her pimply, sallow cheeks, the flush of shame stood out like consumptive spots. Now she spoke very excitedly, but still in a whisper.

"A Spanish comb," she said. "I bought it from her. I gave her a shilling for it. I'm going to buy her dress as well."

Again she glanced at her brother, defiantly, as if daring him to prevent her buying the dress. There was malice in her glance. She, too, had her moments of rebellion when she desired revenge for the contumelies heaped upon her. The revenge she took was always imaginary. In her mind she subjected her enemies to extraordinary physical tortures, chiefly consisting in "making them so ugly that no one would look at them any more." It was her ugliness that afflicted her most. That was why she was now so excited at the prospect of securing Mary's wedding dress and the beautiful comb. With this finery, she fondly thought, she would acquire Mary's beauty.

"Her dress?" said the doctor. "So you are buying her dress? Why so?"

"So you think like them all," said Bridget, "that I should have nothing? You grudge me buying it? But I have a right to do what I like with my own money that I have saved. I earned it hard, the little that I got from lodgers. I never get a dress. I have the same old one since I was a girl. I'm ashamed to go to Mass in it. You and Tony have everything. I have saved two sovereigns. You must tell my father I have a right to the dress if he says anything to me about it. You must or I'll…"

She paused, looked at him fiercely, and then dropped her eyes to the floor. The doctor laughed.

"Or you'll do what?" he said.

"I'll tell my father that you are drinking again," Bridget whispered. The doctor was startled by this threat. It was a fact that he had begun to drink again lately, since his visit to the woman who had died of typhus. He told himself that he was doing so to prevent infection. However, if his father came to hear of it, the purchase of Dr. Lawton's practice might never materialise.

"You wouldn't do that, you mad thing?" he whispered. "I'd kill you if I caught you doing it."

Bridget gave vent to another shrill laugh, without raising her eyes from the floor.

"What do I care what you buy?" said the doctor. "I didn't say you couldn't buy the dress. I'll stand by you if your father says anything."

"Oh! God love you," said Bridget, now looking at him boldly, with an excited countenance. "I'm going to give her a sovereign for it. It's worth a lot more. It's a lovely dress. There is a velvet flounce to it. Maybe, I'll get her cloak, too, for another ten shillings, when the hunger comes on her again. It's with the hunger she's selling the dress."

"With the hunger?" said the doctor dreamily.

Suddenly, the mist became very thick in his head and his tongue grew parched, but he had no energy to reach for the pitcher of water by his bed. He fixed his eyes on the bed, where he was twiddling his toes beneath the blanket. He felt terribly hot and ashamed of himself. Why? He did not know why he was ashamed. But he now hated Bridget violently.

"It will be too big for you," he said maliciously.

"I can shorten it," said Bridget. "You'll look at her baby, won't you? She won't give me the dress unless you look at it."

For some reason, the doctor now felt that Mary must be deprived of her dress at all costs. An extraordinary thought entered his mind that her dress could be used as evidence against him in connection with the murder of Chadwick.

"Yes," he said. "I'll look at her baby if you'll stop talking and go away."

"Oh! God love you," Bridget whispered, licking her lips greedily. "Then it's mine. She wanted the two sovereigns for it, but I knew she would take one. You always know when a person will take less. They have a look in their eyes, afraid you won't buy. I pretended I didn't want it. It's not everybody wants to buy clothes these times. And sure enough, she agreed to the offer of a sovereign, but she wouldn't part with the dress unless you looked at her baby. Out of spite, she might walk all the way into Clogher and sell it there."

She said all this at breakneck speed, in a whisper that was scarcely audible, slurring her words and stammering slightly. The doctor had not listened to her. He was beginning to feel dizzy. He was uncomfortable in the bed. He felt in danger there. The image of Ellie Gleeson's breasts now remained constant before his mind, but it was no longer pleasant. For he could now see Chadwick lying next door with bloody towels around his throat, and somebody was screaming somewhere and saying that the police were going to make a bayonet charge. He must get out of bed at once.

"How can I look at her baby if you stand there?" he shouted angrily at Bridget. "Where is this woman?"

"She is down at the back," said Bridget, edging towards the door. "She is in the little room behind the kitchen. I hid her there."

"Be off," said the doctor. "I'll come down to her."

Bridget hurried out of the room, raising her feet high off the floor like a Chinaman. The doctor jumped out of bed. At least he thought he jumped, but in fact he just staggered. He was so weak that he could hardly stand. Yet it seemed imperative to him that he should dress quickly and get out of the room. Ellie's breasts, the bloody towels around Chadwick's throat, and the person screaming about the police were all here, making the place extremely dangerous. He took the pitcher and drank greedily. Then he buried his face in a basin of water. That steadied him a little and for the moment his brain cleared. But the fumes returned with greater force, together with the internal medley of breasts and towels and people screaming. He dressed himself and left the room. The floor seemed to be rising up to meet him. He had to support himself against the banisters as he went downstairs. Yet he was not aware that there was anything seriously the matter with him. He could not think.

Bridget met him at the foot of the stairs. She brought him into the little room off the kitchen. Mary was standing there within the door, against the wall like a beggar. She stood very erect and she had her child within her cloak. She had a bundle in her hand. Through a window, over Mary's shoulder, the doctor could see his aunt scouring a pot in the yard. She was scouring the pot with sand, and the noise grated so much on his senses that he wanted to scream. He saw his aunt's scraggy hair hanging about her face, and he loathed her. He wanted to kill her.

Mary curtseyed slightly, and he noticed that she was looking at him in a very odd fashion. Her eyes were wide open and so was her mouth. She drew back, upwards from her hips, after she had made the curtsey. Then she clutched her child close to her bosom and gaped at him in terror.

The doctor now felt that a heavy weight was pressing on him and that he must make an important announcement or be overcome by the weight, by Ellie's breasts, by the towels, and by the person who was screaming.

"You are hungry," he shouted. "Your child is hungry. Eat. Eat. I can do nothing for you. Eat, I tell you. Eat."

The mist before his eyes was now so thick that he could neither see Mary nor his aunt, but his hearing was more acute than before. The imaginary person was now screaming:

"He has the plague. The plague! Keep him away from my child."

He fell down on the floor, as he heard another voice say: "Leave me the dress, you fool. Here is the money. Give it to me. You promised it to me."

Then everything swam round and round at terrific speed. He himself joined the whirling and he knew no more.

CHAPTER L

THOMSY AWOKE FROM a glorious dream, in which he had seen the man with yellow hair lead an army to victory. He himself was one of that army. The majority were men and women of the people, their feet covered with sacking. Some were soldiers of the Queen, and they cried out that they would not fire on their own flesh and blood. Some were island men, with their boats upturned on their shoulders, marching like black beetles with long legs.

The great horde ascended a mountain, through sweet-smelling heather, towards the summit on which stood the man with yellow hair. In one hand he carried a landlord's head, from which blood dripped. In the other hand he carried a flashing sword, with which he pointed towards the horizon where the golden spears of the rising sun were shining brilliantly. He was pointing towards the land of plenty, which lay beyond the summit of the mountain.

And then, when the ecstasy of victory had reached its height and there was only a short strip of heather between him and the land of plenty, a voice called on Thomsy to halt. He was rooted to the ground by this voice. The multitude swept past him to the land of plenty, while he stood in acute agony listening to the voice, which said:

"He has the plague. He is all covered with spots like a pig. He fell down shouting."

He awoke in great terror. Now he knew that it was Mary shouting in the kitchen. It hurt him violently to sit up on his pallet. He was stiff from walking. That was why he had felt rooted to the ground. Here, in the darkness of the loft, there was no sign of the glorious sun rising on the land of plenty. It was horrible to realise that the man with yellow hair was just a dream. So were the soldiers, saying they would not fire on their own flesh and blood. So was the great multitude of marching men and women.

"I bought all the food the money would fetch," she cried. "I have it here with me. For it's dangerous from now on to go into that shop, with the plague in it. I'm keeping away from the village."

He wanted to lie back once more, to close his eyes and recapture the ecstasy, which had been cut short by her voice. Yet her voice, shrill with fear, prevented him lying down, just as it had prevented him reaching the summit of the mountain. He pitied her. So he got to his feet, groaning with pain. He stumbled to his ladder and climbed down into the kitchen. The old people were there with her. They were all talking excitedly. His mind became confused and he could not understand what they were saying. There was an acute pain across his forehead. His bones ached. His ears had become clogged. These exterior voices were drowned in a great tumult of sound which rose up within him, the sound of singing and of people marching to a mountain top. He must speak and tell her of the great joy there was in store for all mankind, liberated from the fear of famine by the man with yellow hair.

"Can't you wait awhile, treasure?" he said to her gently. "Don't lose heart now, when there are good men going to get you and Martin out of the country. He gave me his word. It will only be a short while now until you get news from the man with yellow hair."

But she turned on him savagely.

"You and your man with yellow hair!" she cried. "A fine story you brought me from the western islands! I sent you where I should have gone myself. It's late now to talk of men with yellow hair. There is nothing to do but to wait here for death. The plague has started. Soon the roads and the streets of the town below, not to mind the village, will be manured with the rotten bodies of the dead. We are surrounded with corruption and we have nothing to depend on but the miserable clothes on our backs. It's there in that bag, all the food I got for my dress. Oh! A fine end, surely, to my wedding. My man on his keeping and my dress gone to be the ornament of an ugly fool. And me here, shrinking from my own skin with the fear that little Michael will catch the plague. Don't talk to me of messages and men with yellow hair. Fitter for you to raise your snout out there on the flag-stones of the threshing-place and howl like a dog, for it's with the hunger you'll die, surely."

She was giving suck to her child on a stool by the hearth. With one hand she held her scarlet cloak about the infant. In the other hand she had a piece of bread. When she had finished speaking she began to eat the bread ravenously, stuffing her mouth with it, as if she felt an urgent necessity to make milk for her child. Her eyes were wild. Her dark hair had become disordered. It was streaming over her thin cheeks. Her bare feet were soiled. Her old dress had a patch on it.

"Oh! Mary, don't harden your heart against me, darling," Thomsy cried. "Is it me that would try to fool you and your loveliness after making this miserable house into a palace for me, since you came into it? Would I tell lies to you that has been kind to me? You pearl of beauty, sure it does make me drunk to watch you walk and to listen to you talk, with your voice like the singing of the river on a summer day. Ah! Indeed, my pulse, you may well know that it's a thorn in my heart to see you part with your lovely dress and the proud comb you had in your hair, for it's a queen I thought was living with us, when you walked out to Mass on Sunday and you wearing them. And now you're sitting there, with your red cloak shining over your misery. Ah! Mary, my treasure, it's not poor Thomsy would be the man to fail you. If it would help you, darling, here on this spot I'd rip my belly with a knife."

He held out his hands towards her in appeal and burst into tears, but she looked at him coldly. She said something which he could not hear, for his ears now refused to catch the sounds. The tumult became louder within him. It was now menacing, this chorus of people who sang and shouted as they climbed through the sweet-smelling heather towards the summit of the promised land. He looked around him in dismay and saw the old man watching him. The old man had always been hostile to him. Now Thomsy understood the real meaning of that hostility. The old man looked on him as a parasite. There was a singing sound in his ears. The tumult within him surged up into his throat and he cried out:

"It's not me will eat what there is."

The old man was leaning on a stick and his head was thrust forward. His left eye was still fierce, but his right eye had faded and shrunk back into his skull. The ruddy colour was dying in his cheeks. His lips were almost without colour. The tips of his ears had withered. His whole frame had become twisted. His strength was gone; all but the left eye which glared fixedly.

"It's high time for you to speak," the old man said.

"It's not for you I'm saying it," cried Thomsy, "but for her and the child. Let it be for her, whatever there is."

And then again the tumult sank down from his throat. His ears became clogged and he could not hear what the two old women said, although he knew they were wailing. Mary rose from her stool, took him by the hand, and spoke to him. He saw that there were tears in her eyes. He did not understand what she said. That did not matter, for her face had again become beautiful, now that there were tears in her eyes. Now the people began to sing once more in triumph, and the soldiers said that they would not fire on their own flesh and blood. The man with yellow hair stood out gloriously on the mountain top. Thomsy stooped and kissed Mary's hand. Then he reached for the infant's hand and kissed that also.

"God bless the two of you," he whispered.

"And you, too, Thomsy, my love," Mary said. "It was the

fear in me that said cruel things to you and not my heart."

He did not hear her words, for the whole house now seemed to crowd in on him and he hurried out into the yard lest he might suffocate. A drizzling rain was falling. He felt it on his face as he walked painfully to the lane, stooping, with his hands clasped behind his back. The touch of the soft rain was soothing. The pain left his forehead. Now he could contemplate his dream once more with pleasure. He walked towards the village, listening to the voices of the people who marched through the sweet heather.

"Let it be all for her," they said, "whatever there is."

Outside O'Hanlon's hut, the three children stood hand in hand. They were crying. He stood and gaped at them. The youngest girl was almost naked. Her little belly was hanging down like a half-filled sack. Her legs were so thin that he could clearly see the joints of her knees. She was leaning against Julia and sobbing. She sobbed in a queer fashion, as if she had hiccoughs.

"Why are ye crying?" Thomsy said to them.

"Our mother is gone," Julia said in a whisper. "She went last night from us."

"Where is she gone?" Thomsy said.

"We don't know," said the child. "The hunger is on us."

"Is it to the village she went?" said Thomsy.

"We don't know," Julia said.

Then she wailed aloud and the other two children also wailed. Their thin, shrill voices brought the pain back to his forehead. The singing of the marchers changed to a fierce roar.

"I'll bring her to ye from the village," he said.

He did not hear his own voice. He walked away towards the village as fast as he could, in order to escape from these little ones, who wanted to share what Mary had in her bag.

"They mustn't get a bite of it," the voices said. "It's all for her and the child. Every bite of it."

As he passed the weaver's cottage, he saw Sally O'Hanlon

come towards him. A heavy rain was now falling. She was barefooted, and she took long steps, like a drunken person that walks unbalanced, bending at the knees. Muddy water squirted from her feet on either side, as she placed them flat upon the streaming road. She trailed her black shawl behind her, its end twisted round the fingers of her left hand. There was something tied in the other end of the shawl. It hopped along the road after her, like a ball, making a wide rut. She kept raising her right hand above her head and saying something which Thomsy could not hear. His ears had become clogged once more.

"Your children are crying for you," he said to her as she passed.

He could not hear his own voice and she could not have heard him speak, nor had she recognised him, for she went past without looking at him, still raising her right hand above her head and crying out repeatedly:

"Dead meat."

He reached the village. A dense crowd stood in front of the courthouse, indifferent to the heavy rain. He halted on the outskirts of the crowd and looked towards the courthouse like the others. "Famine Relief Committee" was written on a sign over the door. The door was closed and there did not seem to be anybody in the courthouse. Yet the crowd waited there in silence, hoping that somebody would open the door and give them relief from hunger. He found it comforting to stand there in silence with this crowd.

Farther up the village, opposite the chapel, somebody was hammering in a shed. After a while, he saw two men come out of the shed carrying a coffin. They went down a lane with it. A small crowd of people followed them. Then a car came along the road from Clogher. The crowd began to murmur when the car appeared. They surged towards it, thinking it brought food to be distributed. But the car halted in front of the hotel and two men descended from it hurriedly. They went into the hotel.

"They came from the town to our doctor," a woman said. "He has the plague."

Thomsy started on hearing the woman's words. Again he felt rooted to the ground and the horde of people surged past him to the summit of the mountain. So he hurried away from the village as fast as he could, lest the plague might touch her and the child. They would become covered with spots and die of swine fever, before they could reach the land of plenty. He began to feel cold and his stomach was hardening into a ball that trailed along the wet road behind him.

Night was falling when he reached the house. He went round by the back and entered the barn, where he lay down in a corner among some straw. He fell asleep at once. The dream did not return. In the morning he awoke to find the old man bending over him.

"What's this?" he cried, prodding at Thomsy with his stick. "Did you get drunk again? Have you no shame in you?"

"Ga! brother, what ails you?" said Thomsy. "Sure I only laid down here for fear I might have the plague. I didn't want to bring the plague into the house. She might get it from me. Leave me alone, old man."

"The plague!" said Brian, stepping back in fright. "What put that notion in your head?"

Thomsy groaned. His bones ached terribly. And yet he had recovered the full use of his senses. He could hear and there was no tumult within him. The dream had vanished.

"I was in the village," he said. "I heard a woman say the doctor had it. Maybe it's spreading among the people."

The old man hurried out of the barn. Thomsy tried to rise from the straw and found he could not move. He sighed and lay back. Then Mary ran into the barn. She had a mug of gruel in her hand.

"Oh, you poor creature!" she said, going on her knees beside him in the straw. "Is it there you spent the night? What talk is this you have of the plague? Or is it how you took it to heart the way I spoke to you yesterday? Poor creature, I'd be a cruel heathen to turn on you, after you going on that terrible journey for me. Drink this, darling. You haven't eaten a bite this long while. You must be perished and you drenched with the rain yesterday. Why didn't you come into the house and warm yourself?"

"Oh! God love you, Mary," Thomsy whispered, as the tears rolled down his cheeks. "You have opened the gates of Heaven for me with your kind words, you lovely creature. Let me touch your face with my hands. Indeed, it's no plague I have, but shame for not bringing Martin back to you. Take away that gruel, treasure. Why would I take the bite out of your mouth? You need it all. All of it. You are young and you have the infant to feed. The two of ye are young. Let ye live. I'm only a carcass of a man, Mary, a poor old drunken man that is better dead. Why should I take the scarce food from the young people that have their lovely lives before them? Ah! sister, it's a lovely thing to touch your pretty face."

He said all this in an exalted tone, stammering and frothing slightly at the mouth. Mary wept listening to him, but she pretended to be angry with him and held the mug of gruel to his lips.

"Don't talk nonsense," she said with energy. "Drink this. It's rambling in your head you are. Drink it and then lie out in the sun. It's a fine sunny day, thank God. The sun will put new life in you. Drink up now."

"Don't put shame on me, woman," cried Thomsy, drawing away from her.

She forced him to eat the gruel, however. He kept protesting between gulps that it would put him to shame, devouring her food "like a scavenger in the night." She stayed with him until he had finished it. Then she made him rise and go out into the sun. The gruel certainly gave him new strength and he was now able to walk, but the internal tumult had returned. The horde of people marching up the mountain were now shouting abuse at him. He walked down to the river and lay on his face in the long grass which grew by the bank. There the shouting ceased and the murmur of the river water became a song of triumph. Now the man with yellow hair stood out against the horizon with his sword, but he had no landlord's head. He was smiling mysteriously.

In the evening Mary came and roused him. She brought him to the house and made him climb into his loft. He lay down and she put a covering over him. He could not sleep. He lay awake all night, brooding over the shame of eating her food. When he heard her move in the morning, he climbed down into the kitchen. She was kindling the fire.

"Are you better now, darling?" she said to him.

She was smiling and she looked happy, although there were dark rings under her eyes. Thomsy stared at her and trembled.

"Oh! I had a lovely dream, Thomsy," she said.

"A dream?" said Thomsy.

"Yes," she said. "It was the same dream I had before; twice running I had it before. This is the third time I had it. So it must be a true one, darling."

"What dream is this?" Thomsy said, staring at her fixedly.

"It was an angel came to me," Mary whispered, "and he took me over the sea in a ship to America and Martin was with me on it. Oh! It was lovely and I am so happy after it."

Then Thomsy went on one knee and took her hand and kissed it. He looked up into her face and said:

"That's right, Mary. A ship. Don't lose heart. The man with yellow hair. He'll send word. Wait for the word."

Mary looked at him with suspicion. Her forehead wrinkled. Thomsy got to his feet and smiled at her strangely. Then he turned round and waddled to the door.

"Where are you going?" she said sharply.

"Nowhere," Thomsy said. "I'm only going out a while."

"Don't be going far," she said, "for I'm getting gruel ready for you."

"I'll not go far," Thomsy said out in the yard.

Now there was a singing sound in his head. Something like a bubble kept swelling out and then bursting inside his head, against his ears on either side. At each step, his body seemed to rise from the ground and then fall down heavily. He was not conscious of movement and he no longer recognised the earth. It was all a blur – the sky, the mountains, the road. Forward! There was no time to lose. He turned to the left near the cabin where Patch Hernon's aunt used to live. Then he began to climb the ravine. Here he had to crawl on his hands and knees. There was considerable froth on his lips and the bubble had now gone into his stomach. There it kept expanding and contracting. Would there be time? He made a mighty effort to crawl faster up the narrow ravine, in order to reach the summit before the bubble burst.

Here was the hut where Martin had taken refuge on the day he fled wounded from the riot in Crom demesne. A stream dropped down the face of a steep rock above the hut and made a pool that was dark and partly overgrown with moss. Tall, green ferns grew from the crevices of the rocks on either side of this pool. The water falling from a height made a deep moaning sound. It was cold here.

He splashed through the mossy ground on his hands and knees. The sound of the water became an almighty roar and the bubble expanded until it pressed stiffly against the walls of his stomach. In great fear, he struggled to his feet and crawled up into the hut. He lay down on the earthen floor and then the bubble burst.

Now there was no more pain and the roar of the water was distant. It was soft and melodious, receding into the distance, where the man with yellow hair stood on the mountain top, his naked sword flashing in the spears of the rising sun.

Now the great horde of marching people called him and he went with them, marching through the sweet-smelling heather to the summit of the promised land.

CHAPTER LI

"I WONDER WHAT'S keeping Thomsy," Mary said, when they sat down to their gruel. "He said he was only going out for a little while. He's been queer, poor man, since he came back from his journey."

None of the old people paid any attention to her remark. They were too hungry to worry about Thomsy. Knowing that they would get no more until the following morning, they devoured their share of the gruel ravenously. By common agreement, they had rationed themselves to one meal a day. Mary herself was immersed in the contemplation of her dream and she finished eating before she again thought of Thomsy. Owing to her nervous exhaustion, the happy dream had made her slightly delirious. She again felt that escape was certain.

"Poor man," she said as she rose from the form, "his gruel will be cold on him."

The old man looked at Thomsy's mug greedily. The sight of it made him feel very hungry.

"He's very likely gone off again," he grumbled. "It's best not to waste it."

He looked at Mary expectantly, hoping she would divide the spare mug.

"It won't be wasted on you," Mary said. "I'll go and call him."

Out in the yard she called Thomsy several times at the top of her voice. There was no answer. Then she began to get worried. She remembered how strange he had been, when he went on his knee and kissed her hand. He had made queer remarks about a ship and about the man with yellow hair. Could he have gone away again to look for Martin? Perhaps he was ashamed of not having brought definite news. She returned to the kitchen, where she found the old people greedily dipping into the mug. She snatched it from them.

"Ye should be ashamed of yerselves," she said.

They looked at her like naughty children and then went to the hearth, where they squatted. Mary put the mug on the dressers, went to the doorway and looked up the Valley. It was going to be a misty day. Already the peaks of the mountains were hidden within the grey clouds that came rolling slowly down the slopes, like an advancing tide. The sun was still visible in the grey sky, but it was like a moon, pale and without warmth. The cold brought by the mist made her shudder. It was a presage of the coming winter, this cold silence sweeping over the barren earth. The silence of death.

"I'd feel that I sent him to his death," she said, "if he went off again to look for Martin. For it would surely be the death of him."

The old people did not speak. They had no interest in Thomsy and were in an ill temper because of their unsatisfied hunger. It was strange how their appetites had increased with their declining strength. Mary went out once more into the yard and shouted. There was no answer. Then she told her mother to keep an eye on the child and hurried over to Sally O'Hanlon's house. Perhaps Sally had seen him pass. She called when she was some distance from the house. Nobody answered her and she found it odd that Sally's children were not in sight. Recently, they were always perched on the fence by the roadside, begging from those who passed. She advanced a little farther and then halted about ten yards from the door, which was wide open. She felt very nervous.

"Oh! Sally," she cried. "Where are you? Did you see our Thomsy?"

There was no reply, but Sally appeared in the doorway after a few moments.

"Mother of Mercy!" cried Mary in fright.

Sally was wearing her shift. Her skirt was thrown about

her shoulders like a cloak. Her eyes glittered. Her cheeks were deadly pale. She was smiling.

"Come in, darling," she said. "They are quiet now. They are all asleep, the little creatures. But don't talk loud or you might waken them. It's a long rest they need."

Then she put her hand to her lips and made a ludicrous grin. Mary approached slowly.

"So this is the dream I had," she thought, as she stared fixedly at Sally. "Now I'm waking from it."

Sally put out her hand in an expressive fashion and whispered:

"It was a bit of meat that I got down in the village. Don't put it against me, Mary, for I got it the same way you got the bacon. Saving your presence, it was the half of a dog and I had to fight for my share of it. These are hard times and it's with luck a person can get any snipther atall, big or little. I put it in the pot and the poor little creatures could hardly wait until it was boiled. It was a long time since they had anything to eat. They thought I was gone from them, but I wasn't. Oh! No, 'faith. I was always a good mother and a good mother I am still, looking after what God sent me. Come on in, treasure, but don't make any noise, for fear you might waken them."

She stepped aside to let Mary pass into the house. Then she pointed to the three children, who lay in a row, side by side, on the pallet, over by the flat rock which was used as a table.

"There they are," she whispered. "The little creatures are as quiet as lambs. All they needed was a bit of meat. At first it sickened them. The little one was the first to get sick, but she soon quietened. Then the other two started. I didn't want them to wake the little one, so I made them lie down beside her and I put the cloth over their heads. They soon stopped crying after that. Now they are quiet as lambs. Look at the little creatures lying asleep there. Sleep on, you little darlings. Your mother is here with you. She's not gone from you atall.

Oh, no. Here she is, my little treasures. Stoop down and look at the darlings, Mary. But don't speak to them, for fear they might wake up again and start to cry."

She looked wildly at Mary and hissed savagely:

"They mustn't start crying again."

But when Mary looked at her in mortal terror, she composed her face once more. Then she grinned and said gently, in a whisper:

"Make the sign of the Cross on them, darling. Then they will sleep well, for I love you and God loves you, too, you pearl of beauty. Bless my little ones in their long sleep."

Mary stooped over the pallet to make the sign of the Cross over the children, in order to humour this mad woman of whom she was now terribly afraid. Instead of making the sign of the Cross, however, she put her hand over the mouth of the little boy, who lay nearest to her. Then she stood erect suddenly, looked wildly at Sally and said:

"But they are dead, Sally. How could I make the sign of the Cross over dead things? The breath of life is gone out of them. They are not asleep, dear woman. They will never wake again. They are dead."

Sally stopped grinning. Now her eyes glittered fiercely. She uttered a harsh laugh. Then she cried in a loud voice:

"What's that to you? Mind your own business. There may be a hole in your own stocking one of these days. Don't pick holes in the stocking of a miserable woman. I say there is nobody killed here. If they are dead they have a right to be."

Mary put her hands to her face and cried hysterically:

"Oh! darling woman, what are you saying?"

She felt that she was going to be sick and she rushed for the door. Sally followed her out into the yard. Mary stooped over the fence.

"I had a right to put them out of their suffering," Sally cried, "and I'll bury them, too, when I have done my share of looking at their little faces. God gave them to me. I couldn't let them lie there screeching with the pain and nobody to help them. Is it with the meat of a dog I would go on filling their mouths and it only making them screech with the pain?"

Mary straightened herself, wiped her mouth and then ran as fast as she could towards home. When she had gone a little way she began to scream for Thomsy. The old people heard her and came out into the yard. She stopped screaming when she reached them. She burst into tears, ran to her mother and threw her arms around the old woman, who nearly fell under the impact.

"What have you done to little Michael?" she whispered in her mother's arms.

"Musha, what ails you, alannah?" said her mother. "Sure, he's asleep in the cradle."

"It's Sally," Mary whispered, releasing her mother and then pointing to where Sally was gesticulating on the road in front of her house. "She killed her children. They are in there lying in a row. All dead."

The old people crossed themselves and looked at Sally with their mouths open. They moved slowly over to the fence and looked towards her. The mist was now quite thick and their failing sight could barely see her. She was shouting, but at that distance it was impossible to hear what she said. The horrid news seemed to have little effect on them. They just gaped out of curiosity, after the manner of very old people whose senses are unable to react critically. At last, when they spoke, it was in a very casual tone.

"She is saying something," Maggie said. "Maybe it's asking us to go to the wake she is."

"Wake!" cried Mary. "Virgin Mother! Ye are all foolish."

"She was always a thief," the old man said solemnly. "I expected something bad would come of her ways."

Mary ran into the house. The child had wakened and he was crying. She took him out of the cradle, sat down by the fire and began to rock him in her arms. She wept copiously.

This calmed her nerves. The fright she had received gradually gave way to a sombre happiness. Now the possession of her child seemed to make everything else of no importance. Here he was, safe in her arms. She crowed to him and raised him up and down on her knee. She began to laugh through her tears. She rubbed her nose against his cheeks. The child stopped crying, drivelled at the mouth and made a little movement with his arms, as if he wanted to embrace her. Delighted by this movement, she began to talk to him.

"You're not going to sleep, little Michael," she cried. "You're going on a big, big ship with your mamma. A great, big ship with white sails and daddy will be there, too. A big, strong daddy that will look after the two of us. And we'll go away, away over the sea to a rich country. Oh! We'll have lots and lots to eat, little Michael. Be good now, treasure, and grow into a great, big, fat baby. Big, big, fat baby."

Suddenly she heard Maggie call out loudly:

"Arrah! Where are you going, Sally?"

She ran out into the yard with her child and joined the old people at the fence. She saw Sally O'Hanlon walking slowly away to the south. She was dragging something after her.

"What is she doing?" Mary said.

"Devilment," said the old man. "I always said so."

Mary stood on top of the stile and looked. Now she could see that Sally had the children rolled up in her shawl and that she was dragging them along the road to bury them.

"Let ye go into the house and not be gaping there at a sick person," she said severely, turning towards the old people.

" 'Faith, you're right," said her mother.

"Did you see any sign of Thomsy?" Maggie said.

"I'll go up a little way and look for him," said Mary. "If I could find him, he might go into the village for the priest. The priest should be told about her."

She went north along the lane for some distance. The mist was now so heavy that it was impossible to see very far. It was also impossible to think. The mist pressed in on her, making sleep seem imperative. Then she saw their dog come towards her. He stopped in the road when she called him. His belly was filled out to a point on either side. He looked at her furtively. Again she called him, but he refused to approach her. Instead, he hid his tail between his hind legs, raised his mane, growled, leaped over the fence and ran down towards the river. She shuddered and turned back home. When she was climbing over the stile into the yard, she glanced towards the river and saw the dog drinking down there.

"Did you see any sign of him?" Maggie said to her when she entered the house.

"I only saw the dog," Mary said in a tired voice. "He mustn't be let into the house any more."

The old man, who was huddled over the fire with his eyes closed, sat up at this remark.

"Why so?" he cried. "The dog is the only comfort I have. Oscar, come here."

He called for the dog in a loud voice, and getting no reply, he went out to look for him. Mary went into her room and sat on the side of the bed.

"I'll go in the morning," she thought. "There is no use waiting any longer for him. It was her white shift I saw in my dream and not a ship with white sails. He'll never come. The food is shrinking in the bag and we are shrinking, too. The baby is getting thin and my headache is getting worse. There is no use waiting any longer, or I wouldn't be able to reach the town with weakness."

This decision gave her no comfort. Instead, it made her shudder. Then she felt very weak and lay down on the bed. She closed her eyes and fell into a stupor of indifference, from which she was roused by the old man's voice in the kitchen.

"What ails that dog?" he grumbled. "He ran away when he saw me. He has been eating some strap. He is worse than the cat."

"The cat is gone," Maggie said. "There has been no sight of him for days now. Poor cat! The dog will go too."

Mary fell into a heavy sleep. In the morning she awoke with a raging headache and did not think of her decision to leave. She had hardly enough strength to rise. There was no more turf to make a fire. She took a hatchet and broke down the empty hen coop. Having made a fire she prepared some gruel. When they had finished eating, they all sat around the fire, throwing pieces of the hen coop on it from time to time. It was getting quite cold outside. The heavy mist still hung over the Valley. Not a word was spoken by any of them. They seemed to be waiting in silence for the approach of death.

Towards noon they heard the dog bark outside. The old man cried out excitedly:

"There he is. I knew he wouldn't go away. Oscar, come here."

Grasping his stick he hobbled to the door with his hand on his hip. He was now completely decrepit. Mary heard footsteps in the lane and jumped to her feet.

"What people are these?" she said. "They have boots on them."

She followed the old man out into the yard. He was looking down the road towards O'Hanlon's house. The dog was running towards the north, barking intermittently.

"It's the peelers," the old man said.

Mary looked and then drew the old man within cover of the house.

"Don't let them see you," she whispered.

The sight of their uniforms made her heart beat wildly. She forced the old man to return to the house with her, just as the sanitary officer appeared around the gable, followed by two policemen.

"She must have been mad to do a thing like that, if she did it," the sanitary officer was saying.

"Devil a bit of it," said one of the policemen. "It was how

she wanted to get into jail, where she would be fed. Sure, these people are half cannibals. They are no better than Hottentots, same as I saw written in a newspaper."

He spoke with a marked Ulster accent. Like the majority of policemen garrisoned among the Catholic population of the South, he was an Ulster Protestant and he hated the Southern "papishes" violently, considering them to be "no better than Hottentots."

Simms, the sanitary officer, was himself a Protestant, but he was of Southern English descent and therefore more civilised in his prejudices.

"Bad scran to that for a story," he said indignantly. "It would be hard to make me believe that an Irish mother, papish or no papish, would kill her own children in the hope of getting a bite of food."

The other policeman laughed and said in a loud voice:

"You'll see worse than that, Mr. Simms, before you are much older. Maybe these murderers know something about it."

They entered the yard and the first policeman called in a loud voice:

"Anybody alive in this house?"

"Don't speak," Mary said to the old people.

They were all again gathered about the hearth. The sanitary officer came to the door and looked into the kitchen. The two policemen peered over his shoulder.

"Are ye dumb?" said the sanitary officer.

"We are not, 'faith," cried the old man, getting to his feet. "We are not dumb, atall. Good day to ye."

Subservient and garrulous, as usual, in the presence of authority, he hobbled to the door and continued to make inane remarks until the sanitary officer cut him short.

"What do you know about the O'Hanlon woman?" said Simms.

Here Mary jumped to her feet and cried angrily:

"We know nothing about her, and let you get out of here. We are bad enough without you putting your stinking nose into our house."

The two policemen laughed and the sanitary officer reddened. The old man was greatly disturbed by Mary's remarks.

"Pay no heed to her, sir," he implored the sanitary officer. "It's how things are happening and we are frightened."

"What things?" said one of the policemen suspiciously. "Speak out, old man."

"Shut your mouth," Mary cried. "Tell them nothing."

"Sure, I have to tell them about Thomsy," said Brian. "And the dog. The dog won't come to me, sir, when I call him."

"Who is this Thomsy?" said the policeman, putting one foot into the doorway and pushing the sanitary officer aside. "What about him?"

Here Maggie got to her feet and said:

"He is my brother, sir. He went off and we lost sight of him."

"There is something queer here," said the policeman. "Let's search the house, McVicker. You never know what we might find."

The other policeman was not anxious to enter the house for fear there might be disease in it.

"Don't we know he's in the County Mayo?" he said. "I'm not going in there. He couldn't be in two places at once."

"Come on," said the first policeman. "He might have come back."

"Ye murderers," shouted Mary. "I wish he was here to choke the two of ye. Oh! I wish he was here."

"Don't worry, woman," said the policeman. "We'll find him. There's none of them escape us. We'll hang him before we're done with him. Come on, McVicker."

The two policemen began to search the house. The sanitary officer, still in the doorway, tried to pacify Mary, who was shouting abuse at them.

"Don't antagonise the law," he said. "These are hard times.
The poor should be humble if they want help. They are dying
like flies in the village. Ye have no chance of getting help here.
Ye should go into Clogher. There is a new poorhouse being
opened there. Why do ye stay here?"

The two policemen finished their search. Then the three
of them left the house and went up the Valley. The three old
people followed them.

"Mother of God!" said Mary, as she sat alone by the hearth.
"So it's in the County Mayo he is. They know where he is and
they'll take him. Then there is no hope for little Michael and
me. A fine dream surely."

For the first time she rebelled against her belief in Divine
Providence. There was no God for her or the other poor people,
who were starving to death. God belonged to the rich, among
whom there was no hunger and no understanding of hunger.
To be afflicted with hunger was considered, in the world of
the rich, a crime which placed the sufferers outside the bounds
of humanity. They were to be pursued by the servants of the
rich, thrown into jail, or bayoneted, or hanged. God was with
these policemen who had searched the house for Martin. He
was guarding the other policemen who were scouring the
western islands for the fugitive.

"I must not let them find out that I'm hungry," she thought
in horror. "Or else they will hang me for killing my children."

Her mind had begun to wander. The heavy mist swelled
up around her like a tide. There was dead silence in the house.
A bumble bee came in the door and buzzed across the floor. It
struck the wall and fell down to the floor, along which it
crawled a little way. Then it rose once more, took wing, circled
around the kitchen several times, buzzing loudly, until it found
the door and escaped into the heavy mist that rose up about
her like a tide. The child slept in his cradle and she knew that
she must not speak aloud, lest it might awake and begin to
scream.

It was a dog that screamed. First of all there was the sound of a shot being fired and then the dog screamed. She sprang to her feet and listened. Another shot was fired. Now the yelping of the dog ceased. She began to tremble and she found difficulty in swallowing her breath. She felt ravenously hungry. It seemed that all the interior of her body had been scooped out of her. There was a pain at the back of her eyes and she wanted to sink to the floor. If she closed her eyes she would sink. At all costs, she felt that she must keep her eyes open lest the dog might get at the child. The dog would run into the house with his tongue hanging, eat the child and then sneak down to the river bank with his tail between his hind legs. She must fill the emptiness within her, in order to prevent the rich from discovering that she was hungry.

She went into her bedroom, took a piece of dried fish from the sack of food and put it on the tongs to fry. When it was cooked a little she ate it. Then she drank a lot of water. That filled the void, but it produced a momentary feeling of stupor, followed by a return of her raging headache. She sat in the straw chair by the fire, her mind fixed on the pain in her forehead. Her eyes kept closing in spite of herself. Her arms hung limply by her sides. She did not raise her head when she heard the footsteps of the sanitary officer and the policemen go southwards along the lane. Then she heard the old women keening. That roused her.

"They found him!" she cried, getting to her feet.

She stood there with her arms stiff by her sides until the old people entered. The old women were still keening as they came into the kitchen and the old man's face was aghast.

"What did ye see up there in the Valley?" Mary said to them.

"We saw the dead buried up there," the old man said. "There were holes dug in the unholy ground and they were thrown into the holes. No one is living in the north."

"And did ye see Thomsy there?" said Mary in a whisper.

"The dogs were at him," Maggie mumbled, as she paused in her keening. "They tore off his head."

Then she threw herself face downwards on the hearth stone and sprinkled yellow ashes on her head.

CHAPTER LII

NEXT MORNING, MARY was awakened by hearing the dog whine out in the yard. She got up and went to open the door at which he had begun to scratch. When she opened it, he did not try to rush into the kitchen. He lay on his belly, looking up at her pathetically. She spat at him and cried:

"Be off! Foet! You dirty thing!"

She reached for the broom which stood behind the door and struck at him. He accepted three blows without moving. Then he yelped and crawled away. She saw that his right hind foot was missing. He was holding the bloody stump up against his belly.

"What's that?" said Brian, coming to the door of his bedroom.

"It's the dog," Mary said. "He has lost one of his feet."

"Ah," said Brian. "The curse of God on them. So it was him they shot."

Wearing only his shirt, he hurried out into the yard and called the dog. The dog halted on his way to the dunghill, looked at his master and whined. But he did not wag his tail or make an attempt to approach. He seemed to have lost faith in humanity. However, when the old man stooped and fondled him, the wounded animal suddenly gave way to a transport of joy. Brian hurried over to the house with him. Mary blocked the doorway.

"Where are you taking him?" she cried. "Is it into the house you want to bring that dirty thing?"

The old man looked at her with his mouth open.

"He's my dog," he said, "and he's sick. All my life I have been tending sick animals. It's what has been my greatest comfort, being able to cure the poor speechless things. It is a gift God gave me. Dirty or not, he's a poor wounded beast in pain."

Mary stared at him coldly.

"My little Michael is in there," she said. "He's more to me than a dog that has been eating…Take him away from this door. I'll let no plague in here."

The old man looked at her pathetically. Then he looked at the dog.

"Have it your own way," he said. "I'll take him into the barn. Hand me the small jar of stockholm and the brush. It's in the chimney corner."

She gave them to him and he went away to the barn with the dog, still wearing only his shirt, although the morning was cold.

She raked out the coals from the ashes and prepared to make a new fire. But when she looked for fresh sods of turf she found there were none left. The turf was all used.

"I must go down to the turf bank to-day and get a basket of sods," she said aloud.

Then she took the hatchet and began to break up the hen coop. She could hear the dog yelping out in the barn. The fire was lit when the old man returned with the jar of stockholm and the brush. He looked happy and excited.

"You needn't be afraid of him now," he said. "I have him tied to the cow's hook. And his leg is in…What's that you're burning?" His expression changed to one of anger, as he looked at the sticks burning on the hearth and then at the hen coop.

"There's no more turf," said Mary wearily.

"Huh!" said the old man. "Breaking up the house, is it? Nice work! To-day I'll go to the turf bank. If we carry on like this we'll soon be left without a stick of furniture."

For a long time he kept muttering about things, "going to rack and ruin." Attending to the wounded animal seemed to have roused his energy. He even made extraordinary remarks, while he was dressing, about getting ready for the fair; just as if he had animals for sale. Mary did not hear a word that he said. She was in a stupor. Nor did the old man's enthusiasm last very long. When breakfast was ready neither of the old women would taste any food. They both stayed in bed and said they were not hungry.

"It was too much for them," said the old man, "what they saw up there at the head of the Valley."

Mary said nothing. She no longer cared about the old people. She sat there trying to make up her mind. But she did not even have sufficient energy to determine the nature of the decision at which she was trying to arrive. Neither she nor the old man said anything further about going to the turf bank. They just sat in the kitchen. It was cold. Now and again one of them put a few more bits of the hen coop on the fire. They were sitting in this way when the curate arrived early in the afternoon.

His appearance caused an extraordinary scene. Mary and the old man went on their knees to the priest, plucked at his dress and cried out to him for help. The old women cried out from their beds. Even the dog, tied to a hook in the barn, was roused by the noise and began to howl. The child wailed. Father Geelan's dark face wore an anguished expression, as he stood in the kitchen, listening to these cries. Tears ran down his cheeks. At last, when Mary and the old man got to their feet and the commotion subsided, he spoke to them.

"This is all the help I have for ye," he said, handing Mary a loaf of bread and a can of milk.

Mary took the bread and the milk. Then there was a painful silence for a little while, except for the howling of the dog and the child's wailing. The old man sat down by the fire. Mary took the child from his cradle. The priest looked all round the kitchen and seemed uncertain as to what to do next. His lips kept moving and he drew in deep breaths, wheezing loudly.

"You have no news, father?" Mary said quietly.

After the tumult her voice sounded faint. The priest seemed

startled by her question. His forehead wrinkled and he looked at her as in anger.

"It would be wrong for me to give ye any hope on this earth," he said harshly. "The people are paying the price of cowardice. Twenty-four died in the village yesterday. John Hynes took his family into Clogher. There is no shop in the village now. They are making coffins in the chapel yard."

Now there was dead silence in the house except for the priest's asthmatic breathing. The infant, rocked in Mary's arms, had ceased to wail. The dog was barking angrily, as if trying to break loose from the hook. The old man got up and left the house. The priest made a movement, as if to prevent him going out, but instead of that he rubbed his palms together clumsily. Mary began to tremble.

"It was about Martin I was thinking," she said, suddenly.

"Martin?" said the priest dreamily. "Did you hear anything?"

"I thought you might hear something, father," she said, staring at him fixedly. "There was some talk of a man with yellow hair."

"A man with yellow hair?" said the priest, raising his voice. "I heard nothing about a man with yellow hair. Who is he? What is this talk you heard?"

He looked at Mary in a puzzled fashion, as if her remarks had disturbed his train of thought. Mary flushed deeply. Then all the colour left her cheeks and she felt faint. The thought that God belonged to the rich, who had no understanding of hunger, again invaded her mind.

"It was only talk, father," she said quietly. "I thought, maybe, you might hear of a body of men out to help the boys that are on their keeping."

Then the priest sighed deeply and looked at the floor.

"There is no body of men in this country now," he said, "that can help Martin. It is time for ye all to be going out of this place."

Then Mary stiffened and thought savagely: 'There is a body of men. It's a lie, what he is saying."

Her eyes flashed as she said to him:

"I know I'll find him and it's here I'll wait for him. There must be a body of men. I know there is. Where would he find me if I went from here?"

The priest raised his hand as if to make the sign of the Cross over her and he opened his mouth to speak. Just then, Mrs. Gleeson called to him from the bedroom. He went into the bedroom. Mary went out into the yard where she found the old man crouched against the wall of the house.

"What did he say?" whispered the old man furtively.

"He said it was time to go from here," Mary said.

"Ah! God help us," the old man said. "Is that all the comfort he had to give us?"

Then he folded his arms and drooped against the wall, as if he were going to sleep. Mary began to walk up and down the yard. She heard the priest's droning voice. He was confessing her mother. The old man came forward and plucked her by the sleeve.

"Let you go with the child, alannah," he said to her. "We are at the end of our journey in any case. Don't wait here for us."

She made no answer, but continued to march up and down the yard with the child in her arms. The old man went into the house. She heard the priest's droning voice in Maggie's room and then in the kitchen, where he heard the old man's confession. Finally he came out into the yard with his stole around his neck. He called to her. She came over and looked at him steadily.

"I'm not going to die here and be thrown into a hole," she said, quietly.

"Don't you want to…?" began the priest, in a whisper.

She shook her head. Then he made the sign of the Cross over her and shook her by the hand. He walked away without speaking. She did not look after him. She went indoors. The old man looked at her timidly and said:

"Little Michael would like that bread and milk, if you made it into a bruitheen for him."

Then Mary burst out laughing and said:

"That's right, old man. Why didn't I think of it? 'Faith, it's yourself has the fine head on you. It's the very thing for him, the little creature. You can't go far on an empty stomach, can you?"

"Ah! God have mercy on us," the old man said.

CHAPTER LIII

AFTER FEEDING THE child, Mary brought some of the bread and milk to her mother. She found that her mother was dead. She lay on her back. Her hands were clasped on her bosom. Her rosary beads were entwined in her fingers. Her lips were parted in a smile. She had obviously composed herself for death after the priest's visit.

Mary called the old man. He showed no surprise when he saw the corpse. He went into the other bedroom to tell his wife. When he returned, he said that Maggie was also near her end.

"She's wandering in her head," he said, "and small wonder, after what we saw yesterday at the head of the Valley, with Thomsy lying there and he…"

"Hush!" said Mary. "Don't speak of it, old man. What are we going to do?"

"We have no candles," the old man said.

"Don't you be talking of a wake," said Mary. "It's of burying her I am thinking."

The old man scratched his head.

"We are alone now in the Valley," he said, "the four of us."

"Well?" said Mary.

"It was in holes they dug that the others were put," said Brian.

"The priest said they were making coffins in the chapel yard," Mary said; "if you had the strength to go into the village. I couldn't leave the child alone and I'd be afraid to bring him where there is the plague."

"But would you get a coffin without money?" said Brian. "And who would bring it back for you? And then…It's best to make a hole."

Mary wanted him to suggest that. She did not want to suggest it herself. Yet she was angry with him for saying it. The idea of putting her dead mother down into a common hole, in a wild field, like an animal, was repugnant to her.

"That would be a fine thing to do with my own mother," she said.

The old man looked at her pathetically. He had become very gentle since the priest had confessed him.

"All right then," he said. "I'll go into the village for you and try to get a coffin."

"I couldn't send you on such a foolish journey," Mary said. "We may as well make a hole."

"In God's name," the old man said, "couldn't we wait till morning?"

Mary shuddered.

"What's the good of waiting?" she said. "I'll get the spade."

The dog growled at her when she went into the barn. She had to pick up a stone and threaten him before he would let her get to the spade. With raised mane and naked jaws he kept snarling until she had left the barn. She took the spade to the little garden behind the house and began to dig. The old man joined her.

"It won't be deep enough here," she said, thrusting the spade down as far as it would go. "There is only a foot of sod on the rock."

"You're right," said Brian. "You couldn't bury a cat here. But wait a while, though. Wasn't there a scailp here that Thomsy and Martin filled with small stones when they were making this garden last winter?"

"There was," she said. "It was over near the well."

"We'll empty out the scailp," he said. "We should have a bite of food first to give us strength. Eh?"

"Let us do that," Mary said.

While they were eating some bread in the kitchen, Maggie cried out that she was hungry. They both went into her room.

She was lying on her back, with her eyes fixed on the ceiling. Now the hair on her upper lip looked quite black. Mary gave her a piece of bread. She took the bread but made no attempt to eat it.

"Why don't you eat it?" Brian said to her.

"I'm hungry," said the old woman in a sing-song voice, without moving.

"What did I tell you?" Brian said to Mary. "She's not right in the head."

When they returned to the garden, Mary took the child with her in the cradle. She did not want to leave him in the house with the corpse. He was sleeping peacefully now after his good meal. She and the old man removed the soil from the crevice and then hauled out the stones with which it had been filled. It was deep enough, but it was crooked and very narrow.

"God forgive us," said Brian, "we'll have to bend her down into it."

"There is no other place," said Mary, "unless we take her to the bog."

"We wouldn't be able to carry her that far," the old man said. "In God's name, let us bury her in this place."

They returned to the house, wrapped the corpse in a shawl, and carried it into the yard. The dead woman was very light and yet the old man was exhausted by the time he reached the yard. He lowered his end of the shawl to the ground and stood with his mouth open, breathing with difficulty.

"Help me to get her on my back," Mary said.

They managed to raise the corpse to the top of the large stone that stood beside the door. Then Mary got it on her back and brought it to the hole.

"We should say a prayer before we put her down," said the old man, "and sprinkle her with holy water."

"All right," Mary said. "I'll get the holy water."

She brought a little bottle of holy water, which she

sprinkled on the corpse and on the crevice. Then they both knelt to pray. Mary could not pray, but she remembered intimate moments with her mother and she felt sick. Then the old man touched her on the elbow and she got to her feet hurriedly.

"That's all we can do," the old man said. "Let us put her down."

It was now getting dark and there was a solitary bird twittering somewhere in the distance. Mary took the corpse by the head. The old man took the feet. They had to bend it in order to get it down into the crevice. They laid the stones carefully over it, after Mary had covered the dead face with the shawl.

"Let you put the earth over her while I go and make a kind of a cross," said the old man. "It's right to have a cross over it."

Mary took the spade and covered the stones with earth, making a little mound. The old man appeared with two strips of wood from the hen coop, nailed together in the form of a cross. He stuck it into the mound.

"God rest her soul," he said. "It's the best we could do for her."

"It is," Mary said. "It will be a nice sunny grave, surely."

Then she turned away quickly, ran to the child, and took him from the cradle. When she had him in her arms she began to sob. The old man brought the cradle into the house, and Mary followed him.

"I'm so hungry," she said.

Mechanically, she picked up the can of milk which the priest had brought. She put it to her lips and drained it without drawing breath. Then, without speaking to the old man, she went into her room and lay down on the bed, placing the child beside her.

"Are you going to bed?" the old man said to her from the kitchen.

She made no answer. She was too tired to speak. She closed her eyes. She heard the old man cough. Then she heard him hobble into his room and speak to Maggie. She felt herself getting dizzy. Her heart seemed to stop beating and her throat became clogged. She sat up in fright. Perspiration stood out on her forehead. It was now very dark.

"I'm not going to die," she whispered. "I won't die."

She sat like this in bed for a long time and then she heard the dog bark. A horrible thought came into her mind. She jumped from the bed, ran into the kitchen, and called the old man.

"Have you let the dog loose?" she said.

While she was waiting for an answer she heard footsteps outside and a man's voice ordering the dog to be quiet. Feverishly, she groped at the door, searching in the darkness for the bolt. At last she found it. She was opening it just as there was a knock on it outside. Throwing it wide open, she saw the figure of a man.

"Who is there?" she cried.

"Are ye the Kilmartins that live here?" the man said.

Mary was too excited to answer him. Brian came up behind her and spoke.

"I'm Brian Kilmartin," he said. "God save you, stranger, and what might bring you at this hour?"

"Would this young woman be the wife of Martin Kilmartin?" the stranger said.

"Oh! What word have you?" whispered Mary, almost inarticulate with excitement. "Speak to me, but for the love of God don't speak of woe. Oh, don't bring bad news, stranger, for the knife of sorrow is inches deep already in my heart. Speak to me, man."

"Don't be afraid," said the stranger in a calm tone. "It's no bad news I am bringing to you. Get your bundle ready and let you be going into Clogher."

"Is he well?" cried Mary. "Where is he?"

"Now listen to me," said the stranger, "while I tell you all I can. When you come to the workhouse outside the town on the sea road you are to wait there at the gate and a person will speak to you. It will be a person that will ask you did you see a man with yellow hair going the road. You will be told by that person where he is and the person will bring you there. Get ready quick and be making the road, for you have to be there shortly after the dawn of day. The person will be there with the dawn."

With that, the figure turned away and began to cross the yard towards the road.

"Oh! Stranger!" Mary cried, as she stepped out into the yard after him; "have you nothing more to tell me about Martin?"

"I can only tell you what I told you," said the dim figure, without pausing on his way.

"But, stranger," Mary cried, running after him, "can't you tell me who you are?"

"I will that and welcome," he said, leaping over the stile into the lane. "I am a man on my keeping that has a long road to make."

"May God go with you," Mary said, stretching out her two arms towards the figure of the man who went north in the darkness.

Then she burst into tears and turned back into the house. The old man was standing in the doorway. She threw her arms around his neck and said:

"Will you give me your blessing, old man, before I go on my journey?"

"I do that, daughter," said the old man softly. "May God go with you."

"There is something left in the bag," she whispered, "along with a piece of the bread that the priest gave us."

"Don't mind us," said Brian. "The two of us are at the fall of night that has no dawn. We are ready to lie down in peace on the sod where we have spent our lives, below the mountains of Black Valley."

She made up her bundle and took leave of them, still weeping aloud. When she was going out the door, the old man gave her a piece of mortar which he had taken from the wall over the fireplace.

"Give that to Martin," he said.

Then he drew his calloused hands over the child's face.

CHAPTER LIV

THE WORKHOUSE WALL sloped outwards to its base, along which ran a grassy ditch. The grass looked brown in the fading gloom of approaching dawn. Dark bodies were strewn along the ditch. They looked like corpses, owing to their uncouth postures and their stillness. Now and again one of them moaned. Then a murmur passed along the recumbent figures, who shifted, formed groups, tossed angrily, fell apart, and became still once more.

At the centre of the wall, the ditch was cut by the half-circle of the gravelled gateway, which sloped downwards, widening, to the narrow road. This road came from Crom and joined the road that ran westwards along the shore towards Clogher. The two roads, joining, made a cross without a head beyond the workhouse grounds. From the gateway, the sea was dimly visible, beyond the wilderness of tall grass with which the upper reaches of the beach were overgrown. All the road, even as far as the gate, was flecked with sand blown up from the beach. Down there the waves broke slowly, with a rolling sound, upon the soft shore.

Far away on the horizon to the east dawn was breaking. From the direction of the dawn there came the sound of many cart-wheels turning and the clatter of steel-shod hooves on the hard road. To the west lay Clogher, a dark uneven mass topped by thin steeples and the masts of ships. Beyond the town a range of mountains ran, undulating, southwards to a precipitous head, around whose black base the sea's rim was whitening with the dawn.

By the tall, closed gate two women sat talking on the ground. One of them was Mary Halloran, who had been Chadwick's housekeeper. She wore a good black dress and thick woollen stockings, but she had neither shoes nor a cloak. The soles of her stockings had almost disappeared. She had obviously sold her shoes and her cloak for food. Her grey hair hung down her back like a girl. It was very short and ragged at the end. Dew glistened on it. She shivered. The approach of dawn had brought a cold breeze.

"It's no good for you to be thinking of going into Clogher," she said to the other woman, "after what happened to the poor people there yesterday. If you are without a penny they won't let you stay in it after sunset. Lord save us! It's enough to make a person lose faith in God, the way the rich are treating the suffering poor. The poor people come into the town from the hungry land, looking for help, but they are driven out again empty. We were all put on carts, I'm telling you. We were taken this far, but the workhouse was full when I got here. The gate was closed. A man said that a few would be let in when the gate opened in the morning, to take the place of whatever dies in there during the night. All these people lying here were driven out of the town with me. I'm telling you, woman, that it's no place for a poor person."

The other woman rocked herself. She was almost completely covered by a black shawl, as she sat crouching on her heels. Only the toes of her bare feet and her nose were visible. She did not wish to believe the housekeeper's story.

"And why would Christian men drive out the poor that way to their death, unless there was cause for it?"

"It's what I'm telling you," the housekeeper said, "and it's only the truth. There was a big fight in the Main Street yesterday between the peelers and the working men. The working men came marching down the street and they carrying flags with words written on them. It was shouting for work they were, the creatures. Then they set on a baker's shop and the peelers began to scatter skin and hair. The soldiers came then and drove into the people. The government is going to kill all the poor of the country. So I was told by them that should know. They go around every morning and they pick up the dead people that are left outside the lodging-houses and they bury the corpses. That's all they do and they wouldn't do that same only for fear of catching the plague. They won't even put the poor corpses in a proper coffin. It's a sliding coffin they have for all of them. When they come to the big hole, they open the bottom of the coffin. The body slides down into the hole. Then they take the coffin back for another dead person."

"I never thought the day would come," the other woman said, "when I would be sitting outside a workhouse gate, waiting for someone to die inside in it, so as to get into the dead person's place. It's a great disgrace, surely. We were the richest people in Garrymore before the famine came. We had a place for two cows."

"Your disgrace is nothing, woman, compared to mine," said the housekeeper. "I was head of the Big House at Crom before the master got killed. With meat every day and a snipther handy to my mouth whenever I felt a wish for it. Big people coming and going the whole time nearly. There was more than fifty rooms under me."

"A fine place we had surely," the other woman said, paying no heed to Mary Halloran's boast. "What didn't come out of the land came out of the sea next door. We always had fish, fresh or salty, with our praties, until the blight came. Then the people came crowding to the seashore from the middle of the land. They brought the fever with them. It was the fever killed us all, brought by the runaways from the hungry places. We were a village of forty houses before the famine, but soon after there were thousands squatting on every corner of the village land, fishing and gathering periwinkles and limpets, so you couldn't get enough to bait a hook by turning the rocks at low tide. The plague tore through them when it started like a mad stallion, lashing all before it. Sorra one belonging to me is left but myself."

"I'm telling you," the housekeeper said once more, "to try for shelter here in the workhouse and not go into the town. It's not a young woman you are that might earn a penny piece whoring with the soldiers, or with the sailors that bring the corn from America. And you'll get a Christian grave in the workhouse."

"True for you," said the woman from Garrymore. "Whist! Is that someone I see walking on the road?"

Now the noise of turning cart-wheels and of hooves came very loudly from the east. It had become a deep rumble that mingled with the soft thunder of the breaking waves.

"It's a woman," said the housekeeper, peering towards the approaching figure. "It must be someone from my village. By the powers, I'd swear it is Ellie Gleeson."

"Who?" said the woman from Garrymore.

The housekeeper made no answer but stared intently at the approaching woman, who came slowly, very erect, tall, slender, with head thrown back. She carried something on her bosom wrapped in a cloak. There was a big bundle on her back. She paused when she came opposite the gate and turned inwards.

"It's Ellie's sister," the housekeeper said.

"Who?" said the woman from Garrymore.

"Is that you, Mary?" the housekeeper said.

Mary started and came to a halt. She stared at the housekeeper in a startled fashion. Then she smiled and hurried forward to the wall by which the two women were sitting.

"If it isn't Mary Halloran from the Big House!" she whispered. "How are you? Is this the workhouse gate?"

"It is," said the housekeeper gruffly.

"Thank God," said Mary.

She sighed heavily and sank down to the ground by the wall, against which she laid her head. The woman from Garrymore leaned towards her and said:

"The poor creature is worn out with walking. Is that a child she is carrying?"

"So it's in here you are going now," said the housekeeper in a tone of morose satisfaction, "to lie in your own dirt like the rest of us. You that were so proud, you and your sister. It was she started it all. Let bygones be bygones. I have no grudge against you for what's done. A beggar's grudge is a fool's grudge. What news have you of the Valley?"

The woman from Garrymore took a corner of Mary's scarlet cloak between her fingers and said:

"Isn't that the lovely cloth! How much was it a yard? And look at himself! A fine baby, 'faith. God bless you, it's good to look at your comely face. What village are you from?"

Mary drew the cloak jealously around the sleeping child and said:

"It's from Black Valley I come, woman. It wouldn't be you that was expecting me?"

Her cheeks were very flushed and she spoke excitedly.

"Arrah! Why would I be expecting you, darling," said the woman from Garrymore, "and I never laying eyes on you before?"

Mary looked all round her anxiously.

"Who are you looking for?" said the housekeeper in a sullen voice. "Maybe it's one of them lying in the ditch?"

Mary looked along the ditch. It was becoming quite light now. The clamour of turning wheels and of hooves was quite near. Pools of light were spreading over the sea.

"It's dawn," Mary said, looking at the housekeeper in a frightened way. "I thought there would be…"

The she bit her lip and wrinkled her forehead, afraid that she had said too much. She laughed.

"Huh!" said the housekeeper angrily. "It's kind sister for you to have little nature in you, laughing in a place like this."

"Ah, no," Mary said, "it's not for a mean reason I am laughing, but I am light in the head. I thought I'd never get here alive. There is no one alive up in Black Valley except Brian and Maggie. The place is empty. I left them something in the bag. That's all. I saw no one in the village, but I heard a great screeching from fighting dogs. It's like a dead place. Father Geelan said that Johnny Hynes is gone."

"The curse of Cromwell on him," said the housekeeper; "it's well I know he is gone. And it's myself that has a right to say it, for he is my second cousin. I went down to the big place his son Tony has on the quays, the place that belonged to Rabbit. I saw Johnny, but he wouldn't know me. Nor would Tony. I thought they would surely give me something to do, now they have a big house to look after. Sorra bit of them. It's the price of him to have the doctor die on him, in spite of all the nursing they bought for him. Money can't buy everything. They have made enough of it on account of this famine. That ship that's taking people to America to-day brought him another load of corn from Philadelphia."

"Is there a ship going to-day?" Mary cried, gripping the housekeeper by the arm.

"There is," said the housekeeper mournfully. "There is one going every few days now. It's over there in America I should be now, only for the sickness that laid me low. The money was gone on lodgings before I got better. Reilly, the groom, is gone and Hegarty, the driver. Everyone is gone that had the passage money. It's the richest of the people that are gone and only the scum left. They will all die."

Mary was now trembling with excitement and she was looking anxiously from side to side.

"I saw dead people on the road," she said, as if thinking aloud. "One person I met said that Colonel Bodkin, the magistrate, is giving out food, but it's only for his tenants. The same person said that Father Roche is as thin as a shadow. He gives his dinner to the beggars every day. Colonel Bodkin has a watchman at his gate. The person said that the government would start the works again, but there would be no one strong enough to work at the tasks."

The noise of cart-wheels and of hooves had now become

mingled with the sharp sound of cracking whips and the shouts of men. The people lying in the ditch were roused by the tumult. Some of them sat up and groaned. Others tossed about on the ground. A few did not move at all. A little girl was shaking her mother, to whom she called piteously.

"Lord save us!" said the woman from Garrymore. "It's like the dead rising from their graves with the break of day. Oh! Look at the red coats on horseback."

Three horsemen came riding from the east, along the edge of the tall shore grass. The hooves of their horses threw up little blobs of sand. At the same time a Spanish ass came trotting from the west, drawing a cart on which sat a man, who wore a tall hat and a grey cape. The ass turned up the road towards the workhouse gate. A convoy of carts followed the horsemen. Soldiers marched on either side of the carts. The men on horseback had swords and the footmen had carbines. Two of the soldiers on horseback were singing. The carts were loaded with sacks.

Suddenly a tall man rose from the far end of the ditch near the shore road. He was half naked. He raised his right hand with the fist clenched. A piece of his sleeve hung down by his naked elbow.

"Robbers!" he cried, as he shook his upraised fist at the convoy. "Ye are taking the people's harvest out of the country. Ye are stealing our corn and we dying of hunger. We are laid low now but we will rise again. We'll crush the tyrants that suck our blood. The people will rise again."

Then an angry murmur, like a cheer of defiance, passed along the ditch. Other figures rose up and threatened the convoy with their clenched fists. Excited by this murmur the half naked man ran forward shouting. One of the soldiers struck him on the head with a carbine. The man fell. The convoy passed on quickly. Now there were many soldiers singing in unison. A woman ran out from the ditch and began to drag the fallen man.

"That's what you get for going against the law," said the housekeeper. "A split skull. It was all this agitation that started the famine."

"Musha," said the woman from Garrymore, "the poor man only spoke the truth. It would be fitter for the people to rise and fight than to die of hunger in the ditch. I wish I had a gun to shoot the thieving murderers that are taking the food of Ireland over the sea."

Mary's eyes were fixed on the man in the cart. He passed the gate and then turned back. He kept looking towards her. She saw him beckon slightly. She stood up and hurried towards the cart. He was an oldish man with a hooked nose and small, sharp eyes.

"Did you see a man with yellow hair?" he whispered to her when she reached the cart.

"Yes," Mary whispered. "It's me you want. Where is he?"

"Get into the cart," said the man. "I'm taking you to him."

She climbed into the cart and he lashed the ass into a gallop. Tears of joy rolled down Mary's cheeks and she began to laugh under her breath. When they turned west towards Clogher, the man said to her:

"We have him safe on board. Sure, it's an easy thing to get a man out of the country these days, on account of the peelers having to be here and there, with all the riots there are. We have him hidden there and the captain is one of us, so you needn't be afraid. If they question you and you going on board, let you cry and say you have given up hope of finding him. That's all you have to do."

"May God reward ye," Mary said, "whoever ye are."

"Them that strike a blow," said the man, "deserve to be looked after. Them that won't fight can die of the hunger and may the devil roast them. Hi up there. We'll follow after these soldiers with the carts. Here is the ticket that you have to show."

He took a ticket from his pocket and gave it to her. She put it to her lips and kissed it.

"Let you not forget," said the man, "when you are out there in America, that the fight for liberty must go on until it's won and help it as much as you can. That's the only thanks we want."

"Oh! I can't believe it," Mary whispered. "It can't be true that I am going to find Martin and that we are going to escape. It can't be true."

When the cart entered the long Main Street in the wake of the convoy, terror took possession of her. The thoroughfare was practically empty at this hour, but the very houses looked menacing and at each moment she expected to feel a hand on her shoulder. They reached the fish market and came in sight of the quays. Here the man told her to dismount from the cart.

"We'll walk from here," he said.

Tying the ass to a post, he set off towards the quays. She followed him. Now she was dizzy with fear. The baby began to cry, startled by a loud wailing in the distance.

"Hush, darling," she whispered to him. "You'll soon see your daddy."

"There is the ship," whispered the man. "Don't forget now what I told you to say if the peelers ask you questions. Hand your ticket to the man at the gangway and go aboard. You will find your husband after the ship sails. Have no fear. Good-bye to you now and let your son grow up in the land of liberty to be a soldier of liberty. God save you."

Mary was now too terrified to say a word to him, as she shook his hand in farewell. Then she went forward towards the ship. It was a three-masted vessel, moored to the pier in front of Tony Hynes's warehouse.

"Oh!" she said aloud. "It hasn't white sails. They are brown."

The fact that the sails were not white, as in her dream, made her feel certain that all was lost. The shouting and wailing of a great crowd added still further to this fear. The convoy of carts, with its military escort, had halted some short distance beyond the emigrant ship. The sacks of grain were being unloaded from the carts and taken aboard another ship, for transport to England. The crowd of people, who had come down to bid farewell to the emigrants, were infuriated by the sight of their food being carried away from them. They were shouting curses at the soldiers. Some of them were wailing aloud, with their hands stretched towards those on the ship. And on the ship's deck, the crowd of emigrants wailed. Among these latter, however, there were a few young men who held up their clenched fists and threatened the soldiers with cries of future vengeance.

Clutching her ticket in her hand, Mary made her way through the crowd until she reached the line of policemen that stood in front of the gangway. None of them made any attempt to stop her and she was allowed on board the ship. There she sank down in a faint on the deck.

When she recovered, she found herself in a tiny room, almost in darkness. Light came through a narrow slit in the wall. Martin was bending over her, rubbing her hands and whispering to her excitedly. She looked up into his dark, bearded face and fainted again. The next time she opened her eyes, she was being laid down by Martin on a coil of rope on the ship's deck in the prow. A woman was sitting there rocking her baby, who was crying angrily. She grabbed her baby from the woman. Then she looked at Martin fiercely and said:

"Where were you all this time?"

"Oh, darling," Martin said, "I was…"

He could say no more, for she suddenly drew his head towards her and kissed him hungrily.

"Never mind," she whispered fiercely, as she kissed him. "We have escaped now. It's all gone, isn't it? Have we escaped?"

"Look," he said.

He put his arm around her shoulder and made her look towards the receding land. Then she went on her knees and crossed herself. Martin also went on his knees. With tears in their eyes they watched the land receding, as the ship rose and fell with the waves.

"And the old people?" Martin said.

Mary took the piece of mortar from her pocket and gave it to him.

"He told me to give it to you," she sobbed. "It's from the hearth."

"I'll try not to disgrace his name," Martin whispered, as he looked at the morsel of clay, "out there in the new world."

CHAPTER LV

HOAR FROST HAD fallen in the night. It shone in the morning light upon the mountain-sides and all along the Valley's bed. It lay in a whitish crust upon the sagging thatch of the empty houses and on the blighted fields that were already falling back into the wilderness. The stone walls, the granite boulders, and the gorse bushes were white with it. It had formed a thin crust of ice on the surface of the Black Lake. The river was the only thing that moved here beneath the grey sky.

Then Brian Kilmartin came from his house carrying a spade and followed by his dog. The old man was wearing only his shirt. He used the spade as a staff to support him. The dog hobbled on three legs. Their feet made clear imprints on the frost. Their breathing made little clouds that went smoking before them. The dog whined and halted now and again, as if trying to arrest the old man's progress.

Brian climbed with great effort over the stile into the paddock. He went to the middle of the little field and halted. He straightened himself and looked about him on the ground. He prodded with the spade.

"I'll make a hole for her in this place," he muttered.

He tried to spit on his hands, but there was no moisture on his lips. Then he thrust the point of the spade at the frosty earth, put his naked foot on the haft, and pressed with all his force. The point did not penetrate. The dog lay down on his belly and whined loudly. The old man closed his lips, gathered himself together, and again thrust the point of his spade at the frosty ground, pressing with his naked foot on the haft. The point again refused to penetrate. He overbalanced with the effort and fell forward over the fallen spade. The dog rose and barked.

The old man lay still for a little while. Then he groaned loudly and struggled to his knees. Leaning on the spade he got to his feet. Now the dog barked angrily and scraped at the frost with his right forefoot. Again the old man tried to spit on his hands, but his mouth remained open and his tongue hung over his lower lip. He clutched the handle of the spade, leaned forward, threatened the frosty earth with the point, and raised his foot. There was a deep, gurgling sound in his throat and he fell forward headlong. The spade skidded away over the frost and rolled into a hollow. The old man lay still with his arms stretched out.

The dog became silent and lay down on his belly. Then he raised his snout and sniffed the air. He shuddered. Then he dragged himself along the ground until he came to the old man's naked foot. He smelt it. He rose slowly to his feet, raised his mane slightly, and advanced, an inch at a time, smelling along the old man's naked shins and thighs. He started and growled when he came to the shirt. Then he made a little circuit, lay down on his belly once more, and dragged himself, whining, to the head. He smelt the face. He whined. He smelt again. His mane dropped.

Suddenly he raised his snout, sat back on his haunches, and uttered a long howl. Then he lay down on his side and nestled against the old man's shoulder.